Celebrate reading with us!

Cover and title page illustrations by David Ray. Cover illustration reprinted by permission of Philomel Books from *Greyling* by Jane Yolen. Illustrations copyright © 1991 by David Ray.

Acknowledgments appear on page 536.

Beyond the Reef

Senior Author
John J. Pikulski

Senior Coordinating Author
J. David Cooper

Senior Consulting Author
William K. Durr

Coordinating Authors
Kathryn H. Au
M. Jean Greenlaw
Marjorie Y. Lipson
Susan E. Page
Sheila W. Valencia
Karen K. Wixson

Authors
Rosalinda B. Barrera
Edwina Bradley
Ruth P. Bunyan
Jacqueline L. Chaparro
Jacqueline C. Comas
Alan N. Crawford
Robert L. Hillerich
Timothy G. Johnson
Jana M. Mason
Pamela A. Mason
William E. Nagy
Joseph S. Renzulli
Alfredo Schifini

Senior Advisor
Richard C. Anderson

Advisors
Christopher J. Baker
Charles Peters
MaryEllen Vogt

HOUGHTON MIFFLIN COMPANY   BOSTON

Atlanta   Dallas   Geneva, Illinois   Palo Alto   Princeton   Toronto

THEME 1
ADVENTURE
13

THE SPIRIT OF SURVIVAL

 18 Boar Out There
from Every Living Thing *by Cynthia Rylant*

22 Slaves No More
from Profiles in Black and White
by Elizabeth F. Chittenden

38 Survival at Sea   *by Ariane Randall*

 50 Long Claws   *by James Houston*

THEME BOOKS
Medicine Walk
by Ardath Mayhar
Courage at Indian Deep
by Jane Resh Thomas

Award Winner

THEME 2
REALISTIC FICTION
79

BECOMING

🏵 82 Sister
from the book by Eloise Greenfield

🏵 88 The Circuit
by Francisco Jiménez

🏵 102 Papa's Parrot
from Every Living Thing *by Cynthia Rylant*

🏵 108 The Bracelet
by Yoshiko Uchida

🏵 120 The Scribe
from Guests in the Promised Land *by Kristin Hunter*

THEME BOOKS
🏵 . . . and now Miguel
by Joseph Krumgold
🏵 Island of the Blue Dolphins
by Scott O'Dell

THEME 3

POETRY

137

MOVING THE WORLD

139 **Myra Cohn Livingston: Breaking Away**

140 A Beginning

141 The Tape

142 Garage Apartment

144 Finding a Way

144 Power Lines

145 The Way Things Are

147 **Pat Mora: Moments in Time**

148 Urban Raccoon

149 Same Song

151 Border Town: 1938

152 Los Ancianos

154 Good-byes

157 **James Berry: Moving Pictures**

158 One

159 Black Kid in a New Place

160 Kept Home

162 It Seems I Test People

163 My Hard Repair Job

164 Dreaming Black Boy

166 When I Dance

THEME 4

PERSONAL NARRATIVE

173

EXPERIENCES

🎗 176 The Figgerin' of Aunt Wilma
from Thurber Country *by James Thurber*

🎗 188 Summer School
from Living Up the Street *by Gary Soto*

200 Daddy
by Yolanda King in collaboration with Hilda R. Tompkins

206 Barrio Boy
from the book by Ernesto Galarza

🎗 222 Homesick: My Own Story
from the book by Jean Fritz

THEME BOOKS
Nisei Daughter
by Monica Sone
Barrio Boy
by Ernesto Galarza

THEME 5

TRADITIONAL TALES

241

TIMELESS TALES

🎗 244 Brer Rabbit and Brer Cooter Race
retold by William J. Faulkner

250 The Hunter Who Wanted Air
retold by Alexandra Whitney

🎗 258 The Very Angry Ghost
told by Spotted Elk and retold by Richard Erdoes

🎗 266 The Headless Rider
from Stories That Must Not Die *retold by Juan Sauvageau*

🎗 272 Old Plott   *retold by Ellis Credle*

286 The Alligator War   *by Horacio Quiroga*

THEME BOOKS

🎗 The Cow-Tail Switch and Other West African Stories
by Harold Courlander and George Herzog
They Dance in the Sky: Native American Star Myths
by Jean Guard Monroe and Ray A. Williamson

THEME 6

NOVEL

313

THE SUMMER OF THE SWANS

 by Betsy Byars

THEME BOOKS

 The House of Wings
by Betsy Byars

 Number the Stars
by Lois Lowry

DISCOVERING
ANCIENT EGYPT

402 *From* A Message of Ancient Days,
a social studies textbook

418 Seeing the Unseen
from Tales Mummies Tell *by Patricia Lauber*

426 The Tomb of Tut-ankh-Amen
from Lost Worlds: The Romance of Archaeology
by Anne Terry White

THEME BOOKS
Mummies, Tombs, and Treasure:
Secrets of Ancient Egypt
by Lila Perl
Pyramid
by David Macaulay

THEME 8

SCIENCE

453

EXPLORING THE OCEANS

❧ 456 Treasure of the *Andrea Doria*
from Treasures of the Deep: Adventures
of Undersea Exploration *by Walter Oleksy*

466 Oceans of the Earth
from Earth Science, *a science textbook*

❧ 476 Discovering the Oceans
from Under the High Seas: New Frontiers in Oceanography
by Margaret Poynter and Donald Collins

❧ 486 Lurkers of the Deep: Life Within the Ocean Depths
from the book by Bruce H. Robison

THEME BOOKS
❧ The Black Pearl *by Scott O'Dell*
❧ The Great Barrier Reef: A Treasure in the Sea
by Alice Gilbreath

GLOSSARY
500

GLOSSARY OF LITERARY TERMS
526

ADVENTURE

THE SPIRIT OF SURVIVAL

Two children confront a grizzly bear, and more

CONTENTS

THE
SPIRIT OF SURVIVAL

18

Boar Out There
by Cynthia Rylant

22

Slaves No More
by Elizabeth F. Chittenden

14

◆ 38

Survival at Sea
by Ariane Randall

◆ 50

Long Claws
by James Houston

Jenny imagined
the beast many times.
To see it
with her own eyes,
though,
would require an act
of special bravery . . .

Boar Out There

by Cynthia Rylant
Illustrated by Susan Guevara

Everyone in Glen Morgan knew there was a wild boar in the woods over by the Miller farm. The boar was out beyond the splintery rail fence and past the old black Dodge that somehow had ended up in the woods and was missing most of its parts.

Jenny would hook her chin over the top rail of the fence, twirl a long green blade of grass in her teeth and whisper, "Boar out there."

And there were times she was sure she heard him. She imagined him running heavily through the trees, ignoring the sharp thorns and briars that raked his back and sprang away trembling.

She thought he might have a golden horn on his terrible head. The boar would run deep into the woods, then rise up on his rear hooves, throw his head toward the stars and cry a long, clear, sure note into the air. The note would glide through the night and spear the heart of the moon. The boar had no fear of the moon, Jenny knew, as she lay in bed, listening.

One hot summer day she went to find the boar. No one in Glen Morgan had ever gone past the old black Dodge and beyond, as far as she knew. But the boar was there somewhere, between those awful trees, and his dark green eyes waited for someone.

Jenny felt it was she.

Moving slowly over damp brown leaves, Jenny could sense her ears tingle and fan out[1] as she listened for thick breathing from the trees. She stopped to pick a teaberry leaf to chew, stood a minute, then went on.

Deep in the woods she kept her eyes to the sky. She needed to be reminded that there was a world above and apart from the trees — a world of space and air, air that didn't linger all about her, didn't press deep into her skin, as forest air did.

Finally, leaning against a tree to rest, she heard him for the first time. She forgot to breathe, standing there listening to the stamping of hooves, and she choked and coughed.

Coughed!

And now the pounding was horrible, too loud and confusing for Jenny. Horrible. She stood stiff with wet eyes and knew she could always pray, but for some reason didn't.

He came through the trees so fast that she had no time to scream or run. And he was there before her.

---

[1] **fan out:** to open or spread like a fan.

His large gray-black body shivered as he waited just beyond the shadow of the tree she held for support. His nostrils glistened, and his eyes; but astonishingly, he was silent. He shivered and glistened and was absolutely silent.

Jenny matched his silence, and her body was rigid, but not her eyes. They traveled along his scarred, bristling back to his thick hind legs. Tears spilling and flooding her face, Jenny stared at the boar's ragged ears, caked with blood. Her tears dropped to the leaves, and the only sound between them was his slow breathing.

Then the boar snorted and jerked. But Jenny did not move.

High in the trees a bluejay yelled, and, suddenly, it was over. Jenny stood like a rock as the boar wildly flung his head and in terror bolted past her.

Past her. . . .

And now, since that summer, Jenny still hooks her chin over the old rail fence, and she still whispers, "Boar out there." But when she leans on the fence, looking into the trees, her eyes are full and she leaves wet patches on the splintery wood. She is sorry for the torn ears of the boar and sorry that he has no golden horn.

But mostly she is sorry that he lives in fear of bluejays and little girls, when everyone in Glen Morgan lives in fear of him.

Responding to "Boar Out There"

Thinking and Discussing

How does Jenny's image of the boar change as a result of her encounter with it in the forest? Is the boar at all like what she had imagined? In what ways?

After her experience, how do Jenny's feelings about the boar differ from the way the townspeople feel about the boar?

Choosing a Creative Response

Talking About Adventures Imagine that you meet up with the boar the same way Jenny did. How would you tell the story to your friends to add to the small legend that has grown up around the animal? Feel free to change the ending or add new events. Then, in a group discussion, tell your story and describe your thoughts and feelings.

Making a Poster With a group, illustrate the scene in which Jenny and the boar face each other in the forest. Base your drawing on the descriptions in the story. You may want to display your poster in the classroom.

Creating Your Own Activity Plan and complete your own activity in response to "Boar Out There."

Exploring Language Notice the details of descriptive language that the author uses to create clear pictures of the forest and the boar. Scan the story and list your favorite descriptive words and phrases. Try some of the words or phrases in sentences of your own, or use them as models to help you create your own descriptive phrases.

SLAVES NO MORE

The year is 1855. Ann Wood, a young slave girl, is planning her escape from a Virginia plantation. Fleeing into the night, Ann leads a group of five young slaves on a daring journey through dark woods and unfamiliar territory.

Suddenly, the teen-agers find themselves in a dangerous situation that could cut short their search for freedom.

by Elizabeth F. Chittenden

Illustrated by Gershom Griffith

"Ann Wood, where you goin'?"

Tilda, a house servant, asked the young, black ladies' maid who was tiptoeing from the feasting and dancing on the front lawn of the Wood plantation in Virginia.

Ann, only sixteen, knew Tilda was critical of her because she enjoyed the company of the field hands who were her own age. Tilda wanted Ann to remember she belonged to the big house. Usually Ann laughed at Tilda's scoldings, but today she must be careful not to annoy her.

It was Christmas Eve, 1855. The Wood slaves were dressed in their warmest clothes, faded and patched but clean. They had come to the big house for the best food they had eaten in a year, the best they would have for another year.

Before breakfast that morning, Mistress Wood had directed, "You people dig a ditch and fill it with big logs."

All morning the slaves had thrown on log after log and watched them burn down until there was a deep bed of glowing coals. They put chickens, wild turkeys, and pigs on skewers, which were laid across the searing trench. Black women kept the roasting meat turning, basting it with spicy sauces.

All the time they had to keep a careful eye on the excited little ones hopping back and forth over the trenches. Tempting odors made their noses twitch and their mouths water.

A little after noon, a caravan of slaves from two neighboring plantations began arriving — some on foot, some mounted on mules. A few of the old and the very young came in carts. They were coming for the frolicking, feasting, and fiddling they had looked forward to since last Christmas. This was the one party of the year their owners allowed them.

Finally, carriages drawn by handsome purebred horses and driven by black coachmen in livery arrived. This year, as they did every Christmas, the owners of nearby plantations came to the family whose turn it was to give the annual supper for the Christmas celebrations. Watching the abandoned eating and dancing of their slaves amused and entertained the white owners.

When the owners and slaves had all arrived and the food was on the tables, Master Wood nodded to old Daniel, who gave the signal to Mollie. "Le's go, everyone!" she called. Mothers lifted restraining hands from the shoulders of the children, and young and old swarmed to the plank tables laid out on sawhorses under the trees.

The food steamed in the cool December air. Besides the meats, there were hot biscuits, squash, carrots, peach tarts, strawberry preserves, and pies — apple, pecan, and pumpkin. Hungrily, they devoured the delicacies. Women and men who all year long had eaten less so their children could have more of the scanty ration of cornmeal and bacon now ate with abandon.

Ann Wood ate fast — a chicken drumstick, biscuits, an apricot tart, for she always seemed to need more. Then a rib of pork, more biscuits, and a gooseberry tart went down. She took a turkey wing and looked around casually as she slipped it into a burlap sack hidden inside her blouse. Her eyes went again and again to old Daniel, whom Master trusted to oversee the gaieties and report if anything unusual was happening. She hated old Daniel for the favors his tattling won him. She kept her eyes on her master and mistress, too. They sat on the gallery, talking with their guests, laughing — probably at their slaves' gobbling of food, Ann thought bitterly. They would have their banquet later, in the large, elegant dining room where it was warmer. Must be tired of it all, Ann surmised,[1] since they were paying more attention to each other than to the feasting of their slaves.

She left the table and wove a seemingly aimless path through the scattered groups, still busy eating. At the edge of the crowded yard, she started for the stable.

"Ann Wood, where you goin'?"

---

[1] **surmised:** guessed from some information.

She jumped at Tilda's question. "Why, I'm . . . I'm . . ." She prayed for words. "Muffin. Had her pups this mornin'. Goin' to see how she's comin'."

"Shore, shore — I forgot," Tilda muttered. She knew how Ann loved that spaniel Mrs. Wood had given her two years ago, when Ann was fourteen. Ann was Mrs. Wood's favorite personal maid. Now Tilda just laughed to herself. Her eyes followed Ann as she moved toward the barn.

What did Tilda mean by "I forgot"? Ann wondered. Forgot the pups? And why did she laugh so knowingly? Did she suspect?

Ann made herself walk slowly in case somebody did suspect and was watching her. She went into the safe darkness inside the barn and to the stall where Muffin lay with her five puppies. She leaned down to pat the dog's head and felt tears begin to form. "I'll miss you, Muff. Wish I could . . ." But she straightened up and shook off her weakness.

She walked to the rear of the barn, where the horses were stabled, and quietly slid open the back entrance. She stepped outside and pushed it closed. Here, hidden behind the barn, was an open field cart.

"Shucks! You had me scared, Ann," young Fred said from behind the cart.

"Sh—sh! Want 'em to hear us, Fred? When'd you come in from the woods?" She felt the canvas cover Fred had put over the rickety frame of the cart. She nodded approval. "Nice, Fred. Hungry? Here." She took a turkey wing and a biscuit out of the burlap sack she pulled from her blouse and watched Fred bolt them down. She threw the sack to him. "You lay these other pickin's by the bacon slabs in the wagon. Fannie's fetchin' more."

"When we startin', Ann?"

"Hold your horses. Hear it? The fiddlin' and dancin' is beginnin'. We gotta dance — dance like we never danced before. Make 'em think we'll never stop!" Seeing Fred's disgruntled face, she drew his head close and whispered in his ear, "'Member, 'fore mornin' we goin' to be, to be on our way. Gotta hurry back now 'fore Missus finds me gone."

Ann crept back into the barn, stopped long enough to cuddle a puppy in her hand and give it back to Muffin, ran to the front door, and moved toward the dancing.

Pete, beside Miss Lively from the Marshalls' plantation, was flying down the outside of the dancers' square and up the middle of it. He leaned back and pranced until he was exhausted. Chuck dashed in. Determined to show Lively he was better than Pete, he leaped, shuffled, and threw himself around until the set ended.

The Woods and their guests applauded from the gallery. The field hands shouted. Even the older house servants who had stayed aloof forgot their dignity and shouted, too. The fiddler's feet wouldn't stay still as his bow swung up, swung down. Those too old or too timid to join the dancing began "patting" — striking their hands on their knees, then clapping their hands together, then slapping the right shoulder with one hand and the left shoulder with the other, all the while keeping time with their feet.

Then someone started to sing and everyone joined in.

Goin' to the ball
Feet de de dibble
Who's goin' to the ball?
Feet de de dibble
Goin' to wear a red gown
Feet de de dibble
Wear a red gown
Feet de de dibble

Even the gallery folk couldn't keep still. They began to sway back and forth to the fiddler's beat and the song's "de de dibble."

Ann was stepping as high as anybody, as she and Nat jigged through the sets — in and around the oaks and back into the center of the patterns of partners.

Finally, while passing, she touched Fannie on the left shoulder. Fannie nodded, finished the set, and melted into the crowd. A few minutes later Ann tapped Sis. "Feelin' fine?" she questioned her as they had agreed earlier. Then she tapped Tom.

Ann and Nat danced on — first to the east, then to the west, as the fiddler called the set. She kept glancing at her mistress and Tilda and old Daniel. But none of them seemed suspicious.

During the next set, Ann excused herself to Nat and slowly walked through the revelers.[2] Just in case Tilda was watching, she'd go to the barn by way of the big house this time. One, two, one, two, she said to herself, measuring each step. Once inside the house, the door closed, she stood panting and listening. Somebody might be in here. In the silence, she forced herself to move slowly and calmly down the wide hallway, past the open stairway. If someone chanced to glance in a window! In the dining room she

---

[2] **revelers:** people at a celebration.

dared to hurry again, into the big kitchen, where women had been baking pies and breads only a few hours ago. She paused to listen. No one.

Into the open shed behind the kitchen she went, looking around before she stepped out into the deep shadow of the house. She stayed close to the house as she crept in the direction of the barn. Between the house and the barn she had to cross a short stretch from which she could see the dancers and where they could see her.

She edged to the rim of the house shadow. "Please, God, please!" Then she walked nonchalantly[3] into the open strip and across it. Within the blessed darkness of the barn, she turned to make sure no one had followed her. She was safe! Over the pounding of her heart, she heard the still steady pulse of fiddle, dancers, and "patters."

She knelt down and ran her hand over Muff's head. "Muff, 'bye, Muff." The cold nose nuzzled her hand.

---

[3]**nonchalantly** (nŏn´ shə länt´ lē): apparently unconcerned.

Ann pulled herself away from her only real possession and ran to the back door, where Tom was waiting to help her with the horses.

"The others are in the cart under the canvas, you say?" she whispered. "You take Tony. Hush, Lady, it's me," she breathed into the mare's ear as she led her out by the halter. Either horse's neighing might betray them.

Silently she and Tom hitched up the horses. Ann climbed into the cart. She burrowed under the seat and brought out the

weapons she had stolen and hidden over the past month. There were three double-barreled pistols and four long daggers. She gave one to each member of the group; for herself she kept a pistol and a dagger.

"Prob'bly won't need 'em, but in case . . ."

She seated herself beside Tom at the front of the cart and took the reins. "Giddap, Lady; giddap, Tony," she called softly. The wagon began moving. "We're goin'," she whispered jubilantly. "Sis, Tom, Fannie, Fred, Nat, Ann. Goin' to the North where we're goin' to be free."

The horses klop-klopped through the meadow; the rolling wheels could carry the six of them out of slavery to freedom or capture — or death.

A dog's bark suddenly broke the night's silence. Nat crawled from the back of the wagon to behind Ann. "They set the dogs on us, Ann?"

"No, that's Muff. I know her yappin'. Tryin' to follow me." Her words were sure, but her voice was trembling with fear and a longing for her dog. Suppose someone heard Muff, investigated her whereabouts, and missed the six of them. "Nothin' to be feared of," she tried to reassure him. "But, Nat, you watch out back, just for sure . . ."

Ann drove the wagon through the dark without a word. No one spoke. The only sounds were the horses' hoofs on the road and the wheels' turning. Once a night owl's hoot made them jump. There was nothing more.

With a growing feeling of safety, Ann called back to Fannie, "Look under the straw by you. There's a map. The one Uncle Solomon made for us." She handed the reins to Tom and studied the map. She was the only one who could read it. "Gotta make Leesburg 'fore light. Robert Purvey, it says here. Ol' friend to Uncle Solomon. He'll hide us all day in his barn an' let us sleep in the hay."

The eastern sky had just begun to turn the black of night to gray as Ann drove Tony and Lady into the Purvey yard. An hour back she'd been fighting sleep. But like a plunge into cold water, excitement at making the first station of their journey tingled through her.

"Wake up!" She roused the four sleeping figures in the wagon and jabbed her elbow into Tom, whose head was drooping.

Robert Purvey and his wife, Susan, hurried out to them and helped Ann drive into the barn. Tom and Mr. Purvey unhitched and fed the weary horses. Susan brought the young people a pail of warm milk, loaves of bread, and johnnycake with fresh-churned butter. They were hungry. Tired too, so tired that even excitement and happiness over their escape couldn't keep them awake after their stomachs were full.

They slept off and on during the day. About four-thirty, the Purveys came to tell them they must be starting to make the most of nighttime. They had to reach the second underground[4] station, the one in Frederick, Maryland, before the following morning.

Horses and passengers were well rested, and the fugitive wagon moved off fast into the evening dusk. All felt secure. They had fooled their masters. Freedom was theirs. To the roll of the wheels through the long night, they sang songs under their breath. They changed the words of one they'd heard the old slaves sing:

> *Massa sleeps in the feather bed,*
> *Slave sleeps on the floor;*
> *When we get to Philadelph'a*
> *We'll be no slaves no more.*

"Listen!"

"Did ya hear?"

From the distance came the beat of galloping horses and the baying of a hound.

"Someone chasin' us?"

"Sounds like it."

"Gettin' closer."

"'Most here!"

There was no point in trying to outrun them. With the loaded wagon, poor Lady and Tony couldn't beat the hunters.

---

[4]**underground**: secret.

"Whoa, Lady; whoa, Tony." Ann's voice trembled. She pulled them to a halt and leaped from the cart, Nat close behind her. "Knives and guns, all of you," she commanded. "Hold the horses, Tom." She motioned Fred to get in the front seat as he started to jump down with her and Nat. "Sis and Fannie stay in the wagon."

They were hardly in their places when the five men pulled up behind them, sprang from their horses, and ran toward them. Each man carried a long rifle which he pointed at the runaways.

"Thought you were smart, eh? Thought you'd given us the slip? All the way to Maryland. Fancy that!" a stranger with a sheriff's badge sneered. "Come here, you . . ." he snarled at Nat, moving toward him. "Did you hear me?"

A pistol shot sounded, and the hound fell on its side. The five men of the posse jumped involuntarily. Fred had aimed well from the front seat.

"What the —"

"Go ahead! Fire!" Ann dared them. The men hesitated. "Think you gonna take us? We be dead first!"

She seemed taller, stronger, than she was.

Standing beside the back of the wagon, she raised her right arm and leveled the pistol at the nearest man. Trembling with anger and fear, she lifted her left arm and waved her dagger.

The man hesitated at the sight of this bold young black woman who had the nerve to threaten him.

"Shoot! Afraid?" she dared them. She was gambling. But she knew the posse didn't want to kill them. You couldn't sell a dead slave on the market.

"Well, I'll be. . . . You baggage!"

It was beginning to grow light. The knife Sis flourished from the rear of the wagon caught the first light of the sun. Fred fired again. The men backed away from the six young blacks. Ann fired her pistol into the ground at their feet. The men ran to their horses.

"We'll be back! We'll get you!" they shouted as they wheeled and sped away.

"We beat 'em. We beat 'em," Fannie said to herself as if she couldn't believe it.

Ann's legs nearly collapsed as relief coursed through her. But there wasn't time to rejoice or relax. They'd be back again with more men and rifles.

"Gotta move, fast. They'll be back. But — Maryland — we're in Maryland, did you hear them say?"

In the growing light they could see a woods, not too far off. Ann pointed to it. Fred shrugged his shoulders. No one knew what to do. They were bewildered, frightened. They turned to Ann Wood.

"Most likely hidin' place I see," she stated in a flat voice. She took her place beside Tom. "You drive, Tom. To the woods."

A short time later the horses were moving slowly through the woods, between the trees and through the undergrowth, on into the cover of thick evergreens which shut out the sun and made the light eerie. The boys followed behind, covering the horse and wagon tracks as best as they could.

All six, hungry and exhausted, ate the remnants of the Christmas food they had toted from the loaded tables — months ago, it seemed now. They took turns keeping guard while the other five slept and then decided to lie in their covert[5] through the next night. Once they heard — or thought they heard — hoof beats.

The second evening after their triumph over the posse, Ann drove the field cart out into open country.

"Headin' for Frederick. We'll get there by mornin'," she announced as she traced their route on the map with her finger.

---

[5]**covert** (kŭv´ ərt *or* kō´ vərt): sheltered place.

To the wagon's jolting rhythm, the refugees sang softly, "We'll be no slaves no more."

Stations of the Underground Railroad harbored them in Frederick and Hagerstown, Maryland, and in Hanover, New Providence, Coatesville and Conshohocken, Pennsylvania.

Three weeks after their flight from the plantation, Ann Wood drove the faithful horses into Philadelphia. The six young blacks were as skittery as the horses at the noise and bustle of the big city. Here, by arrangement through underground "conductors," they were met by Thomas Garret, a white Quaker,[6] and William Still, a free Negro.

"And Ann dared them to fire at you?" their listeners marveled that first evening in Philadelphia. "Astonishing! But who planned the scheme for you to get away?"

"Ann Wood," Nat promptly volunteered.

"And she directed you between stations?"

"Shore did," Fred grunted.

"Not me, not me alone," Ann interrupted. "Uncle Solomon and Fannie's ma and Jen — didn't want us sold. Like they had been. Risked whippin' or worse to help us all slip out. And all of you. Now, thank God, we're here, safe in Philadelphia. Wish they could know."

Softly Ann Wood began singing and the other five joined her in their own hymn of freedom.

Here in Philadelph'a
We'll be no slaves no more.

---

[6]**Quaker:** a member of the Religious Society of Friends.

Responding to "Slaves No More"

Thinking and Discussing

What strengths do the characters in the story draw on to carry out their escape? What do you feel is Ann Wood's greatest strength? What do you learn about Ann through her actions?

How does the author create a sense of urgency and suspense in the story? What techniques does the author use to add to this feeling of suspense? How do these characteristics affect the reader?

Choosing a Creative Response

Composing a Song or Poem   To lift their spirits, the teen-agers sing an old slave song. Create a song about your favorite part of the story. Copy the verses neatly and illustrate them if you wish. Share your song with the group.

Holding a Discussion   The story ends abruptly in Philadelphia, not revealing what happens to Ann and the rest of the group once they reach the North. Create another ending to the story. Then in a group, discuss what you think might have happened to the teen-agers.

Creating Your Own Activity   Plan and complete your own activity in response to "Slaves No More."

Thinking and Writing

Imagine that Ann Wood is telling a friend what it was like to reach the Purvey farm, to be fed and sheltered, and to hide out in the barn all day. Write the conversation as a dialogue between two friends.

SURVIVAL

I wonder if

we will ever be rescued.

The thought of floating

out here until I die

is horrifying.

I think about sharks . . .

AT SEA

My trip to a resort in Haiti began at New York's La Guardia Airport, two weeks after my fourteenth birthday. All the people going to the resort had congregated around the check-in counter. While waiting around, I met Anna Rivera and Delia Clarke, who would be passengers on the doomed plane, and Delia's daughter, Krista. Anna was concerned about how she could get malaria pills.

I had a great time during my week in Haiti, waterskiing, snorkeling, swimming, and suntanning — things I don't get to do much in New York City. During the week, the Haitians went on strike a number of times to protest against the government. At the end of the week American Airlines, on which we were supposed to fly, canceled all flights to and from Haiti indefinitely because of the political unrest.

The resort gave those of us who were supposed to fly home Saturday a choice: Either stay in the village for free until the airline restored service, or go by chartered airplane to Santo Domingo, in the Dominican Republic, and catch a connecting flight from there. I

by Ariane Randall

wanted to stay since I was having such a good time and there would be a July Fourth celebration, but my father decided that we should get out of the country while we still could. This story proves that all parents should listen to their children.

The next day, July 4, twelve guests gathered to wait for the bus. As it turned out, we wouldn't be leaving for another two hours, so I took the opportunity to sunbathe and go for a last dip in the pool. Finally the bus arrived, and I said good-bye to the friends I'd made.

At the airport the plane never came, due to engine trouble. Finally the resort chartered four small planes, and a few hours later four of us — Delia Clarke, Anna Rivera, my father, and I — boarded the last of them. It was a dinky-looking plane, a Piper Cessna, with only three rows of seats. My father and Anna sat backward in the second row, and Delia and I faced them in the third row. Delia was slim and pretty with short brown hair. She told me she'd lost seventy pounds a few years before. (Later I guessed that kind of will-power helped give her strength after we crashed.) Anna was also nice-looking. She was going home to New York.

We took off at 8:36 P.M. It was soon after that my dad looked out the window and noticed the stars were all wrong. From the

40

location of the Big Dipper and other stars, he could tell that we were going west, toward Cuba, as opposed to east, toward Santo Domingo. He asked Anna, who spoke Spanish, to ask the pilot why we were going in the wrong direction, but she was reluctant. She didn't want to question authority. I don't know why I didn't use my Spanish to question him myself. The plane was getting cold, but I went to sleep for two hours, during which time, I have been told, we continued going 180 degrees in the wrong direction.

When I woke up, I noticed that we were over water, with no land in sight. The lights on the wings were not functioning properly. They started and stopped — and then stopped altogether. Most of the instruments on the dashboard were not lit up. This was something I hadn't paid too much attention to before but now scared me. The pilot was not getting a response on his radio, and Anna noticed we were running out of gas. The next thing I knew the pilot was saying, "Mayday! Mayday!"[1] into the radio. Anna cried, "We're going to crash!" I started looking desperately for my life jacket behind and under the seat, but I couldn't find it. Anna found hers. Delia did not. The last thing I saw the pilot doing was tossing his life jacket to my father, who gave it to me and then pulled me on his lap. The plane circled three times around an oil tanker and began the swift descent, gliding toward the sea.

We hit the water, and there is a terrible crashing sound as my side of the plane breaks off and water rushes in. I climb out onto the wing. As I stand there I realize my glasses are gone. I fish around in the water and come up with half the frame. I toss it away. The plane is sinking, and my father comes out with the two ladies but no pilot. We swim away from the wreck as the tail disappears beneath the water. Now we are four people and two life jackets in the vast, dark Caribbean Sea. The pilot is nowhere to be seen.

---

[1]**mayday:** an international radio-telephone signal word used by airplanes and ships in trouble.

The water is warm, and we swim together, realizing it's the safe thing to do and it's comforting. I am the least hurt, having received a blow to the head, probably from my dad's chin. He has a gash on his chin and is bleeding heavily (later we found out he'd lost a quart of blood). And he has bruises, especially on his legs. Delia seems to have broken her nose, and there is blood coming from it. She is not in pain, though. Anna has several cuts about her face, a broken arm, and a concussion that has caused partial amnesia. She keeps asking what has happened, and we tell her that the airplane has crashed. She will ask again the next minute.

Anna and I have inflated our life jackets. They have lights on them that shine brightly. We all hold on to each other, mainly so that the two without life jackets can remain afloat but partly for security. I'm wearing boxer shorts, a T-shirt over my new red bikini, and Chinese slippers, which I keep on the whole time. My father's pants and shoes are bogging him down, so he takes them off.

We think we see a boat light, but it soon disappears. I wonder if we will ever be rescued. The thought of floating out here until I die is horrifying. I think about sharks and ask Anna and Delia not to splash about so much because it will attract "the wrong kind of fish." Sharks can smell blood a mile away, and three of us are bleeding. There is a silent agreement not to mention the pilot or sharks.

Pretty soon we are all telling each other how glad we are to be together and how much we love each other. We talk about ourselves. Anna is single (we find out later she has a sister). She works with bilingual children and has a new job waiting for her on Monday. She is worried that her job won't be kept for her if we are not rescued soon. Delia has two boys back in Connecticut, where she works in a real estate office. She's happy that her daughter, Krista, was not on our flight. My father, Francis, a Russian history professor, will be teaching in the fall. I'll be a sophomore in high school, and if I make it back, I'll have the best what-did-you-do-for-your-summer-vacation essay to hit my teachers in a long time.

All of a sudden a light appears. It looks like a boat light, and we are filled with hope. It appears to be coming steadily toward us. Delia is the only one who can really see since both my father and I have lost our glasses and Anna is fading toward unconsciousness. Anna's injuries are so serious I think she's going to die, but she seems to get better as time goes on. After a half hour (I have my waterproof watch on) the boat light starts to fade. If no boat comes, I decide that I'll swim for land in the morning . . . if there's land anywhere in sight.

We think we see another boat light, but it turns out to be the planet Venus. I feel sick and throw up a lot, which makes me feel better. I drift off into something like sleep. Around 4:30 A.M. Delia spots something that looks like land but might be mist. We wait for dawn to be certain.

When dawn comes, we see it is definitely land. We talk about what to do. Delia and Anna cannot swim well, if at all. If we all go at their pace, there is no way we will reach shore by night. We must make a decision: If my father and I swim for shore, it seems likely we'll make it and be able to tell the Coast Guard where to find Anna and Delia. Or my father might be able to find a boat and come back himself, and in the meantime they could continue to swim. The alternative is to stick together and hope for rescue. My father and I think that splitting up will increase our collective chances of survival. Anna and Delia are reluctant — they feel safer in a group — but they acknowledge that splitting up would be better. Anna and Delia have the better life jacket. We separate, not really saying good-bye because we expect to see each other again soon. Even after we swim far away and can't see them, we hear their voices carrying over the waves.

I keep my father posted on the time. Hours pass, and the nearer we get, the more we realize that we still have many miles to cover. We stop every twenty minutes or so for a rest break, during which I float on my back, which is not so hard to do with a life jacket. I'm not feeling very strong, and I hold on to my dad's shirt-tails and kick or just let him pull me.

It is noon, and we are still a good distance from land. I no longer hear the voices of Delia and Anna. Every now and then my father tells me he loves me a million, trillion times. I say I will tell him how much I love him when we get to land. I'm too tired to speak just now.

It is two o'clock. I have more energy now and a determination to get to land before dark. My dad is getting weaker but still pushes on. I get salt in my mouth all the time, and my tongue is numb from it. It also gets in my eyes, but I have learned to open them quickly afterward, and for some reason this gets rid of the sting. My hair is all matted. We have not had fresh water or food in thirteen hours, but I'm not hungry or thirsty.

It is three o'clock, and I'm starting to hallucinate. I see dolphins, seals, an occasional shark or two, sailboats, and buoys. I say to my dad, "We can do it." And he says, "Yes . . . we can do it." We keep telling each other "I love you" and that we'll make it to shore. I'm guiding my father now, because he keeps his eyes closed most of the time because of the brine[2] and starts to go in the wrong direction unless I correct him. Two pieces of sugarcane float by us, and like the twig brought back to Noah's Ark, they seem like a sign of hope. I think I see palm trees behind me, but they are not really there. At six o'clock we are maybe a mile from shore and feel certain we will make it before nightfall.

But an hour later, with the shore in sight, the sky has become gray with thunderclouds. We think we see thousands of tiny sailboats, and my dad yells for me to swim fast to them. I try hard as the wind blows and it gets stormier. I look back. I can't see my

---

[2]**brine:** water that contains a lot of salt.

dad. "Daddy! Where are you?" I scream. No one answers, and I'm crying for the first time. "Help! Somebody please help! Daddy, where are you?" The rain is coming down hard and fast. I stick my tongue out to see if I can get some. It doesn't work too well. I fight with the waves to keep moving toward land. I ask God why He has put this test before me. I tell Him it won't work: I will come through this with flying colors; I'll ace this test.

When the storm passes, I just want to sleep. The problem is that I then drift with the current, which seems to be going out to sea. Sea snails are biting my legs, but I don't have the strength to brush them off. I don't know what has happened to my father. I try the signal we planned — a high shriek — in case we got separated, but he doesn't answer. I fight to keep awake but slowly drift off.

All the girls I hung out with at the resort are inside my head telling me to swim this way or that. I'm trying to swim toward a hotel, where I can go to sleep. I just want to relax, but I can't because I'll drown. The straps of my life jacket are cutting into me, so I take it off and let it float away. My mouth is burning from the salt — I don't want to die now — if I have to die, can't I at least have a Coke to drink? — something nice-tasting before I drown.

I dream I am destined to drown. Everyone says so, but I'm still trying to find a way out. I dream I inhaled something that burned out my lungs and throat. Then I'm being pulled. I'm being pulled out of the water into a dugout canoe. By two men. Are they capturing me? I must get out. I pick up a piece of wood from the bottom of the boat and try to clobber one of them with it. But he stops me and hits me back.

What a nice way for me to greet my Haitian rescuers — for that's who they were. I saw that they had picked up my dad, too, in another canoe. I heard my dad asking them to start a search for Anna and Delia. The villagers of Bariadelle fed us mangoes and fresh water and crowded around us to watch. They were trying to talk to us in Creole.[3] I could scarcely talk and was confused, but I did manage a *merci beaucoup.*[4]

From Bariadelle we were driven to Dame-Marie and deposited in a French Canadian mission station. By this time my body had gone into shock. I had a high fever, a severe sunburn, and a throat infection that made it difficult to swallow anything without coughing. We were taken to a doctor, but by morning my fever was gone. I found out that I'd lost three pounds. (What a crash diet!) My father had lost fifteen. We were driven to a hospital in Anse-d'Hainault and eventually, passing through fourteen roadblocks and over sixty miles of bumpy mountain roads, to the city of Jérémie. There my father was able to phone my mother and brother and tell them that we were all right. There was still no news of Anna and Delia.

Back in New York the phone never stops ringing. People call to find out if all this really happened to us. Sometimes I ask myself the same question. But what about Anna and Delia? I think of their voices over the waves as we swam away. What happened to them? What will happen to their families?

It is a miracle my father and I survived. When people ask me what I feel about the whole experience, I say that when you've almost missed life, you see it differently. To be with my family and friends, just to be able to go shopping to replace my lost clothes, each day seems like an amazingly good thing.

Shortly after Ariane Randall and her father were rescued, the U.S. Coast Guard began the search for the two missing women and the pilot. The search continued for three days, but Delia Clarke, Anna Rivera, and the pilot, Elia Katime, were never found.

---

[3]**Creole (krē′ōl′):** a language based on French and the native language of Haiti.
[4]**merci beaucoup:** thank you very much.

Responding to "Survival at Sea"

Thinking and Discussing

How do the steps that Ariane and her father take help their chances of survival during the emergency at sea?

How does Ariane's attitude toward life and other people change as a result of the plane crash?

Choosing a Creative Response

Thinking Quickly The author describes how she and the other victims of the crash act quickly during the emergency. In a group discussion, identify their good decisions, and then try to come up with other solutions to the problems they face.

Filming an Adventure Imagine that you plan to film "Survival at Sea." List each person in the story, and name the actor you might cast in the role. Explain what qualities the actor and the character share that make your choice a good one.

Creating Your Own Activity Plan and complete your own activity in response to "Survival at Sea."

Thinking and Writing

Ariane describes being rescued by two Haitians in a dugout canoe. If you were one of her rescuers, what would you do and say? How would you feel? Rewrite the event from the rescuer's point of view.

Hunger made them

think only of food.

They were desperate.

No one in their family

had eaten anything save

that single fish for six

long days.

LONG CLAWS

written and illustrated by James Houston

Pitohok and Upik hurried back into the igloo, shouting, "An owl helped us! Look! We found these fish where it scratched the snow. We dug them up. Four big ones!" Upik clutched the frozen lake trout in her arms, displaying them like precious silver toys. Someone had buried them outside to be eaten later.

50

Upik handed the largest trout to her mother, who held it over the small flame of her stone lamp until it softened slightly.

"I treasure my hunger before a feast," she whispered as she passed the fish and her sharp-curved ulu knife around to the other members of the family. She gazed at her four children — Pitohok and Upik, their small sister Kanajuk and the baby, who was peeking out from the hood of her parka. Then she looked at her old father. Would any of them survive now that her husband was no longer living?

Pitohok, her son, had a smooth brown face and quick, dark eyes. His teeth were square and strong. Like his sister, he wore a fur parka and pants and boots made of caribou skins. Bundled up like that, they both looked plump. Only the dark shadows below their broad cheekbones betrayed their hunger.

Upik's black shiny eyes, white teeth, and wide, clear face were a pleasure to see. When her parka hood was pushed back, her lustrous blue-black hair hung down in two braids thickened by willow sticks and bound stiff with beads.

When the grandfather sniffed the rich smell of thawing fish, he sat up slowly on the fur-covered sleeping platform that was made of snow. Quickly, they each ate their share of the fish.

"Grandfather," Pitohok said, "the fish will give us enough strength to travel. Tell me where the last caribou is buried so that I may go and find it."

"Oh, it is far from here," his grandfather answered. "Too great a distance for you to go alone."

Pitohok looked at his sister and wondered if she had enough strength to walk with him on such a journey.

"Tell me where it lies," Pitohok asked again.

"It is three days' hard walking west of here," his grandfather said, "near the short hill that stands before the Crooked River. Out on that plain last autumn a young male caribou fell before my rifle. A strong wind was blowing and it began to snow. A great feeling of weakness came over me. I had no way to carry home that last caribou and no time to build a proper cache[1] to hide it. I knew that the heavy snows would drift over its body, hiding all but its horns from sight. So I turned its antlers high hoping that someone might find it later." He looked at Pitohok. "It is too great a journey for one person without dogs."

"I will go with him," said Upik.

"Yes, she could help him," said their mother.

Their grandfather closed his eyes in pain. "It is our only chance. If you two make such a journey, you must first search for the Crooked River. Beyond it stands the pointed hill. If you find that hill, climb to its peak and carefully study the land. I believe that you will see that caribou's antlers standing wind-blown, clear of snow. It is bad that we had to break up the sled and burn its wood in the coldest days of winter. It is sad that the dogs are gone," he

---

[1]**cache** (kăsh): a hiding place for a supply of provisions and other items.

said. "But it is good that we are all alive! I will try hard to think of some way to make a sled for you."

"We will need to dig for that caribou," Pitohok said, "but we cannot find the shovel."

"Of course, you cannot find the snow shovel," their grandfather said. "I warned all of you that that shovel should have been left lying flat. Someone in this camp stood it upright in the snow. I saw it," the old man said. "It was standing like a human. That shovel has a soul like any one of us, like birds, like caribou, like fish, like every other thing. When someone left it standing, it did just what you or I would do. As soon as it grew dark, that shovel ran away. Why not? It doesn't like to stand out there in the cold waiting to be a slave to any one of us!"

Pitohok and his sister did not pause long to puzzle over their grandfather's old-fashioned ideas. Hunger made them think only of food. They were desperate. No one in their family had eaten anything save that single fish for six long days.

Upik looked into her mother's eyes. She could see hunger there and fear that the caribou herds, which were their main food, would not come again in time to save their lives.

"Sleep well," their mother told them. "Only tomorrow when your grandfather looks at the sky will it be decided whether you will go or stay."

"If you cannot find the shovel," their grandfather told Pitohok, "take the hand axe and my old snow knife. You can dig with them."

That night the grandfather asked Pitohok's mother to soak two caribou skins in water. When she had done this, he carefully folded each of them lengthwise six times and turned them up on the ends until they took on the rough appearance of a pair of sled runners. These he placed outside to freeze.

Upik's mother stayed awake sewing by her lamp throughout the night so that she could give her two older children each a pair of

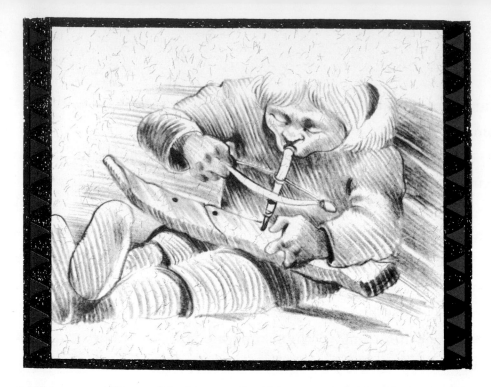

warm, new caribou-skin boots. In the morning the wind was down, but it was bitter cold.

"Bring in the frozen runners," said the grandfather. "If they are hard enough, I shall show you how to build a small sled, using only what we have."

The old man examined the two frozen skins that he had so carefully shaped into sled runners. They were straight and not much longer than his outstretched arms. They were frozen as hard as wood.

Taking an old-fashioned bowdrill, the grandfather placed between his teeth a small bone with a hole in it, shaped just large and deep enough to hold one end of the arrowlike drill shaft. He twisted the string of a short bow around this shaft. By drawing the short bow swiftly back and forth with his right hand in a sawing motion, he made the shaft whirl around so that the sharp nail in its lower end became a drill. Pressing hard, he drilled three holes near the top of each folded caribou-skin runner and forced strong braided caribou sinew through each of these holes.

"Hand me those last three frozen fish," the old man said.

Pitohok passed them to his grandfather.

The grandfather carefully lashed the three stiffly frozen trout on top of the runners so they would serve as cross bars. In this way he was able to bind together a sturdy makeshift sled.

"Now hand me those pulling straps," he said to Upik's mother.

He drilled two more holes in the runners and attached the long leather straps to the front of the sled. Pitohok stood before him while he adjusted this harness to fit Pitohok's shoulders.

"Now," said their grandfather, "here is my old rifle and the only two brass cartridges left to us. I have loaded these with the last two pinches of gunpowder we possess. We have no more lead to make bullets, so I have carved two bullets of stone to fit into these cartridge casings. Stone bullets are strong enough, but I must warn you that they sometimes break and fly apart. Go with strength." Their grandfather sighed. "If you can find that buried caribou, we may all live to see the summer come again."

Upik and Pitohok pulled on their warmest clothing and tied up a roll of caribou sleeping skins.

"We won't come back until we have the meat," Pitohok told his grandfather.

Upik and Pitohok bent low as they went out the long snow tunnel that protected their igloo from the Arctic winds. Their mother followed them outside, but they could find no words to say between them. She held Kanajuk's hand as she watched Upik and Pitohok trudge away, dragging the small frozen sled behind them. Tears filled her eyes, for she wondered whether she would ever see her children again.

Beyond the igloo, the vast flat white snow plain stretched all around them. Far to the east lay Hudson Bay, to the south frozen Kasba Lake. To the north and west the land continued endlessly toward distant, blue, snow-covered mountains and oceans that they had never seen.

Upik and Pitohok traveled steadily westward. The late winter sun faded and soon the whole sky was hidden by a heavy blanket of gray clouds that stretched to the far horizons of the enormous snow-covered land. Only the painful squeal of snow beneath their soft skin boots broke the silence that hung around them.

As it grew dark, the first snowflakes floated down from the western sky. Then gusts of wind swept moaning across the land, driving the fine snow upward into whirling, twisting forms that drifted toward them, then scurried away like ghosts across the lonely plain.

Pitohok stopped at once and drew the snow knife from beneath the lashings of the sled. He licked both sides of the long thin antler blade until it was glazed with ice and would slice smoothly into the hard snow beneath his feet. Carefully he cut out snow blocks and stood them around him in a small circle, cleverly piling them until they curved in at the top to form a dome. Upik stayed outside and packed dry snow into the chinks between the blocks. She could feel the cold wind's force increasing and knew that any weakness in their igloo might allow it to be broken and torn to pieces. Their house of snow was just big enough for the two of them. Upik wondered if it would stand firm.

She stuffed their caribou sleeping robes through the low entrance, and Pitohok yelled to her against the howling wind.

"Push the sled inside as well. We may have to eat it before this storm has ended."

He was right. The blizzard raged and screamed over their small shelter for three long, gloomy days and terrifying nights, leaving them weak with fear and hunger. Their igloo trembled like a frightened rabbit during the awful storm. But it held.

On the fourth morning the wind died out. Pitohok looked at the three frozen trout that formed their small sled. "Tomorrow we will have to eat one of the fish, or we will not have the strength to travel. Two fish will be just enough to hold the sled together."

That night Upik unlashed the lake trout that had been the sled's center crossbar and placed it between herself and the caribou robe beneath her. She slept on top of it all night. In the morning her body heat had thawed the fish enough for them to eat. They shared it with the eagerness of wild animals.

All that day they traveled, then built another igloo and slept again. When they crawled out at dawn, Pitohok pointed into the west. "Do you see something strange over there?"

He cupped his mittened hands together and boosted his sister high. She shaded her eyes and examined the flat horizon.

"It's the hill!" she cried. "And beyond it I can see a long windswept streak that looks like ice. That must be the Crooked River."

"Hurry," said Pitohok. "We must find that caribou while the light is strong."

It was almost evening when they reached the pointed hill. It was not much taller than two men standing one on the shoulders of the other, but in this dead-flat land it looked like an enormous mountain. Eagerly Pitohok climbed it. As he reached the top, he disturbed a snowy owl that took flight across the plain.

Upik, seeing it, crouched down and sang her secret song:

"White owl, I sing to you.

Softly I sing to you,

Owl, my helping spirit."

"Look! Look out there where she is flying," called Pitohok. "I can see the caribou antlers standing upright in the snow. But do you see something moving toward the antlers through the blue shadows of the snowdrift?"

"Yes, I see it," Upik called up to him. "It's dark brown and humped over like a dog."

"It's Kugvik, the wolverine!" said Pitohok. "Look at the way that one moves and digs. They're the worst meat robbers in the world. Quick! I need the rifle."

Upik untied their grandfather's old rifle from the sled and carried it up to her brother. Pitohok sat down on the snow. From his small leather bag, he took out the two precious brass cartridges and examined the stone bullets. He chose one, opened the rifle, and placed the cartridge in its breech.

He held his grandfather's heavy rifle steady by resting his elbows on his knees. With one eye closed, he took careful aim at the wolverine that was digging with its sharp claws through the hard-packed snow, trying to get at the caribou.

Upik jumped back as the heavy rifle boomed and echoed across the wide snow plain.

"I missed," said Pitohok, his voice full of disappointment.

"That's no wonder," Upik called to him. "The bullet that you fired broke into three small pieces. I saw the bits of stone fall onto the snow. But the noise of the rifle frightened the wolverine. He is running away!"

Pitohok came leaping down the hill and lashed the rifle onto the sled again. "Follow me!" he said, snatching up the long straps. "We must reach that caribou before night comes."

The first stars twinkled in the western sky as they came up to the caribou antlers that stood above the snow.

Pitohok stared in wonder at his sister. "Is that grandfather's shovel standing in the snow beside the antlers?" he whispered. "Are we seeing something magic?"

"Is it truly ours?" asked Upik.

"Yes, it's ours," said Pitohok, bending to look closely at its familiar wooden shape and its worn leather stitching. "I'd know that snow shovel anywhere. I've dug with it so many times."

"Grandfather must have left it here last autumn," Upik said, "when he was growing weak and it was dark and storming."

Pitohok drew the snow knife from beneath the lashings of the sled and paced out a circle for their igloo.

"I am going to build it right on top of the caribou, leaving only its horns outside," Pitohok said, "so that wolverines can't come back here in the night and steal the meat from us."

When their new igloo was completed, Upik looked up and saw the cold-faced winter moon rising in the eastern sky. As Pitohok crawled into the igloo, he sighed and said, "Perhaps we don't have to eat. My belly feels full just knowing that we're going to sleep on top of all this rich caribou meat." He patted their snow floor. "Imagine how glad our family will be when we return with such a treasure."

They rose early in the morning and tried again to forget their hunger as they broke the igloo's side walls. Using the snow knife and the shovel, they dug up the frozen caribou and lashed it onto the small sled.

Before they left, Pitohok carefully stood the shovel upright in the snow. He smiled and said, "If you can walk, please hurry home to our grandfather and tell him we are coming."

The snow shovel did not move or seem to hear his words.

Pitohok took up the long pulling straps and together they headed back toward their home. They hauled the welcome weight of meat behind them, following their own footprints eastward, hurrying until it was almost dark. Then they built a small igloo and slept exhausted.

Many times the following morning Upik looked back at the precious caribou lashed to the creaking sled. She tried to fight off her hunger by saying, "Just think of the wonderful smell that meat will make as it simmers in our mother's pot."

The morning sun had risen high above the plain when Pitohok stopped and pushed up his wooden goggles. He shaded his eyes, then pointed at a small dark speck far away. "Do you see it?"

"Yes, what is it?" Upik asked him as she watched it moving slowly toward them across the endless plain of snow.

"I don't know," said Pitohok as he pulled down his goggles to protect his eyes again. "It's not a caribou or a man. But it is certainly something that's alive."

"Let us hurry home," said Upik. "I don't like the look of that moving spot. It sways from side to side in a heavy way that frightens me."

By midafternoon the brown speck had grown much larger.

"It is moving faster than we can walk. What is it?" Upik asked her brother.

"I am not sure," he said, handing her one of the straps. "Let us run for a little while together, then walk, and run again. Perhaps it will turn and go away."

In the late afternoon they had to stop and rest because their legs were too tired to go on.

"Can you tell now what it is," Upik asked, "that thing that is coming closer to us?"

"Yes," Pitohok said. "It is Akla, a barren-ground grizzly bear. It is moving in our footprints, following our scent."

"I am afraid," said Upik. "I have never seen an akla, but I have heard terrible things about them. Hunters call them 'Long Claws.'"

"Let us walk fast again," said Pitohok.

When the sun started to sink into the west, Pitohok knew that they could not get away from the huge, hump-shouldered grizzly that came shambling after them, rolling its enormous hips, gaining on them with every step it took.

"We've got to do something," Pitohok gasped, and now his voice was full of fear. "That akla's going to catch us no matter how fast we walk. And if we run now, it may get excited and attack. Grizzlies are tireless in following their prey and can make short, fast bursts of speed. Grandfather has told me that strong aklas in their prime can sometimes catch a running caribou."

"What shall we do?" Upik asked him, and Pitohok could tell by her voice that she was almost crying.

Pitohok stopped and drew his grandfather's rifle out from under the sled lashings. He put their last stone-nosed cartridge inside its barrel. Looking at his sister, he said, "I hope we won't have to use it."

He stood the rifle upright in the snow. Then quickly he bent and unlashed the frozen caribou and rolled it off the sled. With his short, sharp knife he cut the bindings that held the sled together. As it fell apart, Pitohok grabbed one of the runners. Whirling it around his head, he threw it as far as he could along the trail toward the oncoming grizzly. The second runner he flung far to the right, hoping to draw the big bear away from their path.

The akla stopped, raised its massive head and stared at the two human creatures. Pitohok and Upik could hear its stomach rumbling with hunger as it ambled forward and sniffed the folded caribou skin. Placing one paw upon it, the grizzly tore it into pieces with its teeth and began devouring it.

Pitohok knelt down beside the frozen caribou and grasped it by its front and rear legs. "Quick!" he said to Upik. "Help me heave this meat onto my shoulders."

She did so, scarcely able to believe how heavy it was.

As soon as Pitohok rose to his feet, he started walking, hurrying once more along their own trail that would lead them home.

"You bring the rifle and the snow knife and the last two fish," he called back to his sister. "One sleeping robe will have to do us. Tie it around yourself. Leave the other one. Move!" Upik could hear a sound of horror creeping into his voice again. "Don't let that Long Claws near you!"

Upik's legs ached with tiredness, but she hurried after him, afraid to look back, afraid she would find the grizzly close behind her.

The evening sun turned red as it slid down and touched the long, flat white horizon. Pitohok looked back then and groaned beneath the heavy weight of caribou. "Long Claws is still coming after us. Give him a fish. Hurry and fling it back toward him."

Upik did as she was told. Pitohok looked again, then slowed his pace. "He's lying down," Pitohok gasped. "He's eaten the trout.

He looks now as if he's going to sleep." It was growing dark and Pitohok was staggering with weariness. "Hold onto me," he groaned. "Help me. I've got to make my feet carry me over that next snow ridge so the akla won't see us stop to build our igloo."

When they were beyond the huge bear's sight, Pitohok collapsed, letting the caribou fall to the snow. Upik helped him up, but Pitohok was so exhausted that he could scarcely rise. With the snow knife Upik cut a shallow gravelike hole and they slid the caribou in and carefully covered it with snow. They built their igloo on top of it.

Once inside, Pitohok wedged a snow block firmly into place, trying to jam the entrance. "Let us share our one last fish," he said. "I have never been so hungry or so tired in all my life."

Even while they were eating, they listened carefully. But they did not hear the akla. Upik could not finish her share of the fish, so exhausted was she from their terrible journey. They rolled themselves into the caribou robe and slept, not knowing if the akla would let them live to see the next day dawn.

When Pitohok awoke, he said, "The weather's changed. Can you not smell and feel spring's dampness in the air?"

Cautiously he cut away the entrance block and crawled outside. Upik followed him. The land was blanketed in lead-gray fog that hung heavily above the snow, hiding everything from view. The huge akla might have been very close to them or very far away.

Pitohok dug up the caribou and cutting a larger entrance in their igloo, shoved the frozen animal outside.

"There is Long Claws. He is waiting for us," Upik whispered with terror in her voice.

Pitohok looked up and saw the dark outline of the akla standing watching them. It was less than a stone's throw away, its wide back glistening with silver hoarfrost, which made the coarse hair on its massive shoulders bristle like countless needles.

"Shall I try to shoot him now?" Pitohok whispered to his sister.

"No," she said. "No! I'm afraid that last bullet will break and the noise will only anger him."

"Then hurry," he cried. "Help me get this caribou up onto my back. I don't know how far I can carry it today. My legs feel weak as water. But we've got to get it home."

Swaying its huge head back and forth, the grizzly let a low growl rumble in its throat. It was so close now that for the first time Upik could see the akla's long, sharp claws. They cut deep furrows in the snow when it came shambling toward them. Its beady black eyes watched every move they made.

"Leave our caribou sleeping skin in front of the igloo. That may fool him," Pitohok whispered. "If he goes inside, he will surely smell the place where the caribou lay last night. He may stay there digging long enough for us to lose him."

Together they hurried away, trying to hide themselves from Long Claws in the heavy ice fog. They walked and walked until they came to a riverbed that seemed familiar to them. Violent winds had blown one bank free of snow, but in the swirling fog they could not tell where it would lead them. Pitohok struggled up onto the stones that formed the bank of the frozen river. His sister had to help him by pushing at his back.

"Be careful not to leave a single track up here," Pitohok gasped. "Step from rock to rock," he warned her. "The wind is at our back. If the akla cannot see us or smell our footprints, we may lose him."

Together they traveled on the stony river bank until about midday, following a twisted course, leaving no path behind them.

"I hope we are far enough away from him," Pitohok gasped. "I can walk no farther."

He sank to his knees and let the heavy weight of the caribou sag down until it rested on the wind-cleared stones. He lay against it, his chest heaving as he tried to catch his breath. Although the air was stinging cold, Upik had to kneel and wipe the frost-white sweat from her brother's face.

"He's gone." Upik sighed, glad to rest the heavy rifle in the snow. She looked around in the still-thick fog. "Which way do we go now?"

Pitohok peered over his shoulder and felt cold sweat trickling down his spine. He could see no sign of the sun. Everything was hidden by a wall of fog.

"I . . . I don't know," he admitted. "I was trying so hard to get away from the akla that now . . . we're lost!"

Pitohok struggled painfully onto his knees and looked in all directions. He saw nothing but gray ice fog that drifted in phantom swirls along the frozen river.

"Oh, I wish someone would help us," Upik whispered aloud, and as if in answer to her words, the snowy owl came toward her, winging low out of the fog. Upik saw the owl turn its head as though it had seen the bear, then stare at her with its huge golden-yellow eyes. Suddenly the owl changed its wingbeat, hovering as if by magic at the very edge of the smokelike mists. It seemed to signal Upik. Then, turning sharply to the right, it flew off, cutting a dark trail through the ice-cold wall of fog.

Upik stood up, and, using all her strength, helped her brother heave the caribou onto his back. She struggled to ease the heavy burden as she stood upright.

"We should follow her," said Upik. "I think she knows the way."

Her brother's answer was a moan when the full weight of the frozen caribou settled on his tired, cramped shoulders. "Yes, follow the owl," he whispered.

Upik tried to steady Pitohok while they walked. She looked back only once at the zigzag trail they left in the snow as her brother's strength grew less and less. Both of them had lost all sense of distance and of time. Upik followed the owl's course through the dense fog, wondering if they would ever reach their home.

They had not gone far before Upik heard the sound of heavy breathing. She turned, then screamed in terror. The huge grizzly, its heavy head rolling, its tongue lolling out of its mouth, came padding after them. It was only a pace behind Pitohok. Upik saw Long Claws raise its head and sniff at the rich burden of caribou, which had softened a little because of the heat of Pitohok's body. The grizzly stretched out its neck and licked the frosted nostrils of the caribou.

"What's the matter?" Pitohok asked her. Then turning, he, too, saw the bear. His voice caught in his throat. "You've got to . . . to try and shoot him," Pitohok gasped. "I can't do it. My arms are too tired. My whole body is trembling from carrying this weight. Let him get close to you," he said, "then shoot him . . . in the head."

Upik stopped, raised the heavy rifle and tried to sight along its wavering barrel. "I can't," she said. "I am afraid . . . afraid this

last stone bullet will break." She was weeping. "Drop the caribou," Upik begged her brother. "Let Long Claws take it. We can walk away alive. It will stop and eat. Please drop the caribou. I am afraid that the akla is going to kill you for that meat."

Pitohok hunched his shoulders and struggled forward, as if he had not heard her plea. But now Upik could see that he held his short knife in his hand and that he would not give up their prize of meat without a fight.

Once more she heard an angry rumble in the grizzly's throat and saw it reach out with one terrible paw and rake the caribou along the whole length of its back. As its claws hooked against the caribou's antlers, Pitohok was thrown off balance and stumbled sideways, falling onto his knees. The big bear moved closer. Driven by fear and desperation, Pitohok rose and continued walking, his eyes narrowed, his mouth drawn down with strain.

The huge akla, with lips drawn back to show its enormous teeth, came after him again. Upik once more raised her grandfather's rifle and looked along its sights. The bear must have heard the safety catch click off, for it stopped, turned its head and stared straight up the gun barrel at her. At that moment, looking into its eyes, Upik realized that the bear was neither good nor evil. It was a hunter like themselves, desperate to feed itself and remain alive in the lonely, snow-filled wilderness. She lowered the rifle. She could not bring herself to try to kill the bear.

At that moment, Pitohok whispered hoarsely, "I see the owl again! She's sitting on our family's empty food cache. Can it be?" he sobbed. "Are we . . . almost home?"

The bear moved in again behind him and, raising up on its hind feet, struck out angrily at the caribou's plump haunches. Pitohok reeled from the heavy blow and staggered to his knees. He tried to rise, then sank back onto the snow.

"I can't go on," he said. "I'm finished." He had lost his knife. There were tears in his eyes, but his teeth were clenched in anger. He tightened his grip upon the caribou.

"Let go," Upik begged her brother. "Let him have the meat."

"No," Pitohok said. "If I lose this caribou to that bear and return home with nothing, none of us will live, and I, myself, would die of shame."

He turned away from the hot breath of the snarling grizzly whose great swaying head was not more than an arm's length from his face.

"Run!" Pitohok whispered to his sister. "Run for the igloo and save yourself."

Upik bent and grabbed her brother underneath the arms, trying to help him up, but he was too weak. Then she turned around so that she stood directly between him and the akla's gaping jaws.

"No — don't do that," Pitohok gasped. He was hunched over like an old man. "Put the rifle under the caribou to help me support this weight," he moaned, "or I . . . shall never rise. You run!" he begged his sister. Pitohok wept aloud as he whispered, "I can't do any more. All my strength has gone. It's going black . . . I'm going to . . ."

"You are coming with me, now!" cried Upik. "I can see our igloo. It's not far from us. Can you not see it through the fog?"

The big grizzly raked its claws through the snow. Upik put her left shoulder underneath the caribou and her arm around her brother's waist and strained with all her might. Together they rose from the snow and staggered off toward their family's house. Pitohok stumbled once again and fell onto one knee. He hung there gasping for breath.

The akla snarled and opened its mouth wide to take the caribou's leg and Pitohok's mitted hand between its crushing jaws.

"*Unalook! Kukikotak!*" Upik screamed at the bear. "We shared our fish with you. Don't you dare to harm my brother. He must take this food home to our family. They are starving . . . don't you understand?"

The huge bear let go of Pitohok's hand and the caribou's leg and stood there glaring back at her.

"Quick! Get back on your feet," Upik whispered. "We have only a little way to go."

The grizzly must have seen the snowhouse, too, for suddenly it shambled around in front of them, blocking Pitohok's way.

"I warned you not to hurt my brother," Upik screamed again.

As if ruled by magic, the huge bear stepped back and let them pass.

"Mother! Mother! Come and help us!" Upik wailed.

Long Claws turned its head and stared at her when Upik's mother burst out of their igloo entrance. She saw the great humped shoulders of the akla and, like her daughter, screamed at it, then turned and rushed inside again.

Upik tried to take half of the caribou's weight on her own shoulders while pulling Pitohok to his feet. Slowly he rose, but his knees would scarcely support him.

"Don't drop it now," Upik said in a stern voice. "We're almost there."

Together they staggered painfully toward the igloo.

"Everything is whirling around," cried Pitohok. "It's going black again . . . I'm falling. . . ."

Because she no longer had the strength to hold him, Upik and her brother collapsed together on the snow. She shook him, but Pitohok seemed to have lost the power to hear or move or speak. Upik tried to drag him toward the igloo, but his arms remained locked tight around their precious burden of meat.

Long Claws turned once more and shambled after them, snarling like a huge and angry dog. It grasped the caribou's neck in its powerful jaws and started backing away, dragging the carcass and Pitohok, pulling both of them into the swirling fog.

The snow knife, the rifle and Pitohok's short knife were gone. Upik had no weapons but her hands and teeth. She turned and saw her grandfather crawling out of the igloo on his hands and knees. In his left mitt he held his huge curved bow and in his mouth a pair of arrows. Right behind him came their mother, her parka hood puffed out with icy wind, screaming aloud, raging to protect her children, ready to do battle with the enormous bear. Her hands outstretched like claws, their mother raced forward to attack.

Upik heard her grandfather call out, "Stop, woman. Hold! If you help me, we can pierce him right from here."

The grandfather knelt unsteadily and notched an arrow to the braided string. His hands shook with strain when he tried to draw the powerful bow. But he could not. In desperation Upik's mother knelt and helped to draw the heavy weapon almost to full curve. The point of the arrow wavered wildly when the grandfather tried to aim.

"Don't!" Upik cried, spreading her arms and running between her grandfather's unsteady arrow and the bear. "You might hit Pitohok."

Looking back, she saw her brother still being dragged across the snow behind the bear. In sudden anger she whirled around and ran straight between her brother and the akla, screaming, *"You let go of him! Let go!"*

Surprised, the huge grizzly released the caribou for a moment and raised its head.

"Here, this is for you," she yelled and reaching into her parka hood, she snatched out the last piece of frozen trout that she had saved and flung it beyond the bear.

The akla looked at her, grunted, then turned and moved away from Pitohok, who still clasped the caribou as fiercely as an Arctic crab. The grizzly snatched up the piece of fish. Then, with its hips and frosted shoulders rolling, it disappeared into the silver wall of icy fog.

Pitohok's mother and his grandfather knelt beside him, trying to unlock his arms from the caribou.

Pitohok opened his eyes and stared at them. "I thought that akla would surely snatch the caribou away from me," he whispered.

"I, too, believed that he would take it from you," his grandfather agreed. "But no human knows exactly what the animals will do."

"Upik was afraid of the akla. We were both afraid of him, and yet she ran and put her body between me and the grizzly's snarling jaws. Grandfather, did you believe my sister would do that?"

"No. I did not know what she would do. Nobody knows the strength or courage that humans possess until real danger comes to test them."

Thinking and Discussing

In what ways does the author of *Long Claws* describe nature as being threatening? As being helpful? What do you think the author may be suggesting about the relationship between the Inuit people and nature?

Choosing a Creative Response

Composing a Song or Poem To remember their dangerous adventure, Upik and Pitohok might have made up a song or poem. Write your favorite part of the story as they might have recited or sung it.

Carving an Animal Figure The Inuit people are famous for their carvings. Make an illustration of an animal, bird, or person that Upik or Pitohok might have carved. You might want to do the actual carving on your own later.

Renaming Animals The grizzly bear in the story was also known by the descriptive name Long Claws. Invent descriptive names for the owl, the wolverine, and other animals that Upik and Pitohok could have seen during their adventure.

Creating Your Own Activity Plan and complete your own activity in response to *Long Claws*.

Thinking and Writing

At the end of the story, Grandfather says, "Nobody knows the strength or courage that humans possess until real danger comes to test them." Think about someone you have known or heard about who discovered great strength in the face of danger. Write a description of the way the person was tested, and tell how unexpected courage and strength led to safety.

ABOUT THE AUTHORS

James Houston was born in Canada in 1921. After studying art in Paris, he returned home looking for interesting subjects to draw. By chance he visited an Inuit settlement on the northeast coast of Hudson Bay. He stayed in the Arctic for fourteen years.

Houston used his knowledge of Eskimo life and legends to write books for young people.

He was awarded the Canadian Library Association Book of the Year Award for *Tikta'liktak* and *The White Archer*. He also received the American Library Association Notable Books Award for *The White Archer*, *Akavak*, and *The White Dawn*. Houston now lives in Rhode Island.

Elizabeth F. Chittenden was born in Vermont in 1903. She earned degrees from Smith College and the University of Buffalo and went on to a forty-year career as an English teacher.

After retiring from teaching, she began free-lance writing. The topics of her writings include women's rights and freedom fighters.

Talking about reading, Chittenden has said she is grateful "for the joy of losing 'me' in somebody else's life through a good tale, fiction or biography."

Cynthia Rylant is an award-winning author of picture books, novels, short stories, and poetry. How she writes depends on the genre. "Picture books and poetry come fast," she explains. "Longer books take me about six months to write. . . . When I sit down to write a short story, I usually know I'm going to finish it in four or five pages. Even if I just write the first line, I can tear four or five pages out of the notebook." Rylant was born in Hopewell, Virginia, on June 6, 1954, and was raised in West Virginia.

Ariane Randall, the daughter of two college professors, was a student at Hunter College High School when she wrote about her terrifying experience in the ocean off Haiti. Ariane had gone with her father, Francis, for a week's vacation in Haiti while her older brother and mother stayed home in New York City. "Survival at Sea" is Ariane's account of her disastrous return journey.

OTHER SURVIVORS

Medicine Walk
by Ardath Mayhar
(Atheneum, 1985)

Twelve-year-old Burr Henderson is excited about a birthday flight with his father in their small airplane. When the flight ends in tragedy, however, Burr must make his way on foot out of the forbidding desert — alone. Through his incredible journey Burr learns about the ancient Apache way of life and about himself.

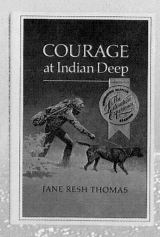

Courage at Indian Deep
by Jane Resh Thomas
(Clarion, 1984)

In the midst of a blizzard, Cass notices a distress call from a sinking ship on Lake Superior. He shows unusual courage as he and his dog and a former school rival help rescue people from the ship.

Wild Timothy
by Gary L. Blackwood
(Atheneum, 1987)

Timothy's father takes him deep into the woods on his first camping trip. When his father sends him out to chop firewood, Timothy becomes hopelessly lost. Alone in the woods, he tries to remember the survival tactics he's only read about.

Hatchet
by Gary Paulsen
(Bradbury, 1987)

Using only a hatchet, Brian spends fifty-four days surviving in the wilderness following a plane crash. In the sequel, *The River* (Delacorte, 1991), a survival reenactment turns into a race against death when Brian's companion is struck by lightning.

Night of the Twisters
by Ivy Ruckman
(Crowell, 1984)

Dan is in charge of the house and his younger brother while his parents are away. He's managing well when suddenly he hears sirens shriek out a tornado alert. Dan rushes his brother and a visiting friend into the basement. They huddle in the shower stall while the twisters strike.

Devil Storm
by Theresa Nelson
(Orchard, 1987)

As storm winds and flood waters rise on the Bolivar Peninsula in Texas, thirteen-year-old Walter Carrol waits for his father to return to the family. His father, however, is trapped miles away in Galveston. To save his mother and sisters, Walter must trust a mysterious, perhaps dangerous, tramp named Old Tom.

REALISTIC FICTION

BECOMING

C O N T E N T S

From *Sister*   82
by Eloise Greenfield

The Circuit   88
by Francisco Jiménez

Papa's Parrot   102
by Cynthia Rylant

The Bracelet   108
by Yoshiko Uchida

The Scribe   120
by Kristin Hunter

The turning point in

the process of

growing up is when

you discover the core

of strength within you

that survives all

hurt.

— *Max Lerner*

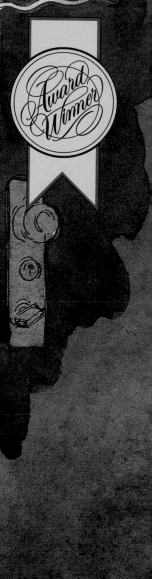

Sister

BY

ELOISE GREENFIELD

Award Winner

Doretha lives with her mother and older sister. Because her mother went to work when Doretha's father died, Doretha helps out by doing chores and most of the cooking. When Doretha was nine, she started a memory book — one page to remind her of each important memory. Now she is thirteen, and the book is filled with memories. One time when Aunt Mae came over . . .

"Sister! You deaf?" Aunt Mae called from the front room.

"I didn't hear you, Aunt Mae," Doretha called back. She folded the dishtowel and hung it over the rack.

"I guess not, the way you singing and carrying on. I said how long you going to take, washing those little bit of dishes?" She lowered her voice when she saw Doretha come into the room. "About time. The movie's coming on, and I hate to watch T.V. by myself." She turned several knobs on the television set. "How the devil you get this thing to stand still?"

Doretha made a fist and banged on the top of the set. The picture slid around once more and stopped. "I'm glad you came over," she said. "Mama's working late today."

"Thelma's going to let those folks at the laundry work her to death, you know that?" Aunt Mae sat down in the stuffed chair and crossed her legs. "Hey, why don't you run down to the corner and get us some potato chips? Keep me from biting my nails down to the quick[1] while I'm watching the movie. It's a murder mystery." She got her shoulder bag from the sofa and gave Doretha some change.

Doretha went to the closet for her coat. She put it on, tied a triangular scarf around her neck to hide the worn collar, opened the front door, and stopped suddenly.

---

[1] **quick** (kwĭk): the sensitive, tender flesh under the fingernails.

Illustrated by James Noel Smith

"Why you just standing there?" Aunt Mae asked.

Doretha closed the door quietly. "They over there on Bernard's front," she said.

"Who?" Aunt Mae went to the window and lifted the yellow nylon curtain.

"The boys," Doretha said. "Aunt Mae! Don't let them see you looking!"

Aunt Mae dropped the curtain and stepped back. She put her hands on her hips. "Now, Sister," she said, "I know you not scared of boys."

"I'm not scared of them, I just don't like to walk by them. Coley's over there, and he acts so . . . so funny. Most of the time he doesn't even speak unless he's by himself."

"He knows you crazy about him, that's why," Aunt Mae said. She leaned her head to one side and widened her large eyes at Doretha. "And I guess when he feels like opening his mouth, you talk to him?"

Doretha didn't answer. She started taking her coat off.

"Put that coat right back on, Sister!"

"But, Aunt Mae . . ."

"I mean it. Put it on right now." She pulled the coat up on Doretha's shoulders. "I never heard anything so simple[2] in all my life. Can't go out your own house unless somebody goes out there first to see if the street's clear of boys. Now, all you got to do is like this. Watch me now." She walked across the room with a little bounce, making her accordion-pleated skirt swing. She was the size Doretha wanted to be, not really slim, but not fat either. "How you doing?" she said to the floor lamp standing beside the sofa. She waved her arm and kept walking. "Now you do it," she told Doretha.

---

[2]**simple**: having little common sense.

"I can't walk like you," Doretha said.

"Well, walk the way you walk, just don't draw all up like something's going to bite you."

Doretha felt silly, but she tried to imitate her aunt. She walked across the room and waved her arm. "How you doing?" she said.

"That's good, that's good," Aunt Mae said. "Now do it again and say it louder."

After the fourth time, Aunt Mae told her she was ready. "I'll be right here behind the curtain, watching," she said.

"They still there?" Doretha asked.

"Yeah, they still there, and if they weren't, I'd go find them. Thelma let you sit around here daydreaming all the time, you won't never learn how to deal."

Doretha put her hand on the doorknob, and a sudden thought made her panic. "What about when I'm coming back?" she asked.

"When you coming back, think about how good those potato chips going to be, and don't even look over there unless somebody says something to you."

When she got outside, Doretha didn't look across the street right away. She was concentrating on how she was walking. Not too fast, not too slow. She didn't hear a break in their laughing and talking, but when she turned her head to look at them, the boys were looking at her.

"How you doing?" she said with a quick wave.

"Hey Doretha, hey baby." Walter and Larry spoke, and Bernard gave her the black salute. But Coley stood still and cool with his hands in his pockets and his feet turned in just slightly. Doretha turned her head away.

At the store, she bought the potato chips from Mr. Carter and started back. She looked straight ahead and walked in rhythm with her thoughts. "Potato chips, potato chips." As soon as she passed the boys, she started to grin. Aunt Mae was laughing when she opened the door for her, and they leaned on it and closed it together. "I did it, I did it!" Doretha said, laughing and hugging her aunt.

Aunt Mae put her hands on her hips. "You bet your Aunt Mae's applecake you did it. And the next time that sometimey, jive joker tries to speak to you, you tell him where to go and what to do when he gets there. Now, come on watch the movie. You missed one murder already."

Thinking and Discussing

What dialogue and actions in "Sister" make the character of Doretha seem like a real person, someone you might know?

At the beginning of "Sister," Doretha's answer to Aunt Mae's questions show how shy she is. How does the author use Doretha's dialogue with the boys and Aunt Mae to show Doretha's increased self-confidence?

Choosing a Creative Response

Giving Advice If Aunt Mae had a radio program called "Ask Aunt Mae," what kind of advice do you think she would give? With a partner, role-play one of Doretha's friends calling to "Ask Aunt Mae" about a problem, and Aunt Mae giving advice.

Creating Your Own Activity Plan and complete your own activity in response to "Sister."

Thinking and Writing

Think of an incident that you would like to share with your classmates, and like Doretha, write your own memory page describing the incident. Say as much or as little as you wish, but try to make your writing clear and lively.

THE CIRCUIT

by Francisco Jiménez

Illustrated by Carlos Llerena-Aguirre

It was that time of year again. Ito, the strawberry sharecropper, did not smile. It was natural. The peak of the strawberry season was over and the last few days the workers, most of them braceros,[1] were not picking as many boxes as they had during the months of June and July.

As the last days of August disappeared, so did the number of braceros. Sunday, only one — the best picker — came to work. I liked him. Sometimes we talked during our half-hour lunch break. That is how I found out he was from Jalisco, the same state in Mexico my family was from. That Sunday was the last time I saw him.

When the sun had tired and sunk behind the mountains, Ito signaled us that it was time to go home. "Ya esora,"[2] he yelled in his broken Spanish. Those were the words I waited for twelve hours a day, everyday, seven days a week, week after week. And the thought of not hearing them again saddened me.

---

[1] **braceros** (brä **sä´**rōs): unskilled farm workers or day laborers.
[2] **"Ya esora"** (yä âs **ō´**rä): loosely, "It's time!"

As we drove home Papa did not say a word. With both hands on the wheel, he stared at the dirt road. My older brother, Roberto, was also silent. He leaned his head back and closed his eyes. Once in a while he cleared from his throat the dust that blew in from outside.

Yes, it was that time of year. When I opened the front door to the shack, I stopped. Everything we owned was neatly packed in cardboard boxes. Suddenly I felt even more the weight of hours, days, weeks, and months of work. I sat down on a box. The thought of having to move to Fresno and knowing what was in store for me there brought tears to my eyes.

That night I could not sleep. I lay in bed thinking about how much I hated this move.

A little before five o'clock in the morning, Papa woke everyone up. A few minutes later, the yelling and screaming of my little brothers and sisters, for whom the move was a great adventure, broke the silence of dawn. Shortly, the barking of the dogs accompanied them.

While we packed the breakfast dishes, Papa went outside to start the "Carcanchita." That was the name Papa gave his old '38 black Plymouth. He bought it in a used-car lot in Santa Rosa in the winter of 1949. Papa was very proud of his car. "Mi Carcanchita," my little jalopy, he called it. He had a right to be proud of it. He spent a lot of time looking at other cars before buying this one. When he finally chose the "Carcanchita," he checked it thoroughly before driving it out of the car lot. He examined every inch of the car. He listened to the motor, tilting his head from side to side like a parrot, trying to detect any noises that spelled car trouble. After being satisfied with the looks and sounds of the car, Papa then insisted on knowing who the original owner was. He never did find out from the car salesman. But he bought the car anyway. Papa figured the original owner must have been an important man because behind the rear seat of the car he found a blue necktie.

Papa parked the car out in front and left the motor running. "Listo" (ready), he yelled. Without saying a word, Roberto and I began to carry the boxes out to the car. Roberto carried the two big boxes and I carried the two smaller ones. Papa then threw the mattress on top of the car roof and tied it with ropes to the front and rear bumpers.

Everything was packed except Mama's pot. It was an old large galvanized pot she had picked up at an army surplus store in Santa Maria the year I was born. The pot was full of dents and nicks, and the more dents and nicks it had, the more Mama liked it. "Mi olla" (my pot), she used to say proudly.

I held the front door open as Mama carefully carried out her pot by both handles, making sure not to spill the cooked beans. When she got to the car, Papa reached out to help her with it.

Roberto opened the rear car door and Papa gently placed it on the floor behind the front seat. All of us then climbed in. Papa sighed, wiped the sweat off his forehead with his sleeve, and said wearily: "Es todo" (that's it).

As we drove away, I felt a lump in my throat. I turned around and looked at our little shack for the last time.

At sunset we drove into a labor camp near Fresno. Since Papa did not speak English, Mama asked the camp foreman if he needed any more workers. "We don't need no more," said the foreman, scratching his head. "Check with Sullivan down the road. Can't miss him. He lives in a big white house with a fence around it."

When we got there, Mama walked up to the house. She went through a white gate, past a row of rose bushes, up the stairs to the front door. She rang the doorbell. The porch light went on and a tall husky man came out. They exchanged a few words. After the man went in, Mama clasped her hands and hurried back to the car.

"We have work! Mr. Sullivan said we can stay there the whole season," she said gasping and pointing to an old garage near the stables.

The garage was worn out by the years. It had no windows. The walls, eaten by termites, strained to support the roof full of holes. The loose dirt floor, populated by earth worms, looked like a gray road map.

That night, by the light of a kerosene lamp, we unpacked and cleaned our new home. Roberto swept away the loose dirt, leaving the hard ground. Papa plugged the holes in the walls with old newspapers and tin can tops. Mama fed my little brothers and sisters. Papa and Roberto then brought in the mattress and placed it on the far corner of the garage. "Mama, you and the little ones sleep on the mattress. Roberto, Panchito, and I will sleep outside under the trees," Papa said.

Early next morning Mr. Sullivan showed us where his crop was, and after breakfast, Papa, Roberto, and I headed for the vineyard to pick.

Around nine o'clock the temperature had risen to almost one hundred degrees. I was completely soaked in sweat and my mouth felt as if I had been chewing on a handkerchief. I walked over to the end of the row, picked up the jug of water we had brought, and began drinking. "Don't drink too much; you'll get sick," Roberto shouted. No sooner had he said that than I felt sick to my stomach. I dropped to my knees and let the jug roll off my hands. I remained motionless with my eyes glued on the hot sandy ground. All I could hear was the drone of insects. Slowly I began to recover. I poured water over my face and neck and watched the black mud run down my arms and hit the ground.

I still felt a little dizzy when we took a break to eat lunch. It was past two o'clock and we sat underneath a large walnut tree that was on the side of the road. While we ate, Papa jotted down the number of boxes we had picked. Roberto drew designs on the ground with a stick. Suddenly I noticed Papa's face turn pale as he looked down the road. "Here comes the school bus," he whispered loudly in alarm. Instinctively, Roberto and I ran and hid in the vineyards. We did not want to get in trouble for not going to school. The yellow bus stopped in front of Mr. Sullivan's house. Two neatly dressed boys about my age got off. They carried books under their arms. After they crossed the street, the bus drove away. Roberto and I came out from hiding and joined Papa. "Tienen que tener cuidado" (you have to be careful), he warned us.

After lunch we went back to work. The sun kept beating down. The buzzing insects, the wet sweat, and the hot dry dust made the afternoon seem to last forever. Finally the mountains around the valley reached out and swallowed the sun. Within an hour it was too dark to continue picking. The vines blanketed the grapes, making it difficult to see the bunches. "Vámonos,"[3] said Papa, signaling to us that it was time to quit work. Papa then took out a pencil and began to figure out how much we had earned our first day. He wrote down numbers, crossed some out, wrote down some more. "Quince"[4] (fifteen dollars), he murmured.

When we arrived home, we took a cold shower underneath a waterhose. We then sat down to eat dinner around some wooden crates that served as a table. Mama had cooked a special meal for us. We had rice and tortillas with "carne con chile," my favorite dish.

The next morning I could hardly move. My body ached all over. I felt little control over my arms and legs. This feeling went on every morning for days until my muscles finally got used to the work.

---

[3] **"Vámonos"** (bä´mō nōs): "Let's go."
[4] **"Quince"** (kēn´sā): "Fifteen."

It was Monday, the first week of November. The grape season was over and I could now go to school. I woke up early that morning and lay in bed, looking at the stars and savoring the thought of not going to work and of starting sixth grade for the first time that year. Since I could not sleep, I decided to get up and join Papa and Roberto at breakfast. I sat at the table across from Roberto, but I kept my head down. I did not want to look up and face him. I knew he was sad. He was not going to school today. He was not going tomorrow, or next week, or next month. He would not go until the cotton season was over, and that was sometime in February. I rubbed my hands together and watched the dry, acid stained skin fall to the floor in little rolls.

When Papa and Roberto left for work, I felt relief. I walked to the top of a small grade next to the shack and watched the "Carcanchita" disappear in the distance in a cloud of dust.

Two hours later, around eight o'clock, I stood by the side of the road waiting for school bus number twenty. When it arrived I climbed in. No one noticed me. Everyone was busy either talking or yelling. I sat in an empty seat in the back.

When the bus stopped in front of the school, I felt very nervous. I looked out the bus window and saw boys and girls carrying books under their arms. I felt empty. I put my hands in my pants pocket and walked to the principal's office. When I entered I heard a woman's voice say: "May I help you?" I was startled. I had not heard English for months. For a few seconds I remained speechless. I looked at the lady who waited for an answer. My first instinct was to answer her in Spanish, but I held back. Finally, after struggling for English words I managed to tell her that I wanted to enroll in the sixth grade. After answering many questions, I was led to the classroom.

Mr. Lema, the sixth grade teacher, greeted me and assigned me a desk. He then introduced me to the class. I was so nervous and scared at that moment when everyone's eyes were on me that I wished I were with Papa and Roberto picking cotton. After taking roll, Mr. Lema gave the class the assignment for the first hour. "The first thing we have to do this morning is finish reading the story we began yesterday," he said enthusiastically. He walked up to me, handed me an English book, and asked me to read. "We are on page 125," he said politely. When I heard this, I felt my blood rush to my head; I felt dizzy. "Would you like to read?" he asked hesitantly. I opened the book to page 125. My mouth was dry. My eyes began to water. I could not begin. "You can read later," Mr. Lema said understandingly.

For the rest of the reading period I kept getting angrier and angrier with myself. I should have read, I thought to myself.

During recess I went into the restroom and opened my English book to page 125. I began to read in a low voice, pretending I was in class. There were many words I did not know. I closed the book and headed back to the classroom.

Mr. Lema was sitting at his desk correcting papers. When I entered he looked up at me and smiled. I felt better. I walked up to him and asked if he could help me with the new words. "Gladly," he said.

The rest of the month I spent my lunch hours working on English with Mr. Lema, my best friend at school.

One Friday during lunch hour Mr. Lema asked me to take a walk with him to the music room. "Do you like music?" he asked me as we entered the building.

"Yes, I like Mexican corridos,"[5] I answered. He then picked up a trumpet, blew on it and handed it to me. The sound gave me goose bumps. I knew that sound. I had heard it in many Mexican

---

[5]**corridos** (kō rē´thōs): Mexican folk ballads.

corridos. "How would you like to learn how to play it?" he asked. He must have read my face because before I could answer, he added: "I'll teach you how to play it during our lunch hours."

That day I could hardly wait to get home to tell Papa and Mama the great news. As I got off the bus, my little brothers and sisters ran up to meet me. They were yelling and screaming. I thought they were happy to see me, but when I opened the door to our shack, I saw that everything we owned was neatly packed in cardboard boxes.

Thinking and Discussing

The story begins with Panchito's family finishing the strawberry-picking job and moving on to find work in Fresno. How do the events described in this opening section lay the groundwork for the rest of the story? How do those events affect the ending?

How do the family members respond differently to the move and to finding work? What do you think the reasons are for their differing reactions?

How do you think Panchito feels at the very end of the story? Describe the ways in which you think Panchito will deal with having to move again.

What do Panchito's responses to school and to Mr. Lema's encouragement tell you about Panchito's character?

Choosing a Creative Response

Listing Personal Possessions   Panchito's whole family puts everything they own into four boxes. Imagine that you are moving to a new town and that you can pack only one medium-sized box. Make a list of what you would take and what you would leave behind. What reasons would you have to support your choices?

Advertising Your School   Panchito's new school evidently offers a music program. Select an extracurricular program that your school offers or that you would like it to offer (drama club, soccer, music, etc.). Create a poster advertising the program. Display the poster in the classroom.

Creating Your Own Activity   Plan and complete your own activity in response to "The Circuit."

Thinking and Writing

Panchito feels sad when his family has to move; he has become used to the family's current home, and he dreads trying to make his way in a new town. If you were to move, what would you miss about your home and your town? How would you deal with the lonely feeling you might have in your new town? Write a personal essay about the things you would not like to leave behind and about what your feelings might be in a new place. Share your essay with a friend or relative.

MIGRANT FARM WORKERS

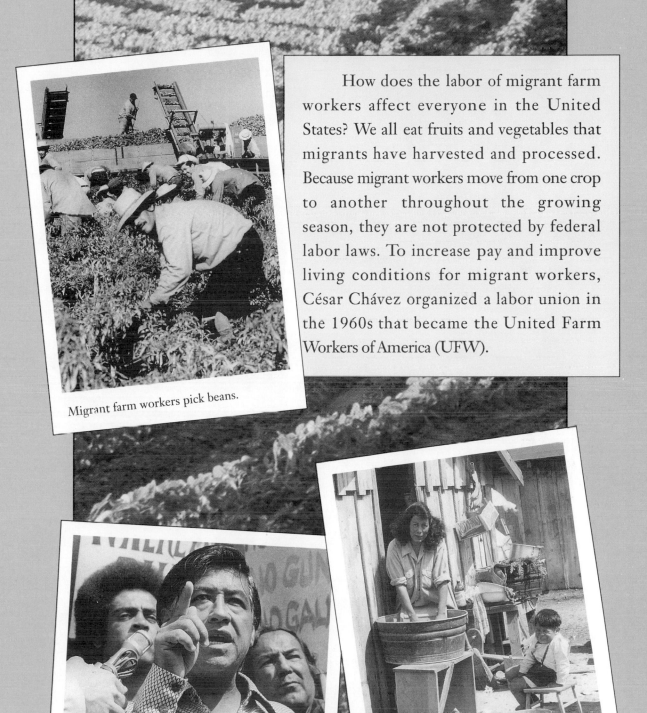

How does the labor of migrant farm workers affect everyone in the United States? We all eat fruits and vegetables that migrants have harvested and processed. Because migrant workers move from one crop to another throughout the growing season, they are not protected by federal labor laws. To increase pay and improve living conditions for migrant workers, César Chávez organized a labor union in the 1960s that became the United Farm Workers of America (UFW).

Migrant farm workers pick beans.

César Chávez heads the United Farm Workers.

A woman washes clothes in a camp.

A worker picks grapes in a vineyard.

This man writes contracts with growers.

Farm workers own this co-op.

The labor union holds a rally.

Striking farm workers demonstrate.

Supporters wave the UFW flag.

by Cynthia Rylant

Though his father was fat and merely owned a candy and nut shop, Harry Tillian liked his papa. Harry stopped liking candy and nuts when he was around seven, but, in spite of this, he and Mr. Tillian had remained friends and were still friends the year Harry turned twelve.

For years, after school, Harry had always stopped in to see his father at work. Many of Harry's friends stopped there, too, to spend a few cents choosing penny candy from the giant bins or to sample Mr. Tillian's latest batch of roasted peanuts. Mr. Tillian looked forward to seeing his son and his son's friends every day. He liked the company.

When Harry entered junior high school, though, he didn't come by the candy and nut shop as often. Nor did his friends. They were older and they had more spending money. They went to a burger place. They played video games. They shopped for records. None of them were much interested in candy and nuts anymore.

Illustrated by Margaret Kasahara

A new group of children came to Mr. Tillian's shop now. But not Harry Tillian and his friends.

The year Harry turned twelve was also the year Mr. Tillian got a parrot. He went to a pet store one day and bought one for more money than he could really afford. He brought the parrot to his shop, set its cage near the sign for maple clusters and named it Rocky.

Harry thought this was the strangest thing his father had ever done, and he told him so, but Mr. Tillian just ignored him.

Rocky was good company for Mr. Tillian. When business was slow, Mr. Tillian would turn on a small color television he had sitting in a corner, and he and Rocky would watch the soap operas. Rocky liked to scream when the romantic music came on, and Mr. Tillian would yell at him to shut up, but they seemed to enjoy themselves.

The more Mr. Tillian grew to like his parrot, and the more he talked to it instead of to people, the more embarrassed Harry became. Harry would stroll past the shop, on his way somewhere else, and he'd take a quick look inside to see what his dad was doing. Mr. Tillian was always talking to the bird. So Harry kept walking.

At home things were different. Harry and his father joked with each other at the dinner table as they always had — Mr. Tillian teasing Harry about his smelly socks; Harry teasing Mr. Tillian about his blubbery stomach. At home things seemed all right.

But one day, Mr. Tillian became ill. He had been at work, unpacking boxes of caramels, when he had grabbed his chest and fallen over on top of the candy. A customer had found him, and he was taken to the hospital in an ambulance.

Mr. Tillian couldn't leave the hospital. He lay in bed, tubes in his arms, and he worried about his shop. New shipments of candy and nuts would be arriving. Rocky would be hungry. Who would take care of things?

Harry said he would. Harry told his father that he would go to the store every day after school and unpack boxes. He would sort out all the candy and nuts. He would even feed Rocky.

So, the next morning, while Mr. Tillian lay in his hospital bed, Harry took the shop key to school with him. After school he left his friends and walked to the empty shop alone. In all the days of his life, Harry had never seen the shop closed after school. Harry didn't even remember what the CLOSED sign looked like. The key stuck in the lock three times, and inside he had to search all the walls for the light switch.

The shop was as his father had left it. Even the caramels were still spilled on the floor. Harry bent down and picked them up one by one, dropping them back in the boxes. The bird in its cage watched him silently.

Harry opened the new boxes his father hadn't gotten to. Peppermints. Jawbreakers. Toffee creams. Strawberry kisses. Harry traveled from bin to bin, putting the candies where they belonged.

"Hello!"

Harry jumped, spilling a box of jawbreakers.

"Hello, Rocky!"

Harry stared at the parrot. He had forgotten it was there. The bird had been so quiet, and Harry had been thinking only of the candy.

"Hello," Harry said.

"Hello, Rocky!" answered the parrot.

Harry walked slowly over to the cage. The parrot's food cup was empty. Its water was dirty. The bottom of the cage was a mess.

Harry carried the cage into the back room.

"Hello, Rocky!"

"Is that all you can say, you dumb bird?" Harry mumbled. The bird said nothing else.

Harry cleaned the bottom of the cage, refilled the food and water cups, then put the cage back in its place and resumed sorting the candy.

"Where's Harry?"

Harry looked up.

"Where's Harry?"

Harry stared at the parrot.

"Where's Harry?"

Chills ran down Harry's back. What could the bird mean? It was like something from "The Twilight Zone."

"Where's Harry?"

Harry swallowed and said, "I'm here. I'm here, you stupid bird."

"You stupid bird!" said the parrot.

Well, at least he's got one thing straight, thought Harry.

"Miss him! Miss him! Where's Harry? You stupid bird!"

Harry stood with a handful of peppermints.

"*What?*" he asked.

"Where's Harry?" said the parrot.

"I'm *here*, you stupid bird! I'm here!" Harry yelled. He threw the peppermints at the cage, and the bird screamed and clung to its perch.

Harry sobbed, "I'm here." The tears were coming.

Harry leaned over the glass counter.

"Papa." Harry buried his face in his arms.

"Where's Harry?" repeated the bird.

Harry sighed and wiped his face on his sleeve. He watched the parrot. He understood now: someone had been saying, for a long time, "Where's Harry? Miss him."

Harry finished his unpacking, then swept the floor of the shop. He checked the furnace so the bird wouldn't get cold. Then he left to go visit his papa.

Thinking and Discussing

Why is it more effective for the boy to learn how his father feels through the parrot than directly from the father?

How does Harry's changing attitude toward candy reflect his changing feelings as he begins growing up?

Choosing a Creative Response

Performing a Puppet Play With a partner, create a puppet show that features Harry and the parrot. Write a dialogue in which the puppets act out their feelings about the situation with the father. Perform the skit in front of the class.

Creating Your Own Activity Plan and complete your own activity in response to "Papa's Parrot."

Thinking and Writing

Imagine that you are Harry, and you must create a sign explaining your father's absence from the store. How might you let people know about your father's situation? Write a large sign explaining why the store is closed.

108

*April 21, 1942, was a typical day for most American families liv-
ing on the West Coast. For thousands of Japanese Americans, however,
April 21 would be remembered as a day of sorrow. A few months after the
bombing of Pearl Harbor, President Franklin D. Roosevelt had signed
Evacuation Order 9066, which commanded that all Japanese Americans
relocate to concentration camps for the duration of World War II.*

*The United States government had given Ruri's family less than
twenty-four hours' notice to evacuate their home. Ruri's mother and older
sister were still packing when the doorbell rang.*

THE BRACELET
BY YOSHIKO UCHIDA
ILLUSTRATED BY CAROL INOUYE

"Mama; is it time to go?"

I hadn't planned to cry, but the tears came suddenly, and I
wiped them away with the back of my hand. I didn't want my older
sister to see me crying.

"It's almost time, Ruri," my mother said gently. Her face was
filled with a kind of sadness I had never seen before.

I looked around at my empty room. The clothes that Mama
always told me to hang up in the closet, the junk piled on my dresser, the old rag doll I could never bear to part with; they were

all gone. There was nothing left in my room, and there was nothing left in the rest of the house. The rugs and furniture were gone, the pictures and drapes were down, and the closets and cupboards were empty. The house was like a gift box after the nice thing inside was gone; just a lot of nothingness.

It was almost time to leave our home, but we weren't moving to a nicer house or to a new town. It was April 21, 1942. The United States and Japan were at war, and every Japanese person on the West Coast was being evacuated by the government to a concentration camp.[1] Mama, my sister Keiko and I were being sent from our home, and out of Berkeley, and eventually, out of California.

The doorbell rang, and I ran to answer it before my sister could. I thought maybe by some miracle, a messenger from the government might be standing there, tall and proper and buttoned into a uniform, come to tell us it was all a terrible mistake; that we wouldn't have to leave after all. Or maybe the messenger would have a telegram from Papa, who was interned[2] in a prisoner-of-war camp in Montana because he had worked for a Japanese business firm.

The FBI had come to pick up Papa and hundreds of other Japanese community leaders on the very day that Japanese planes had bombed Pearl Harbor. The government thought they were dangerous enemy aliens. If it weren't so sad, it would have been funny. Papa could no more be dangerous than the mayor of our city, and he was every bit as loyal to the United States. He had lived here since 1917.

When I opened the door, it wasn't a messenger from anywhere. It was my best friend, Laurie Madison, from next door. She

---

[1]**concentration camp:** a camp for imprisoning people, such as prisoners of war, who are or seem to be a threat to the government.

[2]**interned** (ĭn tûrnd´): forcibly imprisoned, especially in wartime.

was holding a package wrapped up like a birthday present, but she wasn't wearing her party dress, and her face drooped like a wilted tulip.

"Hi," she said. "I came to say good-bye."

She thrust the present at me and told me it was something to take to camp. "It's a bracelet," she said before I could open the package. "Put it on so you won't have to pack it." She knew I didn't have one inch of space left in my suitcase. We had been instructed to take only what we could carry into camp, and Mama had told us that we could each take only two suitcases.

"Then how are we ever going to pack the dishes and blankets and sheets they've told us to bring with us?" Keiko worried.

"I don't really know," Mama said, and she simply began packing those big impossible things into an enormous duffel bag — along with umbrellas, boots, a kettle, hot plate, and flashlight.

"Who's going to carry that huge sack?" I asked.

But Mama didn't worry about things like that. "Someone will help us," she said. "Don't worry." So I didn't.

Laurie wanted me to open her package and put on the bracelet before she left. It was a thin gold chain with a heart dangling on it. She helped me put it on, and I told her I'd never take it off, ever.

"Well, good-bye then," Laurie said awkwardly. "Come home soon."

"I will," I said, although I didn't know if I would ever get back to Berkeley again.

I watched Laurie go down the block, her long blond pigtails bouncing as she walked. I wondered who would be sitting in my desk at Lincoln Junior High now that I was gone. Laurie kept turning and waving, even walking backwards for a while, until she got to the corner. I didn't want to watch anymore, and I slammed the door shut.

The next time the doorbell rang, it was Mrs. Simpson, our other neighbor. She was going to drive us to the Congregational church, which was the Civil Control Station where all the Japanese of Berkeley were supposed to report.

It was time to go. "Come on, Ruri. Get your things," my sister called to me.

It was a warm day, but I put on a sweater and my coat so I wouldn't have to carry them, and I picked up my two suitcases. Each one had a tag with my name and our family number on it. Every Japanese family had to register and get a number. We were Family Number 13453.

Mama was taking one last look around our house. She was going from room to room, as though she were trying to take a mental picture of the house she had lived in for fifteen years, so she would never forget it.

I saw her take a long last look at the garden that Papa loved. The irises beside the fish pond were just beginning to bloom. If Papa had been home, he would have cut the first iris blossom and brought it inside to Mama. "This one is for you," he would have said. And Mama would have smiled and said, "Thank you, Papa San," and put it in her favorite cut-glass vase.

But the garden looked shabby and forsaken now that Papa was gone and Mama was too busy to take care of it. It looked the way I felt, sort of empty and lonely and abandoned.

When Mrs. Simpson took us to the Civil Control Station, I felt even worse. I was scared, and for a minute I thought I was going to lose my breakfast right in front of everybody. There must have been over a thousand Japanese people gathered at the church. Some were old and some were young. Some were talking and laughing, and some were crying. I guess everybody else was scared too. No one knew exactly what was going to happen to us.

We just knew we were being taken to the Tanforan Racetracks, which the army had turned into a camp for the Japanese. There were fourteen other camps like ours along the West Coast.

What scared me most were the soldiers standing at the doorway of the church hall. They were carrying guns with mounted bayonets. I wondered if they thought we would try to run away, and whether they'd shoot us or come after us with their bayonets if we did.

A long line of buses waited to take us to camp. There were trucks, too, for our baggage. And Mama was right; some men were there to help us load our duffel bag. When it was time to board the buses, I sat with Keiko and Mama sat behind us. The bus went down Grove Street and passed the small Japanese food store where Mama used to order her bean-curd cakes and pickled radish. The windows were all boarded up, but there was a sign still hanging on the door that read, "We are loyal Americans."

The crazy thing about the whole evacuation was that we were all loyal Americans. Most of us were citizens because we had been born here. But our parents, who had come from Japan, couldn't become citizens because there was a law that prevented any Asian from becoming a citizen. Now everybody with a Japanese face was being shipped off to concentration camps.

"It's stupid," Keiko muttered as we saw the racetrack looming up[3] beside the highway. "If there were any Japanese spies around, they'd have gone back to Japan long ago."

"I'll say," I agreed. My sister was in high school and she ought to know, I thought.

When the bus turned into Tanforan, there were more armed guards at the gate, and I saw barbed wire strung around the entire

---

[3]**looming up:** towering close by.

grounds. I felt as though I were going into a prison, but I hadn't done anything wrong.

We streamed off the buses and poured into a huge room, where doctors looked down our throats and peeled back our eyelids to see if we had any diseases. Then we were given our housing assignments. The man in charge gave Mama a slip of paper. We were in Barrack 16, Apartment 40.

"Mama!" I said. "We're going to live in an apartment!" The only apartment I had ever seen was the one my piano teacher lived in. It was in an enormous building in San Francisco with an elevator and thick carpeted hallways. I thought how wonderful it would be to have our own elevator. A house was all right, but an apartment seemed elegant and special.

We walked down the racetrack looking for Barrack 16. Mr. Noma, a friend of Papa's, helped us carry our bags. I was so busy looking around, I slipped and almost fell on the muddy track. Army barracks had been built everywhere, all around the racetrack and even in the center oval.

Mr. Noma pointed beyond the track toward the horse stables. "I think your barrack is out there."

He was right. We came to a long stable that had once housed the horses of Tanforan, and we climbed up the wide ramp. Each stall had a number painted on it, and when we got to 40, Mr. Noma pushed open the door.

"Well, here it is," he said, "Apartment 40."

The stall was narrow and empty and dark. There were two small windows on each side of the door. Three folded army cots were on the dust-covered floor and one light bulb dangled from the ceiling. That was all. This was our apartment, and it still smelled of horses.

Mama looked at my sister and then at me. "It won't be so bad when we fix it up," she began. "I'll ask Mrs. Simpson to send me

some material for curtains. I could make some cushions too, and . . . well. . . ." She stopped. She couldn't think of anything more to say.

Mr. Noma said he'd go get some mattresses for us. "I'd better hurry before they're all gone." He rushed off. I think he wanted to leave so that he wouldn't have to see Mama cry. But he needn't have run off, because Mama didn't cry. She just went out to borrow a broom and began sweeping out the dust and dirt. "Will you girls set up the cots?" she asked.

It was only after we'd put up the last cot that I noticed my bracelet was gone. "I've lost Laurie's bracelet!" I screamed. "My bracelet's gone!"

We looked all over the stall and even down the ramp. I wanted to run back down the track and go over every inch of ground we'd walked on, but it was getting dark and Mama wouldn't let me.

I thought of what I'd promised Laurie. I wasn't ever going to take the bracelet off, not even when I went to take a shower. And now I had lost it on my very first day in camp. I wanted to cry.

I kept looking for it all the time we were in Tanforan. I didn't stop looking until the day we were sent to another camp, called Topaz, in the middle of a desert in Utah. And then I gave up.

But Mama told me never mind. She said I didn't need a bracelet to remember Laurie, just as I didn't need anything to remember Papa or our home in Berkeley or all the people and things we loved and had left behind.

"Those are things we can carry in our hearts and take with us no matter where we are sent," she said.

And I guess she was right. I've never forgotten Laurie, even now.

Thinking and Discussing

In "The Bracelet," the reader gets to know the characters through Ruri's telling of the story. What do you learn about Ruri and Laurie? What do you learn about the mother's character through her reactions to the evacuation and the concentration camp?

Although the events described in "The Bracelet" actually happened to thousands of Japanese Americans during World War II, Ruri and her family are made-up characters. What techniques does the author employ to make the story seem realistic?

Choosing a Creative Response

Creating a Bulletin Board Display   Do you have a keepsake, like Ruri's bracelet, that has special memories? Write a few paragraphs about your keepsake, telling how and when you got it, and why it is important to you. You may want to include a drawing with your writing. When you and your classmates have finished, work together to create a bulletin board display.

Preparing a Scene   Imagine that you are writing a play about life in the concentration camps. Review "The Bracelet" for ideas, and then work with a partner to prepare a scene for the play. Write down ideas about how the characters will act and describe what the setting will be like.

Creating Your Own Activity   Plan and complete your own activity in response to "The Bracelet."

Thinking and Writing

Imagine that you have traded places with Ruri and that you are now living at Tanforan. Write a letter to Laurie telling her about your experiences.

QUICK DOLLAR
CHECK CASHING
— SERVICE —

MAINE

THE SCRIBE

BY KRISTIN HUNTER

ILLUSTRATED BY AMANDA SCHAFFER

*W*e been living in the apartment over the Quick Dollar Check Cashing Service five years. But I never had any reason to go in there till two days ago, when Mom had to go to the Wash-a-Mat and asked me to get some change.

And man! Are those people who come in there in some bad shape.

Old man Quick and old man Dollar, who own the place, have signs tacked up everywhere:

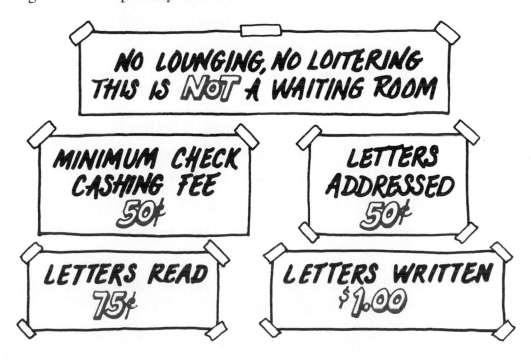

NO LOUNGING, NO LOITERING
THIS IS NOT A WAITING ROOM

MINIMUM CHECK CASHING FEE 50¢

LETTERS ADDRESSED 50¢

LETTERS READ 75¢

LETTERS WRITTEN $1.00

And everybody who comes in there to cash a check gets their picture taken like they're some kind of criminal.

After I got my change, I stood around for a while digging the action. First comes an old lady with some kind of long form to fill out. The mean old man behind the counter points to the "One Dollar" sign. She nods. So he starts to fill it out for her.

"Name?"

"Muskogee Marie Lawson."

"SPELL it!" he hollers.

"M, m, u, s — well, I don't exactly know, sir."

"I'll put down 'Marie,' then. Age?"

"Sixty-three my last birthday."

"Date of birth?"

"March twenty-third" — a pause — "I think, 1900."

"Look, Marie," he says, which makes me mad, hearing him first-name a dignified old gray-haired lady like that, "if you'd been born in 1900, you'd be seventy-two. Either I put that down, or I put 1910."

"Whatever you think best, sir," she says timidly.

He sighs, rolls his eyes to the ceiling, and bangs his fist on the form angrily. Then he fills out the rest.

"One dollar," he says when he's finished. She pays like she's grateful to him for taking the trouble.

Next is a man with a cane, a veteran who has to let the government know he moved. He wants old man Quick to do this for him, but he doesn't want him to know he can't do it himself.

"My eyes are kind of bad, sir, will you fill this thing out for me? Tell them I moved from 121 South 15th Street to 203 North Decatur Street."

Old man Quick doesn't blink an eye. Just fills out the form, and charges the crippled man a dollar.

And it goes on like that. People who can't read or write or count their change. People who don't know how to pay their gas bills, don't know how to fill out forms, don't know how to address envelopes. And old man Quick and old man Dollar cleaning up on all of them. It's pitiful. It's disgusting. Makes me so mad I want to yell.

And I do, but mostly at Mom. "Mom, did you know there are hundreds of people in this city who can't read and write?"

Mom isn't upset. She's a wise woman. "Of course, James," she says. "A lot of the older people around here haven't had your advantages. They came from down South, and they had to quit school very young to go to work.

"In the old days, nobody cared whether our people got an education. They were only interested in getting the crops in." She sighed. "Sometimes I think they *still* don't care. If we hadn't gotten you into that good school, you might not be able to read so well either. A lot of boys and girls your age can't, you know."

"But that's awful!" I say. "How do they expect us to make it in a big city? You can't even cross the streets if you can't read the WALK and DON'T WALK signs."

"It's hard," Mom says, "but the important thing to remember is it's no disgrace. There was a time in history when nobody could read or write except a special class of people."

And Mom takes down her Bible. She has three Bible study certificates and is always giving me lessons from Bible history. I don't exactly go for all the stuff she believes in, but sometimes it *is* interesting.

"In ancient times," she says, "no one could read or write except a special class of people known as *scribes*. It was their job to write down the laws given by the rabbis and the judges. No one else could do it.

"Jesus criticized the scribes," she goes on, "because they were so proud of themselves. But he needed them to write down his teachings."

"Man," I said when she finished, "that's something."

My mind was working double-time. I'm the best reader and writer in our class. Also it was summertime. I had nothing much to do except go to the park or hang around the library and read till my eyeballs were ready to fall out, and I was tired of doing both.

So the next morning, after my parents went to work, I took Mom's card table and a folding chair down to the sidewalk. I lettered a sign with a Magic Marker, and I was in business. My sign said:

I set my table up in front of the Quick Dollar and waited for business. Only one thing bothered me. If the people couldn't read, how would they know what I was there for?

But five minutes had hardly passed when an old lady stopped and asked me to read her grandson's letter. She explained that she had just broken her glasses. I knew she was fibbing, but I kept quiet.

I read the grandson's letter. It said he was having a fine time in California, but was a little short. He would send her some money as soon as he made another payday. I handed the letter back to her.

"Thank you, son," she said, and gave me a quarter.

I handed that back to her too.

The word got around. By noontime I had a whole crowd of customers around my table. I was kept busy writing letters, addressing envelopes, filling out forms, and explaining official-looking letters that scared people half to death.

I didn't blame them. The language in some of those letters — "Establish whether your disability is one-fourth, one-third, one-half, or total, and substantiate[1] in paragraph 3 (b) below" — would upset anybody. I mean, why can't the government write English like everybody else?

Most of my customers were old, but there were a few young ones too. Like the girl who had gotten a letter about her baby from the Health Service and didn't know what "immunization" meant.

At noontime one old lady brought me some iced tea and a peach, and another gave me some fried chicken wings. I was really having a good time, when the shade of all the people standing around me suddenly vanished. The sun hit me like a ton of hot bricks.

Only one long shadow fell across my table. The shadow of a tall, heavy, blue-eyed cop. In our neighborhood, when they see a cop, people scatter. That was why the back of my neck was burning.

"What are you trying to do here, sonny?" the cop asks.

"Help people out," I tell him calmly, though my knees are knocking together under the table.

"Well, you know," he says, "Mr. Quick and Mr. Dollar have been in business a long time on this corner. They are very respected men in this neighborhood. Are you trying to run them out of business?"

"I'm not charging anybody," I pointed out.

"That," the cop says, "is exactly what they don't like. Mr. Quick says he is glad to have some help with the letter-writing. Mr. Dollar says it's only a nuisance to them anyway and takes up too much time. But if you don't charge for your services, it's unfair competition."

---

[1] **substantiate:** prove.

Well, why not? I thought. After all, I could use a little profit. "All right," I tell him. "I'll charge a quarter."

"Then it is my duty to warn you," the cop says, "that it's against the law to conduct a business without a license. The first time you accept a fee, I'll close you up and run you off this corner."

He really had me there. What did I know about licenses? I'm only thirteen, after all. Suddenly I didn't feel like the big black businessman anymore. I felt like a little kid who wanted to holler for his mother. But she was at work, and so was Daddy.

"I'll leave," I said, and did, with all the cool I could muster. But inside I was burning up, and not from the sun.

One little old lady hollered "You big bully!" and shook her umbrella at the cop. But the rest of those people were so beaten-down they didn't say anything. Just shuffled back on inside to give Mr. Quick and Mr. Dollar their hard-earned money like they always did.

I was so mad I didn't know what to do with myself that afternoon. I couldn't watch TV. It was all soap operas anyway, and they seemed dumber than ever. The library didn't appeal to me either. It's not air-conditioned, and the day was hot and muggy.

Finally I went to the park and threw stones at the swans in the lake. I was careful not to hit them, but they made good targets because they were so fat and white. Then after a while the sun got lower. I kind of cooled off and came to my senses. They were just big, dumb, beautiful birds, and not my enemies. I threw them some crumbs from my sandwich and went home.

"Daddy," I asked that night, "how come you and Mom never cash checks downstairs in the Quick Dollar?"

"Because," he said, "we have an account at the bank, where they cash our checks free."

"Well, why doesn't everybody do that?" I wanted to know.

"Because some people want all their money right away," he said. "The bank insists that you leave them a minimum balance."[2]

"How much?" I asked him.

"Only five dollars."

"But that five dollars still belongs to you after you leave it there?"

"Sure," he says. "And if it's in a savings account, it earns interest."

"So why can't people see they lose money when they *pay* to have their checks cashed?"

"A lot of *our* people," Mom said, "are scared of banks, period. Some of them remember the Depression,[3] when all the banks closed and the people couldn't get their money out. And others think banks are only for white people. They think they'll be insulted, or maybe even arrested, if they go in there."

Wow. The more I learned, the more pitiful it was. "Are there any black people working at our bank?"

"There didn't used to be," Mom said, "but now they have Mr. Lovejoy and Mrs. Adams. You know Mrs. Adams, she's nice. She has a daughter your age."

"Hmmm," I said, and shut up before my folks started to wonder why I was asking all those questions.

The next morning, when the Quick Dollar opened, I was right there. I hung around near the door, pretending to read a copy of *Jet* magazine.

"Psst," I said to each person who came in. "I know where you can cash checks *free*."

It wasn't easy convincing them. A man with a wine bottle in a paper bag blinked his red eyes at me like he didn't believe he had

---

[2]**balance:** supply of unspent money.

[3]**Depression:** the Great Depression of the 1930s, a period of widespread unemployment and hardship.

heard right. A carpenter with tools hanging all around his belt said he was on his lunch hour and didn't have time. And a big fat lady with two shopping bags pushed past me and almost knocked me down, she was in such a hurry to give Mr. Quick and Mr. Dollar her money.

But finally I had a little group who were interested. It wasn't much. Just three people. Two men — one young, one old — and the little old lady who'd asked me to read her the letter from California. Seemed the grandson had made his payday and sent her a money order.

"How far is this place?" asked the young man.

"Not far. Just six blocks," I told him.

"Aw shoot. I ain't walking all that way just to save fifty cents."

So then I only had two. I was careful not to tell them where we were going. When we finally got to the Establishment Trust National Bank, I said, "This is the place."

"I ain't goin' in there," said the old man. "No sir. Not me. You ain't gettin' me in *there*." And he walked away quickly, going back in the direction we had come.

To tell the truth, the bank did look kind of scary. It was a big building with tall white marble pillars. A lot of Brink's armored trucks and Cadillacs were parked out front. Uniformed guards walked back and forth inside with guns. It might as well have had a "Colored Keep Out" sign.

Whereas the Quick Dollar is small and dark and funky and dirty. It has trash on the floors and tape across the broken windows. People going in there feel right at home. I looked at the little old lady. She smiled back bravely.

"Well, we've come this far, son," she said. "Let's not turn back now."

So I took her inside. Fortunately Mrs. Adams' window was near the front.

"Hi, James," she said.

"I've brought you a customer," I told her.

Mrs. Adams took the old lady to a desk to fill out some forms. They were gone a long time, but finally they came back.

"Now, when you have more business with the bank, Mrs. Franklin, just bring it to me," Mrs. Adams said.

"I'll do that," the old lady said. She held out her shiny new bankbook. "Son, do me a favor and read that to me."

"Mrs. Minnie Franklin," I read aloud. "July 9, 1972. Thirty-seven dollars."

"That sounds real nice," Mrs. Franklin said. "I guess now I have a bankbook, I'll have to get me some glasses."

Mrs. Adams winked at me over the old lady's head, and I winked back.

"Do you want me to walk you home?" I asked Mrs. Franklin.

"No thank you, son," she said. "I can cross streets by myself all right. I know red from green."

And then she winked at both of us, letting us know she knew what was happening.

"Son," she went on, "don't ever be afraid to try a thing just because you've never done it before. I took a bus up here from Alabama by myself forty-four years ago. I ain't thought once about going back. But I've stayed too long in one neighborhood since I've been in this city. Now I think I'll go out and take a look at *this* part of town."

Then she was gone. But she had really started me thinking. If an old lady like that wasn't afraid to go in a bank and open an account for the first time in her life, why should *I* be afraid to go up to City Hall and apply for a license?

Wonder how much they charge you to be a scribe?

Responding to "The Scribe"

Thinking and Discussing

The author depicts the main character's way of learning by observation. How does James's encounter with the policeman lead to a better understanding of the lives of others around him?

Reread the dialogue between James and his mother. Why do you think the author places so much emphasis on their interaction and relationship?

Choosing a Creative Response

Designing a Mural   In a small group, design a mural in which you illustrate several of your favorite scenes from "The Scribe." When you have completed the mural, display it in your classroom.

Helping Out in Your Community   With your group, think about the problems your community faces. Choose one problem and brainstorm to come up with a solution to the problem. What steps would you take to carry out the solution?

Creating Your Own Activity   Plan and complete your own activity in response to "The Scribe."

About the Authors

Eloise Greenfield was born in Parmele, North Carolina, in 1929. She has written biographies of Rosa Parks, Paul Robeson, and Mary McLeod Bethune. Other books by Greenfield include *Honey, I Love, and Other Love Poems*, which was named an ALA Notable Book; *Africa Dream*, which won the Coretta Scott King Award in 1978; and *Childtimes: A Three-Generation Memoir*, a book of memories recalled by Eloise Greenfield, her mother, and her grandmother.

Kristin Hunter began writing professionally in 1945, at age fourteen, with a column for teen-agers in her hometown (Philadelphia) paper. Her adult jobs also involved writing: advertising copywriter; researcher; creative-writing teacher; and writer of poems, short stories, reviews, articles, and novels. She is married, with four stepchildren. But, Hunter points out, "It has often seemed to me that I have hundreds of children— thousands—who have formed intense personal bonds with my characters, and then with me through letters."

Francisco Jiménez was born in Tlaquepaque, Mexico, in 1943. He came to the United States when he was four years old and became a naturalized citizen in 1965.

The son of laborers, Jiménez pursued a career in literature and higher education. After graduating from the University of Santa Clara in California, he earned M.A. and Ph.D. degrees in Latin American literature at Columbia University in New York City.

Cynthia Rylant's first book, *When I Was Young in the Mountains*, won four awards. Other books of hers include *Waiting to Waltz: A Childhood*, *Every Living Thing*, *A Blue-Eyed Daisy*, *The Relatives Came*, and *A Fine White Dust*, which was a Newbery Honor Book in 1987.

Yoshiko Uchida was born on November 24, 1921, in California. The award-winning author of picture books, folktales, historical fiction, and contemporary fiction for children, Uchida has been a writer for most of her life. "I've been interested in books and writing for as long as I can remember," she explains. "I was writing stories when I was ten. . . . I wrote them on brown wrapping paper which I cut up and bound into booklets. . . . I still have them." Two of her novels, *Journey to Topaz* and *Journey Home*, grew out of her experiences during World War II, when she and her family were sent to a relocation center in the Utah desert.

. . . and now Miguel by Joseph Krumgold (Crowell, 1953). Miguel lives on a sheep farm in New Mexico. He longs to join the men when they take the sheep to the Sangre de Cristo Mountains. The trip promises to be exciting — and dangerous.

Island of the Blue Dolphins by Scott O'Dell (Houghton, 1990). By a terrible mistake, Karana's Native American tribe leave her behind when they have to evacuate their island off the California coast. This award-winning story tells how she not only stays alive for the next eighteen years but also finds happiness.

Queen of Hearts by Vera and Bill Cleaver (Lippincott, 1978). Wilma spends the summer living with her strong-minded grandmother. As the two come to understand each other, they share good times and make some difficult adjustments.

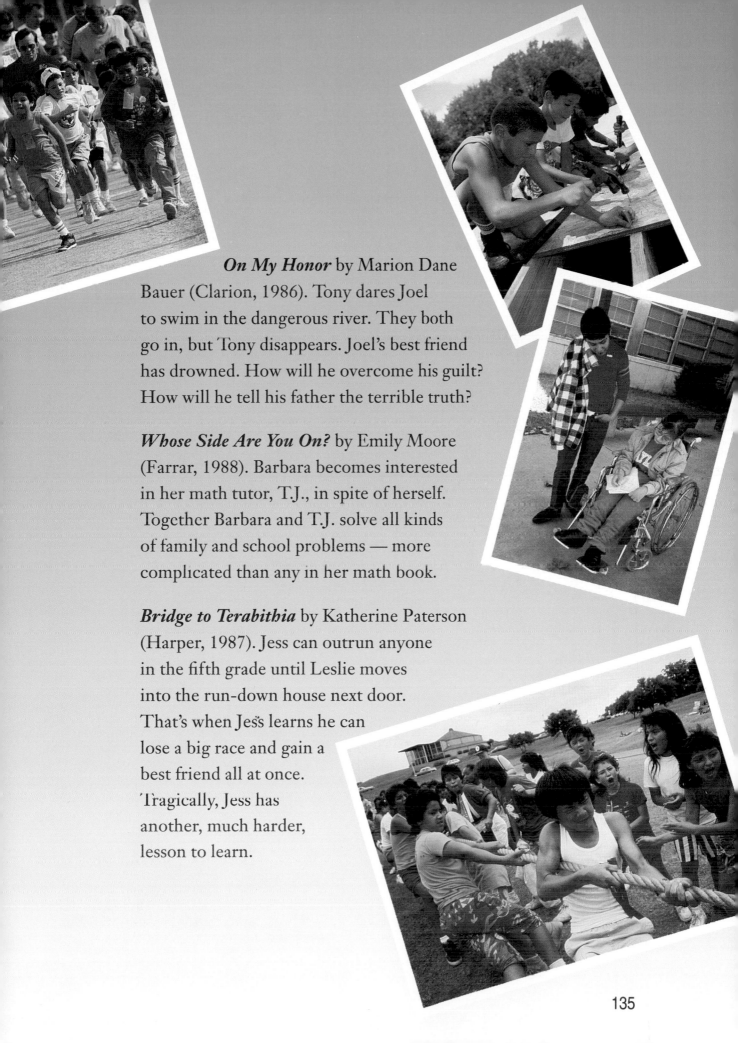

On My Honor by Marion Dane Bauer (Clarion, 1986). Tony dares Joel to swim in the dangerous river. They both go in, but Tony disappears. Joel's best friend has drowned. How will he overcome his guilt? How will he tell his father the terrible truth?

Whose Side Are You On? by Emily Moore (Farrar, 1988). Barbara becomes interested in her math tutor, T.J., in spite of herself. Together Barbara and T.J. solve all kinds of family and school problems — more complicated than any in her math book.

Bridge to Terabithia by Katherine Paterson (Harper, 1987). Jess can outrun anyone in the fifth grade until Leslie moves into the run-down house next door. That's when Jess learns he can lose a big race and gain a best friend all at once. Tragically, Jess has another, much harder, lesson to learn.

POETRY

MOVING THE WORLD

Myra Cohn Livingston: Breaking Away

A Beginning	**140**
The Tape	**141**
Garage Apartment	**142**
Finding a Way	**144**
Power Lines	**144**
The Way Things Are	**145**

Poetry can move you to laughter, move you to tears, or move you to dance. Whether the poet's words reach us from the south-western desert, the heart of the city, or a place of pure imagination, we can celebrate a world of rhythms, and understand what moves us all.

Pat Mora: MOMENTS IN TIME

Urban Raccoon	**148**
Same Song	**149**
Border Town: 1938	**151**
Los Ancianos	**152**
Good-byes	**154**

James Berry: MOVING PICTURES

One	**158**
Black Kid in a New Place	**159**
Kept Home	**160**
It Seems I Test People	**162**
My Hard Repair Job	**163**
Dreaming Black Boy	**164**
When I Dance	**166**

Breaking Away

Illustrated by Rhonda Voo

Myra Cohn Livingston uses traditional rhythm and rhyme, but dares us not to play the same old tune. She creates a world of dreaming, becoming, and breaking out of isolation. Her words help make the human connection. She'll encourage you to be the voice that cuts the silence, to take the rough road, to go "everywhere./anywhere/You need/to go."

A Beginning

Think about the way we'll meet.
I'll be walking down the street.

Suddenly you'll see my eyes,
Look at me with such surprise.

I'll ask, "Do I know your name?"
You'll stop short and do the same.

We'll stand there and then you'll say
How you're glad we met today.

I'll leave soon and hurry home.
You'll call on the telephone

Saying "Hi, how have you been?"
That's the way we can begin.

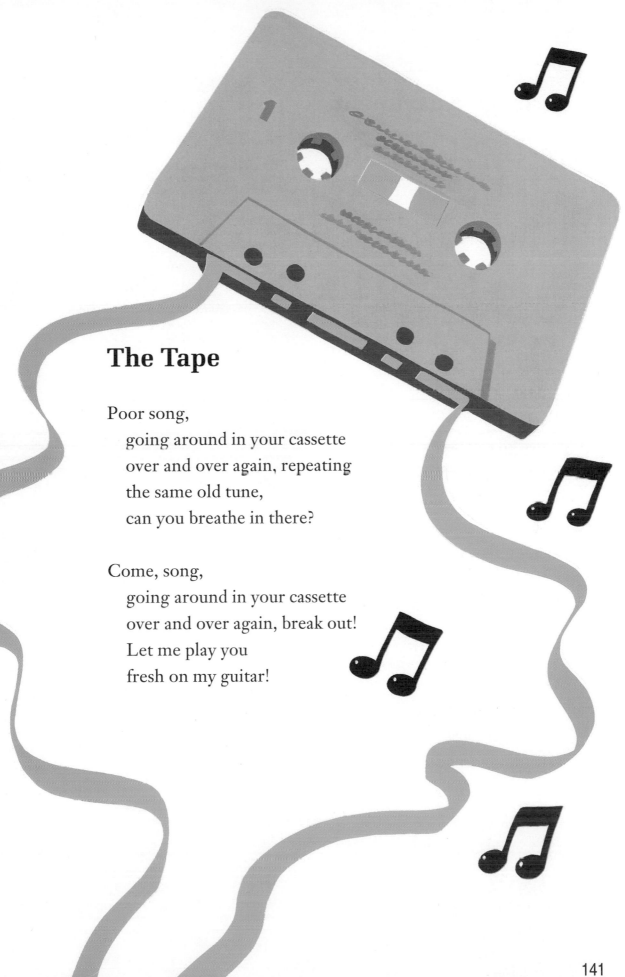

The Tape

Poor song,
   going around in your cassette
   over and over again, repeating
   the same old tune,
   can you breathe in there?

Come, song,
   going around in your cassette
   over and over again, break out!
   Let me play you
   fresh on my guitar!

Garage Apartment

Right on the alley
   is our place.
We have one room.
   There's not much space

but there's a park
   twelve blocks away
and I sleep on
   the rollaway.

Each week
   we go to Family Aid
to get food stamps.
   Our rent is paid.

Mom took a job
   from 3 to 9.
She does her chores
   and I do mine.

One day, I dream,
   we'll have a place
nearer the park
   with lots of space.

Finding a Way

I'd like you for a friend.
I'd like to find the way
Of asking you to be my friend.
I don't know what to say.

What would you like to hear?
What is it I can do?
There has to be some word, some look
Connecting me to you.

Power Lines

Thin robots,
Spun of wire lace,
Plant their feet down
Each in one place.

Standing tall
In a measured row,
Watching over
Highways below.

Holding hands
With steel strand rope,
Gray, faceless.
No fear. No hope.

144

The Way Things Are

It's today,
   This road,
   This knowing the road is there.
   A few brambles,
   A few tangles,
   A few scratches,
   A rough stone against your toe,
   But still, you've got to go
   And take it.
   Fast, sometimes,
   Or slow,
   But go —

           everywhere.
           anywhere
           You need
           to go.

Responding to "Myra Cohn Livingston: Breaking Away"

Thinking and Discussing

What is the message of the poem "Finding a Way"? What kind of mood do the rhythm and rhyme help create? Do you think the mood is right for the poem's subject? Explain.

In what ways is "The Tape" a humorous poem? What might be the more serious message of the poem?

Myra Cohn Livingston's poems often show us things from a different angle. Find some examples of her unique view. How might that view affect the way you think about her poems and also things in daily life?

Choosing a Creative Response

Bringing an Object to Life   The poems "The Tape" and "Power Lines" give human traits to objects that are not alive. Think of an object that interests you and imagine that the object has human traits. Then write a poem, draw a cartoon, or write a description expressing the object's personality.

Meeting Poetry   Myra Cohn Livingston writes poems about human connections. Think of an interesting encounter with a friend that helped you see something in a new way. Then write a poem expressing your ideas about the experience.

Creating Your Own Activity   Plan and complete your own activity in response to the poems in "Myra Cohn Livingston: Breaking Away."

MOMENTS IN TIME

Award Winner

Illustrated by Ed Martinez

PAT MORA captures moments in time, like snapshots that tell stories. Her words form images we clearly see and feel. She lets us enter private worlds, read others' thoughts, listen so closely we can almost hear the beating of their hearts.

Urban Raccoon

Somewhere underneath her thick coat she knows —
autumn, and her paws return to the old tree,
to the abandoned chimney. She climbs the branches,
her outdoor staircase, gold, leafy stories   a stretch
onto the roof and she ambles along the drain pipe,
pudgy tight-rope walker, eyes mysteriously masked.

A flourish of her ringed tail and she settles
on her spot, rubs her roundness on the chimney corner,
without a hurry scratches, ignores cars, sirens. Yawns.

Somewhere underneath her thick coat she knows wind
spins round and around her penthouse, spins
stories all night long about the reddest, sweetest
berries in the world, and she smacks her lips,
pours herself head first into her dark, safe hole,
curls into her furry dreams.

Same Song

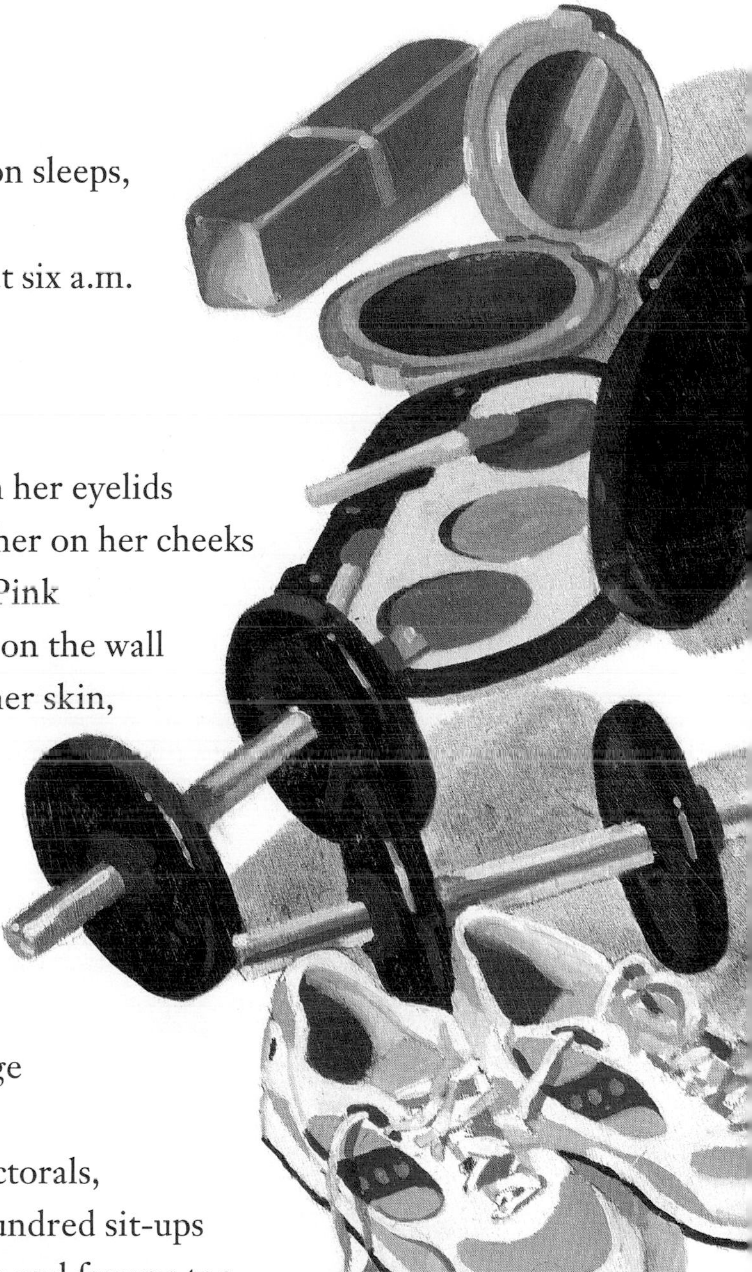

While my sixteen-year-old son sleeps,
my twelve-year-old daughter
stumbles into the bathroom at six a.m.
plugs in the curling iron
squeezes into faded jeans
curls her hair carefully
strokes Aztec Blue shadow on her eyelids
smooths Frosted Mauve blusher on her cheeks
outlines her mouth in Neon Pink
peers into the mirror, mirror on the wall
frowns at her face, her eyes, her skin,
not fair.

At night this daughter
stumbles off to bed at nine
eyes half-shut while my son
jogs a mile in the cold dark
then lifts weights in the garage
curls and bench presses
expanding biceps, triceps, pectorals,
one-handed push-ups, one hundred sit-ups
peers into that mirror, mirror and frowns too.

for Libby

Border Town: 1938

She counts cement cracks
little Esperanza with the long brown braids,
counts so as not to hear
the girls in the playground singing,
       "the farmer's in the dell
        the farmer's in the dell"
laughing and running round-round
while little Esperanza walks head down
eyes full of tears.
       "The nurse takes the child"
but Esperanza walks alone across the loud
street, through the graveyard gates
down the dirt path, walks faster,
faster . . . away
from ghosts with long arms,
no "hi-ho the dairy-o" here,
runs to that other school
for Mexicans
every day wanting to stay close to home,
every day wanting to be the farmer in the dell,
little Esperanza in the long brown braids
counts cement cracks
                ocho, nueve, diez.[1]

---

[1] **ocho, nueve, diez** (ō′chō, nwā′bā, dyäs): eight, nine, ten.

151

Los Ancianos

They hold hands
as they walk with slow steps.
Careful together they cross the plaza
both slightly stooped, bodies returning to the land,
he in faded khaki and straw hat,
she wrapped in soft clothes, black
rebozo[2] round her head and shoulders.

Tourists in halter tops and shorts
pose by flame trees and fountains,
but the old couple walks step by step
on the edge.
Even in the heat, only their wrinkled
hands and faces show.   They know
of moving through a crowd at their own pace.

I watch him help her
off the curb and I smell love
like dried flowers, old love
of holding hands with one man for fifty years.

---

[2]**rebozo** (rā bō´sō): a shawl or type of cape or scarf.

ood-byes

How loud they are
our silent hugs
outroar the airport's blare

                heart to heart

we seek to hide
the sting of tears
                our insides
                        out

spilling on smiles
we so long to invent.

Little troupers we
laugh and mouth
our studied lines

step apart deaf
from our heavy pulse.

                for Mother

RESPONDING TO "PAT MORA: MOMENTS IN TIME"

Thinking and Discussing

Pat Mora's poems tell stories of simple events that take place in a fast-paced world. Look again at one of the poems and tell how the modern world affects the lives of the characters.

In "Same Song," Pat Mora refers to a fairy tale. In "Border Town: 1938," she includes lines from a nursery rhyme. How do these references add meaning to the poems?

Pat Mora chooses words carefully to help us picture her characters and their actions. Using words like *ambles*, *pudgy*, and *flourish*, for instance, she creates an easy-to-imagine "Urban Raccoon." Find other examples of words or phrases that create clear, vivid images.

Choosing a Creative Response

Getting into the Character   Choose a character from one of the poems — the old woman who is crossing the plaza, for example, or the boy who looks into the mirror and frowns. Imagine that you are that character. Write a poem that tells the story from that person's point of view.

Picturing Stories   Using a picture in a magazine or newspaper, imagine a story that could be told about what is going on in the picture. Write out the story and create a display of the story and the picture.

Creating Your Own Activity   Plan and complete your own activity in response to "Pat Mora: Moments in Time."

MOVING PICTURES

Photo-illustrations by Dan Morrill

JAMES BERRY fills our hearts and minds with vivid feelings, moving pictures. His words are explosive, high-impact — filled with motion, color, and sounds that jump out at your senses like graffiti-covered walls.

157

one

Only one of me
and nobody can get a second one
from a photocopy machine.

Nobody has the fingerprints I have.
Nobody can cry my tears, or laugh my laugh
or have my expectancy when I wait.

But anybody can mimic my dance with my dog.
Anybody can howl how I sing out of tune.
And mirrors can show me multiplied
many times, say, dressed up in red
or dressed up in grey.

Nobody can get into my clothes for me
or feel my fall for me, or do my running.
Nobody hears my music for me, either.

I am just this one.
Nobody else makes the words
I shape with sound, when I talk.

But anybody can act how I stutter in a rage.
Anybody can copy echoes I make.
And mirrors can show me multiplied
many times, say, dressed up in green
or dressed up in blue.

BLACK KID IN A NEW PLACE

I'm here, I see
I make a part of a little planet
here, with some of everybody now.

I stretch myself, I see
I'm like a migrant bird
who will not return from here.

I shake out colorful wings.
I set up a palmtree bluesky
here, where winter mists were.

Using what time tucked in me, I see
my body pops with dance.
Streets break out in carnival.

Rooms echo my voice. I see
I was not a migrant bird. I am
a transplanted sapling, here, blossoming.

• •

KEPT HOME

• •

I look out of my high up window.
I see chimney tops, fences, scattered trees,
in this sunny summer-Saturday.

Our white cat strolls
across the neighbour's newly cut grass.
Birds are noisy.
A wind teases branches
and gardens of flowers.

I can't see far on my left.
The silver birch spreads
elegant branches before me,
fluttering its leaves like
a lady's shiny frills in sunlight.

Girls and boys play football,
smaller ones are swinging,
in the playground
and view of the church . . .

Out and out, past all streets
and housetops and trees, the sky
touches our Lookfar Hill,
with a smoky white light surrounding.

When holidays come, any day now,
and I'm well, fit again,
I shall clamber up
Lookfar's hillside tracks . . .

An iron bird roars . . .
Aeroplane breaks the clouds.
It sails in open space.
Who are on board?
Who? I wonder . . .

Travelling or staying at home,
people wait to get somewhere —
wait for something to happen,
something to end, begin or develop . . .

Sunlight floods my room suddenly.
Shadows move on one wall
like reflections
of a busy open flame.

Sounds of motor cars get louder.
Every day our world is its own
moving-picture show . . .
What new character can I add? . . .

IT SEEMS I TEST PEOPLE

My skin sun-mixed like basic earth

my voice having tones of thunder

my laughter working all of me as I laugh

my walk motioning strong swings

it seems I test people

Always awaiting a move

waiting always to recreate my view

my eyes packed with hellos behind them

my arrival bringing departures

it seems I test people

My Hard Repair Job

In the awful quarrel
we had, my temper burnt
our friendship to cinders.
How can I make it whole again?

This way, that way,
that time, this time,
I pick up the burnt bits,
trying to change them back.

Dreaming Black Boy

I wish my teacher's eyes wouldn't
go past me today. Wish he'd know
it's okay to hug me when I kick
a goal. Wish I myself wouldn't
hold back when an answer comes.
I'm no woodchopper now
like all ancestors.

I wish I could be educated
to the best of tune up, and earn
good money and not sink to lick
boots. I wish I could go on every
crisscross way of the globe
and no persons or powers or
hotel keepers would make it a waste.

I wish life wouldn't spend me out
opposing. Wish same way creation
would have me stand it would have
me stretch, and hold high, my voice
Paul Robeson's,[1] my inside eye
a sun. Nobody wants to say
hello to nasty answers.

I wish torch throwers of night
would burn lights for decent times.
Wish plotters in pyjamas would pray
for themselves. Wish people wouldn't
talk as if I dropped from Mars.

I wish only boys were scared
behind bravados, for I could suffer.
I could suffer a big big lot.
I wish nobody would want to earn
the terrible burden I can suffer.

---

[1]**Paul Robeson:** 1898–1976. An African American singer,
actor, and political activist.

When I Dance

· ·

When I dance it isn't merely
That music absorbs my shyness,
My laughter settles in my eyes,
My swings of arms convert my frills
As timing tunes my feet with floor
As if I never just looked on.

It is that when I dance
O music expands my hearing
And it wants no mathematics,
It wants no thinking, no speaking,
It only wants all my feeling
In with animation of place.

When I dance it isn't merely
That surprises dictate movements,
Other rhythms move my rhythms,
I uncradle rocking-memory
And skipping, hopping and running
All mix movements I balance in.

It is that when I dance
I'm costumed in a rainbow mood,
I'm okay at any angle,
Outfit of drums crowds madness round,
Talking winds and plucked strings conspire,
Beat after beat warms me like sun.

When I dance it isn't merely
I shift bodyweight balances
As movement amasses my show,
I celebrate each dancer here,
No sleep invades me now at all
And I see how I am tireless.

It is that when I dance
I gather up all my senses
Well into hearing and feeling,
With body's flexible postures
Telling their poetry in movement
And I celebrate all rhythms.

RESPONDING TO "JAMES BERRY: MOVING PICTURES"

Thinking and Discussing

James Berry uses strong and unusual images such as "palmtree bluesky" and "I make a part of a little planet." Look at his poems again. Which images are the most powerful? How do they help get across the meaning of the poem?

Think about the poem "My Hard Repair Job." What feelings is James Berry writing about? What words show that it will be hard to repair the friendship? Now select another poem. What words does Berry use to help create the mood in that poem?

Choose one of Berry's poems and read it again. What do you notice in the poem that you didn't notice before?

Choosing a Creative Response

Dancing Poetically   Write your own poem called "When I Dance." Write as many lines as you like, but begin each line with the phrase *When I dance.* Tell how dancing makes you feel or what it makes you think of.

Writing Like Anything   James Berry often compares one thing to another in unexpected ways — "I'm like a migrant bird," for example, or "leaves like a lady's shiny frills in sunlight." Think of things familiar to you. What other things might they be compared to? Write a poem in which you include some unusual comparisons.

Creating Your Own Activity   Plan and complete your own activity in response to "James Berry: Moving Pictures."

About the Poets

Poet/author **James Berry,** Jamaican-born and living in Britain, writes from the experience of his Caribbean youth and his transition to another culture. He is the author of two collections of short stories for young people, the Coretta Scott King Award honor book *A Thief in the Village*, set in Jamaica, and *The Girls and Yanga Marshall*, set in London and the Caribbean. Berry has also introduced readers to Caribbean folktales of West African origin.

Myra Cohn Livingston has published over thirty collections of her own poems and has edited anthologies of poems by other writers. Her many books include *The Way Things Are and Other Poems* and *4-Way Stop and other poems*. Livingston has said that the important thing is not what we encounter but "the humanness with which we meet, apprehend, and possibly comprehend it."

Pat Mora, from El Paso, Texas, describes the Southwestern landscape as "my world, my point of reference . . . the subject that has chosen me." A public school and university English teacher, she has written two books of poetry, *Chants* and *Borders*. Mora says, "I am compelled to write by the pleasure I find in words and by my determination to preserve the Mexican American experience." She is the recipient of many awards, including honors from the National Association of Chicano Studies and the Southwest Council of Latin American Studies.

MOVING BEYOND YOUR WORLD

The Dream Keeper and Other Poems
by Langston Hughes (Knopf, 1932, 1986) uses songs, blues, and lyrical poems to show the hopes and concerns of African Americans.

I Like You, If You Like Me: Poems of Friendship
selected by Myra Cohn Livingston (McElderry, 1987) includes poems from many cultures on all aspects of friendship.

Sports Pages
by Arnold Adoff (Lippincott, 1986) covers all types of players and sports, using blank verse that moves with the power and grace of a fine athlete.

Soda Jerk
by Cynthia Rylant (Orchard, 1990) presents a series of poems spoken by a young man who works in a small-town drugstore and observes the people and events around him.

You Come Too: Favorite Poems for Young People
by Robert Frost (Holt, 1959, 1967) brings together this popular poet's better-known verses about nature and people.

PERSONAL NARRATIVE

EXPERIENCES

173

EXPERIENCES

The Figgerin' of Aunt Wilma
by James Thurber   176

Summer School
by Gary Soto   188

Daddy
by Yolanda King in collaboration with
Hilda R. Tompkins   200

From *Barrio Boy*
by Ernesto Galarza   206

From *Homesick: My Own Story*
by Jean Fritz   222

175

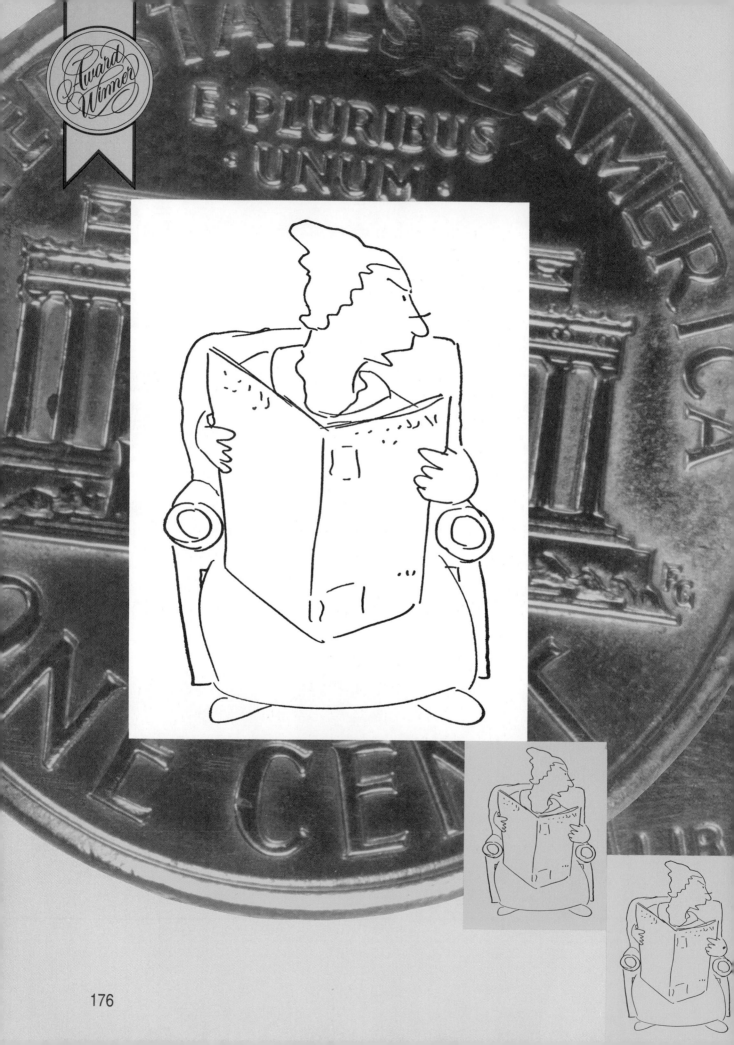

THE FIGGERIN' OF AUNT WILMA

written and illustrated by James Thurber

When I was a boy, John Hance's grocery stood on the south side of Town Street, just east of Fourth, in the Central Market region of Columbus, Ohio. It was an old store even then, forty-five years ago, and its wide oak floor boards had been worn pleasantly smooth by the shoe soles of three generations of customers. The place smelled of coffee, peppermint, vinegar, and spices. Just inside the door on the left, a counter with a rounded glass front held all the old-fashioned penny candies — gumdrops, licorice whips, horehound, and the rest — some of them a little pale with age. On the rear wall, between a barrel of dill pickles and a keg of salt mackerel in brine, there was an iron coffee grinder, whose handle I was sometimes allowed to turn.

Once, Mr. Hance gave me a stick of Yucatan gum, an astonishing act of generosity, since he had a sharp sense of the value of a penny. Thrift was John Hance's

religion. His store was run on a strictly cash basis. He shared the cost of his telephone with the Hays Carriage Shop, next door. The instrument was set in a movable wooden cubicle that could be whirled through an opening in the west wall of the store. When I was ten, I used to hang around the grocery on Saturday afternoons, waiting for the telephone to disappear into the wall. Then I would wait for it to swing back again. It was a kind of magic, and I was disappointed to learn of its mundane[1] purpose — the saving of a few dollars a month.

Mr. Hance was nearly seventy, a short man with white hair and a white mustache and the most alert eyes that I can remember, except perhaps Aunt Wilma Hudson's. Aunt Wilma lived on South Sixth Street and always shopped at Mr. Hance's store. Mr. Hance's eyes were blue and capable of a keen concentration that could make you squirm. Aunt Wilma had black agate eyes that moved restlessly and scrutinized everybody with bright suspicion. In church, her glance would dart around the congregation seeking out irreverent men and women whose expressions showed that they were occupied with worldly concerns, or even carnal thoughts, in the holy place. If she lighted on a culprit, her heavy, dark brows would lower, and her mouth would tighten in righteous disapproval. Aunt Wilma was as honest as the day is long and as easily confused, when it came to what she called figgerin', as the night is dark. Her clashes with Mr. Hance had become a family legend. He was a swift and competent calculator, and nearly fifty years of constant practice had enabled him to add up a column of figures almost at a glance. He set down his columns swiftly on an empty paper sack with a stubby black pencil. Aunt Wilma, on the other hand, was slow and painstaking when it came to figgerin'. She would go over and over a column of numbers, her glasses far down on her nose, her lips moving soundlessly. To her,

---
[1] **mundane:** practical; worldly.

rapid calculation, like all the other reckless and impulsive habits of men, was tainted with a kind of godlessness. Mr. Hance always sighed when he looked up and saw her coming into his store. He knew that she could lift a simple dollar transaction into a dim and mystic realm of confusion all her own.

I was fortunate enough to be present one day in 1905 when Mr. Hance's calculating and Aunt Wilma's figgerin' came together in memorable single combat. She had wheedled me into carrying her market basket, on the ground that it was going to be too heavy for her to manage. Her two grandsons, boys around my own age, had skipped out when I came to call at their house, and Aunt Wilma promptly seized on me. A young'un, as she called everybody under seventeen, was not worth his salt[2] if he couldn't help a body about the house. I had shopped with her before, under duress, and I knew her accustomed and invariable route on Saturday mornings, when Fourth Street, from Main to State, was lined with the stands of truck gardeners. Prices were incredibly low in those days, but Aunt Wilma questioned the cost, the quality, and the measure of everything. By the time she had finished her long and tedious purchases of fresh produce from the country, and we had turned east into Town Street and headed for Mr. Hance's store, the weight of the market basket was beginning to pain my arm. "Come along, child, come along," Aunt Wilma snapped, her eyes shining with the look of the Middle Western housewife engaged in hard but virtuous battle with the wicked forces of the merchandising world.

I saw Mr. Hance make a small involuntary gesture with his right hand as he spied Aunt Wilma coming through the door. He had just finished with a customer, and since his assistant was busy,

---

[2]**worth his salt:** worth feeding and supporting.

he knew he was in for it. It took a good half hour for Aunt Wilma to complete her shopping for groceries, but at length everything she wanted was stacked on the counter in sacks and cans and boxes. Mr. Hance set deftly to work with his paper sack and pencil, jotting down the price of each article as he fitted it into the basket. Aunt Wilma watched his expert movements closely, like a hostile baseball fan waiting for an error in the infield. She regarded adroitness in a man as "slick" rather than skillful.

Aunt Wilma's purchases amounted to ninety-eight cents. After writing down this sum, Mr. Hance, knowing my aunt, whisked the paper bag around on the counter so that she could examine his addition. It took her some time, bending over and peering through her glasses, to arrive at a faintly reluctant corroboration[3] of his figgerin'. Even when she was satisfied that all was in order, she had another go at the column of numbers, her lips moving silently as she added them up for the third time. Mr. Hance waited patiently, the flat of his hands on the counter. He seemed to be fascinated by the movement of her lips. "Well, I guess it's all right," said Aunt Wilma, at last, "but everything *is* so dear." What she had bought for less than a dollar made the market basket bulge. Aunt Wilma took her purse out of her bag and drew out a dollar bill slowly and handed it over, as if it were a hundred dollars she would never see again.

Mr. Hance deftly pushed the proper keys of the cash register, and the red hand on the indicator pointed to $.98. He studied the cash drawer, which had shot out at him. "Well, well," he said, and then, "Hmm. Looks like I haven't got any pennies." He turned back to Aunt Wilma. "Have you got three cents, Mrs. Hudson?" he asked.

That started it.

---

[3] **corroboration** (kə rŏb´ə rā´shən): an agreement that a person's statement is correct.

Aunt Wilma gave him a quick look of distrust. Her Sunday suspicion gleamed in her eyes. "*You* owe *me two* cents," she said sharply.

"I know that, Mrs. Hudson," he sighed, "but I'm out of pennies. Now, if you'll give me three cents, I'll give you a nickel."

Aunt Wilma stared at him cautiously.

"It's all right if you give him three cents and he gives you a nickel," I said.

"Hush up," said Aunt Wilma. "I'm figgerin'." She figgered for several moments, her mouth working again.

Mr. Hance slipped a nickel out of the drawer and placed it on the counter. "There is your nickel," he said firmly. "Now you just have to give me three cents."

Aunt Wilma pecked about in her purse and located three pennies, which she brought out carefully, one at a time. She laid them on the counter beside the nickel, and Mr. Hance reached for them. Aunt Wilma was too quick for him. She covered the eight cents with a lean hand. "Wait, now!" she said, and she took her hand away slowly. She frowned over the four coins as if they were a difficult hand in bridge whist.[4] She ran her lower lip against her upper teeth. "Maybe if I give you a dime," she said, "and take the eight cents . . . It is *two* cents you're short, ain't it?"

Mr. Hance began to show signs of agitation. One or two amused customers were now taking in the scene out of the corners of their eyes. "No, no," said Mr. Hance. "That way, you would be making me a present of seven cents!" This was too much for Aunt Wilma. She couldn't understand the new and preposterous sum of seven cents that had suddenly leaped at her from nowhere. The notion that she was about to do herself out of some money staggered her, and her eyes glazed for a moment like a groggy

---

[4]**bridge whist:** a card game.

prizefighter's. Neither Mr. Hance nor I said anything, out of fear of deepening the tangle. She made an uncertain move of her right hand and I had the wild thought that she was going to give Mr. Hance one of the pennies and scoop up the seven cents, but she didn't. She fell into a silent clinch with the situation and then her eyes cleared. "Why, of *course*!" she cried brightly. "I don't know what got into me! You take the eight cents and give me a dime. Then I'll have the two cents that's coming to me." One of the customers laughed, and Aunt Wilma cut him down with a swift glare. The diversion gave me time to figure out that whereas Mr. Hance had been about to gain seven cents, he was now going to lose a nickel. "That way, *I* would be making *you* a present of *five* cents, Mrs. Hudson," he said stiffly. They stood motionless for several seconds, each trying to stare the other down.

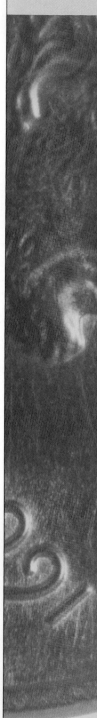

"Now, here," said Mr. Hance, turning and taking her dollar out of the still open cash drawer. He laid it beside the nickel and the pennies. "Now, here," he said again. "You gave me a dollar three, but you don't owe me a dollar three — you owe me five cents less than that. Here is the five cents." He snatched it up and handed it to her. She held the nickel between thumb and forefinger, and her eyes gleamed briefly, as if she at last comprehended the peculiar deal, but the gleam faded. Suddenly she handed him his nickel and picked up her dollar and her three cents. She put the pennies back in her purse. "I've rung up the ninety-eight cents, Mrs. Hudson," said Mr. Hance quickly. "I must put the dollar back in the till." He turned and pointed at the $.98 on the indicator. "I tell you what. If you'll give me the dollar, I'll give you the nickel and we'll call it square." She obviously didn't want to take the nickel or give up the dollar, but she did, finally. I was astounded at first, for here was the penny-careful Mr. Hance knocking three cents off a bill, but then I realized he was afraid of losing the dollar and was willing to settle for the lesser of two evils.

"Well," said Aunt Wilma irritably, "I'm sure I don't know what you're trying to do."

I was a timid boy, but I had to plunge into the snarl, if only on behalf of the family honor. "Gee, Aunt Wilma," I told her, "if you keep the nickel, he's giving you everything for ninety-five cents."

Mr. Hance scowled hard at me. He was afraid I was going to get him in deeper than he already was. "It's all right, son," he said. "It's all right." He put the dollar in the till and shoved the drawer shut with a decisive bang, but I wasn't going to give up.

"Gee whizz, Aunt Wilma," I complained, "you still owe him three cents. Don't you see that?"

She gave me the pitying glance of a superior and tired intelligence. "I never owed him three cents in my life," she said tartly. "He owes me two cents. You stay out of things you don't understand."

"It's all right," said Mr. Hance again, in a weary voice. He was sure that if she scrabbled in her purse again for the three pennies, she would want her dollar back, and they would be right where they had started. I gave my aunt a look of disenchantment.

"Now, wait!" she cried suddenly. "Maybe I have the exact change! I don't know what's got into me I didn't think of that! I think I have the right change after all." She put back on the counter the nickel she had been clutching in her left hand, and then she began to peck at the coins in her purse and, after a good minute, arranged two quarters, four dimes, Mr. Hance's nickel, and three pennies on the counter. "There," she said, her eyes flashing triumph. "Now you give me my dollar back."

Mr. Hance sighed deeply, rang out the cash drawer by pushing "No Sale," and handed her the dollar. Then he hastily scraped up the change, deposited each coin in its proper place in the till, and slammed the drawer shut again. I was only ten, and mathematics was not my best study, but it wasn't hard to figure that Mr. Hance, who in the previous arrangement had been out three cents, was now out five cents. "Good day, Mrs. Hudson," he said grimly. He felt my sympathetic eyes on him, and we exchanged a brief, knowing masculine glance of private understanding.

"Good day, Mr. Hance," said Aunt Wilma, and her tone was as grim as the grocer's.

I took the basket from the counter, and Mr. Hance sighed again, this time with relief. "Goodbye, goodbye," he said with false heartiness, glad to see us on our way. I felt I should slip him the parsley, or whatever sack in the basket had cost a nickel.

"Come on, child," said Aunt Wilma. "It's dreadfully late. I declare it's taken hours to shop today." She muttered plaintively all the way out of the store.

I noticed as I closed the door behind us that Mr. Hance was waiting on a man customer. The man was laughing. Mr. Hance frowned and shrugged.

As we walked east on Town Street, Aunt Wilma let herself go. "I never heard of such a thing in all the born days of my life," she said. "I don't know where John Hance got his schooling, if he got any. The very idea — a grown man like that getting so mixed up. Why, I could have spent the whole day in that store and he'd never of figgered it out. Let him keep the two cents, then. It was worth it to get out of that store."

"*What* two cents, Aunt Wilma?" I almost squealed.

"Why, the two cents he still owes me!" she said. "I don't know what they teach you young'uns nowadays. Of course he owes me two cents. It come to ninety-eight cents and I give him a dollar. He owed me two cents in the beginning and he still owes me two cents. Your Uncle Herbert will explain it to you. Any man in the world could figger it out except John Hance."

I walked on beside her in silence, thinking of Uncle Herbert, a balding, choleric[5] man of high impatience and quick temper.

"Now, you let *me* explain it to your Uncle Herbert, child," she said. "I declare you were as mixed up as John Hance was. If I'd of listened to you and given him the three cents, like you said, I'd never of got my dollar back. He'd owe me five cents instead of two. Why, it's as plain as day."

I thought I had the solution for her now, and I leaped at it. "That's right, Aunt Wilma," I almost yelled. "He owed you a nickel and he gave you the nickel."

Aunt Wilma stabbed me with her indignation. "I gave *him* the nickel," she said. "I put it on the counter right there under your very eyes, and you saw him scoop it up."

I shifted the market basket to my left arm. "I know, Aunt Wilma," I said, "but it was *his* nickel all the time."

She snorted. "Well, he's got his precious nickel, ain't he?" she demanded. I shifted the basket again. I thought I detected a faint trace of uneasiness in her tone. She fell silent and quickened her cadence, and it was hard for me to keep up with her. As we turned south into Sixth Street, I glanced up and saw that she was frowning and that her lips were moving again. She was rehearsing the story of the strange transaction for Uncle Herbert. I began to whistle. "Hush up, child," she said. "I'm figgerin'."

Uncle Herbert was sitting in the living room, eating an apple. I could tell from his expression that he was in one of his rare

---

[5] **choleric (kol´ ər ĭk):** bad-tempered.

amiable moods. Aunt Wilma grabbed the basket away from me. "Now, you let me explain it to your uncle," she said. "You wait till I get back." She sailed out of the room on her way to the kitchen.

A little breathlessly, I told Uncle Herbert the saga of Aunt Wilma's complicated financial quandary. He was chuckling when she came back into the room.

Uncle Herbert's amusement nettled her. "The boy got it wrong," she said accusingly. "He didn't tell it right. He was ever' bit as mixed up as John Hance." Uncle Herbert's chuckle increased to full and open laughter. Aunt Wilma glared at him until he subsided. "Now, Herbert, you listen to me," she began, but he cut in on her.

"If Hance ever gives you that two cents he owes you, Wilma," he said, "I tell you what you have to do to square accounts. Someday you're going to have to give him a dime for three cents." He began to laugh again.

Aunt Wilma Hudson stared at each of us in turn, with a look of fine, cold scorn, and then she raised both her hands and let them fall helplessly. "I declare," she said, "I don't know how the world gets along with the men runnin' it."

RESPONDING TO "THE FIGGERIN' OF AUNT WILMA"

THINKING AND DISCUSSING

How do you think the author feels about Aunt Wilma and Mr. Hance? What do the details in the author's descriptions of Aunt Wilma and Mr. Hance suggest about his opinion of them?

How does the author use detail to make this memory seem real?

Why do you think the author chose to write about this incident? How does the story help reveal the author's views about life?

CHOOSING A CREATIVE RESPONSE

Reading for Laughs   The author uses humorous dialogue to help create this amusing story. With a partner or two, choose a passage that you find funny. Select a part you would like to read: Aunt Wilma's part, Mr. Hance's part, or perhaps the role of the narrator. Practice reading the passage aloud, and then read it to the class. Try to express the humor of the passage by using gestures and by varying your tone of voice to suit the various characters.

Holding a Discussion   "The Figgerin' of Aunt Wilma" provides the reader with a glimpse of life during the early 1900s. How has daily life changed since the author was a boy? How would Aunt Wilma's old-fashioned opinions be received today? In a small group, discuss these changes and differences. Then share what you found with the class.

Creating Your Own Activity   Plan and complete your own activity in response to "The Figgerin' of Aunt Wilma."

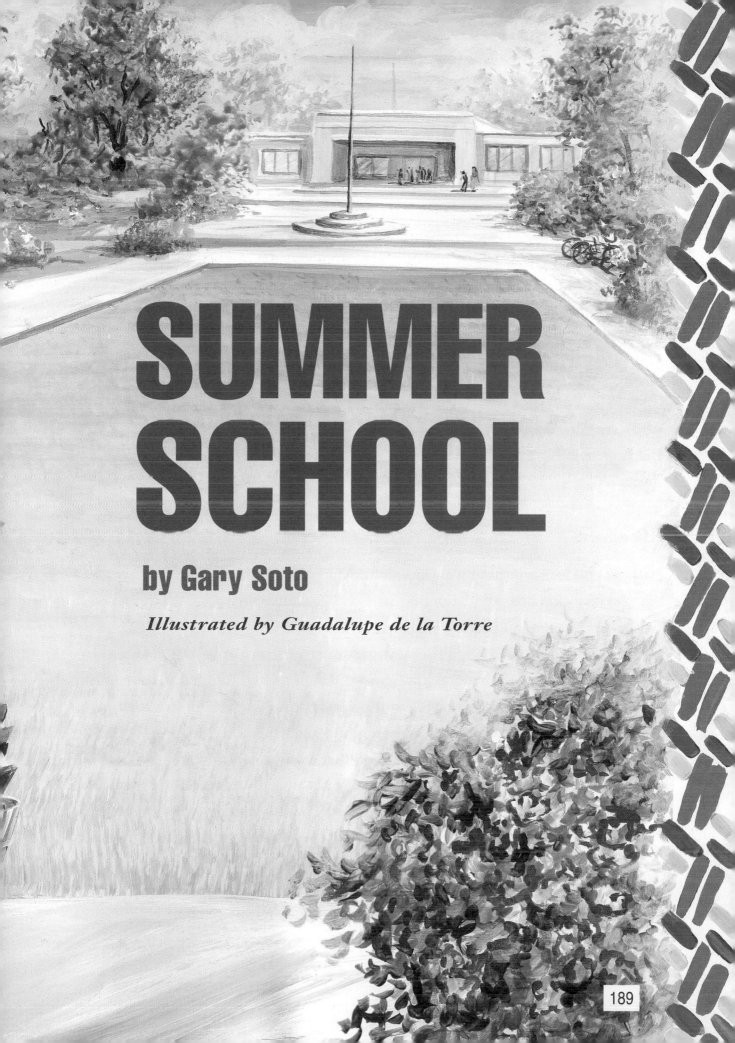

SUMMER SCHOOL

by Gary Soto

Illustrated by Guadalupe de la Torre

The summer before I entered sixth grade I decided to go to summer school. I had never gone, and it was either school or mope around the house with a tumbler of Kool-Aid and watch TV, flipping the channels from exercise programs to soap operas to game shows until something looked right.

My sister decided to go to summer school too, so the two of us hopped onto our bikes and rode off to Heaton Elementary, which was three miles away, and asked around until we were pointed to the right rooms. I ran off without saying good-bye to Debra.

These were the home rooms where the teachers would check roll, announce bulletins, and read us a story before we dashed off to other classes. That morning I came in breathing hard, smiling a set of teeth that were fit for an adult, and took a seat behind a fat kid named Yodelman so I couldn't be seen.

The teacher, whose name is forgotten, told us that summer school classes were all electives — that we could choose anything we wanted. She had written them on the blackboard, and from her list I chose science, history, German, and square dancing.

Little John, a friend from our street, sat across the room. I had not seen him at first, which miffed him because he thought I was playing stuck-up for some reason, and so he threw an acorn at me that bounced harmlessly off Yodelman's shoulder. Yodelman turned his head slowly, turtle-like, blinked his small dull eyes, and then turned his head back to the teacher who was telling us that we had to fill out cards. She had two monitors pass out pencils, and we hovered and strained over the card: Date of birth, address, grade, career goals. At the last one I thought for the longest time, pencil poised and somewhat worried, before I raised my hand to ask the teacher how to spell paleontology.[1] Surprised, as if someone had presented her flowers, she opened her mouth, searched the ceiling with her eyes, and gave it a stab: p-a-y-e-n-t-o-l-o-g-y. I wrote it in uneven capitals and then wrote "bone collector" in the margin.

Little John glared at me, made a fist, and wet his lips. When class was dismissed he punched me softly in the arm and together the two of us walked out of class talking loudly, happy that we were together.

While Little John went to typing I went to science class. The teacher stood before us in a white shirt, yardstick in hand, surrounded by jars of animal parts floating in clear liquids. This scared me, as did a replica of a skeleton hanging like a frayed coat in the corner. On the first day we looked carefully at leaves in groups of threes, after which the teacher asked us to describe the differences.

"This one is dried up and this one is not so dried up," one kid offered, a leaf in each hand.

The teacher, who was kind, said that that was a start. He raised his yardstick and pointed to someone else.

From there I went to history, a class I enjoyed immensely because it was the first one ever in which I would earn an A. This resulted from reading thirty books — pamphlets to be more exact. I was a page turner, and my index finger touched each paragraph before the thumb peeled a new page, as I became familiar with Edison, Carnegie, MacArthur, Eli Whitney . . . At the end of the five-week summer school, the teacher would call me to the front of the class to tell about the books I had read. He

---

[1] **paleontology** (pā´lē ən **tŏl´** ə jē): the scientific study of fossils and ancient forms of life.

stood behind the lectern, looking down at his watch now and then, and beamed at me like a flashlight.

"Who was Pike?"

"Oh, he was the guy that liked to go around in the mountains."

"Who was Genghis Khan?"

"He was a real good fighter. In China."

With each answer the teacher smiled and nodded his head at me. He smiled at the class and some of the students turned their heads away, mad that I knew so much. Little John made a fist and wet his lips.

From history we were released to the playground where we played softball, sucked on popsicles, and fooled around on the monkey bars. We returned to our classes sweating like the popsicles we had sucked to a rugged stick. I went to German where, for five weeks, we sang songs we didn't understand, though we loved them and loved our teacher who paraded around the room and closed his eyes on the high notes. On the best days he rolled up his sleeves, undid his tie, and sweated profusely as he belted out songs so loudly that we heard people pounding on the wall for quiet from the adjoining classroom. Still, he went on with great vigor:

> Mein Hut der hat drei Ecken
> Drei Ecken hat mein Hut
> Und wenn er das nicht hatte
> Dann war's auch nicht mein Hut[2]

---

[2]**Mein Hut der hat . . . :**   My hat has three corners,
Three corners has my hat,
If it didn't have three corners,
It wouldn't be my hat.

And we joined in every time, faces pink from a wonderful beauty that rose effortlessly from the heart.

I left, humming, for square dancing. Debra was in that class with me, fresh from science class. Even though Debra didn't want to do it, we paired off the first day. We made ugly faces at each other as we clicked our heels, swished for a few steps, and clicked again.

It was in that class that I fell in love with my corner gal who looked like Hayley Mills, except she was not as boyish. I was primed to fall in love because of the afternoon movies I watched on television, most of which were stories about women and men coming together, parting with harsh feelings, and embracing in the end to marry and drive big cars.

Day after day we'd pass through do-si-does,[3] form Texas stars,[4] spin, click heels, and bounce about the room, released from our rigid school children lives to let our bodies find their rhythm. As we danced I longed openly for her, smiling like a lantern and wanting very badly for her eyes to lock onto mine and think deep feelings. She swung around my arm, happy as the music, and hooked onto the next kid, oblivious to my yearning.

When I became sick and missed school for three days, my desire for her didn't sputter out. In bed with a comic book, I became dreamy as a cat and closed my eyes to the image of her allemanding[5] left to *The Red River Valley*, a favorite of the class's, her long hair flipping about on her

---

[3] **do-si-does** (dō´ sē dōz´): square-dance steps in which the partners circle one another back to back.

[4] **Texas stars:** square dances in which couples join hands in the middle of their figures to form stars.

[5] **allemanding** (ăl´ ə man´ dĭng): swinging in a half-circle while linking arms with another square-dancer.

precious shoulders. By Friday I was well, but instead of
going to school I stayed home to play "jump and die" with
the neighbor kids, a game in which we'd repeatedly climb a
tree and jump until someone went home crying from a hurt
leg or arm. We played way into the dark.

On Monday I was back at school, stiff as new rope, but
once again excited by science, history, the guttural[6] sounds
of German, and square dancing! By Sunday I had almost

---

[6]**guttural:** produced in the throat.

forgotten my gal, so when I walked into class my heart was sputtering its usual tiny, blue flame. It picked up, however, when I saw the girls come in, pink from the afternoon heat, and line up against the wall. When the teacher clapped her hands, announced something or another, and asked us to pair off, my heart was roaring like a well-stoked fire as I approached a girl that *looked* like my girlfriend. I searched her face, but it wasn't her. I looked around as we galloped about the room but I couldn't spot her. Where is she? Is that her? I asked myself. No, no, my girlfriend has a cute nose. Well, then, is that her? I wondered girl after girl and, for a moment in the dizziness of spinning, I even thought my sister was my girlfriend. So it was. All afternoon I searched for *her* by staring openly into the faces of girls with long hair, and when class was dismissed I walked away bewildered that I had forgotten what the love of my life looked like. The next day I was desperate and stared even more boldly, until the teacher pulled me aside to shake a finger and told me to knock it off.

But I recovered from lost love as quickly as I recovered from jumping from trees, especially when it was announced, in the fourth week of classes, that there would be a talent show — that everyone was welcome to join in. I approached Little John to ask if he'd be willing to sing with me — *Michael Row the Boat Ashore*, *If I Had a Hammer*, or *Sugar Shack* — anything that would bring applause and momentary fame.

"C'mon, I know they'll like it," I whined at him as he stood in center field. He told me to leave him alone, and when a fly ball sailed in his direction he raced for it but missed by several feet. Two runs scored, and he turned angrily at me: "See what you did!"

I thought of square dancing with Debra, but I had the feeling that she would screw up her face into an ugly knot if I should ask. She would tell her friends and they would ride their bikes talking about me. So I decided that I'd just watch the show with my arms crossed.

The talent show was held on the lawn, and we were herded grade by grade into an outline of a horseshoe: The first and second grades sat cross-legged, the third and fourth graders squatted on their haunches, and the fifth and sixth graders stood with their arms across their chests. The first act was two girls — sisters I guessed — singing a song about weather: Their fingers made the shape of falling rain, their arching arms made rainbows, and finally their hands cupped around smiling faces made sunshine. We applauded like rain while some of the kids whistled like wind from a mountain pass.

This was followed with a skit about personal hygiene — bathing and brushing one's teeth. Then there was a juggling act, another singing duo, and then a jazz tap dancer who, because he was performing on the grass, appeared to be stamping mud off his shoes. After each act my eyes drifted to a long table of typewriters. What could they possibly be for? I asked myself. They were such commanding machines, big as boulders lugged from rivers. Finally, just as the tap routine was coming to an end, kids began to show up behind them to fit clean sheets of paper into the rollers. They adjusted their chairs as they looked at one another, whispering. A teacher called our attention to the typewriters and we whistled like mountain wind again.

"All summer we have practiced learning how to type," the teacher said in a clear, deliberate speech. "Not only have we learned to type letters, but also to sing with the typewriters. If you listen carefully, I am sure that you will hear songs that you are familiar with." She turned to the kids, whose hands rested like crabs on the keys, raised a pencil, and then began waving it around. Click — clickclick — click — click — click, and I recognized *The Star Spangled Banner* — and recognized Little John straining over his keyboard. Darn him, I thought, jealous that everyone was looking at him. They then played *Waltzing Matilda*, and this made me even angrier because it sounded beautiful and because Little John was enjoying himself. Click-click-click, and they were playing *Michael Row the Boat Ashore*, and this made me even more mad. I edged my way in front of Little John and, when he looked up, I made a fist and wet my lips. Smiling, he wet his own lips and shaped a cuss word, which meant we would have a fight afterward, when the music was gone and there were no typewriters to hide behind.

Responding to "Summer School"

THINKING AND DISCUSSING

Gary Soto's narrative moves back and forth in time. He includes not only what happens at each class on the first day, but also memorable events that occur in some of the classes over the five-week summer session. How does this affect the story? At what point in the narrative does Gary leave this structure to tell a straight-ahead story?

At what point does Gary begin to enjoy summer school? How can you tell?

CHOOSING A CREATIVE RESPONSE

CREATING A COMIC STRIP   Do you have a favorite episode or humorous incident from "Summer School"? Draw a comic strip illustrating the part you like the best. Share your comic strip with the class.

PLANNING A PERFORMANCE   The performance put on by Little John's typing class was a tremendous success at the summer school talent show. Get together in a small group and brainstorm ideas to plan a special group performance. If time permits, you may want to practice your entertainment and present it to the class.

CREATING YOUR OWN ACTIVITY   Plan and complete your own activity in response to "Summer School."

THINKING AND WRITING

Imagine that you are a newspaper reporter assigned to conduct an interview with Gary Soto about his experience at summer school. Think of important questions to ask him. (What did he learn? How did his feelings about summer school change?) Make a list of six to eight interview questions that you would ask. Then write the answers in the way you think Soto would respond.

EXPLORING LANGUAGE

Gary Soto uses comparisons to great effect in "Summer School." He tells us that the typewriters used in the talent show were "big as boulders lugged from rivers." Look through the story and find other comparisons. Using those comparisons as models, write a few of your own and try them out on a friend.

daddy

The daughter of one of our nation's greatest leaders remembers how his sense of right and wrong applied to individual behavior.

It still tickles me to think about the excitement two little words brought to our household. Anytime we heard the words "Daddy's home," all previous activity stopped and all eight of our feet scurried toward the door. "Daddy, Daddy," we all yelled at the top of our voices, each of us hoping to be the first he would answer.

Although the routine was the same, each time felt like the very first time. Daddy picked us up one by one so we could kiss him on our "sugar spot."

Showing off his baby girl, Daddy often asked Bunny to identify everybody's sugar spot with a kiss. "Where's Mary's sugar spot?" he would ask, and she would kiss Daddy's right cheek. "Where's Yoki's sugar spot?" he would continue, until he went through the entire family. Bunny was always eager to answer Daddy, knowing she would get them all right. But we also knew that she really just enjoyed

by YOLANDA KING

in collaboration with Hilda R. Tompkins

kissing Daddy on everybody else's sugar spot.

The kissing went on a couple of minutes or until there was an interruption such as a phone call for Daddy. But as soon as we were able to get Daddy's attention again, the fun and games continued. "Martin, don't," Mother would admonish[1] as we all gathered in the kitchen around the refrigerator. "Martin, *please*," she would continue. But in spite of all her concern and protest, the game went on as usual — Daddy putting us on top of the refrigerator and shouting, "Jump!"

What a feeling, soaring through the air and landing in Daddy's arms. And each time I jumped, Daddy's arms were right where they were supposed to be, strong, safe, and secure. This was one of the best feelings I experienced as a child. I had no idea at the time that these moments with Daddy would become so precious to me.

Daddy was always a lot of fun, and he seemed to enjoy being with me as much as I enjoyed being with him. Of all the things that Daddy and I did together, traveling with him was one of my favorites. The two of us on a big plane in the sky headed for who-knows-where. I don't remember all of the places we traveled to or all of the things we did once we got there, but one thing was always the same: No matter where we were, what we were doing, or who we were with, crowds of people always tried to get close to my Daddy.

"Dr. King, Dr. King, can I just shake your hand?" "Dr. King, please, may I just have a picture with you?" And some of the ladies wouldn't even ask, they would just push their way through the

---

[1] **admonish:** warn.

crowd and kiss Daddy without ever saying a word. But why? I knew why Daddy was special to me; he was my daddy, and I loved him and he loved me. But what made him so special to other people?

Mother explained that Daddy's work was important to everybody because he was working for freedom and equality. People wanted to touch him and be in his presence because they appreciated so much the things he was trying to do. He wanted to make the world better for everyone.

I understood what mother was saying. It made me proud to have a father that was so devoted to the cause of human rights. People believed in Daddy. They trusted him and learned from his example. I know I did.

One of the most important lessons I learned happened while I was traveling with Daddy. I remember it like it was yesterday, although I was only seven years old. Daddy and I were strolling through the airport hand in hand. Still having a few minutes before takeoff, Daddy decided to stop in one of the airport gift shops to buy a newspaper and some other reading material. While waiting for Daddy to make his choices, I started to look around for something for me.

Browsing the different counters led me to a delectable[2] row of candy and gum. Just as I picked up the candy bar I wanted, Daddy called, "Come on, Yoki." He took my hand and hurried me to the gate. The candy bar that had been in my hand was now in my purse.

We were settled on the plane when I remembered the treat I had for myself. Without giving it much thought, I reached in my purse and took out the candy bar. Before I could get the wrapper off, Daddy asked, "Where did you get that candy?"

---

[2]**delectable:** very tasty; wonderful.

"From the gift shop," I answered.

"You had money?" he asked.

"No," I replied.

"Then how did you pay for it?" he asked.

"Well," I said, "there was no time, so I just put it in my purse."

Calmly, Daddy took the candy bar out of my hand and put it back in my purse. Daddy looked at me with his serious eyes and slowly said, "You will take this back to the store when we return and apologize for taking it. Do you understand me?"

"Yes, sir," I replied, as I sank down in my seat and turned my face to the window.

What Daddy told me I had to do stayed with me the entire time we were away. As the time approached for us to make our return trip, I was hoping that he had either forgotten or changed his mind about returning the candy. But no such luck. When the plane landed, Daddy took my hand and escorted me to the gift shop.

Nervous, embarrassed, and humble, I approached the cashier. "Excuse me, ma'am," I said politely. "I took this candy bar without paying for it, and now I want to return it. I'm sorry." As I handed her the still-wrapped chocolate bar, she extended her hand with a smile and said, "Thank you. Your apology is accepted."

This part of the ordeal had been relatively easy, but I still had to face Daddy. As I turned from the cashier, I expected him to have an angry or disappointed look on his face. To my surprise, he, too, was smiling.

I waved good-bye to the lady, and Daddy took my hand. He looked at me with a real sense of pride. As we walked away, I remember thinking how good it felt to do something right.

RESPONDING TO "DADDY"

THINKING AND DISCUSSING

In "Daddy," Yolanda King provides a personal glimpse of her father, Dr. Martin Luther King, Jr. What do you learn about Dr. King that you would not read in a history book or an encyclopedia?

The author says she did not realize at the time that her "moments with Daddy would become so precious." What does she mean?

Dr. King probably took the trip to make an important public appearance or to give a speech. What do you think it says about him that he did not forget the candy-bar episode?

CHOOSING A CREATIVE RESPONSE

Advising the Author　Imagine that Yolanda King is a friend of yours. She has taken the candy bar from the gift shop, but neither her father nor anyone else knows about it. She has realized her mistake and has come to you for advice. What suggestions might you give her? Jot down some notes about what you would say to her.

Creating Your Own Activity　Plan and complete your own activity in response to "Daddy."

THINKING AND WRITING

Do you know a young person who has had an experience in which he or she made a mistake and an older person helped to correct it? What did the young person learn from it? Imagine that you are that young person and write a brief personal narrative about the experience.

BARRIO BOY

BY ERNESTO GALARZA

From Jalcocotán, a mountain village in Mexico, Ernesto's family moves many times, seeking work and safety from the Mexican Revolution. Ernesto and his mother, Doña Henriqueta, finally settle in a barrio, a Spanish-speaking neighborhood, in Sacramento, California. The ways of Americans, or gringos, seem strange to the new immigrants. But this land offers many new possibilities for Ernesto, possibilities that could brighten his future.

We found the Americans as strange in their customs as they probably found us. Immediately we discovered that there were no *mercados* and that when shopping you did not put the groceries in a *chiquihuite*. Instead everything was in cans or in cardboard boxes or each item was put in a brown paper bag. There were neighborhood grocery stores at the corners and some big ones uptown, but no *mercado*. The grocers did not give children a *pilón*, they did not stand at the door and coax you to come in and buy, as they did in Mazatlán. The fruits and vegetables were displayed on counters instead of being piled up on the floor. The stores smelled of fly spray and oiled floors, not of fresh pineapple and limes.

Neither was there a plaza, only parks which had no bandstands, no concerts every Thursday, and no promenades of boys going one way and girls the other. There were no parks in the *barrio;* and the ones uptown were cold and rainy in winter, and in summer

Illustrated by B. J. Johnson

there was no place to sit except on the grass. When there were celebrations nobody set off rockets in the parks, much less on the street in front of your house to announce to the neighborhood that a wedding or a baptism was taking place. Sacramento did not have a *mercado* and a plaza with the cathedral to one side and the Palacio de Gobierno[1] on another to make it obvious that there and nowhere else was the center of the town.

It was just as puzzling that the Americans did not live in *vecindades,*[2] like our block on Leandro Valle. Even in the alleys, where people knew one another better, the houses were fenced apart, without central courts to wash clothes, talk and play with the other children. Like the city, the Sacramento *barrio* did not have a place which was the middle of things for everyone.

In more personal ways we had to get used to the Americans. They did not listen if you did not speak loudly, as they always did. In the Mexican style, people would know that you were enjoying their jokes tremendously if you merely smiled and shook a little, as if you were trying to swallow your mirth. In the American style there was little difference between a laugh and a roar, and until you got used to them, you could hardly tell whether the boisterous Americans were roaring mad or roaring happy.

It was Doña[3] Henriqueta more than Gustavo or José [my cousins] who talked of these oddities and classified them as agreeable or deplorable. It was she also who pointed out the pleasant surprises of the American way. When a box of rolled oats with a picture of red carnations on the side was emptied, there was a plate or a bowl or a cup with blue designs. We ate the strange stuff regularly for breakfast and we soon had a set of the beautiful dishes. Rice and beans we bought in cotton bags of colored prints. The

---

[1]**Palacio de Gobierno:** a government office building; City Hall.
[2]**vecindades:** neighborhoods; communities.
[3]**Doña:** a title of respect before a woman's given name.

bags were unsewed, washed, ironed, and made into gaily designed towels, napkins, and handkerchiefs. The American stores also gave small green stamps which were pasted in a book to exchange for prizes. We didn't have to run to the corner with the garbage; a collector came for it.

With remarkable fairness and never-ending wonder we kept adding to our list the pleasant and the repulsive in the ways of the Americans. It was my second acculturation.[4]

The older people of the *barrio*, except in those things which they had to do like the Americans because they had no choice, remained Mexican. Their language at home was Spanish. They were continuously taking up collections to pay somebody's funeral expenses or to help someone who had had a serious accident. Cards were sent to you to attend a burial where you would throw a handful of dirt on top of the coffin and listen to tearful speeches at the graveside. At every baptism a new *compadre*[5] and a new *comadre*[6] joined the family circle. New Year greeting cards were exchanged, showing angels and cherubs in bright colors sprinkled with grains of mica so that they glistened like gold dust. At the family parties the huge pot of steaming tamales was still the center of attention, the *atole* served on the side with chunks of brown sugar for sucking and crunching. If the party lasted long enough, someone produced a guitar, the men took over and the singing of *corridos* began.

In the *barrio* there were no individuals who had official titles or who were otherwise recognized by everybody as important people. The reason must have been that there was no place in the public business of the city of Sacramento for the Mexican immigrants. We only rented a corner of the city and as long as we paid the rent on time everything else was decided at City Hall or the County

---

[4]**acculturation:** the process by which someone becomes part of the culture of a particular society.

[5]**compadre:** godfather.

[6]**comadre:** godmother.

Court House, where Mexicans went only when they were in trouble. Nobody from the *barrio* ever ran for mayor or city council-man. For us the most important public officials were the policemen who walked their beats, stopped fights, and hauled drunks to jail in a paddy wagon we called *La Julia*.

The one institution we had that gave the *colonia* some kind of image was the *Comisión Honorífica*, a committee picked by the Mexi-can Consul in San Francisco to organize the celebration of the *Cinco de Mayo*[7] and the Sixteenth of September, the anniversaries of the battle of Puebla and the beginning of our War of Independence. These were the two events which stirred everyone in the *barrio*, for what we were celebrating was not only the heroes of Mexico but also the feeling that we were still Mexicans ourselves. On these occasions there was a dance preceded by speeches and a concert. For both the *cinco* and the sixteenth queens were elected to preside over the ceremonies.

Between celebrations neither the politicians uptown nor the *Comisión Honorífica* attended to the daily needs of the *barrio*. This was done by volunteers — the ones who knew enough English to interpret in court, on a visit to the doctor, a call at the county hospital, and who could help make out a postal money order. By the time I had finished the third grade at the Lincoln School I was one of these volunteers. My services were not professional but they were free, except for the IOU's I accumulated from families who always thanked me with "God will pay you for it."

My clients were not *pochos*, Mexicans who had grown up in California, probably had even been born in the United States. They had learned to speak English of sorts and could still speak Spanish, also of sorts. They knew much more about the Americans than we did, and much less about us. The *chicanos* and the *pochos* had certain feelings about one another. Concerning the *pochos*, the

---

[7]**Cinco de Mayo:** Fifth of May.

chicanos suspected that they considered themselves too good for the *barrio* but were not, for some reason, good enough for the Americans. Toward the *chicanos*, the *pochos* acted superior, amused at our confusions but not especially interested in explaining them to us. In our family when I forgot my manners, my mother would ask me if I was turning *pochito*.

Turning *pocho* was a half-step toward turning American. And America was all around us, in and out of the *barrio*. Abruptly we had to forget the ways of shopping in a *mercado* and learn those of shopping in a corner grocery or in a department store. The Americans paid no attention to the Sixteenth of September, but they made a great commotion about the Fourth of July. In Mazatlán Don Salvador had told us, saluting and marching as he talked to our class, that the *Cinco de Mayo* was the most glorious date in human history. The Americans had not even heard about it.

In Tucson, when I had asked my mother again if the Americans were having a revolution, the answer was: "No, but they have good schools, and you are going to one of them." We were by now settled at 418 L Street and the time had come for me to exchange a revolution for an American education.

The two of us walked south on Fifth Street one morning to the corner of Q Street and turned right. Half of the block was occupied by the Lincoln School. It was a three-story wooden building, with two wings that gave it the shape of a double-T connected by a central hall. It was a new building, painted yellow, with a shingled roof that was not like the red tile of the school in Mazatlán. I noticed other differences, none of them very reassuring.

We walked up the wide staircase hand in hand and through the door, which closed by itself. A mechanical contraption screwed to the top shut it behind us quietly.

Up to this point the adventure of enrolling me in the school had been carefully rehearsed. Mrs. Dodson [our friend] had told us

how to find it and we had circled it several times on our walks. Friends in the *barrio* explained that the director was called a principal, and that it was a lady and not a man. They assured us that there was always a person at the school who could speak Spanish.

Exactly as we had been told, there was a sign on the door in both Spanish and English: "Principal." We crossed the hall and entered the office of Miss Nettie Hopley.

Miss Hopley was at a roll-top desk to one side, sitting in a swivel chair that moved on wheels. There was a sofa against the opposite wall, flanked by two windows and a door that opened on a small balcony. Chairs were set around a table and framed pictures hung on the walls of a man with long white hair and another with a sad face and a black beard.

The principal half turned in the swivel chair to look at us over the pinch glasses crossed on the ridge of her nose. To do this she had to duck her head slightly as if she were about to step through a low doorway.

What Miss Hopley said to us we did not know but we saw in her eyes a warm welcome and when she took off her glasses and straightened up she smiled wholeheartedly, like Mrs. Dodson. We were, of course, saying nothing, only catching the friendliness of her voice and the sparkle in her eyes while she said words we did not understand. She signaled us to the table. Almost tiptoeing across the office, I maneuvered myself to keep my mother between me and the gringo lady. In a matter of seconds I had to decide whether she was a possible friend or a menace. We sat down.

Then Miss Hopley did a formidable[8] thing. She stood up. Had she been standing when we entered she would have seemed tall. But rising from her chair she soared. And what she carried up and up with her was a buxom superstructure, firm shoulders, a straight sharp nose, full cheeks slightly molded by a curved line along the nostrils, thin lips that moved like steel springs, and a high forehead topped by hair gathered in a bun. Miss Hopley was not a giant in body but when she mobilized it to a standing position she seemed a match for giants. I decided I liked her.

She strode to a door in the far corner of the office, opened it and called a name. A boy of about ten years appeared in the doorway. He sat down at one end of the table. He was brown like us, a plump kid with shiny black hair combed straight back, neat, cool, and faintly obnoxious.[9]

Miss Hopley joined us with a large book and some papers in her hand. She, too, sat down and the questions and answers began by way of our interpreter. My name was Ernesto. My mother's name was Henriqueta. My birth certificate was in San Blas. Here was my last report card from the Escuela Municipal Numero 3 para Varones of Mazatlán, and so forth. Miss Hopley put things down in the book and my mother signed a card.

---

[8]**formidable** (fôr′mĭ də bəl): inspiring respectful fear.
[9]**obnoxious** (əb nŏk′shəs): extremely unpleasant or annoying.

As long as the questions continued, Doña Henriqueta could stay and I was secure. Now that they were over, Miss Hopley saw her to the door, dismissed our interpreter and without further ado took me by the hand and strode down the hall to Miss Ryan's first grade.

Miss Ryan took me to a seat at the front of the room, into which I shrank — the better to survey her. She was, to skinny, somewhat runty me, of a withering height when she patrolled the class. And when I least expected it, there she was, crouching by my desk, her blond radiant face level with mine, her voice patiently maneuvering me over the awful[10] idiocies of the English language.

During the next few weeks Miss Ryan overcame my fears of tall, energetic teachers as she bent over my desk to help me with a word in the pre-primer. Step by step, she loosened me and my classmates from the safe anchorage of the desks for recitations at the blackboard and consultations at her desk. Frequently she burst into happy announcements to the whole class. "Ito can read a sentence," and small Japanese Ito, squint-eyed and shy, slowly read aloud while the class listened in wonder: "Come, Skipper, come. Come and run." The Korean, Portuguese, Italian, and Polish first graders had similar moments of glory, no less shining than mine the day I conquered "butterfly," which I had been persistently pronouncing in standard Spanish as boo-ter-flee. "Children," Miss Ryan called for attention. "Ernesto has learned how to pronounce *butterfly*!" And I proved it with a perfect imitation of Miss Ryan. From that celebrated success, I was soon able to match Ito's progress as a sentence reader with "Come, butterfly, come fly with me."

Like Ito and several other first graders who did not know English, I received private lessons from Miss Ryan in the closet, a narrow hall off the classroom with a door at each end. Next to one

---

[10]**awful:** inspiring wonder, respect, or fear.

of these doors Miss Ryan placed a large chair for herself and a small one for me. Keeping an eye on the class through the open door she read with me about sheep in the meadow and a frightened chicken going to see the king, coaching me out of my phonetic ruts in words like *pasture*, *bow-wow-wow*, *hay*, and *pretty*, which to my Mexican ear and eye had so many unnecessary sounds and letters. She made me watch her lips and then close my eyes as she repeated words I found hard to read. When we came to know each other better, I tried interrupting to tell Miss Ryan how we said it in Spanish. It didn't work. She only said "oh" and went on with *pasture*, *bow-wow-wow*, and *pretty*. It was as if in that closet we were both discovering together the secrets of the English language and grieving together over the tragedies of Bo-Peep. The main reason I was graduated with honors from the first grade was that I had fallen in love with Miss Ryan. Her radiant no-nonsense character made us either afraid not to love her or love her so we would not be afraid, I am not sure which. It was not only that we sensed she was with it, but also that she was with us.

Like the first grade, the rest of the Lincoln School was a sampling of the lower part of town where many races made their home. My pals in the second grade were Kazushi, whose parents spoke only Japanese; Matti, a skinny Italian boy; and Manuel, a fat Portuguese who would never get into a fight but wrestled you to the ground and just sat on you. Our assortment of nationalities included Koreans, Yugoslavs, Poles, Irish, and home-grown Americans.

Miss Hopley and her teachers never let us forget why we were at Lincoln: for those who were alien, to become good Americans; for those who were so born, to accept the rest of us. Off the school grounds we traded the same insults we heard from our elders. On the playground we were sure to be marched up to the principal's office for calling someone a wop, a chink, a dago, or a greaser. The school was not so much a melting pot as a griddle where Miss

Hopley and her helpers warmed knowledge into us and roasted racial hatreds out of us.

At Lincoln, making us into Americans did not mean scrubbing away what made us originally foreign. The teachers called us as our parents did, or as close as they could pronounce our names in Spanish or Japanese. No one was ever scolded or punished for speaking in his native tongue on the playground. Matti told the class about his mother's down quilt, which she had made in Italy with the fine feathers of a thousand geese. Encarnación acted out how boys learned to fish in the Philippines. I astounded the third grade with the story of my travels on a stagecoach, which nobody else in the class had seen except in the museum at Sutter's Fort. After a visit to the Crocker Art Gallery and its collection of heroic paintings of the golden age of California, someone showed a silk scroll with a Chinese painting. Miss Hopley herself had a way of expressing wonder over these matters before a class, her eyes wide open until they popped slightly. It was easy for me to feel that

becoming a proud American, as she said we should, did not mean feeling ashamed of being a Mexican.

The Americanization of Mexican me was no smooth matter. I had to fight one lout who made fun of my travels on the *diligencia*, and my barbaric translation of the word into "diligence." He doubled up with laughter over the word until I straightened him out with a kick. In class I made points explaining that in Mexico roosters said "qui-qui-ri-qui" and not "cock-a-doodle-doo," but after school I had to put up with the taunts of a big Yugoslav who said Mexican roosters were crazy.

But it was Homer who gave me the most lasting lesson for a future American.

Homer was a chunky Irishman who dressed as if every day was Sunday. He slicked his hair between a crew cut and a pompadour. And Homer was smart, as he clearly showed when he and I ran for president of the third grade.

Everyone understood that this was to be a demonstration of how the American people vote for president. In an election, the teacher explained, the candidates could be generous and vote for each other. We cast our ballots in a shoe box and Homer won by two votes. I polled my supporters and came to the conclusion that I had voted for Homer and so had he. After class he didn't deny it, reminding me of what the teacher had said — we could vote for each other but didn't have to.

The lower part of town was a collage of nationalities in the middle of which Miss Nettie Hopley kept school with discipline and compassion. She called assemblies in the upper hall to introduce celebrities like the police sergeant or the fire chief, to lay down the law of the school, to present awards to our athletic champions, and to make important announcements. One of these was that I had been proposed by my school and accepted as a member of the newly formed Sacramento Boys Band. "Now, isn't that a wonderful

thing?" Miss Hopley asked the assembled school, all eyes on me. And everyone answered in a chorus, including myself, "Yes, Miss Hopley."

It was not only the parents who were summoned to her office and boys and girls who served sentences there who knew that Nettie Hopley meant business. The entire school witnessed her sizzling Americanism in its awful majesty one morning at flag salute.

All the grades, as usual, were lined up in the courtyard between the wings of the building, ready to march to classes after the opening bell. Miss Shand was on the balcony of the second floor off Miss Hopley's office, conducting us in our lusty singing of "My Country tiz-a-thee." Our principal, as always, stood there like us, at attention, her right hand over her heart, joining in the song.

Halfway through the second stanza she stepped forward, held up her arm in a sign of command, and called loud and clear: "Stop the singing." Miss Shand looked flabbergasted. We were frozen with shock.

Miss Hopley was now standing at the rail of the balcony, her eyes sparking, her voice low and resonant, the words coming down to us distinctly and loaded with indignation.

"There are two gentlemen walking on the school grounds with their hats on while we are singing," she said, sweeping our ranks with her eyes. "We will remain silent until the gentlemen come to attention and remove their hats." A minute of awful silence ended when Miss Hopley, her gaze fixed on something behind us, signaled Miss Shand and we began once more the familiar hymn. That afternoon, when school was out, the word spread. The two gentlemen were the Superintendent of Schools and an important guest on an inspection.

I came back to the Lincoln School after every summer, moving up through the grades with Miss Campbell, Miss Beakey, Mrs. Wood, Miss Applegate, and Miss Delahunty. I sat in the classroom

adjoining the principal's office and had my turn answering her telephone when she was about the building repeating the message to the teacher, who made a note of it. Miss Campbell read to us during the last period of the week about King Arthur, Columbus, Buffalo Bill, and Daniel Boone, who came to life in the reverie of the class through the magic of her voice. And it was Miss Campbell who introduced me to the public library on Eye Street, where I became a regular customer.

All of Lincoln School mourned together when Eddie, the blond boy everybody liked, was killed by a freight train as he crawled across the tracks going home one day. We assembled to say good-bye to Miss Applegate, who was off to Alaska to be married. Now it was my turn to be excused from class to interpret for a parent enrolling a new student fresh from Mexico. Graduates from Lincoln came back now and then to tell us about high school. A naturalist entertained us in assembly, imitating the calls of the meadow lark, the water ouzel, the oriole, and the killdeer. I decided to become a bird man after I left Lincoln.

In the years we lived in the lower part of town, La Leen-Con, as my family called it, became a benchmark in our lives, like the purple light of the Lyric Theater and the golden dome of the Palacio de Gobierno gleaming above Capitol Park.

Despite many obstacles, Ernesto finishes junior high and, with the help and advice of José and his friends, goes on to high school and college. Overcoming many misfortunes, and still proudly Mexican, he embraces America's possibilities.

RESPONDING TO *BARRIO BOY*

THINKING AND DISCUSSING

What images and words does the author of *Barrio Boy* use to describe his first impressions of his new world? At what point in the story does he begin getting used to this world? How can you tell?

The author uses a number of Spanish words such as *mercado* and *barrio* in the beginning of the selection, but he uses fewer Spanish words as the selection continues. Why?

How does the author reveal Ernesto's strengths in the story?

CHOOSING A CREATIVE RESPONSE

Making a Booklet Ernesto might have felt more comfortable if someone had given him tips on how to get along in his new world. Make a booklet of "Tips for New Kids" that would help new students adjust to your school and town.

Creating Your Own Activity   Plan and complete your own activity in response to *Barrio Boy*.

THINKING AND WRITING

Imagine that you are Ernesto, and you are going to graduate from Lincoln School. In a farewell graduation speech, explain how the teachers helped you.

EXPLORING LANGUAGE

Look through the story to find Spanish words that have become familiar in English. List them with their meanings. Then add other Spanish words that you might use in your daily speech.

HOMESICK:
My Own Story

by Jean Fritz

Illustrated by Fred Lynch

Jean Fritz had never set foot in her own country. She had lived all of her twelve years in China, where her mother and father worked for the YMCA. Jean's grandparents and other relatives lived in Washington, Pennsylvania, and Jean and her grandmother had always written to each other — but Jean longed to see her grandmother in person.

Finally Jean's family set sail for California. On the voyage over, Jean and her friend Andrea talked of their hopes and fears. They tried to imagine what their new lives would be like. Jean realized she was actually going to meet her grandmother: Oh Grandma, *she* thought, ready or not, here I come!

Between California and Pennsylvania, however, lay most of a continent. With Jean's father at the wheel of their new car, the trip across America promised to be one Jean would never forget.

The morning we were due to arrive in San Francisco, all the passengers came on deck early, but I was the first. I skipped breakfast and went to the very front of the ship where the railing comes to a point. That morning I would be the "eyes" of the *President Taft*, searching the horizon for the first speck of land. My private ceremony of greeting, however, would not come until we were closer, until we were sailing through the Golden Gate. For years I had heard about the Golden Gate, a narrow stretch of water connecting the Pacific Ocean to San Francisco Bay. And for years I had planned my entrance.

Dressed in my navy skirt, white blouse, and silk stockings, I felt every bit as neat as Columbus or Balboa[1] and every bit as heroic when I finally spotted America in the distance. The decks had filled with passengers by now, and as I watched the land come closer, I had to tell myself over and over that I was HERE. At last.

Then the ship entered the narrow stretch of the Golden Gate and I could see American hills on my left and American houses on my right, and I took a deep breath of American air.

"'Breathes there the man, with soul so dead,'"[2] I cried,

"'Who never to himself hath said,

This is my own, my native land!'"

I forgot that there were people behind and around me until I heard a few snickers and a scattering of claps, but I didn't care. I wasn't reciting for anyone's benefit but my own.

Next for my first steps on American soil, but when the time came, I forgot all about them. As soon as we were on the dock, we were jostled from line to line. Believe it or not, after crossing thousands of miles of ocean to get here, we had to prove that it was O.K. for us to come into the U.S.A. We had to show that we were honest-to-goodness citizens and not spies. We had to open our baggage and let inspectors see that we weren't smuggling in opium or anything else

---

[1] **Balboa** (băl bōʹə), **Vasco de:** 1475–1517. A Spanish explorer; discovered the Pacific Ocean (1513).

[2] **Breathes there the man . . . .** from *The Lay of the Last Minstrel* (1805), by Scottish writer Sir Walter Scott.

illegal. We even had to prove that we were germ-free, that we didn't have smallpox or any dire disease that would infect the country. After we had finally passed the tests, I expected to feel one-hundred-percent American. Instead, stepping from the dock into the city of San Francisco, I felt dizzy and unreal, as if I were a made-up character in a book I had read too many times to believe it wasn't still a book.

As we walked the Hulls to the car that their Aunt Kay had driven up from Los Angeles, I told Andrea about my crazy feeling.

"I'm kind of funny in the head," I said. "As if I'm not really me. As if this isn't really happening."

"Me too," Andrea agreed. "I guess our brains haven't caught up to us yet. But my brains better get going. Guess what?"

"What?"

"Aunt Kay says our house in Los Angeles is not far from Hollywood."

Then suddenly the scene speeded up and the Hulls were in the car, ready to leave for Los Angeles, while I was still stuck in a book without having said any of the things I wanted to. I ran after the car as it started.

"Give my love to John Gilbert,"[3] I yelled to Andrea.

She stuck her head out the window. "And how!" she yelled back.

My mother, father, and I were going to stay in a hotel overnight and start across the continent the next morning, May 24, in our new Dodge. The first thing we did now was to go to a drugstore where my father ordered three ice-cream sodas. "As tall as you can make them," he said. "We have to make up for lost time."

---

[3]**John Gilbert:** an American movie actor in the silent-film era of the 1920s.

My first American soda was chocolate and it was a whopper. While we sucked away on our straws, my father read to us from the latest newspaper. The big story was about America's new hero, an aviator named Charles Lindbergh who had just made the first solo flight across the Atlantic Ocean. Of course I admired him for having done such a brave and scary thing, but I bet he wasn't any more surprised to have made it across one ocean than I was to have finally made it across another. I looked at his picture. His goggles were pushed back on his helmet and he was grinning. He had it all over John Gilbert, I decided. I might even consider having a crush on him — that is, if and when I ever felt the urge. Right now I was coming to the bottom of my soda and I was trying to slurp up the last drops when my mother told me to quit; I was making too much noise.

The rest of the afternoon we spent sight-seeing, riding up and down seesaw hills in cable cars, walking in and out of American stores. Every once in a while I found myself smiling at total strangers because I knew that if I were to speak to them in English, they'd answer in English. We were all Americans. Yet I still felt as if I were telling myself a story. America didn't become completely real for me until the next day after we'd left San Francisco and were out in the country.

My father had told my mother and me that since he wasn't used to our new car or to American highways, we should be quiet and let him concentrate. My mother concentrated too. Sitting in the front seat, she flinched every time she saw another car, a crossroad, a stray dog, but she never said a word. I paid no attention to the road. I just kept looking out the window until all at once there on my right was a white picket fence and a meadow, fresh and green as if it had just this minute been created. Two black-and-white cows were grazing slowly over the grass as if they had all the time in the world, as if they knew that no matter how much they ate, there'd always be more, as if in their quiet munching way they understood that they had nothing, nothing whatsoever to worry about. I poked my mother, pointed, and whispered, "Cows." I had never seen cows in China but it was not the cows themselves that impressed me. It was the whole scene. The perfect greenness. The washed-clean look. The peacefulness. Oh, *now*! I thought. Now I was in America. Every last inch of me.

By the second day my father acted as if he'd been driving the car all his life. He not only talked, he sang, and if he felt like hitching up his trousers, he just took his hands off the wheel and hitched. But as my father relaxed, my mother became more tense. "Arthur," she finally said, "you are going forty-five."

My father laughed. "Well, we're headed for the stable, Myrtle. You never heard of a horse that dawdled on its way home, did you?"

My mother's lips went tight and thin. "The whole point of driving across the continent," she said, "was so we could see the country."

"Well, it's all there." My father swept his hand from one side of the car to the other. "All you have to do is to take your eyes off the road and look." He honked his horn at the car in front of him and swung around it.

At the end of the day, after we were settled in an overnight cabin, my father  took a new notebook from his pocket. I watched as he wrote: "May 24. 260 miles."

Just as I'd suspected, my father was out to break records. I bet that before long we'd be making 300 miles or more a day. I bet we'd be in Washington, P.A., long before July.

The trouble with record breaking is that it can lead to Narrow Squeaks, and while we were still in California we had our first one. Driving along a back road that my father had figured out was a shortcut, we came to a bridge with a barrier across it and a sign in front: THIS BRIDGE CONDEMNED. DO NOT PASS. There was no other road marked DETOUR, so obviously the only thing to do was to turn around and go back about five miles to the last town and take the regular highway. My father stopped the car. "You'd think they'd warn you in advance," he muttered. He slammed the door, jumped over the barrier, and walked onto the bridge. Then he climbed down the riverbank and looked up at the bridge from below. When he came back up the bank, he

pushed the barrier aside, got in the car, and started it up. "We can make it," he said.

It hadn't occurred to me that he'd try to drive across. My mother put her hand on his arm. "Please, Arthur," she begged, but I didn't bother with any "pleases." If he wanted to kill himself, he didn't have to kill Mother and me too. "Let Mother and me walk across," I shouted. "Let us out. Let us OUT."

My father had already revved up the motor. "A car can have only one driver," he snapped. "I'm it." He backed up so he could get a flying start and then we whooped across the bridge, our wheels clattering across the loose boards, space gaping below. Well, we did reach the other side and when I looked back, I saw that the bridge was still there.

"You see?" my father crowed. "You see how much time we saved?"

All I could see was that we'd risked our lives because

he was so pigheaded. Right then I hated my father. I felt rotten hating someone I really loved but I couldn't help it. I knew the loving would come back but I had to wait several hours.

There were days, however, particularly across the long, flat stretches of Texas, when nothing out-of-the-way happened. We just drove on and on, and although my father reported at the end of the day that we'd gone 350 miles, the scenery was the same at the end as at the beginning, so it didn't feel as if we'd moved at all. Other times we ran into storms or into road construction and we were lucky if we made 200 miles. But the best day of the whole trip, at least as far as my mother and I were concerned, was the day that we had a flat tire in the Ozark Mountains. The spare tire and jack were buried in the trunk under all our luggage, so everything had to be taken out before my father could even begin work on the tire. There was no point in offering to help because my father had a system for loading and unloading which only he understood, so my mother and I set off up the mountainside, looking for wild flowers.

"Watch out for snakes," my mother said, but her voice was so happy, I knew she wasn't thinking about snakes.

As soon as I stepped out of the car, I fell in love with the day. With the sky — fresh, blotting-paper blue. With the mountains, warm and piney and polka-dotted with flowers we would never have seen from the window of a car. We decided to pick one of each kind and press them in my gray geography book which I had in the car. My mother held out her skirt, making a hollow out of it, while I dropped in the flowers and she named them: forget-me-not, wintergreen, pink, wild rose. When we didn't know the name, I'd make one up: pagoda plant, wild confetti, French knot. My mother's skirt was

atumble with color when we suddenly realized how far we'd walked. Holding her skirt high, my mother led the way back, running and laughing. We arrived at the car, out of breath, just as my father was loading the last of the luggage into the trunk. He glared at us, his face streaming with perspiration. "I don't have a dry stitch on me," he said, as if it were our fault that he sweat so much. Then he looked at the flowers in Mother's skirt and his face softened. He took out his handkerchief and wiped his face and neck and finally he smiled. "I guess I picked a good place to have a flat tire, didn't I?" he said.

The farther we went, the better mileage we made, so that by the middle of June we were almost to the West Virginia state line. My father said we'd get to Washington,

P.A., the day after the next, sometime in the afternoon. He called my grandmother on the phone, grinning because he knew how surprised she'd be. I stood close so I could hear her voice.

"Mother?" he said when she answered. "How about stirring up a batch of flannel cakes?"

"Arthur!" (She sounded just the way I knew she would.) "Well, land's sakes, Arthur, where are you?"

"About ready to cross into West Virginia."

My grandmother was so excited that her words fell over each other as she tried to relay the news to my grandfather and Aunt Margaret and talk over the phone at the same time.

The next day it poured rain and although that didn't slow us down, my mother started worrying. Shirls Avenue, my grandparents' street, apparently turned into a dirt road just before plunging down a steep hill to their

house and farm. In wet weather the road became one big sea of mud which, according to my mother, would be "worth your life to drive through."

"If it looks bad," my mother suggested, "we can park at the top of the hill and walk down in our galoshes."

My father sighed. "Myrtle," he said, "we've driven across the Mohave Desert.[4] We've been through thick and thin for over three thousand miles and here you are worrying about Shirls Avenue."

The next day the sun was out, but when we came to Shirls Avenue, I could see that the sun hadn't done a thing to dry up the hill. My father put the car into low, my mother closed her eyes, and down we went, sloshing up to our hubcaps, careening[5] from one rut to another, while my father kept one hand down hard on the horn to announce our arrival.

By the time we were at the bottom of the hill and had parked beside the house, my grandmother, my grandfather, and Aunt Margaret were all outside, looking exactly the way they had in the calendar picture. I ran right into my grandmother's arms as if I'd been doing this every day.

"Welcome home! Oh, welcome home!" my grandmother cried.

I hadn't known it but this was exactly what I'd wanted her to say. I needed to hear it said out loud. I was home.

---

[4] **Mohave Desert** also **Mojave** (mō hä´vē): a desert in southern California that covers thousands of square miles.
[5] **careening:** swerving.

RESPONDING TO
Homesick: My Own Story

THINKING AND DISCUSSING

Once the author has sailed through the Golden Gate and stepped onto American soil, she feels "dizzy and unreal." Why is she slightly numb and dazed at the way things are going?

Describe how the author's mother and father react differently to their cross-country trip.

Why do you think Jean's father was willing to chance driving over the condemned bridge? Were his actions worth the risk or not? Explain your answers.

CHOOSING A CREATIVE RESPONSE

Bringing the Story Home   With your group, present an extended version of the homecoming scene that closes the story. Members of the group can take the parts of Jean, her parents, her grandparents, and her Aunt Margaret. In writing the scene, begin with the slippery trip down the muddy hill, and include the grandmother's greeting. Then write further dialogue and action to show all the characters greeting one another.

Sharing Jean Fritz's Story   Tell the class or your group about the incident in the story that you find the most interesting, exciting, or enjoyable. Tell how you might have responded if you had been in Jean's place.

Creating Your Own Activity   Plan and complete your own activity in response to *Homesick: My Own Story*.

ABOUT THE AUTHORS

JEAN FRITZ

Jean Fritz spent her childhood in Hankow, China, where she was born in 1915 to missionary parents. Interest in her American roots, as well as her love for China, led Fritz to explore both countries in her writings.

A leading author of biography and historical fiction, Fritz received the Laura Ingalls Wilder Medal in 1986 for her "lasting contribution to literature for children."

Ernesto Galarza was born in 1905 in Jalcocotán, Mexico. To escape the violence of the Mexican Revolution, Galarza's family moved frequently, settling down in Sacramento, California. Galarza wrote several books on the history of farm workers in America, a volume of poetry, and *Barrio Boy*, his autobiography. Galarza died in San Jose, California, in 1984.

ERNESTO GALARZA

Yolanda King was born in 1955, the eldest child of Rev. Martin Luther King, Jr., and Coretta Scott King. Yolanda King became an actress, producer, and director. She and Attallah Shabazz, daughter of the African American leader Malcolm X, have toured together in the theater company they founded.

YOLANDA KING

GARY SOTO

Gary Soto was born in 1952 in Fresno, California, and grew up among farm workers. As a college student, he studied poetry and earned an advanced degree in creative writing from the University of California.

An award-winning poet, Soto began publishing essays and stories in 1977. Soto's poems often deal with his own experience as a Mexican American.

James Thurber is considered one of the world's great humorists. He spent most of his life in New York City. In spite of losing his sight, he created hundreds of humorous stories and countless cartoons. He also wrote plays. Many of his stories, such as "The Secret Life of Walter Mitty," were made into movies. Thurber died in 1961.

JAMES THURBER

BARRIO BOY by Ernesto Galarza (University of Notre Dame Press, 1971)

After Ernesto had spent his early childhood in a Mexican mountain village, his family moved to a barrio in Sacramento, California. He gradually learned to feel at home in his adopted country and, in the process, moved from boyhood toward manhood.

NISEI DAUGHTER by Monica Sone (University of Washington Press, 1979)

Living in Seattle, Monica Sone felt more American than Japanese. After the Japanese attack on Pearl Harbor, however, Monica was shipped with her family to a prison camp for people of Japanese descent. Despite that painful experience, Monica finally found peace with both parts of her Japanese American heritage.

OWLS IN THE FAMILY by Farley Mowat (Bantam, 1981)

In this delightful recollection of his childhood, author Farley Mowat writes about growing up in Canada with two pet owls. From the time he took Wol home after a storm and rescued Weeps from an old oil barrel, life at home — and around the neighborhood — was never the same.

CHILDTIMES: *A Three-Generation Memoir* by Eloise Greenfield and Lessie Jones Little (Crowell, 1979)

Three women — a grandmother, a mother, and a daughter — recall their childhoods. Their recollections, ranging from the 1880s to the 1950s, center on family life within the context of the African American struggle for freedom and equality.

HOMESICK: My Own Story by Jean Fritz (Putnam, 1982)

Born and raised in China, young Jean Fritz felt fiercely American and longed for a land she had never seen. As a result, she developed an enthusiasm for American history and as an author made it the subject of much of her writing. In this lively narrative, she provides her early personal history.

TRADITIONAL TALES

THEME 5

TIMELESS TALES

TIMELESS TALES

244   BRER RABBIT AND BRER COOTER RACE retold by
William J. Faulkner (United States — African American)

250   THE HUNTER WHO WANTED AIR retold by Alexandra
Whitney (South America — South American Indian)

258   THE VERY ANGRY GHOST told by Spotted Elk and retold
by Richard Erdoes (United States — Sioux)

266   THE HEADLESS RIDER from *Stories That Must Not Die*
retold by Juan Sauvageau (United States — Hispanic)

272   OLD PLOTT retold by Ellis Credle
        (United States — Appalachia)

286   THE ALLIGATOR WAR by Horacio Quiroga
        (South America — Hispanic)

Brer Rabbit
and Brer Cooter
Race

RETOLD BY WILLIAM J. FAULKNER

Along time ago, when the creatures lived together in villages the way people do today, Brer[1] Rabbit and Brer Box Cooter were neighbors. But Brer Rabbit used to poke fun at Brer Cooter because, like all turtles, he had to carry his house on his back wherever he went and he always moved about so slowly.

"Brer Cooter, I feel sorry for you sometimes," said Brer Rabbit one day. "You travel around so slowly on those short legs of yours that it's a wonder you can get out of a shower of rain. And you look so funny carrying your house on your back. I declare there isn't but one other creature in the whole world that's slower than you — and he carries his house on his back, too. It's Brer Snail. Ho! Ho! Ho! That is funny! You and Brer Snail are the slowest creatures in the world." And Brer Rabbit doubled up with laughter as he looked down at Brer Cooter. This hurt Brer Cooter's feelings and made him angry.

"Hold on there, Mister Smart-Aleck," said Brer Box Cooter. "Don't talk too fast. The old folks say, 'An empty wagging makes a heap of fuss.' And that's what I think about you. Just because your legs are long and you can pick them up quick, it doesn't mean you can outrun me in a footrace. In a fair race, man to man, I'll run your long ears off you," challenged Brer Cooter.

This was more than Brer Rabbit could stand. His ears were big and long, but for once he was too amazed to believe them. The idea of Brer Cooter, the slowest creature in town, outrunning Brer Rabbit, the fastest runner in town except possibly for Brer Deer,

---

[1]**Brer** (brûr): a southern expression meaning "brother." Also used to refer to a friend or comrade.

Illustrated by Michael McCurdy

was just too much for Brer Rabbit. He rolled over and over on the ground and laughed and laughed until he looked silly.

Finally he caught his breath and managed to say, "Brer Cooter, that's too funny to be sensible. Fact is, it's impossible. Cooter outrun rabbit in a footrace? No living creature's ever heard tell of such a thing. Why, Brer Cooter, it's so impossible that I'll bet you a whole bushel of pinders[2] that you can't outrun me. And I'll even let you lay out the racetrack and set up the mile posts yourself."

Brer Box Cooter appeared to be well pleased to run a race with Brer Rabbit. Especially since Brer Fox and Brer Wolf and other creatures of the village had come up and overheard much of the big talk, and Brer Rabbit was strutting all around the street, boasting of his speed before the crowd. Brer Cooter's pride would not let him back out of the race now.

"All right, Brer Rabbit," he said, "we'll run the race this coming Saturday afternoon, straight across the field for two miles. And I'll set up the mileposts myself."

Now, it did not take long for such exciting news to spread all over the countryside, and by Saturday morning the creatures from miles around began gathering for the footrace. Brer Cooter had laid out the racecourse very carefully, taking special care to run it across a few gullies[3] and high places.

Brer Rabbit paid no attention to all of this, but spent his time boasting of how he would beat Brer Cooter. He went so far as to tell his wife to be on the front piazza[4] to watch him raise dust when he

---

[2]**pinder (pĭn′dər):** peanut.
[3]**gully (gŭl′ē):** a ditch or channel cut in the earth by running water, especially after a rain.
[4]**piazza** (pē ăz′ə): a porch.

passed Brer Cooter on the way to the last milepost. For, you see, Brer Cooter had placed three posts in the ground a mile apart: the first one at the start, the second one in the middle, and the last one at the end.

Everybody from the Deep Woods and the villages nearby was on hand to see the race and to root for his or her favorite. At the signal to go, Brer Rabbit and Brer Cooter dashed away from the first post at top speed. In an instant, Brer Rabbit had passed Brer Cooter and kicked up dust in his face. Brer Cooter went steadily on.

Brer Rabbit soon was so far ahead that he said to himself, "Aw shucks, I've left Brer Box Cooter so far behind, I'm going to lie down and take a nap."

And he did. And while he was asleep, Brer Cooter disappeared in a gully.

After a while, Brer Rabbit awoke and dashed off across the field toward the second post. Brer Cooter was nowhere in sight. So, as Brer Rabbit neared the post, he called out, "Hello there, Brer Cooter! Where are you?"

Instantly Brer Cooter struck his shell against the post and said, "Here I am, Brer Rabbit! I've been here so long my head is in my house." And his head actually was in his shell.

Brer Rabbit was so surprised he couldn't believe what he saw. Nevertheless, he said to Brer Cooter, "Come on, slowpoke. I slept too long back there. But you won't beat me to the last post. Good-bye, I'm gone."

With that, Brer Rabbit left the turtle far behind again as he galloped across the field. But Brer Rabbit had not gone very far before he came to his house, and then he stopped.

"Hello, honey!" he said to his wife. "I just thought I'd stop by and

talk with you a bit. You see, I left that old slowpoke of a cooter so far behind, he couldn't see me for my dust."

"Come on in, dear, and sit down on the piazza for a spell," encouraged his wife. "You must be hot and tired from running on a day like this. I'll bring you some lemonade." So Brer Rabbit took a seat on the piazza and soon lost track of time as he talked and drank lemonade.

Finally he remembered the race, ran down the steps, jumped over the fence, and was off again at top speed. He looked like a whirlwind coming across the field, he was raising so much dust. Not seeing Brer Box Cooter again, he yelled out as he neared the milepost, "Where are you, Brer Cooter?"

Instantly came back the answer, "Here I am, Brer Rabbit. I've been here so long my head is in my house." And Brer Cooter rapped the milepost with his shell as Brer Rabbit dashed up just a moment too late to win the race.

So Brer Cooter won the footrace and the bushel of pinders, while Brer Rabbit became the laughingstock of all the creatures for miles around. And, strange to say, Brer Rabbit never found out that Brer Box Cooter had planted one of his cousins in the ground with only his head showing at the last two posts.

When the cousins had seen Brer Rabbit coming, they'd jumped out of the ground and said, "Here I am, Brer Rabbit. I've been here so long my head is in my house."

And from this race with Brer Cooter, Brer Rabbit learned a good lesson — that it never pays to brag or to poke fun at another creature.

RESPONDING TO

Brer Rabbit and Brer Cooter Race

How is the behavior of the animals in this tale similar to human behavior? What conclusions can you then draw about human nature from this story?

CHOOSING A CREATIVE RESPONSE

Drawing a Map Create a map showing all the events of the race between Brer Rabbit and Brer Cooter.

Holding a Debate Divide your group into two teams and debate the following question: "Who really wins the race?" Have one team defend Brer Cooter and the other team defend Brer Rabbit.

Creating Your Own Activity Plan and complete your own activity in response to "Brer Rabbit and Brer Cooter Race."

THINKING AND WRITING

Write a sports article about the race between Brer Rabbit and Brer Cooter. Include an interview with one of the two competitors telling why he won or lost.

THE HUNTER WHO WANTED AIR

RETOLD BY
ALEXANDRA WHITNEY

ILLUSTRATED BY
ENRIQUE SANCHEZ

The first time Mapuri the hunter noticed Tafeela, she was weaving a basket under a shelter of thatched grass. So enchanted was he by her grace and beauty that he immediately strode into the nearby hut of her father, Okono, and asked for permission to marry Tafeela.

"I shall let Tafeela decide for herself whether or not she will marry you," said Okono, as he went to the doorway and summoned his daughter.

When Tafeela entered the hut, Okono explained the reason for Mapuri's presence. Tafeela peered intently at her suitor. Then she stood on tiptoe and whispered in her father's ear.

"Tafeela thinks you are handsome," Okono told Mapuri, "but she says she will only marry someone who possesses a quality such as wisdom. You are known to be an expert hunter and a skilled fisherman, but —" Okono hesitated, somewhat embarrassed, "I seriously doubt if anyone would call you wise."

"Then I shall become wise at once!" Mapuri said airily.

"And just how do you plan to accomplish that?" Okono wanted to know.

"Very simply," declared Mapuri. "I have heard that Mankato, chieftain of the tribe that lives upriver by the waterfall, is great in wisdom. I shall go to him, and when he has taught me all that he knows, I shall return and marry Tafeela!"

Mapuri went off merrily whistling an imitation of the honeybird's song.

Early the following morning Mapuri ran to the river and leaped into his *corial*, the dugout canoe he had carved from a tree trunk. Then he paddled strenuously upstream until he heard the thunderous torrent of the waterfall.

When he had pulled his dugout onto a sandy cove, he hastened toward a cluster of beehive-shaped huts set back from the riverbank. Amid the excited barking of dogs, he exchanged greetings with a group of villagers and told them he had come to see Mankato.

Mapuri was led to a large thatched hut, roofed with pale-yellow palm straws that swept gracefully to the ground. Seated cross-legged in the entrance was an ancient man with a magnificent head of graying hair.

Mapuri stood before him and came to the point at once: "Mankato, I wish to learn how to be wise."

The old chieftain's eyes twinkled from behind half-closed lids. "Before one can acquire wisdom, one must truly desire it," he said.

"I desire it more than anything else at the moment!" cried Mapuri.

"Then you shall have your first lesson," said Mankato, rising slowly to his feet. "Come, let us walk to the river."

When the pair arrived at the riverbank, Mankato told Mapuri to kneel in the shallow water. But as soon as Mapuri had done so, Mankato firmly pushed the young man's head underwater and held it there for a moment or two.

Choking and spluttering, Mapuri raised his head out of the river. Then he drew in great gulps of air.

"What did you think about while your head was underwater?" asked Mankato, seemingly unaware of his would-be pupil's distress.

"Air!" wheezed Mapuri.

"What!" exclaimed Mankato. "Did you not think of your prowess[1] in the hunt?"

"No!" gasped Mapuri. "All I could think of was air!"

"Did you not think of your nets brimming with fish?" persisted Mankato.

"No," said Mapuri, "I thought only of air!"

"When you want wisdom as much as you wanted air, then shall you become wise," said Mankato. And without a backward glance at Mapuri, the old man walked away.

The long shadows of early evening lay on the river when Mapuri returned to his village. As he trod wearily past Okono's hut, Tafeela emerged from the doorway.

"Did you learn how to be wise, Mapuri?" she asked.

Mapuri hung his head and looked forlornly at his toes. "Alas, Tafeela, I have learned only one thing," he said. "Air is more important to me than wisdom."

Tafeela's eyes sparkled beneath her fringe of glossy black hair. "In that case," she said, "I shall accept your offer of marriage."

Mapuri could scarcely believe his ears. "*Kiriwani!* Impossible!" he cried. "Surely you must realize that many, many moons and many, many suns will come and go before I will be able to claim wisdom!"

Tafeela laughed softly. "That may be true, but you possess another quality more valuable than all the game in our forest, more priceless than all the fish in our river: honesty. And honesty, Mapuri, is the first step on the path to wisdom," said Tafeela.

---

[1]**prowess** (prou′ĭs): skillfulness.

THE HUNTER WHO WANTED AIR

THINKING AND DISCUSSING

Mapuri tells the old chieftain that he desires wisdom above all else. What does the old chieftain guess about Mapuri's desire that causes him to hold Mapuri's head underwater? What does Mapuri learn?

Tafeela tells Mapuri that honesty is the first step on the path to wisdom. Make a list of other qualities a person might need to attain wisdom. Compare your list with the lists of your classmates.

CHOOSING A CREATIVE RESPONSE

TRACKING TRAVELS   With a partner, create a collage or a map showing Mapuri's travels through the jungle. Display your completed project in the classroom.

EXPLAINING YOUR DECISION   At the end of the story, Tafeela changes her mind about Mapuri even though he has not yet become wise. Imagine that you are Tafeela and that you are writing a letter to a friend describing the incident. Summarize what has happened, and then tell why you have decided to give Mapuri a chance. Share your letter with a partner or your group.

CREATING YOUR OWN ACTIVITY   Plan and complete your own activity in response to "The Hunter Who Wanted Air."

tories are handed on from the older generation to the younger. It is all done by word of mouth — the art is in the telling, the pleasure in listening. Each speaker is an individualist telling the story in his own way. Some legends are sacred, and whoever relates them will make an effort to tell the story just as he heard it from his grandfather, in the same words if possible. Others are fun stories which can be improved upon with each telling. One family tells a legend one way, another family knows it differently. Some stories die because there is nobody left to tell them and nobody to remember. Luckily that does not happen very often. . . .

RICHARD ERDOES
The Sound of Flutes and Other Indian Legends

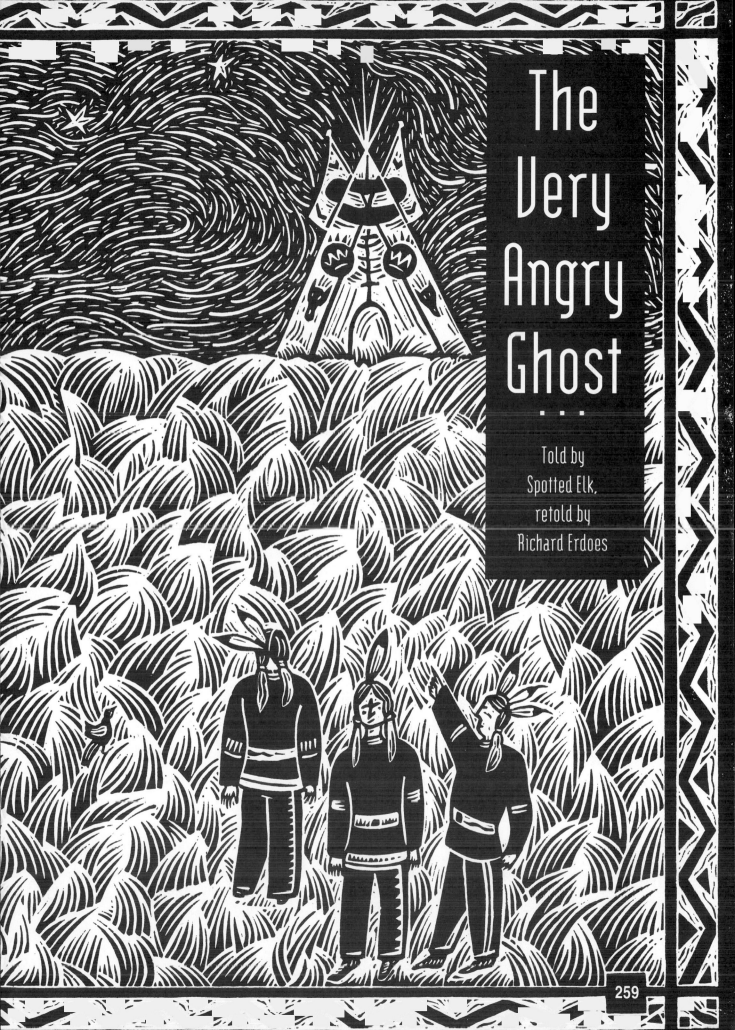

The Very Angry Ghost

Told by Spotted Elk, retold by Richard Erdoes

Y ▪ ▪ ▪ oung men never know how to behave themselves. They should learn good manners from
their elders, but they seldom do.

One day, long ago, an old warrior who
had counted many coups[1] in his days took
three young braves with him on a raid to steal
▪ ▪ ▪ horses from the Pawnees, ancient enemies
of the Sioux.

"Stealing horses" — this is what the white men call
it. But it was really a sport practiced by all the Plains
tribes. To creep into an enemy village noiselessly,
unseen, and to make off with their herd right under the
noses of the horse guards — to outwit, outthink, and
outride them — took great skill and brought fame and
honor to a warrior.

On this raid, though, the four Sioux had no luck.
They were discovered by the enemy before they could
even get near the horse herd. They had to be happy to
get out of this scrape alive by running away and hiding
themselves in a ravine. They had left on foot, and on
foot they went home. Their moccasins had holes in
them from their many days of hard walking. They were
hungry, tired, and empty-handed.

---

[1] **counted coups (koun'tĭd ko͞oz):** In battle, the Plains Indians "counted coup"
on an enemy by touching him with a "coup stick." This was considered to
require more bravery than killing an enemy.

Halfway home, they passed a hill on top of which they spied a lonely tipi,[2] all by itself, and without any signs of life. They wondered what it was doing there on the wild prairie, and went up to investigate. They found that it was a burial tipi — a splendid one made of sixteen large buffalo hides and painted all over with pictures of war and hunting.

Inside they found the body of a man, his face painted in the sacred scarlet color, lying in state in a resplendent war shirt and beautifully beaded leggings. His fine weapons, his quilled moccasins, and all his other possessions were spread about him to take along to the spirit world.

The young men looked admiringly at all these fine things. "What a stroke of luck," they said. "We will take all this to bring home, turning failure into success."

"A fine success," chided the old warrior. "To steal horses from an enemy brings honor, but to rob the dead is shameful. How wrong I was to pick youths of low mind like you to accompany me. Don't you know that only great chiefs and famous warriors are buried thus?"

They left and went down the hill again, making their camp near a stream. But the young men were still thinking of all the splendid things left in the lone tipi.

---

[2]**tipi (tē′pē):** a form of the word teepee; a tent.

"I think it was stupid to leave it all there," said one of them. "We should have taken everything," said the second. "Let us go right now and do it," said the third.

"I really showed bad judgment in picking you to go with me on a raid," the old man told them. "I will never be able to make good warriors out of you!"

But the young men would not listen. "Old one, show some sense," they answered him. "Those fine things are of no use to one who is dead, but they are of much use to us who are alive."

"Well, I guess you better go without me then," said the old warrior. So they left him to go up that hill again. Quickly the old man ran to the stream and smeared himself all over with cold mud. He took a fur pouch he wore, made two holes in it, and put it over his head as a mask. He looked like a ghost from another world. He ran fast, circling the hill, coming up on the far side, and sat down in the entrance of the lone tipi before the three young braves arrived.

When they got there, they heard an eerie hollow voice, resounding from the tipi. "Who has come here to rob a great chief? I will take them to the spirit world with me." Out from under the entrance flap rose the specter of a frightful ghost, the pale moonlight making it look still more terrible to the young men, who were so petrified with fright that their hair stood on end.

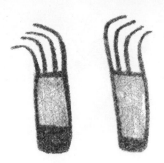

They stood stock-still and open-mouthed for a few seconds. Then, all together, they dropped their bows, turned around, and took to their heels, running down the hill as fast as their feet would carry them.

It was not very fast. They were so scared, they didn't know where to put their feet. They stumbled, they stepped on cactus and prickly pear, they got stuck in the underbrush. The ghost got nearer and nearer, gaining on them fast. At last the hindmost felt a cold, clammy hand touching his bare shoulder and a hollow voice whispering in his ear, "Friend, I have come for you!" The young man was so frightened he fell down in a dead faint.

Then it was the next young man's turn to feel the icy hand, and to hear the ghostlike voice. He, too, fainted. And so did the third and last one.

The old man got back to the campsite well ahead of them. He took off his mask and washed the mud from his body in the cold stream. He was warming himself by the fire as the bedraggled young men came in one by one.

"Where are all those fine things you wanted to take from that dead chief?" asked the old warrior.

"We did not find the tipi," said the young men. "And we did not feel like taking those things after all."

The old warrior said nothing.

Back home in their village, the three young men were sitting in the camp circle telling the people about their raid. Suddenly the old warrior came and sat down among the others. He put on his fur mask and laid a muddy hand on a pretty girl's shoulder. "Does that frighten you, *wincincala*?"[3] he asked the girl.

"You are a funny old man," said the girl, giggling.

"There are some here who were very frightened," said the old warrior, "so frightened that they fainted." And he told the story of how he had fooled them.

Everybody had a good laugh at the young men's expense. They were shamed, but this was good for them. It taught them a lesson, how to act and how to behave, so that they turned out to be good men and brave warriors.

Opening illustration by Patti Green
In–text illustrations by Paul Goble

---

[3]**wincincala:** a young girl.

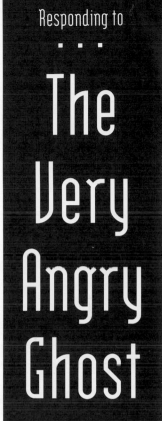

Thinking and Discussing

Why did the old warrior trick the young men?
Did he achieve his purpose? Why or why not?

Choosing a Creative Response

Holding a Trial Plan and hold a mock trial to judge
the three young warriors. Members of your group
can take the parts of the jury, judge, lawyers, and witnesses.
At the end of the trial, the jury can decide whether or not the
young men are guilty of a crime. The judge can come up with
a just punishment if they are found guilty.

Creating Your Own Activity Plan and complete your own activity in response to "The Very Angry Ghost."

Thinking and Writing

Suppose the three young braves were humble men of honor.
How would they respond to their unsuccessful raid? How
would the story's outcome be affected? Write a summary of
the plot as it would take place this way.

The Headless Rider

from *Stories That Must Not Die*
retold by Juan Sauvageau
illustrated by Alfredo Cruz

El jinete sin cabeza

de *Stories That Must Not Die*
recopilado por Juan Sauvageau
ilustrado por Alfredo Cruz

San Diego
1917

The friend who told me the following anecdote swears that it is not a story but an authentic fact.

"This happened in 1917 in Duval County.

"My wife and I left our little ranch to go and visit my uncle who lived close to San Diego. We traveled the whole day in our wagon pulled by two mules. We even continued after dark for a while, looking for a place to camp for the night.

"We saw a campfire in the distance. I told my wife, 'We must be getting close to Dead Man's Lagoon. I am glad we're going to have company for the night. I feel safer this way.'

"But the fire got smaller and smaller as we got closer to the lagoon. By the time we got there, only embers were left. Nobody around . . . not even tracks on the ground.

"I didn't feel good about the situation, especially about the fire diminishing at our approach, but I did not say anything in order to not frighten my wife. We decided to camp right there under a big oak tree. It was too dark by this time to continue anyway.

"We got what we needed for the night out of the wagon and I threw some wood upon the coals. As the fire started to burn again, we heard the galloping of a horse in the distance. It was coming faster and faster. We heard branches cracking in front of us.

La Laguna del Muerto

Les voy a contar una historia que me relató un amigo mío. Jura él que no es cuento sino la purita verdad.

—Esto aconteció en el condado de Duval en 1917.

Mi esposa y yo salimos de nuestro ranchito para ir a visitar a mi tío que vivía cerca de San Diego. En nuestro carretón, estirado por dos mulas, viajamos todo el día. Seguimos adelante aún después de acostarse el sol, buscando un lugar para campar esa noche.

Vimos una lumbre a lo lejos. Le dije a mi esposa, "Creo que nos estamos acercando a La Laguna del Muerto. Me da gusto que haya gente ya. Me siento más seguro así que si estuviéramos solos".

Pues más nos acercábamos a la laguna, más se bajaban las llamas del fuego. Cuando llegamos, nada más quedaban las brasas. No había nadie... ni se veían huellas en el suelo.

Esto del fuego apagado me molestaba en algo pero no quise decir nada a mi señora para no asustarla. Decidimos campar allá mismo debajo de un enorme encino. Era ya demasiado oscuro para seguir adelante.

Sacamos del carretón lo que necesitábamos para la noche. Eché leña encima de las brasas y prendió la lumbre de vuelta.

"We saw the most frightening sight of our lives, a tall grey horse running at full speed right in front of us . . . upon the horse, a headless rider. We saw him as clearly as I see you now. He planted his spurs in the flanks of the animal as he passed in front of us.

"My wife fainted at that moment.

"The horse continued towards the lagoon and ran over it, all the way across, as if it were on cement. I could hear the hoofs on the other side of the lagoon.

"The sound stopped suddenly and at the same time the fire in front of me went out.

"As the moon had come out from behind the clouds, I decided we should leave immediately and find another place for the rest of the night. I marked the spot carefully before leaving, hanging rags on the branches of the oak tree.

"When we arrived at my uncle's ranch, we told him immediately what had frightened us so much the night before.

"He smiled like he knew exactly what the whole thing was about.

"'Well,' he said, 'you were at the Dead Man's Lagoon. I've heard lots of rumors about that place.'

"Many years ago, I was told, four ranchers got together on the side of the lagoon for a race. Each man was convinced he had the best horse. They bet everything they had, money, ranches, cattle. Mr. Dickson had a tall grey stallion called Hercules. Well, Hercules won the race with such ease that the other men, furious and humiliated, not only refused to pay their debt but even killed Mr. Dickson with a machete, cutting his head off. Since then, according to what people say, he and Hercules have been running that race over and over again.

"As soon as my uncle finished the story, he and I went back to the spot I had marked the night before. There was not a track on the ground, not even in the soft mud on the side of the lagoon. Nobody could even tell there had been a fire, no coals, no ashes, nothing. Even the rags I had used to mark the place were gone."

Al momento en que se levantaban las llamas, empezamos a oír un caballo que venía a galope a lo lejos. Venía hacia nosotros más y más aprisa. Oímos las ramas que se quebraban. Y entonces fuimos testigos de la cosa la más espantosa: en mero frente de nosotros, un caballo alto, gris, corriendo a toda velocidad; montado sobre el caballo, un jinete sin cabeza. Lo vimos tan claramente como le veo a usted en este momento. Al pasar en frente de nosotros, clavó sus espuelas en los lados del animal. Mi mujer se desmayó en este momento.

El jinete siguió hacia la laguna; el caballo corrió encima del agua como si hubiera sido cemento. Todavía pude oír el ruido de los cascos del animal al otro lado de la laguna.

De repente se paró el ruido; al mismo tiempo se apagó el fuego en frente de mí.

Como la luna ya había salido de entre las nubes, decidí dejar aquel lugar inmediatamente y buscar otro sitio para pasar la noche. Antes de irme, sin embargo, marqué el lugar con trapos que colgué en las ramas del encino.

El día siguiente, al llegar a la casa del tío, le contamos, naturalmente, lo que nos había asustado tanto la noche de antes.

Se sonrió el tío como si supiera muy bien de qué se trataba. "Bueno", dijo él, "estaban al lado de La Laguna del Muerto. He oído muchos rumores tocante a ese lugar". Dicen que, hace muchos años, se juntaron cuatro propietarios de rancho para ver quién tenía el mejor caballo. Cada uno de los hombres estaba convencido que su caballo ganaría. Tan seguros estaban que apostaron todo lo que tenían, dinero, ranchos y ganado.

El señor Dickson tenía un caballo gris, alto y poderoso, que se llamaba Hércules. Pues, Hércules se ganó la carrera con tanta facilidad que los otros hombres, humillados, se enojaron. No solamente rehusaron pagar sus apuestas, sino que se echaron encima de él y le mataron con un machete, cortándole la cabeza.

Desde entonces se dice que el señor Dickson y Hércules vuelven a correr de nuevo la misma carrera cada noche.

Luego que terminó mi tío, salimos él y yo para La Laguna del Muerto. Volvimos al lugar exacto al lado de la laguna. Ni siquiera una huella en el suelo, aun en el lodo al lado de la laguna. No quedaba nada del fuego, ni brasas, ni cenizas; aun los trapos que yo había dejado en las ramas habían desaparecido.

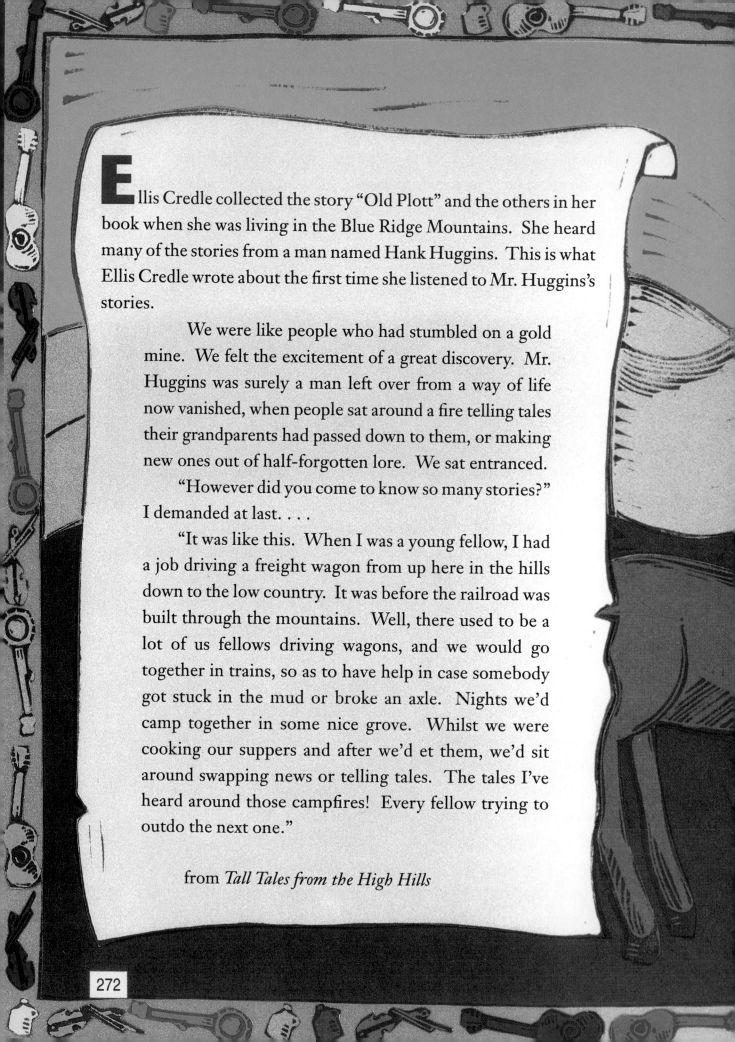

Ellis Credle collected the story "Old Plott" and the others in her book when she was living in the Blue Ridge Mountains. She heard many of the stories from a man named Hank Huggins. This is what Ellis Credle wrote about the first time she listened to Mr. Huggins's stories.

We were like people who had stumbled on a gold mine. We felt the excitement of a great discovery. Mr. Huggins was surely a man left over from a way of life now vanished, when people sat around a fire telling tales their grandparents had passed down to them, or making new ones out of half-forgotten lore. We sat entranced.

"However did you come to know so many stories?" I demanded at last. . . .

"It was like this. When I was a young fellow, I had a job driving a freight wagon from up here in the hills down to the low country. It was before the railroad was built through the mountains. Well, there used to be a lot of us fellows driving wagons, and we would go together in trains, so as to have help in case somebody got stuck in the mud or broke an axle. Nights we'd camp together in some nice grove. Whilst we were cooking our suppers and after we'd et them, we'd sit around swapping news or telling tales. The tales I've heard around those campfires! Every fellow trying to outdo the next one."

from *Tall Tales from the High Hills*

Old Plott

retold by Ellis Credle

Illustrated by Randall Enos

For as long as he could remember, young Jess Honeycutt had been hearing about the train. It passed through the city forty miles on yonder side of the mountain. Everybody that came back from there had something to tell about it.

"She's a sight to behold," they said. "She's got one eye right in the middle of her forehead. Go to see her in the nighttime. There she comes, down the track, glaring like a one-eyed wildcat staring into a pine torch. And racket. Whee! She comes a-raring[1] like a square dance on a tin roof!"

Jess sure did have a hankering[2] to see that train-critter, and one time when his wife went off to visit her folks he allowed it was

---

[1] **a-raring:** eager.
[2] **hankering:** longing, craving.

his chance and he was a-going. He stuck the frying pan up the chimney, hid the ax in a crotch of the tree, whistled up old Plott, his bear dog, and off he put. As he trudged on down the trail Jess got to thinking that it might not be a good idea to take his dog along. How could he prepare old Plott's mind for the sight of the train? The thing might scarify him to the point of addling his wits. He might run clean away and never come back. Jess didn't want anything like that to happen. Old Plott was the best bear dog anywhere in the Blue Ridge Mountains. Everybody knew it, and Jess loved him like a brother.

By this time, Jess had got down the mountain as far as the cabin where old man Gruber lived. The idea came to him that he might ask the old man to keep Plott until he got back from his

travels. Yes, that's what he'd do. No use taking chances with such a valuable dog.

He opened the front gate, walked up to Mr. Gruber's cabin and knocked at the door. It opened a crack and a gun barrel came poking through.

Young Jess gave a start. He backed away. "Hold on there, Mr. Gruber, hold on a minute. I don't mean you no harm."

"Who is it then?" came old man Gruber's voice from inside and it sounded mighty mean.

"It's me, Jess Honeycutt."

"Oh, so it's you, young Jess!" Old man Gruber stuck his head out the door. "Where are your raisings, young feller? That ain't no way to act, to come a-knocking at the door without even a whoop or a holler. How's a man to know if it's friend or foe? Mind your manners next time and give a holler before you open the gate."

"Yes, sir, Mr. Gruber, I sure will. I beg your pardon for giving you a scare."

"All right then, young Jess, all right. Now what is it you've come for?"

"I'm off for a trip, Mr. Gruber and I just wondered if you'd do me a favor while I'm away in foreign parts?"

"A favor? I don't know about that." Old man Gruber drew in his head and began to shut the door.

"I'll pay you well if you'll help me out, Mr. Gruber!" cried young Jess.

"Oh, that's different now." Mr. Gruber looked out again. "What is it you want me to do? What's the favor?"

"I was going to ask you to keep old Plott for me while I'm away."

"Old Plott? You want me to keep old Plott whilst you're away?" A greedy gleam came into old man Gruber's eyes. "Bring him right in, Jess. That's a favor I won't charge you for. I'll keep him here and treat him as kindly as if he were my own child. I sure will."

"That's mighty nice of you, Mr. Gruber." Jess was real pleased. He whistled old Plott into the cabin and shut the door on him. Then he went along on his journey, satisfied and easy in his mind. He clean forgot what folks said about old man Gruber, that he would steal the pennies outen a blind beggar's hat; that he was the meanest, stingiest, cheatin'est old man in seven counties.

A few days later, down the trail again came young Jess. He was footsore and dusty. He'd been over the mountain to the city.

He'd seen the train and he'd had enough of traveling. He stopped at old man Gruber's gate and gave a whoop and a holler.

Old man Gruber stuck his head out the door.

"Heigh-oh there, Mr. Gruber. Well, I'm back from my trip." He opened the gate and walked up the path.

"Howdy, young Jess, howdy. I reckon you've seen a sight, I reckon you have. Well, come around and tell me all about it one of these days." Old man Gruber drew in his head and began to shut the door.

"Hold on there, Mr. Gruber, hold on!" Young Jess stuck his foot in the crack. "What about my dog Plott? Where's old Plott? I've come for him."

"Old Plott, old Plott?" Mr. Gruber scratched his head and pretended to think. "Oh, yes, I declare I near 'bout forgot old Plott. Son, I sure am sorry to have to tell you about old Plott."

"What's the matter? What's happened? He ain't run away, has he?"

"Worse than that, son —"

"He ain't been hurt now, has he?"

Old man Gruber didn't say anything. He just looked down at the ground and shook his head in a mournful way.

"You ain't trying to tell me old Plott is dead now, are you, Mr. Gruber?" cried young Jess.

"I'm sorry to have to tell you, son, but he sure is. Dead as a doornail."

Tears came to young Jess' eyes. He felt as though a mule had kicked him right in the middle of his stomach. "Don't tell me, Mr. Gruber. That dog was everything to me. I wouldn't have taken a pretty[3] for him."

"Well, son, it's the truth. He's dead."

"How did it happen, Mr. Gruber?"

"Why, son, the day you left I shut old Plott up in a little old house here on the place. I'd been renting it to some powerful dirty folks and they'd left it chockablock[4] full of bedbugs. Those bugs hadn't had nothing to eat for the longest time. I reckon they were mortal hungry. Anyway, they set onto old Plott in the night and ate him up, hair, hide, and all. Wasn't anything left but his bones."

Jess turned about to go home. "Those bugs don't know what they've done to me!" He stumbled down the path with hanging head. He glanced back as he opened the gate. Mr. Gruber was grinning from ear to ear, as though he had done something mighty smart and was real pleased with himself.

That set young Jess to studying. He stood a minute with his hand on the gate, then he turned around and walked up the path again.

---

[3] **pretty:** a toy or decorative object.

[4] **chockablock (chŏk′ə blŏk′):** squeezed together.

"Mr. Gruber, I declare to goodness, this has hit me mighty hard. And I'm clean wore out with traveling. I feel so bad I don't know as I can get home. You know it's a mighty steep climb from here up to my cabin there on the mountain. Wouldn't you lend me your mule to ride on the rest of the way?"

"I don't know about that, now, young Jess. I need my mule here to home. Got to do some plowing today. Got to plow every day this week."

Young Jess stepped up on the porch. "Well then, Mr. Gruber, I reckon you'll just have to give me some dinner and some supper later on and put me up for the night. I haven't got the strength to go a step farther."

"Now, now, young Jess, you ain't that bad off." Mr. Gruber looked worried.

"I sure am, Mr. Gruber, I'm laid low. I'll have to stay the night with you, I sure will."

"No, young Jess, you can't do that. No, you can't. Maybe I'd better lend you my mule after all. Will you bring him back tomorrow sure and certain?"

"Sure as shootin', Mr. Gruber. Why would you ask such a thing? You know I'm as honest as the day is long, just like Pap and my old grandpap before me."

Old man Gruber led out his mule. Young Jess straddled him and off he went, plodding up the trail toward home.

On the following day, old man Gruber got up bright and early. He looked up the trail to see if young Jess was on the way with his mule. Not a sign of him did he see.

"Now, that's no way to do — to keep my mule till half the day is gone! Maybe he won't get here till afternoon," he grumbled to himself and he found some work to do around the house.

When nighttime came and still no Jess and no mule, old man Gruber fussed and fumed. "That young scamp, a-keeping my mule right now during planting time. What's he up to, I'd like to know?"

The next day he leaped up as soon as the sun peeped over the ridge and ran out to see if young Jess was on the way. No, he wasn't. And the next day he didn't come either. Old man Gruber was mad a sight. "That cheating young rascal, I'll have the law on him, that I will. He'll pay me hard money for every day he keeps my mule!"

Well, day by day went by with never a sign of Jess and the mule. With his creaky joints, old man Gruber knew well enough he'd never make it up the steep trail to the cabin where Jess lived, and every day that passed he got madder and madder.

Then one morning, after the sun was well up in the sky, he looked out the window and there was young Jess sauntering along the road as though he didn't have a care in the world nor a thought for Mr. Gruber's mule.

Old man Gruber ran out of the house without even stopping to put his shoes on. "Oh there you are, you young scallawag! Where's my mule, now, where is he, I'd like to know?"

Young Jess stopped in the middle of the road. He looked at Mr. Gruber in a surprised sort of way. Then he scratched his head and pretended to think. "Your mule, Mr. Gruber? Oh, yes, I

declare I near 'bout forgot your mule. I sure am sorry to have to tell you about him, Mr. Gruber."

"What do you mean? What's happened to my mule?"

Young Jess didn't answer. He just looked down at the ground and shook his head in a mournful way.

"You haven't lost my mule in the mountains? You haven't let him fall off a cliff, have you?" shouted old man Gruber.

"Worse than that, Mr. Gruber. Worse than that," Jess said sadly.

"You ain't trying to tell me my mule is dead now, are you?" screamed the old man.

"I've got a mighty strong suspicion he is — dead as a doornail. But I don't know for sure, Mr. Gruber. No, I don't. A mighty curious thing happened to your mule. It sure did."

"I don't believe it! I don't believe nary a word you say, Jess Honeycutt. You've stole my mule and I'll have you jailed!" screeched old man Gruber. "Come on now, come right on. I'm going to haul you down the road to Squire Meekins' house. He'll fix you for stealing my mule." He grabbed young Jess by the arm and began to drag him down the road.

When they got to the crossroads where Squire Meekins lived, old man Gruber stood at his gate and hollered, "Squire Meekins! Come out, come out here right now. I want you to 'tend to this mule-thief!" And there he stood a-shouting and a-vaporing[5] until Squire Meekins came out on the porch to see what all the racket was about.

"I want you to throw young Jess in the jailhouse, Squire!" Old man Gruber shook his fist in the air and stomped his bare feet. "I want you to haul him off to jail right now!"

"Now, now, Mr. Gruber —" began Squire Meekins in a kindly voice.

"He stole my mule!" shrieked old man Gruber.

"He borrowed my mule and won't bring him back. He says something curious happened to him. 'T ain't so. He's stole him. He's a plain mule-thief and I want the law on him!"

Squire Meekins held up his hand. "Calm yourself, Mr. Gruber, calm yourself. Let's get at both sides of this dispute. What's this all about, young Jess, what's happened to Mr. Gruber's mule? You tell me now, straight out."

"Well, it happened like this, Squire Meekins. As I was a-riding along home the other day after Mr. Gruber lent me that mule, I saw some turkey buzzards sort of sailing around up there in the sky. They kept circling lower and lower. I never thought nothing about it until they were right over my head. It came to me then that it was mighty peculiar how close they'd come. I could have reached

---

[5]**a-vaporing:** fuming with rage.

282

up and grabbed one. All of a sudden one of 'em swooped down. He grabbed Mr. Gruber's mule by the tail. He upended that mule and heaved me off, right over the critter's head. Then he went sailing off with that mule, a-flying fast and a-crowing like a rooster!"

"Hold on there, young Jess," exclaimed Squire Meekins. "I've seen many a turkey buzzard in my life, but nary one that could crow like a rooster!"

"As I'm a-living, that buzzard went a-flying off with that mule," young Jess insisted. "And with all the other buzzards following after. Last I saw of 'em they were a-clearing the top of Old Baldy Mountain. I reckon those buzzards hadn't had anything to eat in the longest time and they was mortal hungry. By this time you can be sure they've eaten Mr. Gruber's mule and picked his bones."

"You hear that, Squire Meekins?" yelled old man Gruber. "He expects us to believe a gally-whopper[6] like that. He stands there and tells such buncombe[7] with a straight face!"

"If a bunch of hungry bedbugs can eat up a full-grown dog like what happened to my old Plott, then a bunch of hungry buzzards can fly off with a mule and pick his bones," said young Jess.

It all came out then, how old man Gruber had acted about old Plott.

[6]**gally-whopper** (găl′ē-wŏp′ər): tall tale; lie.
[7]**buncombe** (bŭng′kəm): original form of the word *bunk*, "lies."

"What's sauce for the goose is sauce for the gander," said young Jess. "If my dog comes back after being eat by bedbugs, then maybe the mule will come back after being eat by the buzzards."

And that's just how it turned out. Squire Meekins made old man Gruber fetch Plott from the woods where he'd hid him and then young Jess brought back the mule. Maybe you think old man Gruber learned a lesson from all this. But no, folks in the mountains say he's still as mean and stingy and cheating as ever.

Responding to "Old Plott"

Thinking and Discussing

In what other ways could Jess have made Mr. Gruber reveal the truth about old Plott? Do you think that the way Jess chose was the best way to do it? Why?

Why do you think Mr. Gruber does not learn a lesson from the events in this tale?

Choosing a Creative Response

Reading Aloud   Which sentences and short passages capture the speech rhythms of the region especially well? With other students, take turns reading aloud these passages. You might also enjoy reading them to younger students.

Creating Your Own Activity   Plan and complete your own activity in response to "Old Plott."

Thinking and Writing

Mr. Gruber's explanation of old Plott's disappearance and Jess's explanation of the mule's fate are humorous and exaggerated. Such stories are often told in everyday life. Sometimes they form the basis of urban legends. Think of similar exaggerated stories that you've heard. Choose your favorite, and write a brief retelling of it, adding your own personal touches. Eventually, you may want to make a collection of these stories to share with your classmates.

The Alligators

WRITTEN BY HORACIO QUIROGA

WAR

ILLUSTRATED BY DARIUS DETWILER

It was a very big river in a region of South America that had never been visited by white men; and in it lived many, many alligators — perhaps a hundred, perhaps a thousand.

287

For dinner they ate fish, which they caught in the stream, and for supper they ate deer and other animals that came down to the waterside to drink. On hot afternoons in summer they stretched out and sunned themselves on the bank. But they liked nights when the moon was shining best of all. Then they swam out into the river and sported and played, lashing the water to foam with their tails, while the spray ran off their beautiful skins in all the colors of the rainbow.

These alligators had lived quite happy lives for a long, long time. But at last one afternoon, when they were all sleeping on the sand, snoring and snoring, one alligator woke up and cocked his ears — the way alligators cock their ears. He listened and listened, and, to be sure, faintly, and from a great distance, came a sound: *Chug! Chug! Chug!*

"Hey!" the alligator called to the alligator sleeping next to him, "Hey! Wake up! Danger!"

"Danger of what?" asked the other, opening his eyes sleepily and getting up.

"I don't know!" replied the first alligator. "That's a noise I never heard before. Listen!"

The other alligator listened: *Chug! Chug! Chug!*

In great alarm the two alligators went calling up and down the riverbank: "Danger! Danger!" And all their sisters and brothers and mothers and fathers and uncles and aunts woke up and began running this way and that with their tails curled up in the air. But the excitement did not serve to calm their fears. *Chug! Chug! Chug!* The noise was growing louder every moment; and at last, away off down the stream, they could see something moving along the surface of the river, leaving a trail of gray smoke behind it and beating the water on either side to foam: *Chush! Chush! Chush!*

The alligators looked at each other in the greatest astonishment: "What on earth is that?"

But there was one old alligator, the wisest and most experienced of them all. He was so old that only two sound teeth were left in his jaws — one in the upper jaw and one in the lower jaw. Once, also, when he was a boy, fond of adventure, he had made a trip down the river all the way to the sea.

"I know what it is," said he. "It's a whale. Whales are big fish, they shoot water up through their noses, and it falls down on them behind."

At this news, the little alligators began to scream at the top of their lungs. "It's a whale! It's a whale! It's a whale!" and they made for the water intending to duck out of sight.

But the big alligator cuffed[1] with his tail a little alligator that was screaming nearby with his mouth open wide. "Dry up!" said he. "There's nothing to be afraid of! I know all about whales! Whales are the afraidest people there are!" And the little alligators stopped their noise.

---

[1] **cuffed:** slapped.

But they grew frightened again a moment afterward. The gray smoke suddenly turned to an inky black, and the *Chush! Chush! Chush!* was now so loud that all the alligators took to the water, with only their eyes and the tips of their noses showing at the surface.

Cho-ash-h-h! Cho-ash-h-h! Cho-ash-h-h! The strange monster came rapidly up the stream. The alligators saw it go crashing past them, belching great clouds of smoke from the middle of its back and splashing into the water heavily with the big revolving things it had on either side.

It was a steamer, the first steamer that had ever made its way up the Paraná.[2] *Chush! Chush! Chush!* It seemed to be getting farther away again. *Chug! Chug! Chug!* It had disappeared from view.

One by one, the alligators climbed up out of the water onto the bank again. They were all quite cross with the old alligator who had told them wrongly that it was a whale.

"It was not a whale!" they shouted in his ear — for he was rather hard of hearing. "Well, what was it that just went by?"

---

[2]**Paraná:** a river in central South America.

The old alligator then explained that it was a steamboat full of fire and that the alligators would all die if the boat continued to go up and down the river.

The other alligators only laughed, however. Why would the alligators die if the boat kept going up and down the river? It had passed by without so much as speaking to them! That old alligator didn't really know so much as he pretended to! And since they were very hungry they all went fishing in the stream. But alas! There was not a fish to be found! The steamboat had frightened every single one of them away.

"Well, what did I tell you?" said the old alligator. "You see, we haven't anything left to eat! All the fish have been frightened away! However — let's just wait till tomorrow. Perhaps the boat won't come back again. In that case, the fish will get over their fright and come back so that we can eat them." But the next day the steamboat came crashing by again on its way back down the river, spouting black smoke as it had done before, and setting the whole river boiling with its paddle wheels.

"Well!" exclaimed the alligators. "What do you think of that? The boat came yesterday. The boat came today. The boat will come tomorrow. The fish will stay away and nothing will come down here at night to drink. We are done for!"

ut an idea occurred to one of the brighter alligators: "Let's dam the river!" he proposed. "The steamboat won't be able to climb a dam!"

"That's the talk! That's the talk! A dam! A dam! Let's build a dam!" And the alligators all made for the shore as fast as they could.

They went up into the woods along the bank and began to cut down trees of the hardest wood they could find — walnut and mahogany, mostly. They felled more than ten thousand of them altogether, sawing the trunks through with the kind of saw that alligators have on the tops of their tails. They dragged the trees down into the water and stood them up about a yard apart, all the way across the river, driving the pointed ends deep into the mud and weaving the branches together. No steamboat, big or little, would ever be able to pass that dam! No one would frighten the fish again! They would have a good dinner the following day and every day! And since it was late at night by the time the dam was done, they all fell sound asleep on the riverbank.

Chug! Chug! Chug! Chush! Chush! Chush! Cho-ash-h-h-h! Cho-ash-h-h-h! Cho-ash-h-h-h!

They were still asleep the next day when the boat came up; but the alligators barely opened their eyes and then tried to go to sleep again. What did they care about the boat? It could make all the noise it wanted but it would never get by the dam!

And that is what happened. Soon the noise from the boat stopped. The men who were steering on the bridge took out their spyglasses and began to study the strange obstruction that had been thrown up across the river. Finally a small boat was sent to look into it more closely. Only then did the alligators get up from where they were sleeping, run down into the water, and swim out behind the dam, where they lay floating and looking downstream between the piles. They could not help laughing, nevertheless, at the joke they had played on the steamboat!

The small boat came up, and the men in it saw how the alligators had made a dam across the river. They went back to the steamer but soon after came rowing up toward the dam again.

"Hey, you alligators!"

"What can we do for you?" answered the alligators, sticking their heads through between the piles in the dam.

"That dam is in our way!" said the men.

"Tell us something we don't know!" answered the alligators.

"But we can't get by!"

"I'll say so!"

"Well, take the old thing out of the way!"

"Nosireesir!"

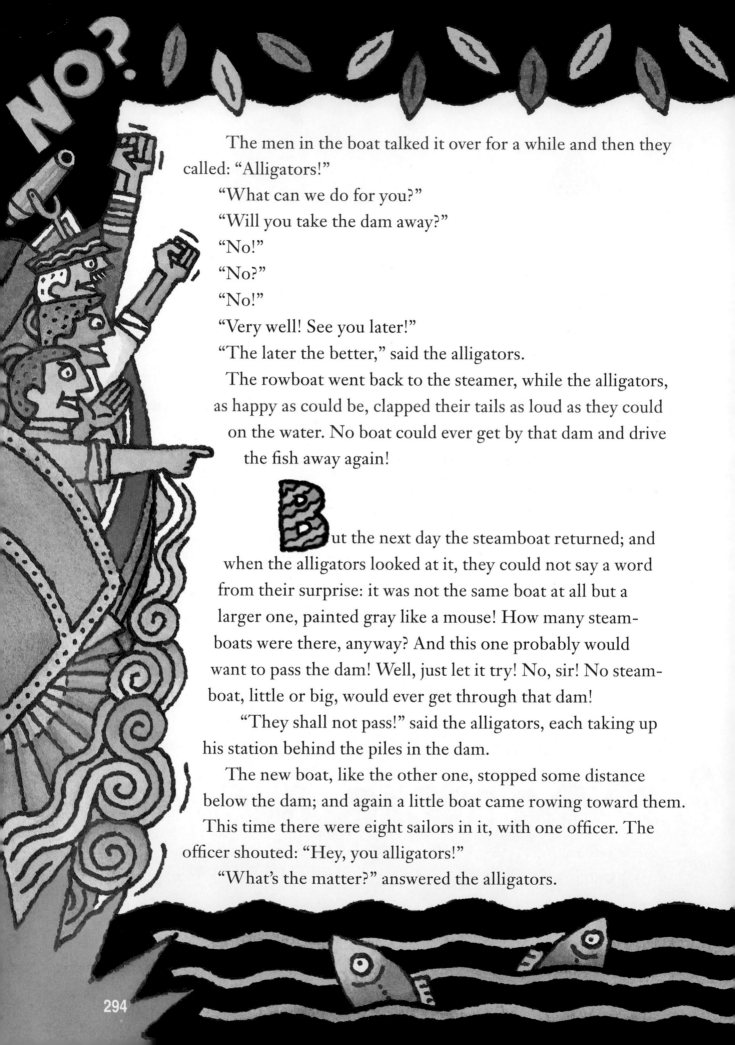

The men in the boat talked it over for a while and then they called: "Alligators!"

"What can we do for you?"

"Will you take the dam away?"

"No!"

"No?"

"No!"

"Very well! See you later!"

"The later the better," said the alligators.

The rowboat went back to the steamer, while the alligators, as happy as could be, clapped their tails as loud as they could on the water. No boat could ever get by that dam and drive the fish away again!

But the next day the steamboat returned; and when the alligators looked at it, they could not say a word from their surprise: it was not the same boat at all but a larger one, painted gray like a mouse! How many steamboats were there, anyway? And this one probably would want to pass the dam! Well, just let it try! No, sir! No steamboat, little or big, would ever get through that dam!

"They shall not pass!" said the alligators, each taking up his station behind the piles in the dam.

The new boat, like the other one, stopped some distance below the dam; and again a little boat came rowing toward them. This time there were eight sailors in it, with one officer. The officer shouted: "Hey, you alligators!"

"What's the matter?" answered the alligators.

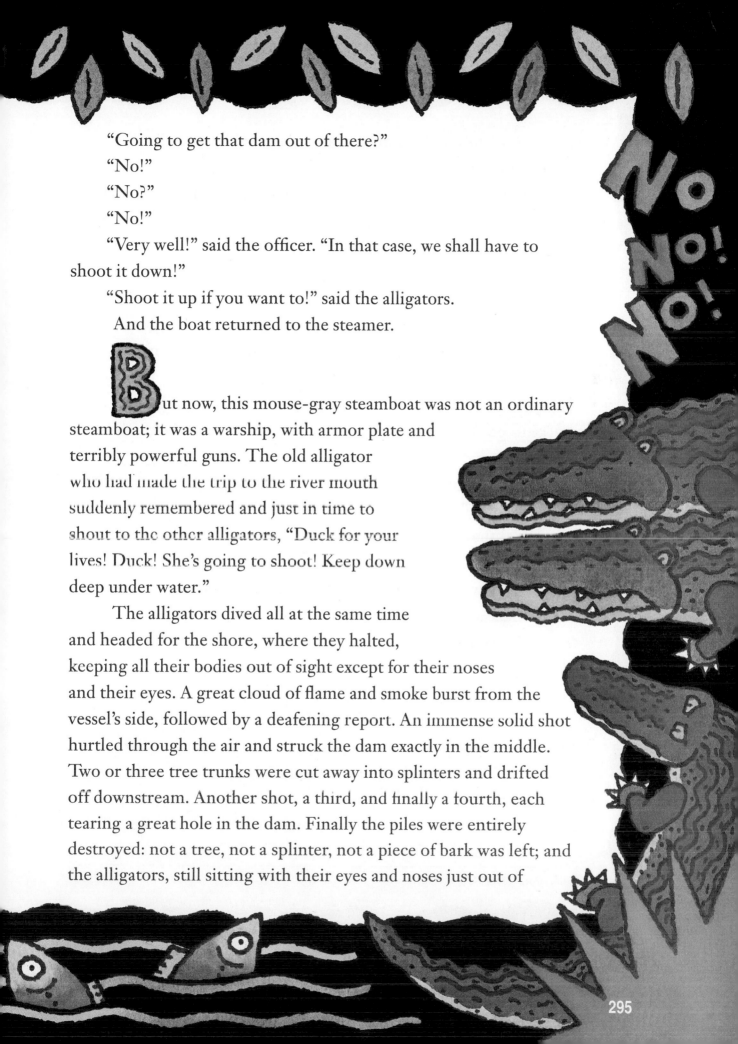

"Going to get that dam out of there?"

"No!"

"No?"

"No!"

"Very well!" said the officer. "In that case, we shall have to shoot it down!"

"Shoot it up if you want to!" said the alligators.

And the boat returned to the steamer.

But now, this mouse-gray steamboat was not an ordinary steamboat; it was a warship, with armor plate and terribly powerful guns. The old alligator who had made the trip to the river mouth suddenly remembered and just in time to shout to the other alligators, "Duck for your lives! Duck! She's going to shoot! Keep down deep under water."

The alligators dived all at the same time and headed for the shore, where they halted, keeping all their bodies out of sight except for their noses and their eyes. A great cloud of flame and smoke burst from the vessel's side, followed by a deafening report. An immense solid shot hurtled through the air and struck the dam exactly in the middle. Two or three tree trunks were cut away into splinters and drifted off downstream. Another shot, a third, and finally a fourth, each tearing a great hole in the dam. Finally the piles were entirely destroyed: not a tree, not a splinter, not a piece of bark was left; and the alligators, still sitting with their eyes and noses just out of water, saw the warship come steaming by and blowing its whistle in derision[3] at them.

Then the alligators came out on the bank and held a council of war. "Our dam was not strong enough," said they; "we must make a new and much thicker one."

So they worked again all that afternoon and night, cutting down the very biggest trees they could find and making a much better dam than they had built before. When the gunboat appeared the next day, they were sleeping soundly and had to hurry to get behind the piles of the dam by the time the rowboat arrived there.

"Hey, alligators!" called the same officer.

"See who's here again!" said the alligators, jeeringly.

"Get that new dam out of there!"

"Never in the world!"

"Well, we'll blow it up, the way we did the other!"

"Blaze away, and good luck to you!"

You see, the alligators talked so big because they were sure the dam they had made this time would hold up against the most terrible cannonballs in the world. And the sailors must have thought so, too; for after they had fired the first shot a tremendous explosion occurred in the dam. The gunboat was using shells, which burst among the timbers of the dam and broke the thickest trees into tiny, tiny bits. A second shell exploded right near the first, and a third near the second. So the shots went all

---

[3]**derision:** (dĭ rĭzh´ən): scorn.

along the dam, each tearing away a long strip of it till nothing, nothing, nothing was left. Again the warship came steaming by, closer in toward shore on this occasion, so that the sailors could make fun of the alligators by putting their hands to their mouths and holloing.

"So that's it!" said the alligators, climbing up out of the water. "We must all die, because the steamboats will keep coming and going, up and down, and leaving us not a fish in the world to eat!"

The littlest alligators were already whimpering, for they had had no dinner for three days; and it was a crowd of very sad alligators that gathered on the river shore to hear what the old alligator now had to say.

"We have only one hope left," he began. "We must go and see the Sturgeon![4] When I was a boy, I took that trip down to the sea along with him. He liked the salt water better than I did and went quite a way out into the ocean. There he saw a sea fight between two of these boats; and he brought home a torpedo[5] that had failed to explode. Suppose we go and ask him to give it to us. It is true the Sturgeon has never liked us alligators; but I got along with him pretty well myself. He is a good fellow, at bottom, and surely he will not want to see us all starve!"

The fact was that some years before an alligator had eaten one of the Sturgeon's favorite grandchildren, and for that reason the Sturgeon had refused ever since to call on the alligators or

---

[4] **sturgeon:** a kind of freshwater or salt-water fish.

[5] **torpedo:** a bomb used underwater.

receive visits from them. Nevertheless, the alligators now trooped off in a body to the big cave under the bank of the river where they knew the Sturgeon stayed, with his torpedo beside him. There are sturgeons as much as six feet long, you know, and this one with the torpedo was of that kind.

"Mr. Sturgeon! Mr. Sturgeon!" called the alligators at the entrance of the cave. No one of them dared go in, you see, on account of that matter of the Sturgeon's grandchild.

"Who is it?" answered the Sturgeon.

"We're the alligators," the latter replied in a chorus.

"I have nothing to do with alligators," grumbled the Sturgeon crossly.

But now the old alligator with the two teeth stepped forward and said, "Why, hello, Sturgy. Don't you remember Ally, your old friend that took that trip down the river when we were boys?"

"Well, well! Where have you been keeping yourself all these years?" said the Sturgeon, surprised and pleased to hear his old friend's voice. "Sorry I didn't know it was you! How goes it? What can I do for you?"

"We've come to ask you for that torpedo you found, remember? You see, there's a warship keeps coming up and down our river scaring all the fish away. She's a whopper, I'll tell you, armor plate, guns, the whole thing! We made one dam and she knocked

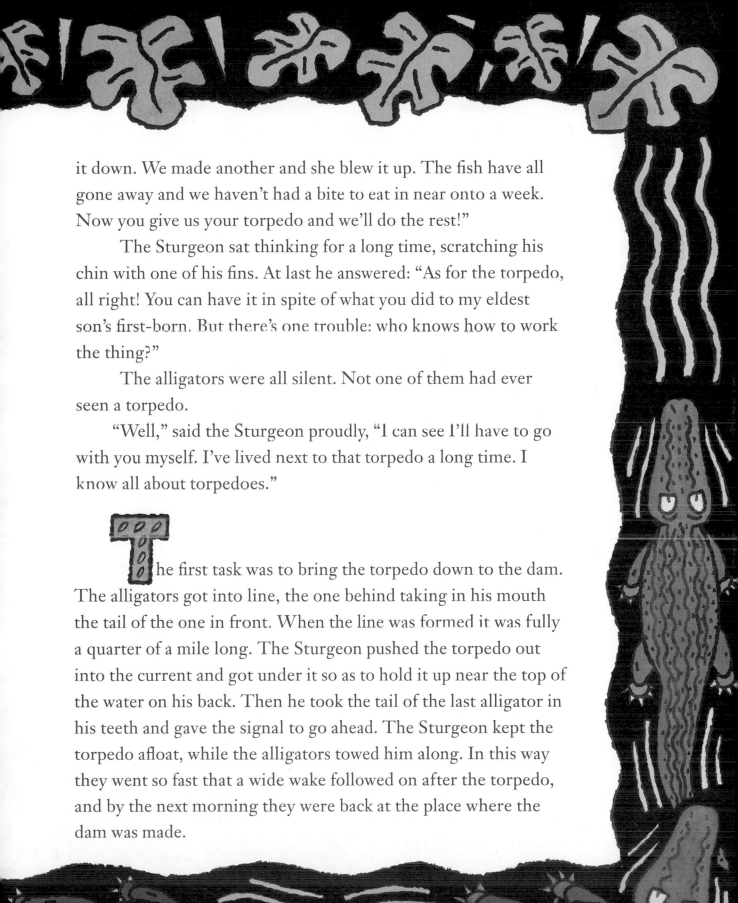

it down. We made another and she blew it up. The fish have all
gone away and we haven't had a bite to eat in near onto a week.
Now you give us your torpedo and we'll do the rest!"

The Sturgeon sat thinking for a long time, scratching his
chin with one of his fins. At last he answered: "As for the torpedo,
all right! You can have it in spite of what you did to my eldest
son's first-born. But there's one trouble: who knows how to work
the thing?"

The alligators were all silent. Not one of them had ever
seen a torpedo.

"Well," said the Sturgeon proudly, "I can see I'll have to go
with you myself. I've lived next to that torpedo a long time. I
know all about torpedoes."

The first task was to bring the torpedo down to the dam.
The alligators got into line, the one behind taking in his mouth
the tail of the one in front. When the line was formed it was fully
a quarter of a mile long. The Sturgeon pushed the torpedo out
into the current and got under it so as to hold it up near the top of
the water on his back. Then he took the tail of the last alligator in
his teeth and gave the signal to go ahead. The Sturgeon kept the
torpedo afloat, while the alligators towed him along. In this way
they went so fast that a wide wake followed on after the torpedo,
and by the next morning they were back at the place where the
dam was made.

As the little alligators who had stayed at home reported, the warship had already gone by upstream. But this pleased the others all the more. Now they would build a new dam, stronger than ever before, and catch the steamer in a trap, so that it would never get home again.

They worked all that day and all the next night, making a thick, almost solid dike, with barely enough room between the piles for the alligators to stick their heads through. They had just finished when the gunboat came into view.

Again the rowboat approached with the eight men and their officer. The alligators crowded behind the dam in great excitement, moving their paws to hold their own with the current, for this time they were downstream.

"Hey, alligators!" called the officer.

"Well?" answered the alligators.

"Still another dam?"

"If at first you don't succeed, try, try, again!"

"Get that dam out of there!"

"No, sir!"

"You won't?"

"We won't!"

"Very well! Now you alligators just listen! If you won't be reasonable, we are going to knock this dam down, too. But to save you the trouble of building a fourth, we are going to shoot every blessed alligator around here. Yes, every single last alligator, women and children, big ones, little ones, fat ones, lean ones, and even that old codger sitting there with only two teeth left in his jaws!"

The old alligator understood that the officer was trying to insult him with that reference to his two teeth, and he answered: "Young man, what you say is true. I have only two teeth left, not counting one or two others that are broken off. But do you know what those two teeth are going to eat for dinner?" As he said this the old alligator opened his mouth wide, wide, wide.

"Well, what are they going to eat?" asked one of the sailors.

"A little dude of a naval officer I see in a boat over there!" — and the old alligator dived under water and disappeared from view.

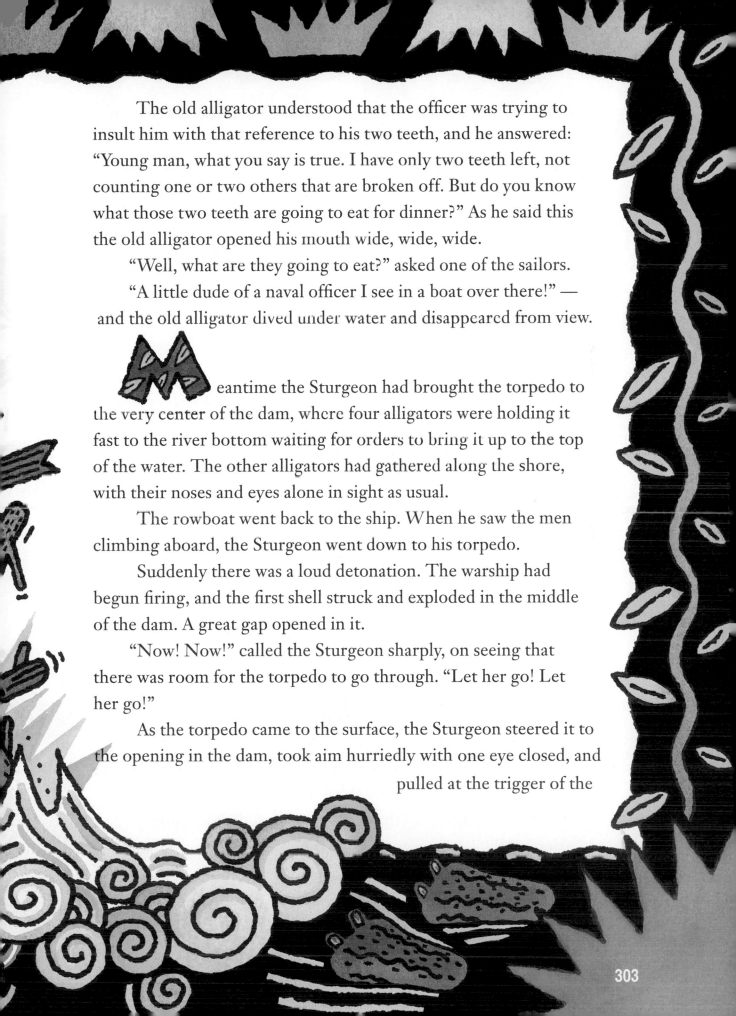eantime the Sturgeon had brought the torpedo to the very center of the dam, where four alligators were holding it fast to the river bottom waiting for orders to bring it up to the top of the water. The other alligators had gathered along the shore, with their noses and eyes alone in sight as usual.

The rowboat went back to the ship. When he saw the men climbing aboard, the Sturgeon went down to his torpedo.

Suddenly there was a loud detonation. The warship had begun firing, and the first shell struck and exploded in the middle of the dam. A great gap opened in it.

"Now! Now!" called the Sturgeon sharply, on seeing that there was room for the torpedo to go through. "Let her go! Let her go!"

As the torpedo came to the surface, the Sturgeon steered it to the opening in the dam, took aim hurriedly with one eye closed, and pulled at the trigger of the torpedo with his teeth. The propeller of the torpedo began to revolve, and it started off upstream toward the gunboat.

And it was high time. At that instant a second shot exploded in the dam, tearing away another large section.

From the wake the torpedo left behind it in the water the men on the vessel saw the danger they were in, but it was too late to do anything about it. The torpedo struck the ship in the middle, and went off.

You can never guess the terrible noise that torpedo made. It blew the warship into fifteen thousand million pieces, tossing guns and smokestacks and shells and rowboats — everything — hundreds and hundreds of yards away.

The alligators all screamed with triumph and made as fast as they could for the dam. Down through the opening bits of wood came floating, with a number of sailors swimming as hard as they could for the shore. As the men passed through, the alligators put their paws to their mouths and holloed, as the men had done to them three days before. They decided not to eat a single one of the sailors, though some of them deserved it without a doubt. Except that when a man dressed in a blue uniform with gold braid came by, the old alligator jumped into the water off the dam and snap! snap! ate him in two mouthfuls.

"Who was that man?" asked an ignorant young alligator, who never learned his lessons in school and never knew what was going on.

"It's the officer of the boat," answered the Sturgeon. "My old friend, Ally, said he was going to eat him, and eaten him he has!"

The alligators tore down the rest of the dam, because they knew that no boats would be coming by that way again.

The Sturgeon, who had quite fallen in love with the gold lace of the officer, asked that it be given him in payment for the use of his torpedo. The alligators said he might have it for the trouble of picking it out of the old alligator's mouth, where it had caught on the two teeth. They also gave him the officer's belt and sword. The Sturgeon put the belt on just behind his front fins and buckled the sword to it. Thus togged out, he swam up and down for more than an hour in front of the assembled alligators, who admired his beautiful spotted skin as something almost as pretty as the coral snake's, and who opened their mouths wide at the splendor of his uniform. Finally they escorted him in honor back to his cave under the riverbank, thanking him over and over again and giving him three cheers as they went off.

When they returned to their usual place they found the fish had already returned. The next day another steamboat came by; but the alligators did not care, because the fish were getting used to it by this time and seemed not to be afraid. Since then the boats have been going back and forth all the time, carrying oranges. And the alligators open their eyes when they hear the *chug! chug! chug!* of a steamboat and laugh at the thought of how scared they were the first time and of how they sank the warship.

But no warship has ever gone up the river since the old alligator ate the officer.

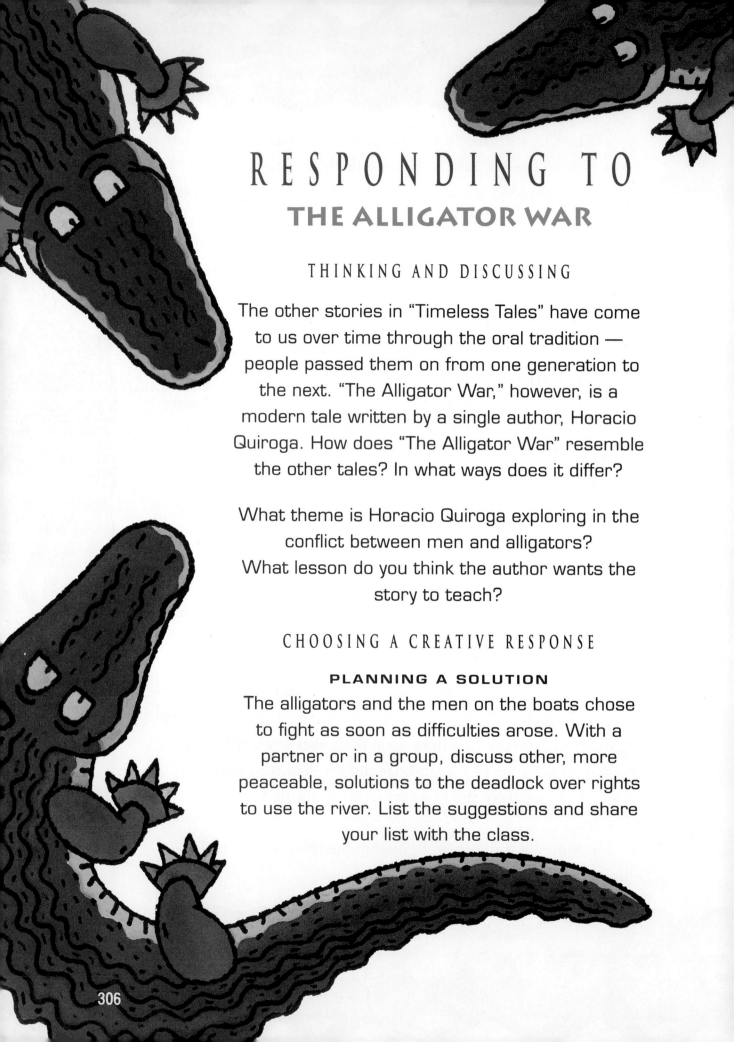

RESPONDING TO
THE ALLIGATOR WAR

THINKING AND DISCUSSING

The other stories in "Timeless Tales" have come to us over time through the oral tradition — people passed them on from one generation to the next. "The Alligator War," however, is a modern tale written by a single author, Horacio Quiroga. How does "The Alligator War" resemble the other tales? In what ways does it differ?

What theme is Horacio Quiroga exploring in the conflict between men and alligators? What lesson do you think the author wants the story to teach?

CHOOSING A CREATIVE RESPONSE

PLANNING A SOLUTION
The alligators and the men on the boats chose to fight as soon as difficulties arose. With a partner or in a group, discuss other, more peaceable, solutions to the deadlock over rights to use the river. List the suggestions and share your list with the class.

WORKING WITH YOUR HANDS

Work with a group to dramatize a scene from the story in a puppet show. You may want to start by creating character sketches of the main characters. Then make puppets based on the sketches, using paper, cardboard, or whatever materials are at hand. As you perform your scene, make sure that the characters behave as they are described in the story. Put on the puppet show for the class.

CREATING YOUR OWN ACTIVITY

Plan and complete your own activity in response to "The Alligator War."

THINKING AND WRITING

Write a newspaper account of the story of "The Alligator War." Before you begin, think of how you would present the events most effectively to a newspaper reader. Write a headline, and then compose an opening paragraph that covers the five *W*'s — Who, What, When, Where, and Why. Fill out the rest of the story with details. Share the story with a partner or with your group.

Ellis Credle was born in 1902 in North Carolina. She was brought up on the North Carolina coast and later lived in the Blue Ridge Mountains. *Down, Down the Mountain* includes tales and sayings of the mountain people. *Tall Tales from the High Hills* is a continuation of Credle's interest in the mountain country of Appalachia.

Richard Erdoes was born in 1912 in Vienna, Austria, but has lived most of his life in the United States. He has had a career as a free-lance artist, illustrator, muralist, photographer, writer, and maker of educational films.

William J. Faulkner came from South Carolina, where as a boy he lived on a small farm with his widowed mother. His love for storytelling stems from his friendship with a former slave named Simon Brown, who told him "stories out of his imagination or the imagination of others he'd heard around the campfire in the slave quarters years ago." In *The Days When the Animals Talked*, Faulkner faithfully recorded the old stories that Simon Brown had told him.

oracio Quiroga was born in 1878 in Uruguay, but he spent most of his life in the tropical jungle in Argentina. Quiroga was interested in the supernatural, and his early writing shows the influence of the American writer Edgar Allan Poe. Later, using the jungle as his setting, he wrote about the ways in which people survive fear and difficulty. In some of Quiroga's stories, animal narrators such as poisonous snakes or wild bulls reveal the writer's true thoughts. His books include *South American Jungle Tales* and *The Exiles and Other Stories*. Quiroga died in 1937.

lexandra Whitney has written books for young people including *Voices in the Wind: Central and South American Legends* and *Once a Bright Red Tiger*. Her writing reflects her lifelong interest in Central and South America and in animals, especially birds. Born in 1922, she has traveled extensively to collect material for her books. A South American parrot named Picchu shares her home in New York City.

TALES AND MORE TALES

The Cow-Tail Switch and Other West African Stories

The seventeen stories in this collection are full of laughter, with tricks played by clever and scheming animals and people. The authors gathered the tales on their trips to West Africa. By Harold Courlander and George Herzog (Holt, 1947, 1987)

They Dance in the Sky: Native American Star Myths

Long ago, storytellers of Native American nations studied the night sky and created these exciting tales about the stars and constellations. By Jean Guard Monroe and Ray A. Williamson (Houghton, 1987)

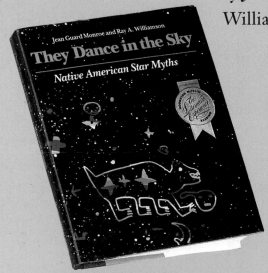

Womenfolk and Fairy Tales

This lively collection of tales from diverse cultures portrays girls and women as active, capable people in a variety of situations and roles. Edited by Rosemary Minard (Houghton, 1975)

The Rainbow People

The twenty Chinese tales retold in this collection are set in a land where magic things happen naturally, and characters range from the foolish to the fantastic. By Laurence Yep (Harper, 1989)

The People Could Fly: American Black Folktales

Animal, fantasy, and supernatural stories, as well as slave tales of freedom, make up a collection by a well-known, award-winning author. Retold by Virginia Hamilton (Knopf, 1985)

NOVEL

THE SUMMER OF THE SWANS

by Betsy Byars
Photo-illustrations by Susan Donath

Sara Godfrey was lying on the bed tying a kerchief on the dog, Boysie. "Hold your chin up, Boysie, will you?" she said as she braced herself on one elbow. The dog was old, slept all the time, and he was lying on his side with his eyes closed while she lifted his head and tied the scarf.

Her sister Wanda was sitting at the dressing table combing her hair. Wanda said, "Why don't you leave Boysie alone?"

"There's nothing else to do," Sara answered without looking up. "You want to see a show?"

"Not particularly."

"It's called 'The Many Faces of Boysie.'"

"Now I know I don't want to see it."

Sara held up the dog with the kerchief neatly tied beneath his chin and said, "The first face of Boysie, proudly presented for your entertainment and amusement, is the Russian Peasant Woman. Taaaaaa-daaaaaa!"

"Leave the dog alone."

"He likes to be in shows, don't you, Boysie?" She untied the scarf, refolded it and set it carefully on top of the dog's head. "And now for the second face of Boysie, we travel halfway around the world to the mysterious East, where we see Boysie the Inscrutable Hindu. Taaaaaaa-daaaaaa!"

With a sigh Wanda turned and looked at the dog. "That's pathetic. In people's age that dog is eighty-four years old." She shook a can of hair spray and sprayed her hair. "And besides, that's my good scarf."

"Oh, all right." Sara fell back heavily against the pillow. "I can't do anything around here."

"Well, if it's going to make you that miserable, I'll watch the show."

"I don't want to do it any more. It's no fun now. This place smells like a perfume factory." She put the scarf over her face and stared up through the thin blue material. Beside her, Boysie lay back down and curled himself into a ball. They lay without moving for a moment and then Sara sat up on the bed and looked down at her long, lanky legs. She said, "I have the biggest feet in my school."

"Honestly, Sara, I hope you are not going to start listing all the millions of things wrong with you because I just don't want to hear it again."

"Well, it's the truth about my feet. One time in Phys Ed the boys started throwing the girls' sneakers around and Bull Durham got my sneakers and put them on and they fit perfectly! How do you think it feels to wear the same size shoe as Bull Durham?"

"People don't notice things like that."

"Huh!"

"No, they don't. I have perfectly terrible hands — look at my fingers — only I don't go around all the time saying, 'Everybody, look at my stubby fingers, I have stubby fingers, everybody,' to *make* people notice. You should just ignore things that are wrong with you. The truth is everyone else is so worried about what's wrong with *them* that —"

"It is very difficult to ignore the fact that you have huge feet when Bull Durham is dancing all over the gym in your shoes. They were not stretched the tiniest little bit when he took them off either."

"You wear the same size shoe as Jackie Kennedy Onassis if that makes you feel any better."

"How do you know?"

"Because one time when she was going into an Indian temple she had to leave her shoes outside and some reporter looked in them to see what size they were." She leaned close to the mirror and looked at her teeth.

"Her feet *look* littler."

"That's because she doesn't wear orange sneakers."

"I like my orange sneakers." Sara sat on the edge of the bed, slipped her feet into the shoes, and held them up. "What's wrong with them?"

"Nothing, except that when you want to hide something, you don't go painting it orange. I've got to go. Frank's coming."

She went out the door and Sara could hear her crossing into the kitchen. Sara lay back on the bed, her head next to Boysie. She looked at the sleeping dog, then covered her face with her hands and began to cry noisily.

"Oh, Boysie, Boysie, I'm crying," she wailed. Years ago, when Boysie was a young dog, he could not bear to hear anyone cry. Sara had only to pretend she was crying and Boysie would come running. He would whine and dig at her with his paws and lick her hands until she stopped. Now he lay with his eyes closed.

"Boysie, I'm crying," she said again. "I'm really crying this time. Boysie doesn't love me."

The dog shifted uneasily without opening his eyes.

"Boysie, Boysie, I'm crying, I'm so sad, Boysie," she wailed, then stopped and sat up abruptly. "You don't care about anybody, do you, Boysie? A person could cry herself to death these days and you wouldn't care."

She got up and left the room. In the hall she heard the tapping noise of Boysie's feet behind her and she said without looking at him, "I don't want you now, Boysie. Go on back in the bedroom. Go on." She went a few steps farther and, when he continued to follow her, turned and looked at him. "In case you are confused, Boysie, a dog is supposed to comfort people and run up and nuzzle them and make them feel better. All you want to do is lie on soft things and hide bones in the house because you are too lazy to go outside. Just go on back in the bedroom."

She started into the kitchen, still followed by Boysie, who could not bear to be left alone, then heard her aunt and Wanda arguing, changed her mind, and went out onto the porch.

Behind her, Boysie scratched at the door and she let him out. "Now quit following me."

Her brother Charlie was sitting on the top step and Sara sat down beside him. She held out her feet, looked at them, and said, "I like my orange sneakers, don't you, Charlie?"

He did not answer. He had been eating a lollipop and the stick had come off and now he was trying to put it back into the red candy. He had been trying for so long that the stick was bent.

"Here," she said, "I'll do it for you." She put the stick in and handed it to him. "Now be careful with it."

She sat without speaking for a moment, then she looked down at her feet and said, "I hate these orange sneakers. I just *hate* them." She leaned back against the porch railing so she wouldn't have to see them and said, "Charlie, I'll tell you something. This has been the worst summer of my life."

She did not know exactly why this was true. She was doing the same things she had done last summer — walk to the Dairy Queen with her friend Mary, baby-sit for Mrs. Hodges, watch television — and yet everything was different. It was as if her life was a huge kaleidoscope, and the kaleidoscope had been turned and now everything was changed. The same stones, shaken, no longer made the same design.

But it was not only one different design, one change; it was a hundred. She could never be really sure of anything this summer. One moment she was happy, and the next, for no reason, she was miserable. An hour ago she had loved her sneakers; now she detested them.

"Charlie, I'll tell you what this awful summer's been like. You remember when that finky Jim Wilson got you on the seesaw, remember that? And he kept bouncing you up and down and then he'd keep you up in the air for a real long time and then he'd drop you down real sudden, and you couldn't get off and you thought you never would? Up and down, up and down, for the rest of your life? Well, that's what this summer's been like for me."

He held out the candy and the stick to her.

"Not again!" She took it from him. "This piece of candy is so gross that I don't even want to touch it, if you want to know the truth." She put the stick back in and handed it to him. "Now if it comes off again — and I mean this, Charlie Godfrey — I'm throwing the candy away."

Charlie looked at the empty sucker stick, reached into his mouth, took out the candy, and held them together in his hand. Sara had said she would throw the candy away if this happened again and so he closed his fist tightly and looked away from her.

Slowly he began to shuffle his feet back and forth on the step. He had done this so many times over the years that two grooves had been worn into the boards. It was a nervous habit that showed he was concerned about something, and Sara recognized it at once.

"All right, Charlie," she said wearily. "Where's your sucker?"

He began to shake his head slowly from side to side. His eyes were squeezed shut.

"I'm not going to take it away from you. I'm going to fix it one more time."

He was unwilling to trust her and continued to shake his head. The movement was steady and mechanical, as if it would continue forever, and she watched him for a moment.

Then, with a sigh, she lifted his hand and attempted to pry his fingers loose. "Honestly, Charlie, you're holding onto this grubby piece of candy like it was a crown jewel or something. Now, let go." He opened his eyes and watched while she took the candy from him and put the stick in. The stick was now bent almost double, and she held it out to him carefully.

"There."

He took the sucker and held it without putting it into his mouth, still troubled by the unsteadiness of the bent stick. Sara looked down at her hands and began to pull at a broken fingernail. There was something similar about them in that moment, the same oval face, round brown eyes, brown hair hanging over the forehead, freckles on the nose. Then Charlie glanced up and the illusion was broken.

Still holding his sucker, he looked across the yard and saw the tent he had made over the clothesline that morning. He had taken an old white blanket out into the yard, hung it over the low clothesline, and then got under it. He had sat there with the blanket blowing against him until

Sara came out and said, "Charlie, you have to fasten the ends down, like this. It isn't a tent if it's just hanging in the wind."

He had thought there was something wrong. He waited beneath the blanket until she came back with some clothespins and hammered them into the hard earth, fastening the edges of the blanket to the ground. "Now, *that's* a tent."

The tent had pleased him. The warmth of the sun coming through the thin cotton blanket, the shadows of the trees moving overhead had made him drowsy and comfortable and now he wanted to be back in the tent.

Sara had started talking about the summer again, but he did not listen. He could tell from the tone of her voice that she was not really talking to him at all. He got up slowly and began to walk across the yard toward the tent.

Sara watched him as he walked, a small figure for his ten years, wearing faded blue jeans and a striped knit shirt that was stretched out of shape. He was holding the sucker in front of him as if it were a candle that might go out at any moment.

Sara said, "Don't drop that candy in the grass now or it's really going to be lost."

She watched while he bent, crawled into the tent, and sat down. The sun was behind the tent now and she could see his silhouette. Carefully he put the sucker back into his mouth.

Then Sara lay back on the hard boards of the porch and looked up at the ceiling.

I n the house Wanda and Aunt Willie were still arguing. Sara could hear every word even out on the porch. Aunt Willie, who had been taking care of them since the death of their mother six years ago, was saying loudly, "No, not on a motorcycle. No motorcycle!"

Sara grimaced. It was not only the loudness of Aunt Willie's voice that she disliked. It was everything — the way she bossed them, the way she never really listened, the way she never cared what she said. She had once announced loud enough for everyone in Carter's Drugstore to hear that Sara needed a good dose of magnesia.

"It isn't a motorcycle, it's a motor *scooter.*" Wanda was speaking patiently, as if to a small child. "They're practically like bicycles."

"No."

"All I want to do is to ride one half mile on this perfectly safe motor scooter —"

"No. It's absolutely and positively no. No!"

"Frank is very careful. He has never had even the tiniest accident."

No answer.

"Aunt Willie, it is perfectly safe. He takes his mother to the grocery store on it. Anyway, I am old enough to go without permission and I wish you'd realize it. I am nineteen years old."

No answer. Sara knew that Aunt Willie would be standing by the sink shaking her head emphatically from side to side.

"Aunt Willie, he's going to be here any minute. He's coming all the way over here just to drive me to the lake to see the swans."

"You don't care *that* for seeing those swans."

"I do too. I love birds."

"All right then, those swans have been on the lake three days, and not once have you gone over to see them. Now all of a sudden you *have* to go, can't wait one minute to get on this devil motorcycle and see those swans."

"For your information, I have been dying to see them, only this is my first chance." She went out of the kitchen and pulled the swinging door shut behind her. "And I'm going," she said over her shoulder.

Wanda came out of the house, slammed the screen door, stepped over Boysie, and sat by Sara on the top step. "She never wants anyone to have any fun."

"I know."

"She makes me so mad. All I want to do is just ride down to see the swans on Frank's motor scooter." She looked at Sara, then broke off and said, "Where did Charlie go?"

"He's over there in his tent."

"I see him now. I wish Frank would hurry up and get here before Aunt Willie comes out." She stood, looked down the street, and sat back on the steps. "Did I tell you what that boy in my psychology class last year said about Charlie?"

Sara straightened. "What boy?"

"This boy Arnold Hampton, in my psychology class. We were discussing children who —"

"You mean you talk about Charlie to perfect strangers? To your class? I think that's awful." She put her feet into the two grooves worn in the steps by Charlie. "What do you say? 'Let me tell you all about my retarded brother — it's so interesting'?" It was the first time in her life that she had used the term "retarded" in connection with her brother, and she looked quickly away from the figure in the white tent. Her face felt suddenly hot and she snapped a leaf from the rhododendron bush by the steps and held it against her forehead.

"No, I don't say that. Honestly, Sara, you —"

"And then do you say, 'And while I'm telling you about my retarded brother, I'll also tell you about my real hung-up sister'?" She moved the leaf to her lips and blew against it angrily.

"No, I don't say that because you're not all that fascinating, if you want to know the truth. Anyway, Arnold Hampton's father happens to be a pediatrician and Arnold is sincerely interested in working with boys like Charlie. He is even helping start a camp which Charlie may get to go to next summer, and all because I talked to him in my psychology class." She sighed. "You're impossible, you know that? I can't imagine why I even try to tell you anything."

"Well, Charlie's our problem."

"He's everybody's. There is no — Oh, here comes Frank." She broke off and got to her feet. "Tell Aunt Willie I'll be home later."

She started quickly down the walk, waving to the boy who was making his way slowly up the street on a green motor scooter.

"Wait, wait, you wait." Aunt Willie came onto the porch drying her hands on a dish towel. She stood at the top of the steps until Frank, a thin boy with red hair, brought the motor scooter to a stop. As he kicked down the stand she called out, "Frank, listen, save yourself some steps. Wanda's not going anywhere on that motorcycle."

"Aw, Aunt Willie," Frank said. He opened the gate and came slowly up the walk. "All we're going to do is go down to the lake. We don't even have to get on the highway for that."

"No motorcycles," she said. "You go break your neck if you want to. That's not my business. Wanda, left in my care, is not going to break her neck on any motorcycle."

"Nobody's going to break his neck. We're just going to have a very uneventful ride down the road to the lake. Then we're going to turn around and have a very uneventful ride back."

"No."

"I tell you what," Frank said. "I'll make a deal with you."

"What deal?"

"Have you ever been on a motor scooter?"

"Me? I never even rode on a bicycle."

"Try it. Come on. I'll ride you down to the Tennents' house and back. Then if you think it's not safe, you say to me, 'Frank, it's not safe,' and I'll take my motor scooter and ride off into the sunset."

She hesitated. There was something about a ride that appealed to her.

Sara said against the rhododendron leaf, "I don't think you ought to. You're too old to be riding up and down the street on a motor scooter."

She knew instantly she had said the wrong thing, for at once Aunt Willie turned to her angrily. "Too old!" She faced Sara with indignation. "I am barely forty years old. May I grow a beard if I'm not." She stepped closer, her voice rising. "Who says I'm so old?" She held the dish towel in front of her, like a matador taunting a bull. The dish towel flicked the air once.

"Nobody said anything," Sara said wearily. She threw the leaf down and brushed it off the steps with her foot.

"Then where did all this talk about my age come from, I'd like to know?"

"Anyway," Frank interrupted, "you're not too old to ride a motor scooter."

"I'll do it." She threw the dish towel across the chair and went down the steps. "I may break my neck but I'll do it."

"Hold on tight, Aunt Willie," Wanda called.

"Hold on! Listen, my hands never held on to anything the way I'm going to hold on to this motorcycle." She laughed, then said to Frank, "I never rode on one of these before, believe me."

"It's just like a motorized baby carriage, Aunt Willie."

"Huh!"

"This ought to be good," Wanda said. She called, "Hey, Charlie," waited until he looked out from the tent, and then said, "Watch Aunt Willie. She's going to ride the motor scooter."

Charlie watched Aunt Willie settle herself sidesaddle on the back of the scooter.

"Ready?" Frank asked.

"I'm as ready as I'll ever be, believe me, go on, go on."

Her words rose into a piercing scream as Frank moved the scooter forward, turned, and then started down the hill. Her scream, shrill as a bird's cry, hung in the still air. "Frank, Frank, Frank, Frankeeeeee!"

At the first cry Charlie staggered to his feet, staring in alarm at Aunt Willie disappearing down the hill. He pulled on one side of the tent as he got to his feet, causing the other to snap loose at the ground and hang limp from the line. He stumbled, then regained his balance.

Wanda saw him and said, "It's all right, Charlie, she's having a good time. She *likes* it. It's all right." She crossed the yard, took him by the hand, and led him to the steps. "What have you got all over yourself?"

"It's a gross red sucker," Sara said. "It's all over me too."

"Come on over to the spigot and let me wash your hands. See, Aunt Willie's coming back now."

In front of the Tennents' house Frank was swinging the scooter around, pivoting on one foot, and Aunt Willie stopped screaming long enough to call to the Tennents, "Bernie, Midge, look who's on a motorcycle!" Then she began screaming again as Frank started the uphill climb. As they came to a stop Aunt Willie's cries changed to laughter. "Huh, old woman, am I! Old woman!" Still laughing, she stepped off the scooter.

"You're all right, Aunt Willie," Frank said.

Sensing a moment of advantage, Wanda moved down the walk. She was shaking the water from her hands. "So can I go, Aunt Willie?"

"Oh, go on, go on," she said, half laughing, half scolding. "It's your own neck. Go on, break your own neck if you want to."

"It's not her neck you have to worry about, it's my arms," Frank said. "Honest, Aunt Willie, there's not a drop of blood circulating in them."

"Oh, go on, go on with you."

"Come on, Little One," Frank said to Wanda.

Aunt Willie came and stood by Sara, and they watched Wanda climb on the back of the motor scooter. As Wanda and Frank drove off, Aunt Willie laughed again and said, "Next thing, *you'll* be going off with some boy on a motorcycle."

Sara had been smiling, but at once she stopped and looked down at her hands. "I don't think you have to worry about that."

"Huh! It will happen, you'll see. You'll be just like Wanda. You'll be —"

"Don't you see that I'm nothing like Wanda at all?" She sat down abruptly and put her lips against her knees. "We are so different. Wanda is a hundred times prettier than I am."

"You are just alike, you two. Sometimes in the kitchen I hear you and I think I'm hearing Wanda. That's how alike you are. May my ears fall off if I can hear the difference."

"Maybe our *voices* are alike, but that's all. I can make my voice sound like a hundred different people. Listen to this and guess who it is. 'N–B–C! Beautiful downtown Burbank.'"

"I'm not in the mood for a guessing game. I'm in the mood to get back to our original conversation. It's not how you look that's important, let me tell you. I had a sister so beautiful you wouldn't believe it."

"Who?"

"Frances, that's who."

"She wasn't all that beautiful. I've seen her and —"

"When she was young she was. So beautiful you wouldn't believe it, but such a devil, and —"

"It is *too* important how you look. Parents are always saying it's not how you look that counts. I've heard that all my life. It doesn't matter how you look. It doesn't matter how you look. Huh! If you want to find out how much it matters, just let your hair get too long or put on too much eye makeup and listen to the screams." She got up abruptly and said, "I think I'll walk over and see the swans myself."

"Well, I have not finished with this conversation yet, young lady."

Sara turned and looked at Aunt Willie, waited with her hands jammed into her back pockets.

"Oh, never mind," Aunt Willie said, picking up her dish towel and shaking it. "I might as well hold a conversation with this towel as with you when you get that look on your face. Go on and see the swans." She broke off. "Hey, Charlie, you want to go with Sara to see the swans?"

"He'll get too tired," Sara said.

"So walk slow."

"I never get to do anything by myself. I have to take him every- where. I have him all day and Wanda all night. In all this whole house I have one drawer to myself. *One drawer.*"

"Get up, Charlie. Sara's going to take you to see the swans."

Sara looked down into his eyes and said, "Oh, come on," and drew him to his feet.

"Wait, there's some bread from supper." Aunt Willie ran into the house and came back with four rolls. "Take them. Here. Let Charlie feed the swans."

"Well, come on, Charlie, or it's going to be dark before we get there."

"Don't you rush him along, hear me, Sara?"

"I won't."

Holding Sara's hand, Charlie went slowly down the walk. He hesitated at the gate and then moved with her onto the sidewalk. As they walked down the hill, his feet made a continuous scratching sound on the concrete.

When they were out of earshot Sara said, "Aunt Willie thinks she knows everything. I get so sick of hearing how I am exactly like Wanda when Wanda is beautiful. I think she's just beautiful. If I could look like anyone in the world, I would want to look like her." She kicked at some high grass by the sidewalk. "And it does too matter how you look, I can tell you that." She walked ahead angrily for a few steps, then waited for Charlie and took his hand again.

"I think how you look is the most important thing in the world. If you *look* cute, you *are* cute; if you *look* smart, you *are* smart, and if you don't look like anything, then you aren't anything.

"I wrote a theme on that one time in school, about looks being the most important thing in the world, and I got a D — a *D*! Which is a terrible grade.

"After class the teacher called me up and told me the same old business about looks not being important, and how some of the ugliest people in the world were the smartest and kindest and cleverest."

They walked past the Tennents' house just as someone inside turned on the television, and they heard Eddie Albert singing, "Greeeeeen acres is —" before it was turned down. Charlie paused a moment, recognizing the beginning of one of his favorite programs, looked up at Sara, and waited.

"Come on," Sara said. "And then there was this girl in my English class named Thelma Louise and she wrote a paper entitled 'Making People Happy' and she got an A. An *A*! Which is as good as you can get. It was sickening. Thelma Louise is a beautiful girl with blond hair and naturally curly eyelashes, so what does she know? Anyway, one time Hazel went over to Thelma Louise's, and she said the rug was worn thin in front of the mirror in Thelma Louise's room because Thelma Louise stood there all the time watching herself."

She sighed and continued to walk. Most of the houses were set close together as if huddled for safety, and on either side of the houses the West Virginia hills rose, black now in the early evening shadows. The hills were as they had been for hundreds of years, rugged forest land, except that strip mining had begun on the hills to the north, and the trees and earth had been hacked away, leaving unnatural cliffs of pale washed earth.

Sara paused. They were now in front of Mary Weicek's house and she said, "Stop a minute. I've got to speak to Mary." She could hear Mary's record player, and she longed to be up in Mary's room, leaning back against the pink dotted bedspread listening to Mary's endless collection of records. "Mary!" she called. "You want to walk to the pond with me and Charlie and see the swans?"

Mary came to the window. "Wait, I'm coming out."

Sara waited on the sidewalk until Mary came out into the yard. "I can't go because my cousin's here and she's going to cut my hair," Mary said, "but did you get your dress yesterday?"

"No."

"Why not? I thought your aunt said you could."

"She did, but when we got in the store and she saw how much it cost she said it was foolish to pay so much for a dress when she could make me one just like it."

"Disappointment."

"Yes, because unfortunately she can't make one *just* like it, she can only make one *kind of* like it. You remember how the stripes came together diagonally in the front of that dress? Well, she already has mine cut out and I can see that not one stripe meets."

"Oh, Sara."

"I could see when she was cutting it that the stripes weren't going to meet and I kept saying, 'It's not right, Aunt Willie, the stripes aren't going to meet,' and all the while I'm screaming, the scissors are flashing and she is muttering, 'The stripes will meet, the stripes will meet,' and then she holds it up in great triumph and not one stripe meets."

"That's awful, because I remember thinking when you showed me the dress that it was the way the stripes met that looked so good."

"I am aware of that. It now makes me look like one half of my body is about two inches lower than the other half."

"Listen, come on in and watch my cousin cut my hair, can you?"

"I better not. I promised Aunt Willie I'd take Charlie to see the swans."

"Well, just come in and see how she's going to cut it. She has a whole book of hair styles."

"Oh, all right, for a minute. Charlie, you sit down right there." She pointed to the steps. "Right there now and don't move, hear me? Don't move off that step. Don't even stand up." Then she went in the house with Mary, saying, "I really can't stay but a minute because I've got to take Charlie down to see the swans and then I've got to get home in time to dye my tennis shoes —"

"Which ones?"

"These, these awful orange things. They make me look like Donald Duck or something."

Charlie sat in the sudden stillness, hunched over his knees, on the bottom step. The whole world seemed to have been turned off when Sara went into the Weiceks' house, and he did not move for a long time. The only sound was the ticking of his watch.

The watch was a great pleasure to him. He had no knowledge of hours or minutes, but he liked to listen to it and to watch the small red hand moving around the dial, counting off the seconds, and it was he who remembered every morning after breakfast to have Aunt Willie wind it for him. Now he rested his arm across his legs and looked at the watch.

He had a lonely feeling. He got this whenever he was by himself in a strange place, and he turned quickly when he heard the screen door open to see if it was Sara. When he saw Mrs. Weicek and another woman he turned back and looked at his watch. As he bent over, a pale half circle of flesh showed between the back of his shirt and his pants.

"Who's the little boy, Allie?"

Mrs. Weicek said, "That's Sara's brother, Charlie. You remember me telling you about him. He's the one that can't talk. Hasn't spoken a word since he was three years old."

"Doesn't talk at all?"

"If he does, no one's ever heard him, not since his illness. He can understand what you say to him, and he goes to school, and they say he can write the alphabet, but he can't talk."

Charlie did not hear them. He put his ear against his watch and listened to the sound. There was something about the rhythmic ticking that never failed to soothe him. The watch was a magic charm whose tiny noise and movements could block out the whole clamoring world.

Mrs. Weicek said, "Ask him what time it is, Ernestine. He is so proud of that watch. Everyone always asks him what time it is." Then without waiting, she herself said, "What time is it, Charlie? What time is it?"

He turned and obediently held out the arm with the watch on it.

"My goodness, it's after eight o'clock," Mrs. Weicek said. "Thank you, Charlie. Charlie keeps everyone informed of the time. We just couldn't get along without him."

The two women sat in the rocking chairs on the porch, moving slowly back and forth. The noise of the chairs and the creaking floor boards made Charlie forget the watch for a moment. He got slowly to his feet and stood looking up the street.

"Sit down, Charlie, and wait for Sara," Mrs. Weicek said.

Without looking at her, he began to walk toward the street.

"Charlie, Sara wants you to wait for her."

"Maybe he doesn't hear you, Allie."

"He hears me all right. Charlie, wait for Sara. Wait now." Then she called, "Sara, your brother's leaving."

Sara looked out the upstairs window and said, "All right, Charlie, I'm coming. Will you wait for a minute? Mary, I've got to go."

She ran out of the house and caught Charlie by the arm. "What are you going home for? Don't you want to see the swans?"

He stood without looking at her.

"Honestly, I leave you alone for one second and off you go. Now come on." She tugged his arm impatiently.

As they started down the hill together she waved to Mary, who was at the window, and said to Charlie, "I hope the swans are worth all this trouble I'm going to."

"We'll probably get there and they'll be gone," she added. They walked in silence. Then Sara said, "Here's where we cut across the field." She waited while he stepped carefully over the narrow ditch, and then the two of them walked across the field side by side, Sara kicking her feet restlessly in the deep grass.

T here was something painfully beautiful about the swans. The whiteness, the elegance of them on this dark lake, the incredible ease of their movements made Sara catch her breath as she and Charlie rounded the clump of pines.

"There they are, Charlie."

She could tell the exact moment he saw them because his hand tightened; he really held her hand for the first time since they had left Mary's. Then he stopped.

"There are the swans."

The six swans seemed motionless on the water, their necks all arched at the same angle, so that it seemed there was only one swan mirrored five times.

"There are the swans," she said again. She felt she would like to stand there pointing out the swans to Charlie for the rest of the summer. She watched as they drifted slowly across the water.

"Hey, Sara!"

She looked across the lake and saw Wanda and Frank, who had come by the road. "Sara, listen, tell Aunt Willie that Frank and I are going over to his sister's to see her new baby."

"All right."

"I'll be home at eleven."

She watched as Wanda and Frank got back on the motor scooter. At the roar of the scooter, the startled swans changed direction and moved toward Sara. She and Charlie walked closer to the lake.

"The swans are coming over here, Charlie. They see you, I believe."

They watched in silence for a moment as the sound of the scooter faded. Then Sara sat down on the grass, crossed her legs yoga style, and picked out a stick which was wedged inside one of the orange tennis shoes.

"Sit down, Charlie. Don't just stand there."

Awkwardly, with his legs angled out in front of him, he sat on the grass. Sara pulled off a piece of a roll and tossed it to the swans. "Now they'll come over here," she said. "They love bread."

She paused, put a piece of roll into her own mouth, and sat chewing for a moment.

"I saw the swans when they flew here, did you know that, Charlie? I was out on our porch last Friday and I looked up, and they were coming over the house and they looked so funny, like frying pans with their necks stretched out." She handed him a roll. "Here. Give the swans something to eat. Look, watch me. Like that."

She watched him, then said, "No, Charlie, small pieces, because swans get things caught in their throats easily. No, that's *too* little. That's just a crumb. Like *that*."

She watched while he threw the bread into the pond, then said, "You know where the swans live most of the time? At the university, which is a big school, and right in the middle of this university is a lake

and that's where the swans live. Only sometimes, for no reason, the swans decide to fly away, and off they go to another pond or another lake. This one isn't half as pretty as the lake at the university, but here they are."

She handed Charlie another roll. "Anyway, that's what Wanda thinks, because the swans at the university are gone."

Charlie turned, motioned that he wanted another roll for the swans, and she gave him the last one. He threw it into the water in four large pieces and put out his hand for another.

"No more. That's all." She showed him her empty hands.

One of the swans dived under the water and rose to shake its feathers. Then it moved across the water. Slowly the other swans followed, dipping their long necks far into the water to catch any remaining pieces of bread.

Sara leaned forward and put her hands on Charlie's shoulders. His body felt soft, as if the muscles had never been used. "The swans are exactly alike," she said. "Exactly. No one can tell them apart."

She began to rub Charlie's back slowly, carefully. Then she stopped abruptly and clapped him on the shoulders. "Well, let's go home."

He sat without moving, still looking at the swans on the other side of the lake.

"Come on, Charlie." She knew he had heard her, yet he still did not move. "Come *on*." She got to her feet and stood looking down at him. She held out her hand to help him up, but he did not even glance at her. He continued to watch the swans.

"Come on, Charlie. Mary may come up later and help me dye my shoes." She looked at him, then snatched a leaf from the limb overhead and threw it at the water. She waited, stuck her hands in her back pockets, and said tiredly, "Come on, Charlie."

He began to shake his head slowly back and forth without looking at her.

"Mary's coming up to help me dye my shoes and if you don't come on we won't have time to do them and I'll end up wearing these same awful Donald Duck shoes all year. Come *on*."

He continued to shake his head back and forth.

"This is why I never want to bring you anywhere, because you won't go home when I'm ready."

With his fingers he began to hold the long grass on either side of him as if this would help him if she tried to pull him to his feet.

"You are really irritating, you know that?" He did not look at her and she sighed and said, "All right, if I stay five more minutes, will you go?" She bent down and showed him on his watch. "That's to right there. When the big hand gets *there*, we go home, all right?"

He nodded.

"Promise?"

He nodded again.

"All right." There was a tree that hung over the water and she went and leaned against it. "All right, Charlie, four more minutes now," she called.

Already he had started shaking his head again, all the while watching the swans gliding across the dark water.

Squinting up at the sky, Sara began to kick her foot back and forth in the deep grass. "In just a month, Charlie, the summer will be over," she said without looking at him, "and I will be so glad."

Up until this year, it seemed, her life had flowed along with rhythmic evenness. The first fourteen years of her life all seemed the same. She had loved her sister without envy, her aunt without finding her coarse, her brother without pity. Now all that was changed. She was filled with a discontent, an anger about herself, her life, her family, that made her think she would never be content again.

She turned and looked at the swans. The sudden, unexpected tears in her eyes blurred the images of the swans into white circles, and she blinked. Then she said aloud, "Three minutes, Charlie."

Sara was lying in bed with the lights out when Wanda came into the bedroom that night. Sara was wearing an old pair of her father's pajamas with the sleeves cut out and the legs rolled up. She watched as Wanda moved quietly across the room and then stumbled over the dressing-table stool. Hobbling on one foot, Wanda opened the closet door and turned on the light.

"You can put on the big light if you want. I'm awake," Sara said.

"*Now* you tell me."

"Did you have a good time, Wanda?"

"Yes."

"Did you get to see the baby?"

"He was so cute. He looked exactly like Frank. You wouldn't have believed it."

"Poor baby."

"No, he was darling, really he was, with little red curls all over his head." She undressed quickly, turned off the closet light, and then got into bed beside Sara. She smoothed her pillow and looked up at the ceiling. "Frank is so nice, don't you think?"

"He's all right."

"Don't you like him?" She rose up on one elbow and looked down at Sara in the big striped pajamas.

"I said he was all right."

"Well, what don't you like?"

"I didn't say I didn't like him."

"I know, but I can tell. What don't you like?"

"For one thing, he never pays any attention to Charlie. When he came up the walk tonight he didn't even speak to him."

"He probably didn't see him in the tent. Anyway, he likes Charlie — he told me so. What else?"

"Oh, nothing, it's just that he's always so affected, the way he calls you Little One and gives you those real meaningful movie-star looks."

"I love it when he calls me Little One. Just wait till someone calls *you* Little One."

"I'd like to know who could call me Little One except the Jolly Green Giant."

"Oh, Sara."

"Well, I'm bigger than everyone I know."

"You'll find someone."

"Yes, maybe if I'm lucky I'll meet somebody from some weird foreign country where men value tall skinny girls with big feet and crooked noses. Every time I see a movie, though, even if it takes place in the weirdest, foreignest country in the world, like where women dance in gauze bloomers and tin bras, the women are still little and beautiful." Then she said, "Anyway, I hate boys. They're all just one big nothing."

"Sara, what's wrong with you?"

"Nothing."

"No, I mean it. What's really wrong?"

"I don't know. I just feel awful."

"Physically awful?"

"Now don't start being the nurse."

"Well, I want to know."

"No, not physically awful, just plain awful. I feel like I want to start screaming and kicking and I want to jump up and tear down the curtains and rip up the sheets and hammer holes in the walls. I want to yank my clothes out of the closet and burn them and —"

"Well, why don't you try it if it would make you feel better?"

"Because it wouldn't." She lifted the top sheet and watched as it billowed in the air and then lowered on her body. She could feel the cloth as it settled on the bare part of her legs. "I just feel like nothing."

"Oh, everybody does at times, Sara."

"Not like me. I'm not anything. I'm not cute, and I'm not pretty, and I'm not a good dancer, and I'm not smart, and I'm not popular. I'm not anything."

"You're a good dishwasher."

"Shut up, Wanda. I don't think that's funny."

"Welllll —"

"You act like you want to talk to me and then you start being funny. You do that to me all the time."

"I'm through being funny, so go on."

"Well, if you could see some of the girls in my school you'd know what I mean. They look like models. Their clothes are so tuff and they're invited to every party, every dance, by about ten boys and when they walk down the hall everybody turns and looks at them."

"Oh, those girls. They hit the peak of their whole lives in junior high school. They look like grown women in eighth grade with the big teased hair and the eye liner and by the time they're in high school they have a used look."

"Well, I certainly don't have to worry about getting a used look."

"I think it is really sad to hit the peak of your whole life in junior high school."

"Girls, quit that arguing," Aunt Willie called from her room. "I can hear you all the way in here."

"We're not arguing," Wanda called back. "We are having a peaceful little discussion."

"I know an argument when I hear one, believe me. That's one thing I've heard plenty of and I'm hearing one right now. Be quiet and go to sleep."

"All right."

They lay in silence. Sara said, "The peak of my whole life so far was in third grade when I got to be milk monitor."

Wanda laughed. "Just give yourself a little time." She reached over, turned on the radio, and waited till it warmed up. "Frank's going to dedicate a song to me on the Diamond Jim show," she said. "Will the radio bother you?"

"No."

"Well, it bothers me," Aunt Willie called from her room. "Maybe you two can sleep with the radio blaring and people arguing, but I can't."

"I have just barely got the radio turned on, Aunt Willie. I have to put my head practically on the table to even hear it." She broke off abruptly. "What was that dedication, did you hear?"

"It was to all the girls on the second floor of Arnold Hall."

"Oh."

"I mean what I say now," Aunt Willie called. "You two get to sleep. Wanda, you've got to be up early to get to your job at the hospital on time, even if Sara can spend the whole day in bed."

"I'd like to know how I can spend the whole day in bed when she gets me up at eight o'clock," Sara grumbled.

"Aunt Willie, I just want to hear my dedication and then I'll go to sleep."

Silence.

Sara turned over on her side with the sheet wrapped tightly around her body and closed her eyes. She was not sleepy now. She could hear the music from the radio, and the sound from the next room of Charlie turning over in his bed, trying to get settled, then turning over again. She pulled the pillow over her head, but she could not block out the noises. Oddly, it was the restless sounds from Charlie's room which seemed loudest.

Charlie was not a good sleeper. When he was three, he had had two illnesses, one following the other, terrible high-fevered illnesses, which had almost taken his life and had damaged his brain. Afterward, he had lain silent and still in his bed, and it had been strange to Sara to see the pale baby that had replaced the hot, flushed, tormented one. The once-bright eyes were slow to follow what was before them, and the hands never reached out, even when Sara held her brother's favorite stuffed dog, Buh-Buh, above him. He rarely cried, never laughed. Now it was as if Charlie wanted to make up for those listless years in bed by never sleeping again.

Sara heard his foot thump against the wall. It was a thing that could continue for hours, a faint sound that no one seemed to hear but Sara, who slept against the wall. With a sigh she put the pillow back beneath her head and looked up at the ceiling.

"That was my dedication. Did you hear it?" Wanda whispered. "To Little One from Frank."

"Vomit."

"Well, I think it was sweet."

The thumping against the wall stopped, then began again. It was a sound that Sara had become used to, but tonight it seemed unusually loud. She found herself thinking how this had been Charlie's first movement after his long illness, a restless kicking out of one foot, a weak movement then that could hardly be noticed beneath the covers, but now, tonight, one that seemed to make the whole house tremble.

"Don't tell me you don't hear that," she said to Wanda. "I don't see how you can all persist in saying that you don't hear Charlie kicking the wall."

Silence.

"Wanda, are you asleep?"

Silence.

"Honestly, I don't see how people can just fall asleep any time they want to. Wanda, are you really asleep?"

She waited, then drew the sheet close about her neck and turned to the wall.

I n his room Charlie lay in bed still kicking his foot against the wall. He was not asleep but was staring up at the ceiling where the shadows were moving. He never went to sleep easily, but tonight he had been concerned because a button was missing from his pajamas, and sleep was impossible. He had shown the place where the button was missing to Aunt Willie when he was ready for bed, but she had patted his shoulder and said, "I'll fix it tomorrow," and gone back to watching a game show on television.

"Look at that," Aunt Willie was saying to herself. "They're never going to guess the name. How can famous celebrities be so stupid?" She had leaned forward and shouted at the panelists, "It's Clark Gable!" Then, "Have they never heard of a person who works in a store? A person who works in a store is a *clerk* — Clerk Gable — the name is *Clerk Gable*!"

Charlie had touched her on the shoulder and tried again to show her the pajamas.

"I'll fix it tomorrow, Charlie." She had waved him away with one hand.

He had gone back into the kitchen, where Sara was dyeing her tennis shoes in the sink.

"Don't show it to me," she said. "I can't look at anything right now. And Mary, quit laughing at my tennis shoes."

"I can't help it. They're so gross."

Sara lifted them out of the sink with two spoons. "I know they're gross, only you should have told me that orange tennis shoes could not be dyed baby blue. Look at that. That is the worst color you have ever seen in your life. Admit it."

"I admit it."

"Well, you don't have to admit it so quickly. They ought to put on the dye wrapper that orange cannot be dyed baby blue. A warning."

"They do."

"Well, they ought to put it in big letters. Look at those shoes. There must be a terrible name for that color."

"There is," Mary said. "Puce."

"What?"

"Puce."

"Mary Weicek, you made that up."

"I did not. It really is a color."

"I have never heard a word that describes anything better. Puce. These just look like puce shoes, don't they?" She set them on newspapers. "They're — Charlie, get out of the way, please, or I'm going to get dye all over you."

He stepped back, still holding his pajama jacket out in front of him. There were times when he could not get anyone's attention no matter what he did. He took Sara's arm and she shrugged free.

"Charlie, there's not a button on anything I own, either, so go on to bed."

Slowly, filled with dissatisfaction, he had gone to his room and got into bed. There he had begun to pull worriedly at the empty buttonhole until the cloth had started to tear, and then he had continued to pull until the whole front of his pajama top was torn and hung open. He was now holding the jacket partly closed with his hands and looking up at the ceiling.

It was one o'clock and Charlie had been lying there for three hours.

He heard a noise outside, and for the first time he forgot about his pajamas. He stopped kicking his foot against the wall, sat up, and looked out the window. There was something white in the bushes; he could see it moving.

He released his pajamas and held onto the window sill tightly, because he thought that he had just seen one of the swans outside his window, gliding slowly through the leaves. The memory of their soft smoothness in the water came to him and warmed him.

He got out of bed and stood by the other window. He heard a cat miaowing and saw the Hutchinsons' white cat from next door, but he paid no attention to it. The swans were fixed with such certainty in his mind that he could not even imagine that what he had seen was only the cat.

Still looking for the swans, he pressed his face against the screen. The beauty of them, the whiteness, the softness, the silent splendor had impressed him greatly, and he felt a longing to be once again by the lake, sitting in the deep grass, throwing bread to the waiting swans.

It occurred to him suddenly that the swan outside the window had come to find him, and with a small pleased smile he went around the bed, sat, and slowly began to put on his bedroom slippers. Then he walked out into the hall. His feet made a quiet shuffling sound as he passed through the linoleumed hall and into the living room, but no one heard him.

The front door had been left open for coolness and only the screen door was latched. Charlie lifted the hook, pushed open the door, and stepped out onto the porch. Boysie, who slept in the kitchen, heard the door shut and came to the living room. He whined softly when he saw Charlie outside on the porch and scratched at the door. He waited, then after a moment went back to the kitchen and curled up on his rug in front of the sink.

Charlie walked across the front porch and sat on the steps. He waited. He was patient at first, for he thought that the swans would come to the steps, but as time passed and they did not come, he began to shuffle his feet impatiently back and forth on the third step.

Suddenly he saw something white in the bushes. He got up and, holding the banister, went down the steps and crossed the yard. He looked into the bushes, but the swans were not there. It was only the cat, crouched down behind the leaves and looking up at him with slitted eyes.

He stood there, looking at the cat, unable to understand what had happened to the swans. He rubbed his hands up and down his pajama tops, pulling at the torn material. The cat darted farther back into the bushes and disappeared.

After a moment Charlie turned and began to walk slowly across the yard. He went to the gate and paused. He had been told again and again that he must never go out of the yard, but those instructions, given in daylight with noisy traffic on the street, seemed to have nothing to do with the present situation.

In the soft darkness all the things that usually confused him — speeding bicycles, loud noises, lawn mowers, barking dogs, shouting children — were gone, replaced by silence and a silvery moonlit darkness. He seemed to belong to this silent world far more than he belonged to the daytime world of feverish activity.

Slowly he opened the gate and went out. He moved past the Hutchinsons' house, past the Tennents', past the Weiceks'. There was a breeze now, and the smell of the Weiceks' flowers filled the air. He walked past the next house and hesitated, suddenly confused. Then he started through the vacant lot by the Akers' house. In the darkness it looked to him like the field he and Sara had crossed earlier in the evening on their way to see the swans.

He crossed the vacant lot, entered the wooded area, and walked slowly through the trees. He was certain that in just a moment he would come into the clearing and see the lake and the white swans gliding on the dark water. He continued walking, looking ahead so that he would see the lake as soon as possible.

The ground was getting rougher. There were stones to stumble over now and rain gullies and unexpected piles of trash. Still the thought of the swans persisted in his mind and he kept walking.

Charlie was getting tired and he knew something was wrong. The lake was gone. He paused and scanned the field, but he could not see anything familiar.

He turned to the right and began to walk up the hill. Suddenly a dog barked behind him. The sound, unexpected and loud, startled him, and he fell back a step and then started to run. Then another dog was barking, and another, and he had no idea where the dogs were. He was terribly frightened and he ran with increasing awkwardness, thrashing at the weeds with his hands, pulling at the air, so that everything about him seemed to be running except his slow feet.

The sound of the dogs seemed to him to be everywhere, all around him, so that he ran first in one direction, then in another, like a wild animal caught in a maze. He ran into a bush and the briers stung his face and arms, and he thought this was somehow connected with the dogs and thrashed his arms out wildly, not even feeling the cuts in his skin.

He turned around and around, trying to free himself, and then staggered on, running and pulling at the air. The dogs' barking had grown fainter now, but in his terror he did not notice. He ran blindly, stumbling over bushes and against trees, catching his clothing on twigs, kicking at unseen rocks. Then he came into a clearing and was able to gain speed for the first time.

He ran for a long way, and then suddenly he came up against a wire fence that cut him sharply across the chest. The surprise of it threw him back on the ground, and he sat holding his hands across his bare chest, gasping for breath.

Far down the hill someone had spoken to the dogs; they had grown quiet, and now there was only the rasping sound of Charlie's own breathing. He sat hunched over until his breathing grew quieter, and then he straightened and noticed his torn pajamas for the first time since he had left the house. He wrapped the frayed edges of the jacket carefully over his chest as if that would soothe the stinging cut.

After a while he got slowly to his feet, paused, and then began walking up the hill beside the fence. He was limping now because when he had fallen he had lost one of his bedroom slippers.

The fence ended abruptly. It was an old one, built long ago, and now only parts remained. Seeing it gone, Charlie felt relieved. It was as if the fence had kept him from his goal, and he stepped over a trailing piece of wire and walked toward the forest beyond.

Being in the trees gave him a good feeling for a while. The moonlight coming through the leaves and the soft sound of the wind in the branches were soothing, but as he went deeper into the forest he became worried. There was something here he didn't know, an unfamiliar smell, noises he had never heard before. He stopped.

He stood beneath the trees without moving and looked around him. He did not know where he was. He did not even know how he had come to be there. The whole night seemed one long struggle, but he could not remember why he had been struggling. He had wanted something; he could not remember what.

His face and arms stung from the brier scratches; his bare foot, tender and unused to walking on the rough ground, was already cut and sore, but most of all he was gripped by hopelessness. He wanted to be back in his room, in his bed, but home seemed lost forever, a place so disconnected from the forest that there was no way to get from one to the other.

He put his wrist to his ear and listened to his watch. Even its steady ticking could not help him tonight and he wrapped the torn pajamas tighter over his chest and began to walk slowly up the hill through the trees. As he walked, he began to cry without noise.

I n the morning Sara arose slowly, letting her feet hang over the edge of the bed for a moment before she stepped onto the floor. Then she walked across the room, and as she passed the dressing table she paused to look at herself in the mirror. She smoothed her hair behind her ears.

One of her greatest mistakes, she thought, looking at herself critically, was cutting her hair. She had gone to the beauty school in Bentley, taking with her a picture from a magazine, and had asked the girl to cut her hair exactly like that.

"And look what she did to me!" she had screamed when she got home. "Look! Ruined!"

"It's not that bad," Wanda had said.

"Tell the truth. Now look at that picture. Look! Tell the truth — do I look anything, anything at *all*, even the tiniest little bit, like that model?"

Wanda and Aunt Willie had had to admit that Sara looked nothing like the blond model.

"I'm ruined, just ruined. Why someone cannot take a perfectly good magazine picture and cut someone's hair the same way without ruining them is something I cannot understand. I hope that girl fails beauty school."

"Actually, your *hair* does sort of look like the picture. It's your face and body that don't."

"Shut up, Wanda. Quit trying to be funny."

"I'm not being funny. It's a fact."

"I didn't make smart remarks the time they gave you that awful permanent."

"You did too. You called me Gentle Ben."

"Well, I meant that as a compliment."

"All right, girls, stop this now. No more arguing. Believe me, I mean it."

Sara now looked at herself, weighing the mistake of the hair, and she thought suddenly: I look exactly like that cartoon cat who is always chasing Tweetie Bird and who has just been run over by a steam roller and made absolutely flat. This hair and my flat face have combined to make me look exactly like —

"Sara!" Aunt Willie called from the kitchen.

"What?"

"Come on and get your breakfast, you and Charlie. I'm not going to be in here fixing one breakfast after another until lunch time."

"All right."

She went into the hall and looked into Charlie's room.

"Charlie!"

He was not in his bed. She walked into the living room. Lately, since he had learned to turn on the television, he would get up early, come in, and watch it by himself, but he was not there either.

"Charlie's already up, Aunt Willie."

In the kitchen Aunt Willie was spooning oatmeal into two bowls.

"Oatmeal again," Sara groaned. "I believe I'll just have some Kool-Aid and toast."

"Don't talk nonsense. Now, where's Charlie?"

"He wasn't in his room."

She sighed. "Well, find him."

"First I've got to see my shoes." She went over to the sink and looked at the sneakers. "Oh, they look awful. Look at them, Aunt Willie. They're gross."

"Well, you should have left them alone. I've learned my lesson about dyeing clothes, let me tell you. You saw me, I hope, when I had to wear that purple dress to your Uncle Bert's funeral."

"What color would you say these were?"

"I haven't got time for that now. Go get your brother."

"No, there's a name for this color. I just want to see if you know it."

"I don't know it, so go get your brother."

"I'll give you three choices. It's either, let me see — it's either pomegranate, Pomeranian, or puce."

"Puce. Now go get your brother."

"How did you know?"

"Because my aunt had twin Pomeranian dogs that rode in a baby carriage and because I once ate a piece of pomegranate. Go get your brother!"

Sara put down the shoes and went back into the hall.

"Charlie!" She looked into his room again. "Oh, Charlie!" She went out onto the front porch and looked at Charlie's tent. It had blown down during the night and she could see that he wasn't there.

Slowly she walked back through the hall, looking into every room, and then into the kitchen.

"I can't find him, Aunt Willie."

"What do you mean, you can't find him?" Aunt Willie, prepared to chide the two children for being late to breakfast, now set the pan of oatmeal down heavily on the table.

"He's not in his room, he's not in the yard, he's not anywhere."

"If this is some kind of a joke —" Aunt Willie began. She brushed past Sara and went into the living room. "Charlie! Where are you, Charlie?" Her voice had begun to rise with the sudden alarm she often felt in connection with Charlie. "Where could he have gone?" She turned and looked at Sara. "If this is a joke . . ."

"It's not a joke."

"Well, I'm remembering last April Fool's Day, that's all."

"He's probably around the neighborhood somewhere, like the time Wanda took him to the store without saying anything."

"Well, Wanda didn't take him this morning." Aunt Willie walked into the hall and stood looking in Charlie's room. She stared at the empty bed. She did not move for a moment as she tried to think of some logical explanation for his absence. "If anything's happened to that boy —"

"Nothing's happened to him."

"All right, where is he?"

Sara did not answer. Charlie had never left the house alone, and Sara could not think of any place he could be either.

"Go outside, Sara. Look! If he's not in the neighborhood, I'm calling the police."

"Don't call until we're sure, Aunt Willie, please."

"I'm calling. Something's wrong here."

Sara was out of her pajamas and into her pants and shirt in a minute. Leaving her pajamas on the floor, she ran barefoot into the yard.

"Charlie! Charlie!" She ran around the house and then stopped. Suddenly she remembered the swans and ran back into the house.

"Aunt Willie, I bet you anything Charlie went down to the lake to see the swans."

Aunt Willie was talking on the telephone and she put one hand over the receiver and said, "Run and see."

"You aren't talking to the police already?" Sara asked in the doorway.

"I'm not talking to the police, but that's what I'm going to do when you get back. Now quit wasting time."

"Just let me get my shoes."

She ran back into the kitchen and put on the sneakers, which were still wet. Then she ran out of the house and down the street. As she passed the Weiceks', Mary came out on the porch.

"What's the hurry?" she called.

"Charlie's missing. I'm going to see if he's down at the lake."

"I'll go with you." She came down the steps, calling over her shoulder, "Mom, I'm going to help Sara look for Charlie."

"Not in those curlers you're not."

"Mom, I've got on a scarf. Nobody can even tell it's rolled."

"Yeah, everyone will just think you have real bumpy hair," Sara said.

"Oh, hush. Now what's all this about Charlie?"

"We couldn't find him this morning and I think he might have got up during the night and gone to see the swans. He acted awful when we had to leave."

"I know. I saw you dragging him up the street last night."

"I had to. It was the only way I could get him home. It was black dark. You couldn't even see the swans and he still wouldn't come home."

"I hope he's all right."

"He's probably sitting down there looking at the swans, holding onto the grass, and I'm going to have to drag him up the hill screaming all over again. He's strong when he wants to be, you know that?"

"Hey, you've got your shoes on."

"Yeah, but they're still wet."

"You'll probably have puce feet before the day's over."

"That's all I need."

They turned and crossed the field at the bottom of the hill.

"Let's hurry because Aunt Willie is at this moment getting ready to call the police."

"Really?"

"She's sitting by the phone now. She's got her little card out with all her emergency numbers on it and her finger is pointing right to *POLICE*."

"Remember that time the old man got lost in the woods? What was his name?"

"Uncle somebody."

"And they organized a posse of college boys and the Red Cross brought coffee and everything, and then they found the old man asleep in his house the next morning. He was on a picnic and had got bored and just went home."

"Don't remind me. Probably as soon as Aunt Willie calls the police we'll find Charlie in the bathroom or somewhere."

They came through the trees and into the clearing around the lake. Neither spoke.

"Yesterday he was sitting right here," Sara said finally. "Charlie! Charlie!"

There was no answer, but the swans turned abruptly and began to glide to the other side of the lake. Sara felt her shoulders sag and she rammed her hands into her back pockets.

"Something really has happened to him," she said. "I know it now."

"Probably not, Sara."

"I *know* it now. Sometimes you just know terrible things. I get a feeling in my neck, like my shoulders have come unhinged or something, when an awful thing happens."

Mary put one hand on her arm. "Maybe he's hiding somewhere."

"He can't even do that right. If he's playing hide-and-seek, as soon as he's hidden he starts looking out to see how the game's going. He just can't —"

"Maybe he's at the store or up at the Dairy Queen. I could run up to the drugstore."

"No, something's happened to him."

They stood at the edge of the water. Sara looked at the swans without seeing them.

Mary called, "Charlie! Charlie!" Her kerchief slipped off and she retied it over her rollers. "Charlie!"

"I was so sure he'd be here," Sara said. "I wasn't even worried because I knew he would be sitting right here. Now I don't know what to do."

"Let's go back to the house. Maybe he's there now."

"I know he won't be."

"Well, don't get discouraged until we see." She took Sara by the arm and started walking through the trees. "You know who you sound like? Remember when Mary Louise was up for class president and she kept saying, 'I know I won't get it. I know I won't get it.' For three days that was all she said."

"And she didn't get it."

"Well, I just meant you sounded like her, your voice or something," Mary explained quickly. "Now, come on."

When Sara entered the house with Mary, Aunt Willie was still sitting at the telephone. She was saying, "And there's not a trace of him." She paused in her conversation to ask, "Did you find him?" and when Sara shook her head, she said into the telephone, "I'm hanging up now, Midge, so I can call the police. Sara just came in and he wasn't at the lake."

She hung up, took her card of emergency phone numbers and began to dial.

There was something final about calling the police and Sara said, "Aunt Willie, don't call yet. Maybe —"

"I'm calling. A hundred elephants couldn't stop me."

"Maybe he's at somebody's house," Mary said. "One time my brother went in the Hutchinsons' to watch TV and we —"

"Hello, is this the police department? I want to report a missing child."

She looked up at Sara, started to say something, then turned back to her telephone conversation. "Yes, a missing child, a boy, ten, Charlie Godfrey. G-o-d-f-r-e-y." Pause. "Eighteen-oh-eight Cass Street. This is Willamina Godfrey, his aunt. I'm in charge." She paused, then said, "Yes, since last night." She listened again. "No, I don't know what time. We woke up this morning, he was gone. That's all." She listened and as she answered again her voice began to rise with concern and anger. "No, I could not ask his friends about him because he doesn't have any friends. His brain was injured when he was three years old and that is why I am so concerned. This is not a ten-year-old boy who can go out and come home when he feels like it. This is not a boy who's going to run out and break street lights and spend the night in some garage, if that's what you're thinking. This is a boy, I'm telling you, who can be lost and afraid three blocks from home and cannot speak one word to ask for help. Now are you going to come out here or aren't you?"

She paused, said, "Yes, yes," then grudgingly, "And thank you." She hung up the receiver and looked at Sara. "They're coming."

"What did they say?"

"They said they're coming. That's all." She rose in agitation and began to walk into the living room. "Oh, why don't they hurry!"

"Aunt Willie, they just hung up the telephone."

"I know." She went to the front door and then came back, nervously slapping her hands together. "Where can he *be*?"

"My brother was always getting lost when he was little," Mary said.

354

"I stood right in this house, in that room," Aunt Willie interrupted. She pointed toward the front bedroom. "And I promised your mother, Sara, that I would look after Charlie all my life. I promised your mother nothing would ever happen to Charlie as long as there was breath in my body, and now look. Look! Where is this boy I'm taking such good care of?" She threw her hands into the air. "Vanished without a trace, that's where."

"Aunt Willie, you can't watch him every minute."

"Why not? Why can't I? What have I got more important in my life than looking after that boy? Only one thing more important than Charlie. Only one thing — that devil television there."

"Aunt Willie —"

"Oh, yes, that devil television. I was sitting right in that chair last night and he wanted me to sew on one button for him but I was too busy with the television. I'll tell you what I should have told your mother six years ago. I should have told her, 'Sure, I'll be glad to look after Charlie except when there's something good on television. I'll be glad to watch him in my spare time.' My tongue should fall out on the floor for promising to look after your brother and not doing it."

She went back to the doorway. "There are a hundred things that could have happened to him. He could have fallen into one of those ravines in the woods. He could be lost up at the old mine. He could be at the bottom of the lake. He could be kidnaped." Sara and Mary stood in silence as she named the tragedies that could have befallen Charlie.

Sara said, "Well, he could not have been kidnaped, because anybody would know we don't have any money for ransom."

"That wouldn't stop some people. Where are those policemen?"

Sara looked down at the table beside the television and saw a picture Charlie had drawn of himself on tablet paper. The head and body were circles of the same size, the ears and eyes overlapping smaller circles, the arms and legs were elongated balloons. He had started printing his name below the picture, but had completed only two letters before he had gone out to make the tent. The *C* was backward.

Wanda had bought him the tablet and crayons two days ago and he had done this one picture with the brown crayon. It gave Sara a sick feeling to see it because something about the picture, the smallness, the unfinished quality, made it look somehow very much like Charlie.

Aunt Willie said, "When you want the police they are always a hundred miles away bothering criminals."

"They're on their way. They said so," Mary said.

"All right then, where are they?"

Mary blinked her eyes at this question to which she had no answer, and settled the rollers beneath her scarf.

"I still can't get it out of my head that Charlie went back to see the swans," Sara said.

"He really was upset about having to go home. I can testify to that," Mary said.

Aunt Willie left the room abruptly. When she came back she was holding a picture of Charlie in one hand. It was a snapshot of him taken in March, sitting on the steps with Boysie in front of the house.

"The police always want a photograph," she said. She held it out so Mary and Sara could see it. "Mrs. Hutchinson took that with her Polaroid."

"It's a real good picture of him," Mary said.

Sara looked at the picture without speaking. Somehow the awkward, unfinished crayon drawing on the table looked more like Charlie than the snapshot.

"It was his birthday," Aunt Willie said mournfully, "and look how proud he was of that watch Wanda bought him, holding his little arm straight out in the picture so everyone would notice it. I fussed so much about Wanda getting him a watch because he couldn't tell time, and then he was so proud just to be wearing it. Everyone would ask him on the street, 'What time is it, Charlie? Have you got the time, Charlie?' just to see how proud he was to show them."

"And then those boys stole it. I think that was the meanest thing," Mary said.

"The watch was lost," Aunt Willie said. "The watch just got lost."

"Stolen," Sara snapped, "by that crook Joe Melby."

"I am the quickest person to accuse somebody, you know that. You saw me, I hope, when I noticed those boys making off with the Hutchinsons' porch chairs last Halloween; but that watch just got lost. Then Joe Melby found it and, to his credit, brought it back."

"Huh!"

"There was no stealing involved."

Mary said, giggling, "Aunt Willie, did Sara ever tell you what she did to Joe?"

"Hush, Mary," Sara said.

"What did she do?"

"She made a little sign that said *FINK* and stuck it on Joe's back in the hall at school and he went around for two periods without knowing it was there."

"It doesn't matter what I did. Nobody's going to pick on my brother and I mean it. That fink stole Charlie's watch and then got scared and told that big lie about finding it on the floor of the school bus."

"You want revenge too much."

"When somebody *deserves* revenge, then —"

"I take my revenge same as anybody," Aunt Willie said, "only I never was one to keep after somebody and keep after somebody the way you do. You take after your Uncle Bert in that."

"I hope I always do."

"No, your Uncle Bert was no good in that way. He would never let a grudge leave him. When he lay dying in the hospital, he was telling us who we weren't to speak to and who we weren't to do business with. His dying words were against Jeep Johnson at the used-car lot."

"Good for Uncle Bert."

"And that nice little Gretchen Wyant who you turned the hose on, and her wearing a silk dress her brother had sent her from Taiwan!"

"That nice little Gretchen Wyant was lucky all she got was water on her silk dress."

"Sara!"

"Well, do you know what that nice little Gretchen Wyant did? I was standing in the bushes by the spigot, turning off the hose, and this nice little Gretchen Wyant didn't see me — all she saw was Charlie at the fence — and she said, 'How's the *retard* today?' only she made it sound even uglier, 'How's the *reeeeetard*,' like that. Nothing ever made me so mad. The best sight of my whole life was nice little Gretchen Wyant standing there in her wet Taiwan silk dress with her mouth hanging open."

"Here come the police," Mary said quickly. "But they're stopping next door."

"Signal to them," Aunt Willie said.

Before Mary could move to the door, Aunt Willie was past her and out on the porch. "Here we are. This is the house." She turned and said over her shoulder to Sara, "Now, God willing, we'll get some action."

Sara sat in the living room wearing her cut-off blue jeans, an old shirt with *Property of State Prison* stamped on the back which Wanda had brought her from the beach, and her puce tennis shoes. She was sitting in the doorway, leaning back against the door with her arms wrapped around her knees, listening to Aunt Willie, who was making a telephone call in the hall.

"It's no use calling," Sara said against her knees. This was the first summer her knees had not been skinned a dozen times, but she could still see the white scars from other summers. Since Aunt Willie did not answer, she said again, "It's no use calling. He won't come."

"You don't know your father," Aunt Willie said.

"That is the truth."

"Not like I do. When he hears that Charlie is missing, he will . . ." Her voice trailed off as she prepared to dial the telephone.

Sara had a strange feeling when she thought of her father. It was the way she felt about people she didn't know well, like the time Miss Marshall, her English teacher, had given her a ride home from school, and Sara had felt uneasy the whole way home, even though she saw Miss Marshall every day.

Her father's remoteness had begun, she thought, with Charlie's illness. There was a picture in the family photograph album of her father laughing and throwing Sara into the air and a picture of her father holding her on his shoulders and a picture of her father sitting on the front steps with Wanda on one knee and Sara on the other. All these pictures of a happy father and his adoring daughters had been taken before Charlie's illness and Sara's mother's death. Afterward there weren't any family pictures at all, happy or sad.

When Sara looked at those early pictures, she remembered a laughing man with black curly hair and a broken tooth who had lived with them for a few short golden years and then had gone away. There was no connection at all between this laughing man in the photograph album and the gray sober man who worked in Ohio and came home to West Virginia on occasional weekends, who sat in the living room and watched baseball or football on television and never started a conversation on his own.

Sara listened while Aunt Willie explained to the operator that the call she was making was an emergency. "That's why I'm not direct dialing," she said, "because I'm so upset I'll get the wrong numbers."

"He won't come," Sara whispered against her knee.

As the operator put through the call and Aunt Willie waited, she turned to Sara, nodded emphatically, and said, "He'll come, you'll see."

Sara got up, walked across the living room and into the kitchen, where the breakfast dishes were still on the table. She looked down at the two bowls of hard, cold oatmeal, and then made herself three pieces of toast and poured herself a cup of cherry Kool-Aid. When she came back eating the toast Aunt Willie was still waiting.

"Didn't the operator tell them it was an emergency, I wonder," Aunt Willie said impatiently.

"Probably."

"Well, if somebody told me I had an emergency call, I would run, let me tell you, to find out what that emergency was. That's no breakfast, Sara."

"It's my lunch."

"Kool-Aid and toast will not sustain you five minutes." She broke off quickly and said in a louder voice, "Sam, is that you?" She nodded to Sara, then turned back to the telephone, bent forward in her concern. "First of all, Sammy, promise me you won't get upset — no, promise me first."

"He won't get upset. Even *I* can promise you that," Sara said with her mouth full of toast.

"Sam, Charlie's missing," Aunt Willie said abruptly.

Unable to listen to any more of the conversation, Sara took her toast and went out onto the front porch. She sat on the front steps and put her feet into the worn grooves that Charlie's feet had made on the third step. Then she ate the last piece of toast and licked the butter off her fingers.

In the corner of the yard, beneath the elm tree, she could see the hole Charlie had dug with a spoon; all one morning he had dug that hole and now Boysie was lying in it for coolness. She walked to the tree and sat in the old rope swing and swung over Boysie. She stretched out her feet and touched Boysie, and he lifted his head and looked around to see who had poked him, then lay back in his hole.

"Boysie, here I am, look, Boysie, look."

He was already asleep again.

"Boysie —" She looked up as Aunt Willie came out on the porch and stood for a minute drying her hands on her apron. For the occasion of Charlie's disappearance she was wearing her best dress, a bright green bonded jersey, which was so hot her face above it was red and shiny. Around her forehead she had tied a handkerchief to absorb the sweat.

Sara swung higher. "Well," she asked, "is he coming?" She paused to pump herself higher. "Or not?"

"He's going to call back tonight."

"Oh," Sara said.

"Don't say 'Oh' to me like that."

"It's what I figured."

"Listen to me, Miss Know-it-all. There is no need in the world for your father to come this exact minute. If he started driving right this second he still wouldn't get here till after dark and he couldn't do anything then, so he just might as well wait till after work and then drive."

"Might as well do the sensible thing." Sara stood up and really began to swing. She had grown so much taller since she had last stood in this swing that her head came almost to the limb from which the swing hung. She caught hold of the limb with her hands, kicked her feet free, and let the swing jerk wildly on its own.

"Anyway," Aunt Willie said, "this is no time to be playing on a swing. What will the neighbors think, with Charlie missing and you having a wonderful time on a swing?"

"I knew he wouldn't come."

"He is going to come," Aunt Willie said in a louder voice. "He is just going to wait till dark, which is reasonable, since by dark Charlie will probably be home anyway."

"It is so reasonable that it makes me sick."

"I won't listen to you being disrespectful to your father, I mean that," she said. "I know what it is to lose a father, let me tell you, and so will you when all you have left of him is an envelope."

Aunt Willie, Sara knew, was speaking of the envelope in her dresser drawer containing all the things her father had had in his pockets when he died. Sara knew them all — the watch, the twenty-seven cents in change, the folded dollar bill, the brown plaid handkerchief, the three-cent stamp, the two bent pipe cleaners, the half pack of stomach mints.

"Yes, wait till you lose your father. Then you'll appreciate him."

"I've already lost him."

"Don't you talk like that. Your father's had to raise two families and all by himself. When Poppa died, Sammy had to go to work and support all of us before he was even out of high school, and now he's got this family to support too. It's not easy, I'm telling you that. *You* raise two families and then I'll listen to what you've got to say against your father."

Sara let herself drop to the ground and said, "I better go. Mary and I are going to look for Charlie."

"Where?"

"Up the hill."

"Well, don't *you* get lost," Aunt Willie called after her.

From the Hutchinsons' yard some children called, "Have you found Charlie yet, Sara?" They were making a garden in the dust, carefully planting flowers without roots in neat rows. Already the first flowers were beginning to wilt in the hot sun.

"I'm going to look for him now."

"Sawa?" It was the youngest Hutchinson boy, who was three and sometimes came over to play with Charlie.

"What?"

"Sawa?"

"What?"

"Sawa?"

"*What?*"

"Sawa, I got gwass." He held up two fists of grass he had just pulled from one of the few remaining clumps in the yard.

"Yes, that's fine. I'll tell Charlie when I see him."

S ara and Mary had decided that they would go to the lake and walk up behind the houses toward the woods. Sara was now on her way to Mary's, passing the vacant lot where a baseball game was in progress. She glanced up and watched as she walked down the sidewalk.

The baseball game had been going on for an hour with the score still zero to zero and the players, dusty and tired, were playing silently, without hope.

She was almost past the field when she heard someone call, "Hey, have you found your brother yet, Sara?"

She recognized the voice of Joe Melby and said, "No," without looking at him.

"What?"

She turned, looked directly at him, and said, "You will be pleased and delighted to learn that we have not." She continued walking down the street. The blood began to pound in her head. Joe Melby was the one person she did not want to see on this particular day. There was something disturbing about him. She did not know him, really, had hardly even spoken to him, and yet she hated him so much the sight of him made her sick.

"Is there anything I can do?"

"No."

"If he's up in the woods, I could help look. I know about as much about those hills as anybody." He left the game and started walking behind her with his hands in his pockets.

"No, thank you."

"I *want* to help."

She swirled around and faced him, her eyes blazing. "I do not want your help." They looked at each other. Something twisted inside her and she felt suddenly ill. She thought she would never drink cherry Kool-Aid again as long as she lived.

Joe Melby did not say anything but moved one foot back and forth on the sidewalk, shuffling at some sand. "Do you —"

"Anybody who would steal a little boy's watch," she said, cutting off his words, and it was a relief to make this accusation to his face at last, "is somebody whose help I can very well do without." Her head was pounding so loudly she could hardly hear her own words. For months, ever since the incident of the stolen watch, she had waited for this moment, had planned exactly what she would say. Now that it was said, she did not feel the triumph she had imagined at all.

"Is that what's wrong with you?" He looked at her. "You think I stole your brother's watch?"

"I know you did."

"How?"

"Because I asked Charlie who stole his watch and I kept asking him and one day on the school bus when I asked him he pointed right straight at you."

"He was confused —"

"He wasn't that confused. You probably thought he wouldn't be able to tell on you because he couldn't talk, but he pointed right —"

"He *was* confused. I gave the watch *back* to him. I didn't take it."

"I don't believe you."

"You believe what you want then, but I didn't take that watch. I thought that matter had been settled."

"Huh!"

She turned and started walking with great speed down the hill. For some reason she was not as sure about Joe Melby as she had been before, and this was even more disturbing. He did take the watch, she said to herself. She could not bear to think that she had been mistaken in this, that she had taken revenge on the wrong person.

Behind her there were sudden cheers as someone hit a home run. The ball went into the street. Joe ran, picked it up, and tossed it to a boy in the field. Sara did not look around.

"Hey, wait a minute," she heard Joe call. "I'm coming."

She did not turn around. She had fallen into that trap before. Once when she had been walking down the street, she had heard a car behind her and the horn sounding and a boy's voice shouting, "Hey, beautiful!" And she had turned around. She! Then, too late, she had seen that the girl they were honking and shouting at was Rosey Camdon on the opposite side of the street, Rosey Camdon who was Miss Batelle District Fair and Miss Buckwheat Queen and a hundred other things. Sara had looked down quickly, not knowing whether anyone had seen her or not, and her face had burned so fiercely she had thought it would be red forever. Now she kept walking quickly with her head down.

"Wait, Sara."

Still she did not turn around or show that she had heard him.

"Wait." He ran, caught up with her, and started walking beside her. "All the boys say they want to help."

She hesitated but kept walking. She could not think of anything to say. She knew how circus men on stilts felt when they walked, because her legs seemed to be moving in the same awkward way, great exaggerated steps that got her nowhere.

She thought she might start crying so she said quickly, "Oh, all right." Then tears did come to her eyes, sudden and hot, and she looked down at her feet.

He said, "Where should we start? Have you got any ideas?"

"I think he's up in the woods. I took him to see the swans yesterday and I think he was looking for them when he got lost."

"Probably up that way."

She nodded.

He paused, then added, "We'll find him."

She did not answer, could not, because tears were spilling down her cheeks, so she turned quickly and walked alone to Mary's house and waited on the sidewalk until Mary came out to join her.

She and Mary were almost across the open field before Sara spoke. Then she said, "Guess who just stopped me and gave me the big sympathy talk about Charlie."

"I don't know. Who?"

"Joe Melby."

"Really? What did he say?"

"He wants to help look for Charlie. He makes me sick."

"I think it's nice that he wants to help."

"Well, maybe if he'd stolen your brother's watch you wouldn't think it was so nice."

Mary was silent for a moment. Then she said, "I probably shouldn't tell you this, but he didn't steal that watch, Sara."

"Huh!"

"No, he really didn't."

Sara looked at her and said, "How do you know?"

"I can't tell you how I know because I promised I wouldn't, but I *know* he didn't."

"How?"

"I can't tell. I promised."

"That never stopped you before. Now, Mary Weicek, you tell me what you know this minute."

"I promised."

"Mary, tell me."

"Mom would kill me if she knew I told you."

"She won't know."

"Well, your aunt went to see Joe Melby's mother."

"What?"

"Aunt Willie went over to see Joe Melby's mother."

"She didn't!"

"Yes, she did too, because my mother was right there when it happened. It was about two weeks after Charlie had gotten the watch back."

"I don't believe you."

"Well, it's the truth. You told Aunt Willie that Joe had stolen the watch — remember, you told everybody — and so Aunt Willie went over to see Joe's mother."

"She wouldn't do such a terrible thing."

"Well, she did."

"And what did Mrs. Melby say?"

"She called Joe into the room and she said, 'Joe, did you steal the little Godfrey boy's watch?' And he said, 'No.'"

"What did you expect him to say in front of his mother? 'Yes, I stole the watch'? Huh! That doesn't prove anything."

"So then she said, 'I want the truth now. Do you know who did take the watch?' and he said that nobody had *stolen* the watch."

"So where did it disappear to for a week, I'd like to know."

"I'm coming to that. He said some of the fellows were out in front of the drugstore and Charlie was standing there waiting for the school bus — you were in the drugstore. Remember it was the day we were getting the stamps for letters to those pen pals who never answered? Remember the stamps wouldn't come out of the machine? Well, anyway, these boys outside the store started teasing Charlie with some candy, and while Charlie was trying to get the candy, one of the boys took off Charlie's watch without Charlie noticing it. Then they were going to ask Charlie what time it was and when he looked down at his watch, he would get upset because the watch would be gone. They were just going to tease him."

"Finks! *Finks!*"

"Only you came out of the drugstore right then and saw what they were doing with the candy and told them off and the bus came and you hustled Charlie on the bus before anybody had a chance to give back the watch. Then they got scared to give it back and that's the whole story. Joe didn't steal the watch at all. He wasn't even in on it. He came up right when you did and didn't even know what had happened. Later, when he found out, he got the watch back and gave it to Charlie, that's all."

"Why didn't you tell me before this?"

"Because I just found out about it at lunch. For four months my mother has known all about this thing and never mentioned it because she said it was one of those things best forgotten."

"Why did she tell you now?"

"That's the way my mom is. We were talking about Charlie at the dinner table, and suddenly she comes up with this. Like one time she casually mentioned that she had had a long talk with Mr. Homer about me. Mr. Homer, the principal! She went over there and they had a long discussion and she never mentioned it for a year."

"That is the worst thing Aunt Willie has ever done."

"Well, don't let on that you know or I'll be in real trouble."

"I won't, but honestly, I could just —"

"You promised."

"I know. You don't have to keep reminding me. It makes me feel terrible though, I can tell you that." She walked with her head bent forward. "Terrible! You know what I just did when I saw him?"

"What?"

"Accused him of stealing the watch."

"Sara, you didn't."

"I did too. I can't help myself. When I think somebody has done something mean to Charlie I can't forgive them. I want to keep after them and keep after them just like Aunt Willie said. I even sort of suspected Joe Melby hadn't really taken that watch and I still kept on —"

"Shh! Be quiet a minute." Mary was carrying her transistor radio and she held it up between them. "Listen."

The announcer was saying: "We have a report of a missing child in the Cass section — ten-year-old Charlie Godfrey, who has been missing from his home since sometime last night. He is wearing blue pajamas and brown felt slippers, has a watch on one wrist and an identification bracelet with his name and address on the other. He is a mentally handicapped child who cannot speak and may become alarmed when approached by a stranger. Please notify the police immediately if you have seen this youngster."

The two girls looked at each other, then continued walking across the field in silence.

Mary and Sara were up in the field by the woods. They had been searching for Charlie for an hour without finding a trace of him.

Mary said, "I don't care how I look. I am taking off this scarf. It must be a hundred degrees out here."

"Charlie!" Sara called as she had been doing from time to time. Her voice had begun to sound strained, she had called so often. "Charlie!"

"Sara, do you know where we are?" Mary asked after a moment.

"Of course. The lake's down there and the old shack's over there and you can see them as soon as we get up a little higher."

"*If* we get up a little higher," Mary said in a tired voice.

"You didn't have to come, you know."

"I wanted to come, only I just want to make sure we don't get lost. I have to go to Bennie Hoffman's party tonight."

"I know. You told me ten times."

"So I don't want to get lost." Mary walked a few steps without speaking. "I still can't figure out why I was invited, because Bennie Hoffman hardly knows me. I've just seen him two times this whole summer at the pool. Why do you think he —"

"Come on, will you?"

"It seems useless, if you ask me, to just keep walking when we don't really know which way he went. Aunt Willie thinks he went in the old coal mine."

368

"I know, but she only thinks that because she associates the mine with tragedy because her uncle and brother were killed in that coal mine. But Charlie wouldn't go in there. Remember that time we went into the Bryants' cellar after they moved out, and he wouldn't even come in there because it was cold and dark and sort of scary."

"Yes, I do remember because I sprained my ankle jumping down from the window and had to wait two hours while you looked through old *Life* magazines."

"I was not looking through old magazines."

"I could hear you. I was down there in that dark cellar with the rats and you were upstairs and I was yelling for help and you kept saying, 'I'm going for help right now,' and I could hear the pages turning and turning and turning."

"Well, I got you out, didn't I?"

"Finally."

Sara paused again. "Charlie! Charlie!" The girls waited in the high grass for an answer, then began to walk again. Mary said, "Maybe we should have waited for the others before we started looking. They're going to have a regular organized posse with everybody walking along together. There may be a helicopter."

"The longer we wait, the harder it will be to find him."

"Well, I've got to get home in time to bathe and take my hair down."

"I know. I *know*. You're going to Bennie Hoffman's party."

"You don't have to sound so mad about it. I didn't *ask* to be invited."

"I am not mad because you were invited to Bennie Hoffman's party. I couldn't care less about Bennie Hoffman's party. I'm just mad because you're slowing me up on this search."

"Well, if I'm slowing you up so much, then maybe I'll just go on home."

"That suits me fine."

They looked at each other without speaking. Between them the radio began announcing: "Volunteers are needed in the Cass area in the search for young Charlie Godfrey, who disappeared from his home sometime during the night. A search of the Cheat woods will begin at three o'clock this afternoon."

Mary said, "Oh, I'll keep looking. I'll try to walk faster."

Sara shrugged, turned, and started walking up the hill, followed by Mary. They came to the old fence that once separated the pasture from the woods. Sara walked slowly beside the fence. "Charlie!" she called.

"Would he come if he heard you, do you think?"

Sara nodded. "But if they get a hundred people out here clomping through the woods and hollering, he's not going to come. He'll be too scared. I know him."

"I don't see how you can be so sure he came up this way."

"I just know. There's something about me that makes me understand Charlie. It's like I know how he feels about things. Like sometimes I'll be walking down the street and I'll pass the jeweler's and I'll think that if Charlie were here he would want to stand right there and look at those watches all afternoon and I know right where he'd stand and how he'd put his hands up on the glass and how his face would look. And yesterday I knew he was going to love the swans so much that he wasn't ever going to want to leave. I know how he feels."

"You just think you do."

"No, I *know*. I was thinking about the sky one night and I was looking up at the stars and I was thinking about how the sky goes on and on forever, and I couldn't understand it no matter how long I thought, and finally I got kind of nauseated and right then I started thinking, Well, this is how Charlie feels about some things. You know how it makes him sick sometimes to try to print letters for a long time and —"

"Look who's coming," Mary interrupted.

"Where?"

"In the trees, walking toward us. Joe Melby."

"You're lying. You're just trying to make me —"

"It is him. Look." She quickly began to tie her scarf over her rollers again. "And you talk about *me* needing eyeglasses."

"Cut across the field, quick!" Sara said. "No, wait, go under the fence. Move, will you, Mary, and leave that scarf alone. Get under the fence. I am not going to face him. I mean it."

"I am not going under any fence. Anyway, it would look worse for us to run away than to just walk by casually."

"I cannot walk by casually after what I said."

"Well, you're going to have to face him sometime, and it might as well be now when everyone feels sorry for you about your brother." She called out, "Hi, Joe, having any luck?"

He came up to them and held out a brown felt slipper and looked at Sara. "Is this Charlie's?"

Sara looked at the familiar object and forgot the incident of the watch for a moment. "Where did you find it?"

"Right up there by the fence. I had just picked it up when I saw you."

She took the slipper and, holding it against her, said, "Oh, I *knew* he came up this way, but it's a relief to have some proof of it."

"I was just talking to Mr. Aker," Joe continued, "and he said he heard his dogs barking up here last night. He had them tied out by the shack and he thought maybe someone was prowling around."

"Probably Charlie," Mary said.

"That's what I figured. Somebody ought to go down to the gas station and tell the people. They're organizing a big search now and half of the men are planning to go up to the mine."

There was a pause and Mary said, "Well, I guess I could go, only I don't know whether I'll have time to get back up here." She looked at Joe. "I promised Bennie Hoffman I'd come to his party tonight. That's why my hair's in rollers."

"Tell them I found the slipper about a half mile up behind the Akers' at the old fence," Joe said.

"Sure. Are you coming to Bennie's tonight?"

"Maybe."

"Come. It's going to be fun."

Sara cleared her throat and said, "Well, I think I'll get on with my search if you two will excuse me." She turned and started walking up the hill again. There seemed to be a long silence in which even the sound of the cicadas in the grass was absent. She thrashed at the high weeds with her tennis shoes and hugged Charlie's slipper to her.

"Wait a minute, Sara, I'll come with you," Joe Melby said.

He joined her and she nodded, still looking down at the slipper. There was a picture of an Indian chief stamped on the top of the shoe and there was a loneliness to the Indian's profile, even stamped crudely on the felt, that she had never noticed before.

She cleared her throat again. "There is just one thing I want to say." Her voice did not even sound familiar, a tape-recorded voice.

He waited, then said, "Go ahead."

She did not speak for a moment but continued walking noisily through the weeds.

"Go ahead."

"If you'll just wait a minute, I'm trying to think how to say this." The words she wanted to say — I'm sorry — would not come out at all.

They continued walking in silence and then Joe said, "You know, I was just reading an article about a guru over in India and he hasn't spoken a word in twenty-eight years. *Twenty-eight years* and he hasn't said one word in all that time. And everyone has been waiting all those years to hear what he's going to say when he finally does speak because it's supposed to be some great wise word, and I thought about this poor guy sitting there and for twenty-eight years he's been trying to think of something to say that would be the least bit great and he can't think of anything and he must be getting really desperate now. And every day it gets worse and worse."

"Is there supposed to be some sort of message in that story?"

"Maybe."

She smiled. "Well, I just wanted to say that I'm sorry." She thought again that she was going to start crying and she said to herself, You are nothing but a big soft snail. Snail!

"That's all right."

"I just found out about Aunt Willie going to see your mother."

He shrugged. "She didn't mean anything by it."

"But it was a terrible thing."

"It wasn't all that bad. At least it was different to be accused of something I *didn't* do for a change."

"But to be called in like that in front of Aunt Willie and Mary's mother. No, it was terrible." She turned and walked into the woods.

"Don't worry about it. I'm tough. I'm indestructible. I'm like that coyote in 'Road Runner' who is always getting flattened and dynamited and crushed and in the next scene is strolling along, completely normal again."

"I just acted too hastily. That's one of my main faults."

"I do that too."

"Not like me."

"Worse probably. Do you remember when we used to get grammar-school report cards, and the grades would be on one part of the card, and on the other side would be personality things the teacher would check, like 'Does not accept criticism constructively'?"

Sara smiled. "I always used to get a check on that one," she said.

"Who didn't? And then they had one, 'Acts impetuously and without consideration for others,' or something like that, and one year I got a double check on that one."

"You didn't."

"Yes, I did. Second grade. Miss McLeod. I remember she told the whole class that this was the first year she had ever had to give double checks to any student, and everyone in the room was scared to open his report card to see if he had got the double checks. And when I opened mine, there they were, two sets of double checks, on acting impetuously and on not accepting criticism, and single checks on everything else."

"Were you crushed?"

"Naturally."

"I thought you were so tough and indestructible."

"Well, I am" — he paused — "I think." He pointed to the left. "Let's go up this way."

She agreed with a nod and went ahead of him between the trees.

There was a ravine in the forest, a deep cut in the earth, and Charlie had made his way into it through an early morning fog. By chance, blindly stepping through the fog with his arms outstretched, he had managed to pick the one path that led into the ravine, and when the sun came out and the fog burned away, he could not find the way out.

All the ravine looked the same in the daylight, the high walls, the masses of weeds and wild berry bushes, the trees. He had wandered around for a while, following the little paths made by dirt washed down from the hillside, but finally he sat down on a log and stared straight ahead without seeing.

After a while he roused enough to wipe his hands over his cheeks where the tears and dirt had dried together and to rub his puffed eyelids. Then he looked down, saw his bare foot, put it on top of his slipper, and sat with his feet overlapped.

There was a dullness about him now. He had had so many scares, heard so many frightening noises, started at so many shadows, been hurt so often that all his senses were worn to a flat hopelessness. He would just sit here forever.

It was not the first time Charlie had been lost, but never before had there been this finality. He had become separated from Aunt Willie once at the county fair and had not even known he was lost until she had come bursting out of the crowd screaming, "Charlie, Charlie," and enveloped him. He had been lost in school once in the hall and could not find his way back to his room, and he had walked up and down the halls, frightened by all the strange children looking out of every door, until one of the boys was sent out to lead him to his room. But in all his life there had never been an experience like this one.

He bent over and looked down at his watch, his eyes on the tiny red hand. For the first time he noticed it was no longer moving. Holding his breath in his concern, he brought the watch closer to his face. The hand was still. For a moment he could not believe it. He watched it closely, waiting. Still the hand did not move. He shook his hand back and forth, as if he were trying to shake the watch off his wrist. He had seen Sara do this to her watch.

Then he held the watch to his ear. It was silent. He had had the watch for five months and never before had it failed him. He had not even known it could fail. And now it was silent and still.

He put his hand over the watch, covering it completely. He waited. His breathing had begun to quicken again. His hand on the watch was almost clammy. He waited, then slowly, cautiously, he removed his hand and looked at the tiny red hand on the dial. It was motionless. The trick had not worked.

Bending over the watch, he looked closely at the stem. Aunt Willie always wound the watch for him every morning after breakfast, but he did not know how she did this. He took the stem in his fingers, pulled at it clumsily, then harder, and it came off. He looked at it. Then, as he attempted to put it back on the watch, it fell to the ground and was lost in the leaves.

A chipmunk ran in front of him and scurried up the bank. Distracted for a moment, Charlie got up and walked toward it. The chipmunk paused and then darted into a hole, leaving Charlie standing in the shadows trying to see where it had gone. He went closer to the bank and pulled at the leaves, but he could not even find the place among the roots where the chipmunk had disappeared.

Suddenly something seemed to explode within Charlie, and he began to cry noisily. He threw himself on the bank and began kicking, flailing at the ground, at the invisible chipmunk, at the silent watch. He wailed, yielding in helplessness to his anguish, and his piercing screams, uttered again and again, seemed to hang in the air so that they overlapped. His fingers tore at the tree roots and dug beneath the leaves and scratched, animal-like, at the dark earth.

His body sagged and he rolled down the bank and was silent. He looked up at the trees, his chest still heaving with sobs, his face strangely still. After a moment, his eyelids drooped and he fell asleep.

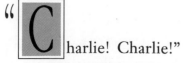"Charlie! Charlie!"

The only answer was the call of a bird in the branches overhead, one long tremulous whistle.

"He's not even within hearing distance," Sara said.

For the past hour she and Joe Melby had been walking deeper and deeper into the forest without pause, and now the trees were so thick that only small spots of sunlight found their way through the heavy foliage.

"Charlie, oh, Charlie!"

She waited, looking down at the ground.

Joe said, "You want to rest for a while?"

Sara shook her head. She suddenly wanted to see her brother so badly that her throat began to close. It was a tight feeling she got sometimes when she wanted something, like the time she had had the measles and had wanted to see her father so much she couldn't even swallow. Now she thought that if she had a whole glass of ice water — and she was thirsty — she probably would not be able to drink a single drop.

"If you can make it a little farther, there's a place at the top of the hill where the strip mining is, and you can see the whole valley from there."

"I can make it."

"Well, we can rest first if —"

"I can make it."

She suddenly felt a little better. She thought that if she could stand up there on top of the hill and look down and see, somewhere in that huge green valley, a small plump figure in blue pajamas, she would ask for nothing more in life. She thought of the valley as a relief map where everything would be shiny and smooth, and her brother would be right where she could spot him at once. Her cry, "There he is!" would ring like a bell over the valley and everyone would hear her and know that Charlie had been found.

She paused, leaned against a tree for a moment, and then continued. Her legs had begun to tremble.

It was the time of afternoon when she usually sat down in front of the television and watched game shows, the shows where the married couples tried to guess things about each other and where girls had to pick out dates they couldn't see. She would sit in the doorway to the hall where she always sat and Charlie would come in and watch with her, and the living room would be dark and smell of the pine-scented cleaner Aunt Willie used.

Then "The Early Show" would come on, and she would sit through the old movie, leaning forward in the doorway, making fun, saying things like, "Now, Charlie, we'll have the old Convict Turning Honest scene," and Charlie, sitting on the stool closer to the television, would nod without understanding.

She was good, too, at joining in the dialogue with the actors. When the cowboy would say something like, "Things are quiet around here tonight," she would join in with, "Yeah, *too* quiet," right on cue. It seemed strange to be out here in the woods with Joe Melby instead of in the living room with Charlie, watching *Flame of Araby*, which was the early movie for that afternoon.

Her progress up the hill seemed slower and slower. It was like the time she had won the slow bicycle race, a race in which she had to go as slow as possible without letting a foot touch the ground, and she had gone slower and slower, all the while feeling a strong compulsion to speed ahead and cross the finish line first. At the end of the race it had been she and T. R. Peters, and they had paused just before the finish line, balancing motionless on their bicycles. The time had seemed endless, and then T.R. lost his balance and his foot touched the ground and Sara was the winner.

She slipped on some dry leaves, went down on her knees, straightened, and paused to catch her breath.

"Are you all right?"

"Yes, I just slipped."

She waited for a moment, bent over her knees, then she called, "Charlie! Charlie," without lifting her head.

"Oh, Charleeeeee," Joe shouted above her.

Sara knew Charlie would shout back if he heard her, the long wailing cry he gave sometimes when he was frightened during the night. It was such a familiar cry that for a moment she thought she heard it.

She waited, still touching the ground with one hand, until she was sure there was no answer.

"Come on," Joe said, holding out his hand.

He pulled her to her feet and she stood looking up at the top of the hill. Machines had cut away the earth there to get at the veins of coal, and the earth had been pushed down the hill to form a huge bank.

"I'll never get up that," she said. She leaned against a tree whose leaves were covered with pale fine dirt which had filtered down when the machines had cut away the hill.

"Sure you will. I've been up it a dozen times."

He took her hand and she started after him, moving sideways up the steep bank. The dirt crumbled beneath her feet and she slid, skinned one knee, and then slipped again. When she had regained her balance she laughed wryly and said, "What's going to happen is that I'll end up pulling you all the way down the hill."

"No, I've got you. Keep coming."

She started again, putting one foot carefully above the other, picking her way over the stones. When she paused, he said, "Keep coming. We're almost there."

"I think it's a trick, like at the dentist's when he says, 'I'm almost through drilling.' Then he drills for another hour and says, 'Now, I'm really almost through drilling,' and he keeps on and then says, 'There's just one more spot and then I'll be practically really through.'"

"We must go to the same dentist."

"I don't think I can make it. There's no skin at all left on the sides of my legs."

"Well, we're really almost practically there now, in the words of your dentist."

She fell across the top of the dirt bank on her stomach, rested for a moment, and then turned and looked down the valley.

She could not speak for a moment. There lay the whole valley in a way she had never imagined it, a tiny finger of civilization set in a sweeping expanse of dark forest. The black treetops seemed to crowd against the yards, the houses, the roads, giving the impression that at any moment the trees would close over the houses like waves and leave nothing but an unbroken line of black-green leaves waving in the sunlight.

Up the valley she could see the intersection where they shopped, the drugstore, the gas station where her mother had once won a set of twenty-four stemmed glasses which Aunt Willie would not allow them to use, the grocery store, the lot where the yellow school buses were parked for the summer. She could look over the valley and see another hill where white cows were all grouped together by a fence and beyond that another hill and then another.

She looked back at the valley and she saw the lake and for the first time since she had stood up on the hill she remembered Charlie.

Raising her hand to her mouth, she called, "Charlie! Charlie! Charlie!" There was a faint echo that seemed to waver in her ears.

"Charlie, oh, Charlie!" Her voice was so loud it seemed to ram into the valley.

Sara waited. She looked down at the forest, and everything was so quiet it seemed to her that the whole valley, the whole world was waiting with her.

"Charlie, hey, Charlie!" Joe shouted.

"Charleeeeee!" She made the sound of it last a long time. "Can you hear meeeeee?"

With her eyes she followed the trail she knew he must have taken — the house, the Akers' vacant lot, the old pasture, the forest. The forest that seemed powerful enough to engulf a whole valley, she thought with a sinking feeling, could certainly swallow up a young boy.

"Charlie! Charlie! Charlie!" There was a waver in the last syllable that betrayed how near she was to tears. She looked down at the Indian slipper she was still holding.

"Charlie, oh, Charlie." She waited. There was not a sound anywhere. "Charlie, where are you?"

"Hey, Charlie!" Joe shouted.

They waited in the same dense silence. A cloud passed in front of the sun and a breeze began to blow through the trees. Then there was silence again.

"Charlie, Charlie, Charlie, Charlie, Charlie."

She paused, listened, then bent abruptly and put Charlie's slipper to her eyes. She waited for the hot tears that had come so often this summer, the tears that had seemed so close only a moment before. Now her eyes remained dry.

I have cried over myself a hundred times this summer, she thought, I have wept over my big feet and my skinny legs and my nose, I have even cried over my stupid shoes, and now when I have a true sadness there are no tears left.

She held the felt side of the slipper against her eyes like a blindfold and stood there, feeling the hot sun on her head and the wind wrapping around her legs, conscious of the height and the valley sweeping down from her feet.

"Listen, just because you can't hear him doesn't mean anything. He could be —"

"Wait a minute." She lowered the slipper and looked down the valley. A sudden wind blew dust into her face and she lifted her hand to shield her eyes.

"I thought I heard something. Charlie! Answer me right this minute."

She waited with the slipper held against her breasts, one hand to her eyes, her whole body motionless, concentrating on her brother. Then she stiffened. She thought again she had heard something — Charlie's long high wail. Charlie could sound sadder than anyone when he cried.

In her anxiety she took the slipper and twisted it again and again as if she were wringing water out. She called, then stopped abruptly and listened. She looked at Joe and he shook his head slowly.

She looked away. A bird rose from the trees below and flew toward the hills in the distance. She waited until she could see it no longer and then slowly, still listening for the call that didn't come, she sank to the ground and sat with her head bent over her knees.

Beside her, Joe scuffed his foot in the dust and sent a cascade of rocks and dirt down the bank. When the sound of it faded, he began to call, "Charlie, hey, Charlie," again and again.

Charlie awoke, but he lay for a moment without opening his eyes. He did not remember where he was, but he had a certain dread of seeing it.

There were great parts of his life that were lost to Charlie, blank spaces that he could never fill in. He would find himself in a strange place and not know how he had got there. Like the time Sara had been hit in the nose with a baseball at the Dairy Queen, and the blood and the sight of Sara kneeling on the ground in helpless pain had frightened him so much that he had turned and run without direction, in a frenzy, dashing headlong up the street, blind to cars and people.

By chance Mr. Weicek had seen him, put him in the car, and driven him home, and Aunt Willie had put him to bed, but later he remembered none of this. He had only awakened in bed and looked at the crumpled bit of ice-cream cone still clenched in his hand and wondered about it.

His whole life had been built on a strict routine, and as long as this routine was kept up, he felt safe and well. The same foods, the same bed, the same furniture in the same place, the same seat on the school bus, the same class procedure were all important to him. But always there could be the unexpected, the dreadful surprise that would topple his carefully constructed life in an instant.

The first thing he became aware of was the twigs pressing into his face, and he put his hand under his cheek. Still he did not open his eyes. Pictures began to drift into his mind; he saw Aunt Willie's cigar box which was filled with old jewelry and buttons and knicknacks, and he found that he could remember every item in that box — the string of white beads without a clasp, the old earrings, the tiny book with souvenir fold-out pictures of New York, the plastic decorations from cakes, the turtle made of sea shells. Every item was so real that he opened his eyes and was surprised to see, instead of the glittering contents of the box, the dull and unfamiliar forest.

He raised his head and immediately felt the aching of his body. Slowly he sat up and looked down at his hands. His fingernails were black with earth, two of them broken below the quick, and he got up slowly and sat on the log behind him and inspected his fingers more closely.

Then he sat up straight. His hands dropped to his lap. His head cocked to the side like a bird listening. Slowly he straightened until he was standing. At his side his fingers twitched at the empty air as if to grasp something. He took a step forward, still with his head to the side. He remained absolutely still.

Then he began to cry out in a hoarse excited voice, again and again, screaming now, because he had just heard someone far away calling his name.

At the top of the hill Sara got slowly to her feet and stood looking down at the forest. She pushed the hair back from her forehead and moistened her lips. The wind dried them as she waited.

Joe started to say something but she reached out one hand and took his arm to stop him. Scarcely daring to believe her ears, she stepped closer to the edge of the bank. Now she heard it unmistakably — the sharp repeated cry — and she knew it was Charlie.

"Charlie!" she shouted with all her might.

She paused and listened, and his cries were louder and she knew he was not far away after all, just down the slope, in the direction of the ravine.

"It's Charlie, it's Charlie!"

A wild joy overtook her and she jumped up and down on the bare earth and she felt that she could crush the whole hill just by jumping if she wanted.

She sat and scooted down the bank, sending earth and pebbles in a cascade before her. She landed on the soft ground, ran a few steps, lost her balance, caught hold of the first tree trunk she could find, and swung around till she stopped.

She let out another whoop of pure joy, turned and ran down the hill in great strides, the puce tennis shoes slapping the ground like rubber paddles, the wind in her face, her hands grabbing one tree trunk after another for support. She felt like a wild creature who had traveled through the forest this way for a lifetime. Nothing could stop her now.

At the edge of the ravine she paused and stood gasping for breath. Her heart was beating so fast it pounded in her ears, and her throat was dry. She leaned against a tree, resting her cheek against the rough bark.

She thought for a minute she was going to faint, a thing she had never done before, not even when she broke her nose. She hadn't even believed people really did faint until this minute when she clung to the tree because her legs were as useless as rubber bands.

There was a ringing in her ears and another sound, a wailing siren-like cry that was painfully familiar.

"Charlie?"

Charlie's crying, like the sound of a cricket, seemed everywhere and nowhere.

She walked along the edge of the ravine, circling the large boulders and trees. Then she looked down into the ravine where the shadows lay, and she felt as if something had turned over inside her because she saw Charlie.

He was standing in his torn pajamas, face turned upward, hands raised, shouting with all his might. His eyes were shut tight. His face was streaked with dirt and tears. His pajama jacket hung in shreds about his scratched chest.

He opened his eyes and as he saw Sara a strange expression came over his face, an expression of wonder and joy and disbelief, and Sara knew that if she lived to be a hundred no one would ever look at her quite that way again.

She paused, looked down at him, and then, sliding on the seat of her pants, went down the bank and took him in her arms.

"Oh, Charlie."

His arms gripped her like steel.

"Oh, Charlie."

She could feel his fingers digging into her back as he clutched her shirt. "It's all right now, Charlie, I'm here and we're going home." His face was buried in her shirt and she patted his head, said again, "It's all right now. Everything's fine."

She held him against her for a moment and now the hot tears were in her eyes and on her cheeks and she didn't even notice.

"I know how you feel," she said. "I know. One time when I had the measles and my fever was real high, I got lost on my way back from the bathroom, right in our house, and it was a terrible feeling, terrible, because I wanted to get back to my bed and I couldn't find it, and finally Aunt Willie heard me and came and you know where I was? In the kitchen. In our kitchen and I couldn't have been more lost if I'd been out in the middle of the wilderness."

She patted the back of his head again and said, "Look, I even brought your bedroom slipper. Isn't that service, huh?"

She tried to show it to him, but he was still clutching her, and she held him against her, patting him. After a moment she said again, "Look, here's your slipper. Let's put it on." She knelt, put his foot into the shoe, and said, "Now, isn't that better?"

He nodded slowly, his chest still heaving with unspent sobs.

"Can you walk home?"

He nodded. She took her shirttail and wiped his tears and smiled at him. "Come on, we'll find a way out of here and go home."

"Hey, over this way," Joe called from the bank of the ravine. Sara had forgotten about him in the excitement of finding Charlie, and she looked up at him for a moment.

"Over this way, around the big tree," Joe called. "That's probably how he got in. The rest of the ravine is a mass of brier bushes."

She put one arm around Charlie and led him around the tree. "Everybody in town's looking for you, you know that?" she said. "Everybody. The police came and all the neighbors are out — there must be a hundred people looking for you. You were on the radio. It's like you were the President of the United States or something. Everybody was saying, 'Where's Charlie?' and 'We got to find Charlie.'"

Suddenly Charlie stopped and held up his hand and Sara looked down. "What is it?"

He pointed to the silent watch.

She smiled. "Charlie, you are something, you know that? Here we are racing down the hill to tell everyone in great triumph that you are found, *found*, and we have to stop and wind your watch first."

She looked at the watch, saw that the stem was missing, and shook her head. "It's broken, Charlie, see, the stem's gone. It's broken."

He held it out again.

"It's *broken*, Charlie. We'll have to take it to the jeweler and have it fixed."

He continued to hold out his arm.

"Hey, Charlie, you want to wear my watch till you get yours fixed?" Joe asked. He slid down the bank and put his watch on Charlie's arm. "There."

Charlie bent his face close and listened.

"Now can we go home?" Sara asked, jamming her hands into her back pockets.

Charlie nodded.

They walked through the woods for a long time, Joe in the lead, picking the best path, with Charlie and Sara following. From time to time Sara turned and hugged Charlie and he smelled of trees and dark earth and tears and she said, "Everybody's going to be so glad to see you it's going to be just like New Year's Eve."

Sara could not understand why she suddenly felt so good. It was a puzzle. The day before she had been miserable. She had wanted to fly away from everything, like the swans to a new lake, and now she didn't want that any more.

Down the hill Mr. Rhodes, one of the searchers, was coming toward them and Joe called out, "Mr. Rhodes, Sara found him!"

"Is he all right?" Mr. Rhodes called back.

"Fine, he's fine."

"Sara found him and he's all right. He's all right." The phrase passed down the hill from Dusty Rhodes, who painted cars at the garage, to Mr. Aker to someone Sara couldn't recognize.

Then all the searchers were joining them, reaching out to pat Charlie and to say to Sara, "Oh, your aunt is going to be so happy," or "Where *was* he?" or "Well, now we can all sleep in peace tonight."

They came through the woods in a big noisy group and out into the late sunlight in the old pasture, Sara and Charlie in the middle, surrounded by all the searchers.

Suddenly Sara sensed a movement above her. She looked up and then grabbed Charlie's arm.

The swans were directly overhead, flying with outstretched necks, their long wings beating the air, an awkward blind sort of flight. They were so low that she thought they might hit the trees, but at the last moment they pulled up and skimmed the air just above the treetops.

"Look, Charlie, look. Those are the swans. Remember? They're going home."

He looked blankly at the sky, unable to associate the heavy awkward birds with the graceful swans he had seen on the water. He squinted at the sky, then looked at Sara, puzzled.

"Charlie, those are the swans. Remember? At the lake?" she said, looking right at him. "They're going home now. Don't you remember? They were —"

"Hey, there's your aunt, Charlie. There's Aunt Willie coming."

Sara was still pulling at Charlie's arm, directing his attention to the sky. It seemed urgent somehow that Charlie see the swans once again. She said, "Charlie, those are —"

He looked instead across the field and he broke away from Sara and started running. She took two steps after him and then stopped. Aunt Willie in her bright green dress seemed to shine like a beacon, and he hurried toward her, an awkward figure in torn blue pajamas, shuffling through the high grass.

There was a joyous yell that was so shrill Sara thought it had come from the swans, but then she knew that it had come from Charlie, for the swans were mute.

"Here he is, Willie," Mrs. Aker called, running behind Charlie to have some part in the reunion.

Aunt Willie was coming as fast as she could on her bad legs. "I never thought to see him again," she was telling everyone and no one. "I thought he was up in that mine. I tell you, I never thought to see him again. Charlie, come here to your Aunt Willie."

Charlie ran like a ball rolling downhill, bouncing with the slope of the land.

"I tell you this has been the blackest day of my life" — Aunt Willie was gasping — "and I include every day I have been on earth. Charlie, my Charlie, let me look at you. Oh, you are a sight."

He fell into Aunt Willie's arms. Over his head Aunt Willie said through her tears to Mrs. Aker, "May you never lose your Bobby, that's all I got to say. May you never lose your Bobby, may none of you ever lose anybody in the woods or in the mine or anywhere."

Sara stood in the pasture by the old gray shack and watched the swans disappear over the hill, and then she watched Charlie and Aunt Willie disappear in the crowd of people, and she felt good and loose and she thought that if she started walking down the hill at that moment, she would walk with the light movements of a puppet and never touch the ground at all.

She thought she would sit down for a moment now that everyone was gone, but when she looked around she saw Joe Melby still standing behind her. "I thought you went with the others."

"Nope."

"It's been a very strange day for me." She looked at the horizon where the swans had disappeared.

"It's been one of my stranger days too."

"Well, I'd better go home."

Joe walked a few steps with her, cleared his throat, and then said, "Do you want to go to Bennie Hoffman's party with me?"

She thought she hadn't heard him right for a moment, or if she had, that it was a mistake, like the boy who shouted, "Hey, beautiful," at Rosey Camdon.

"What?"

"I asked if you wanted to go with me to the party."

"I wasn't invited." She made herself think of the swans. By this time they could probably see the lake at the university and were about to settle down on the water with a great beating of wings and ruffling of feathers. She could almost see the long perfect glide that would bring them to the water.

"I'm inviting you. Bennie said I could bring somebody if I wanted to. He begged me to bring someone, as a matter of fact. He and Sammy and John and Pete have formed this musical group and they're going to make everybody listen to them."

"Well, I don't know."

"Why not? Other than the fact that you're going to have to listen to some terrible guitar playing. Bennie Hoffman has had about one and a half lessons."

"Well . . ."

"It's not any big deal, just sitting in Bennie Hoffman's back yard and watching him louse up with a two-hundred-dollar guitar and amplifier."

"I guess I could go."

"I'll walk over and pick you up in half an hour. It won't matter if we're late. The last fifty songs will sound about the same as the first fifty."

"I'll be ready."

When Sara came up the walk Wanda was standing on the porch. "What is going on around here, will you tell me that? Where is Charlie?"

"We found him. He's with Aunt Willie, wherever that is."

"Do you know how I heard he was lost? I heard it on the car radio when I was coming home. How do you think that made me feel — to hear from some disc jockey that my own brother was missing? I could hardly get here because there are a hundred cars full of people jamming the street down there."

"Well, he's fine."

"So Mr. Aker told me, only I would like to see him and find out what happened."

"He got up during the night sometime — this is what I think happened — to go see the swans and ended up in a ravine crying his heart out."

Wanda stepped off the porch and looked across the street, leaning to see around the foliage by the fence. She said, "Is that them over there on the Carsons' porch?"

Sara looked and nodded.

"Honestly, Charlie still in his pajamas, and Aunt Willie in her good green dress with a handkerchief tied around her forehead to keep her from sweating, and both of them eating watermelon. That beats all."

"At least he's all right."

Wanda started down the walk, then paused. "You want to come?"

"No, I'm going to a party."

"Whose?"

"Bennie Hoffman's."

"I didn't think you were invited."

"Joe Melby's taking me."

"Joe Melby? Your great and terrible enemy?"

"He is not my enemy, Wanda. He is one of the nicest people I know."

"For three months I've been hearing about the evils of Joe Melby. Joe Melby, the thief; Joe Melby, the fink; Joe Melby, the —"

"A person," Sara said coldly, "can occasionally be mistaken." She turned and went into the living room, saw Boysie sleeping by the door and said, "Boysie, we found Charlie." She bent and rubbed him behind the ears. Then she went into the kitchen, made a sandwich, and was starting into the bedroom when the phone rang.

"Hello," she said, her mouth full of food.

"Hello, I have a long-distance call for Miss Willamina Godfrey," the operator said.

"Oh, she's across the street. If you'll wait a minute I'll go get her."

"Operator, I'll just talk to whoever's there," Sara heard her father say.

She said quickly, "No, I'll go get her. Just wait one minute. It won't take any time. She's right across the street."

"Sara? Is this Sara?"

"Yes, this is me." The strange feeling came over her again. "If you wait a minute I'll go get Aunt Willie."

"Sara, did you find Charlie?"

"Yes, we found him, but I don't mind going to get Aunt Willie. They're over on the Carsons' porch."

"Is Charlie all right?"

"He's fine. He's eating watermelon right now."

"Where was he?"

"Well, he went up into the woods and got lost. We found him in a ravine and he was dirty and tired and hungry but he's all right."

"That's good. I was going to come home tonight if he hadn't been found."

"Oh."

"But since everything's all right, I guess I'll just wait until the weekend."

"Sure."

"So I'll probably see you Saturday, then, if nothing turns up."

"Fine."

"Be sure to tell Willie I called."

"I will."

A picture came into her mind of the laughing, curly-headed man with the broken tooth in the photograph album, and she suddenly saw life as a series of huge, uneven steps, and she saw herself on the steps, standing motionless in her prison shirt, and she had just taken an enormous step up out of the shadows, and she was standing, waiting, and there were other steps in front of her, so that she could go as high as the sky, and she saw Charlie on a flight of small difficult steps, and her father down at the bottom of some steps, just sitting and not trying to go further. She saw everyone she knew on those blinding white steps and for a moment everything was clearer than it had ever been.

"Sara?"

"I'm still here."

"Well, that was all I wanted, just to hear that Charlie was all right."

"He's fine."

"And I'll see you on Saturday if nothing happens."

"Sure."

"Good-by."

She sat for a minute still holding the receiver and then she set it back on the telephone and finished her sandwich. Slowly she slipped off her tennis shoes and looked down at her feet, which were dyed blue. Then she got up quickly and went to get ready for the party.

Thinking and Discussing

What details make the Godfreys seem like a real family in the modern-day world? What do you learn about each family member through the dialogue? When and how do you get to know Charlie?

Why are the watch, the sneakers, and the swans important? What makes them meaningful for certain characters?

What does Sara learn from the events in this novel? How does she change?

Choosing a Creative Response

Identifying Personal Treasures Most people own something they keep only because it comforts them. For Charlie, it is a watch. Make a list of things you treasure, and circle your favorite one. Explain why you treasure this item.

Reporting Charlie's Rescue With a group, plan and act out a television newscast covering the story of Charlie's rescue. Take the parts of the story characters, reporters, and camera operators. Then discuss how the portrayal of this event differs in the newscast and the novel.

Creating Your Own Activity Plan and complete your own activity in response to *The Summer of the Swans*.

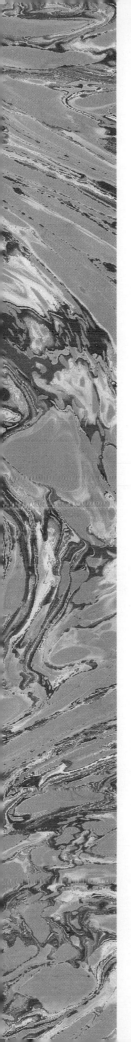

About the Author

Betsy Byars was born in Charlotte, North Carolina, in 1928. She grew up in a family that enjoyed reading, and she herself learned to read when she was only four years old. Byars, however, had no desire to be a writer. She recalls, "Writing seemed boring. You sat in a room all day by yourself and typed." Finding herself home alone with two young children, however, she turned to writing to fill the quiet hours.

Byars's first book was published in 1962, but it was not successful. Still, she pressed on, completing three other stories before writing *The Midnight Fox*, which was published in 1968. Byars says, "This is my favorite book, because it is very personal. A great deal of my own children and their activities went into it, and a great deal of myself. It came closer to what I was trying to do than any of my other books." In 1971 *The Summer of the Swans* won the Newbery Medal as well as several other awards. The idea for this popular story grew out of her actual experiences tutoring children with learning disabilities. Other books for children followed, including *The House of Wings*, *After the Goat Man*, *The Pinballs*, *The Cartoonist*, *The Night Swimmers*, *The Computer Nut*, and *The Not-Just-Anybody Family*. Byars now lives in Clemson, South Carolina, where she spends as much as eight hours a day at a word processor, hammering out her current book.

Taking Flight

The House of Wings by Betsy Byars (Viking, 1972)
Sammy doesn't understand why his eccentric grand-father seems to love only wild animals. It takes a blind and injured crane to teach him about caring.

The Midnight Fox by Betsy Byars (Viking, 1968)
The prospect of spending the summer on a farm is not pleasant for Tommy, who is afraid of animals. But one day he sees a beautiful black fox, and soon his whole life centers around the fox and her cub.

Number the Stars by Lois Lowry (Houghton, 1989)
Annemarie Johansen and her family must endure the hated German occupation of Denmark. When the Nazis begin arresting and deporting Jews, the Johansens try to save their friends the Rosens. Their courage reflects the heroism of the Danish Resistance, which managed to smuggle nearly seven thousand people to safety in Sweden.

Jellybean by Tessa Duder (Viking, 1986)
Geraldine feels invisible in her mother's world of musicians and concert rehearsals until a new friend helps her make a secret ambition come true.

Cassie Binegar by Patricia MacLachlan (Harper, 1982)
Cassie is upset when she moves to a new home by the sea. Embarrassed by her large, noisy family, she decides to find a private space of her own.

DISCOVERING

ANCIENT
EGYPT

The pyramids at Giza

HELP WANTED
Archaeological Dig in Egypt

Discover tombs of the Pharaohs. Break open massive doors of stone. Enter burial chambers and catalogue treasures. Bring the history of ancient Egypt to life.

Discoveries

From *A Message of Ancient Days*,
a social studies textbook
    The Gift of the Nile   402
    Life in Ancient Egypt   409

Seeing the Unseen
from *Tales Mummies Tell*
by Patricia Lauber   418

The Tomb of Tut-ankh-Amen
from *Lost Worlds: The Romance of Archaeology*
by Anne Terry White   426

From *A Message of Ancient Days,* a social studies textbook

The Gift of the Nile

What did the ancient Egyptians accomplish because of the "gifts of the Nile"?

Key Terms

- cataract
- delta
- papyrus
- dynasty
- pharaoh

➤ *In this scene at Aswan in south Egypt, the fertile riverbank contrasts sharply with the barren desert.*

Grain was scarce, and fruit was dried up. People robbed their neighbors. Babies were crying, and old men were sad as they sat on the ground with their legs bent and their arms folded.

So begins an ancient legend about the Nile River. The Egyptians depended on the flooding of the Nile to water their fields. During years of "high Niles," crops grew well and people had plenty to eat. Years of "low Niles" provided barren fields.

The legend tells of a time of low Niles, when Egypt had seven years of famine. This time fell during the reign of King Zoser, who ruled in the 2600's B.C. The king watched the crops withering, and he saw his people starving. He turned to his chief advisor, Imhotep, for help. The answer, said Imhotep, was to learn the name of the god of the Nile so they could pray to him. Later, he told the king that the Nile slept in two caverns below a temple near Egypt's southern border. When it was time, the ram-god Khnum (kə **nōōm´**) opened the floodgates, and the Nile rushed toward Egypt. That night Zoser dreamed that Khnum spoke to him: "I am Khnum. I know the Nile. When it covers the fields, it gives them life. Now the Nile will pour over the land without stopping. Plants will grow, bowing down with fruit. The years

of starvation will be over."

When the king awoke, he told the people that they must honor Khnum by giving a portion of each year's harvest to his temple. The high Niles returned, and the seven years of hunger ended.

The Geography of the Nile

▼ *Some have compared the shape of Egypt with that of a lotus flower. Can you see the flower's blossom and stem?*

Egypt is on the northeastern coast of Africa. Look at the map and locate Egypt on the globe in the inset. Now find the Nile River on the large map.

As the ancient legend shows, the Nile is Egypt's lifeline. Without it, most of the land would be desert. It is the longest river in the world, traveling over 4,000 miles from its source in the lakes and marshes of central Africa to its outlet in the Mediterranean Sea.

At six places along the Nile's winding course, stone cliffs and boulders force its waters through narrow channels. The water rushes through, forming waterfalls and rapids called **cataracts**. The first cataract marked the southern boundary of ancient Egypt. Find it on the map.

From the first cataract, the Nile flows north for about 600 miles. For most of this journey, it flows as a single

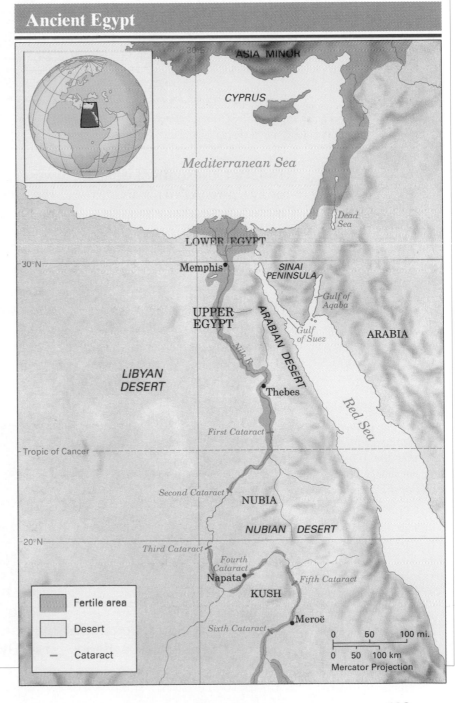

Ancient Egypt

ASIA MINOR
CYPRUS
Mediterranean Sea
Dead Sea
LOWER EGYPT
Memphis
SINAI PENINSULA
Gulf of Aqaba
UPPER EGYPT
ARABIAN DESERT
Gulf of Suez
ARABIA
Nile R.
LIBYAN DESERT
Thebes
Red Sea
First Cataract
Tropic of Cancer
Second Cataract
NUBIA
NUBIAN DESERT
Third Cataract
Fourth Cataract
Napata
Fifth Cataract
KUSH
Meroë
Sixth Cataract

Fertile area
Desert
— Cataract

0   50   100 mi.
0   50 100 km
Mercator Projection

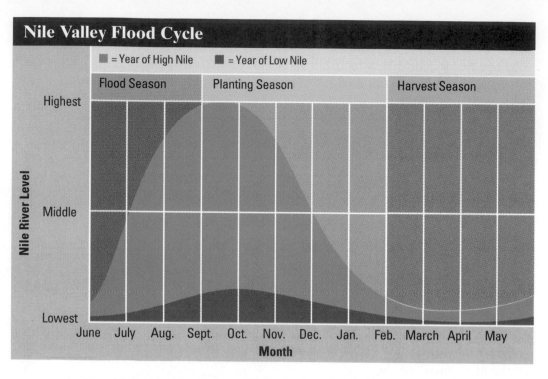

Nile Valley Flood Cycle

■ = Year of High Nile ■ = Year of Low Nile

	Flood Season	Planting Season	Harvest Season

Nile River Level: Highest / Middle / Lowest

Month: June · July · Aug. · Sept. · Oct. · Nov. · Dec. · Jan. · Feb. · March · April · May

▲ *Which months made up each of Egypt's three seasons? How did the years of high Niles differ from the years of low Niles? What might you be doing now if you were a farmer in ancient Egypt?*

➤ *The Egyptians used stone nilometers like this one to measure the yearly flood level of the Nile.*

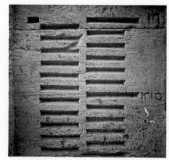

river. But just south of what is today Cairo (**kī´rō**) it divides into many smaller channels and streams. This triangle of marshy wetlands is called the **delta**.

A Dry Climate

From the air much of the Nile looks like a brown snake wriggling north across a vast desert. Its narrow banks are green with crops and palms. Abruptly they turn into desert — red stone and hot sands. The people who lived there 4,000 years ago called their fertile, dark-soiled valley the Black Land. The desert was the Red Land.

Egypt gets almost no rain. The deserts on the east and the

west are parts of the Sahara, the great desert that covers much of North Africa. Desert on two sides, mountains on the south, and the Mediterranean on the north — these natural barriers isolated ancient Egypt and protected it from invaders.

A Seasonal Cycle

In this desert land, the Egyptians depended on the Nile for water and for life. The amount of water the Nile carried on its journey to the Mediterranean varied from season to season. When heavy rains fell in central Africa and snows began to melt high in the mountains of east Africa, the water level of the river rose. By the time the river

the river, dividing the year into three seasons. During the season of flooding, from June through September, the Nile overflowed its banks and covered the fields. When the Nile returned to its normal level, from December to February, the farmers planted their crops. From March until June, with the river at its lowest level, the farmers harvested their crops. This cycle of flooding, planting, and harvesting gave a pattern to Egyptian life.

The River's Gifts

About 2,500 years ago Herodotus (hĭ rŏd´ə təs), a Greek visitor to ancient Egypt, called this land the "gift of the Nile." The Egyptians sang special hymns of praise to the river. The example below was written down in the New Kingdom.

◄ Notice the fine carving and bright coloring in this small wooden statue of a woman carrying an offering.

*H*ail to thee O Nile that issues from the earth and comes to keep Egypt alive! . . . He that waters the meadows which Ra created.
Hymn to the Nile, from papyrus documents, 1350–1100 B.C.

reached Egypt, it overflowed its banks. Egypt's farmers depended on the annual flooding to water their crops.

The floods of Egypt were predictable. They came at about the same time each year. Farmers knew when the Nile would rise, and they planned ahead for that time. In fact, the Egyptians measured time by

To take advantage of the annual flooding of the Nile, the people built irrigation channels to carry water into the fields. They also built dams to hold back the water for use during dry seasons. In some

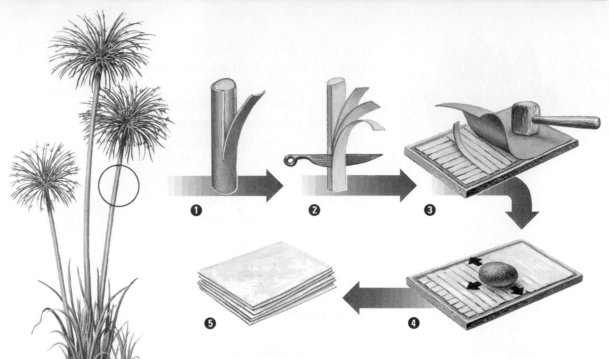

Paper-makers cut the stem of the papyrus and removed the inner pith. This clockwise series of images shows how they cut the pith into strips, put one layer across another, beat the layers into a single sheet, and polished each sheet with a stone and trimmed the edges.

■ Explain how water, mud, plants, and animals were all "gifts of the Nile" to the Egyptians.

ways this was the same thing done by the ancient Sumerians, the people of an older civilization. But the floods were predictable in Egypt, and farming was easier. The Egyptians needed less cooperation than the Sumerians to get the work done. As a result, they did not develop cities until much later.

Besides water, another gift of the Nile was the thick, black mud left behind in the annual flooding. This mud enriched the soil and made the farmland extremely productive.

The Nile gave other gifts as well. Ducks, geese, and other edible water birds made their homes in the marshes of the delta. **Papyrus** (pə pī´rəs), a long, thin reed, grew wild along the riverbanks. The Egyptians harvested the papyrus and made it into baskets, boats, sandals, and a lightweight writing material. Our word *paper* comes from the word *papyrus*.

The Nile also served as a highway. Boats going north traveled swiftly downstream with the current. Boats going south used sails to travel upstream.

The Egyptians used the gifts of the Nile wisely. Here in this land of contrasts—fertile riverbanks and barren deserts, Black Land and Red Land—they built a remarkable civilization. ■

The Union of Two Lands

Ancient Egypt had two parts, Upper Egypt and Lower Egypt. Upper Egypt, the south part, stretched for over 500 miles from Aswan north to the beginning of the Nile Delta.

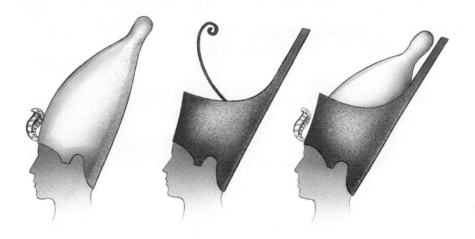

The white crown of Upper Egypt was placed inside the red crown of the king of Lower Egypt, forming the double red and white crown that symbolized the union of the two lands.

Lower Egypt, the north part, was the area of the Nile Delta. Lower Egypt was only 100 miles long but many times wider than Upper Egypt.

Red and White Crowns

By about 3300 B.C., both Upper Egypt and Lower Egypt had kings. The king of Upper Egypt wore a tall, white pear-shaped crown. The king of Lower Egypt wore a short, boxy red crown with a tall spike at the back and a curlicue at the front.

Much of our knowledge of Egypt in this prehistoric time is mixed with legend. One famous legend tells about Menes (mē´nēz), a king of Upper Egypt. Around 3100 B.C., Menes defeated the king of Lower Egypt, united the two lands, and named himself King of Upper and Lower Egypt.

The legend goes on to tell how Menes designed a new crown to celebrate his victory. This double crown, which combined those of Upper and Lower Egypt, stood for the union of the two lands. Menes and his family went on to form the first Egyptian dynasty. A **dynasty** is a series of rulers from the same family. After Menes died, his son became king, and later his grandson.

During its almost 4,000-year history, 30 different dynasties ruled Egypt.

Menes chose the city of Memphis as his capital. Find Memphis on the map on page 403. How do you think the location of Memphis helped Menes keep firm control of both parts of his newly united kingdom?

Over 2,000 Years of History

History for ancient Egypt began around 3000 B.C., with the invention of hieroglyphic writing. Within the history of ancient Egypt, historians have

The slate palette of Narmer is from around 2950 B.C. King Narmer, who is wearing the white crown, is striking a kneeling prisoner.

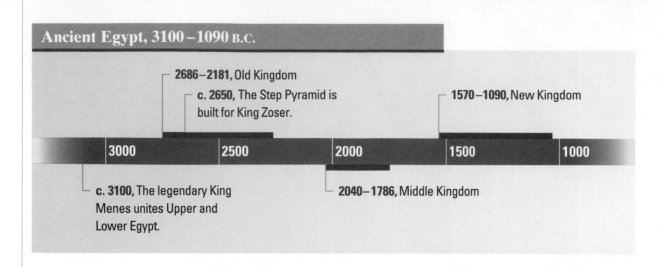

Ancient Egypt, 3100–1090 B.C.

2686–2181, Old Kingdom

c. 2650, The Step Pyramid is built for King Zoser.

1570–1090, New Kingdom

3000 — 2500 — 2000 — 1500 — 1000

c. 3100, The legendary King Menes unites Upper and Lower Egypt.

2040–1786, Middle Kingdom

identified three periods when many important events took place.

In the Old Kingdom, from 2686 to 2181 B.C., the Egyptians built the great pyramids. In the Middle Kingdom, from 2040 to 1786 B.C., Egypt became stronger, and the Egyptians achieved a great deal in literature, art, and architecture. In the New Kingdom, from 1570 to 1090 B.C., Egypt became a world power by conquering other nations and building a great empire. Sometime in the New Kingdom period, the Egyptian people began to call their kings **pharaoh**. In the two earlier periods the word pharaoh, meaning "great house," had been the name for the king's palace. In the New Kingdom,

pharaoh came to mean the king who lived in the palace.

In the years between these periods, weak kings ruled, or foreigners gained control of Egypt. These in-between periods were times of great confusion.

In the 1,000 years before the Old Kingdom began, the Egyptian people accomplished many things. They learned to irrigate their fields, and they raised both grain and livestock. They formed governments, with kings as rulers. They invented hieroglyphic writing. Finally, they created the belief systems and customs that made Egyptian life unique. These early achievements formed the basis of ancient Egyptian society. ■

■ *What were some important early accomplishments of the Egyptians?*

R E V I E W

1. What did the ancient Egyptians accomplish because of the "gifts of the Nile"?
2. Explain how the geography of Egypt affected its early development as a civilization.
3. The ancient Egyptians valued a quiet, orderly life. They did not want things to change. How might these preferences help to explain why the story of Menes was important to them?

Life in Ancient Egypt

The photo below may surprise you if you have seen pictures of pyramids in Egypt. This pyramid is different. It is called the Step Pyramid, and the name fits. To find out more about this unusual structure, we will revisit King Zoser.

Sometime in the middle of the 2600's B.C., King Zoser began to plan for his burial. He called on Imhotep, his chief advisor and also a fine architect, to design his tomb. Until then, a royal tomb was a flat-topped, mud-brick structure built over a burial chamber that lay deep under the ground. Imhotep designed a grander, more permanent tomb for the king, and he did not build it of mud brick, but of stone.

No one knows whether Imhotep planned the design in advance or thought of it as the work went along. At any rate, his builders put one flat-topped structure on top of another. They made each level a few feet smaller than the one below it.

When Imhotep's pyramid was finished, a chamber for the king's body lay about 80 feet under the ground. A mile-long, 30-foot-high stone wall surrounded the tomb. The wall had 14 doors, only one of which actually opened.

Later architects and engineers built on Imhotep's ideas to design and construct

Key Terms

- afterlife
- embalm
- mummy
- hieroglyphics

◄ *Zoser's Step Pyramid, the first large-scale stone structure in the world, was built in the mid-2600's B.C. on a plateau overlooking the ancient city of Memphis.*

409

pyramids even grander than the Step Pyramid. King Zoser had launched an age of pyramid building that would last for more than 1,000 years.

Pyramid building reached its peak during the Old Kingdom. More than 80 pyramids survive as reminders of that distant age.

The Egyptian Religion

King Zoser's pyramid was more than just a new idea in architecture. It reflected the religious beliefs of the Egyptian people. Early Egyptian literature pictured the king climbing to heaven on a stairway formed by the rays of the sun. People may have thought of that stairway when they looked at the Step Pyramid. The shape of the later pyramids might also have seemed like the slope of the sun's rays. In that way, the later pyramids, too, might have pictured a king's passage to heaven.

Preparing for the Afterlife

The Egyptians believed in an **afterlife,** a life that would continue after death. This belief was so strong and important to the people that great preparation was made for death and burial. Pyramid building was just one part of it.

Another was the preparation of the body itself. Before an Egyptian's body was placed in a pyramid or other tomb, it had to be prepared for the afterlife.

The Egyptians believed that without a body, a person's spirit couldn't eat, drink, dance, or enjoy the other pleasures that the afterlife would offer. If the body decayed, the spirit would die too. So the Egyptians developed a process called **embalming**, treating the

➤ *The sky god Horus, depicted with the head of a hawk, was closely connected with the king. In fact, the Egyptians saw their king as Horus on earth. Here Horus is shown standing in his sun boat. With him is an ibis, a sacred bird of ancient Egypt.*

body to protect it from decay. This process preserved the body as a **mummy.**

Once the mummy had been prepared, it was placed into a coffin made of wood or stone. The coffin was left in the tomb along with items for use in the afterlife. These items ranged from food and drink to gold and jewelry. They included many objects that were useful in daily life, such as clothes, games, and hand mirrors. Some tombs even held mummies of cats or baboons. Some contained small carved statues of servants. Some tomb walls were painted with scenes from the everyday life of the dead person.

Most of these objects and paintings were found in the tombs of royal or wealthy families. But even many of the less privileged were buried with some favorite possessions.

According to Egyptian belief, the objects and paintings in the tomb would help ensure that the person would continue to enjoy the good things of this life. The Egyptians loved life in this world. Because they believed the afterlife would be much like this life, they wanted to be buried with the things they would need.

After a mummy was placed in its tomb, priests recited prayers or chanted magic spells. They called on the gods to help the person make the trip from this world to the next. These words appear on the tomb of an Old Kingdom ruler named Pepi: "Gates of sky, open for Pepi, Gates of heaven, open for Pepi, Pepi comes to you, make him live!"

The Book of the Dead

Hymns, prayers, and magic spells from the tombs are found in the Egyptian *Book of the Dead*. One part describes a trial in which the soul of a dead person argues its case before a jury of the gods. "In life, I fed the hungry," says the soul. "I respected my parents."

The soul also tells what it did not do. "I never stole." The gods then weigh the heart of the dead person against the feather of truth. The Egyptians believed the heart was the center of intelligence and memory. If the heart was too heavy with sin, they believed, it died a second death from which there was no returning. But the heart that passed the test would go on to a happy afterlife. Such a judgment scene is shown in the picture on page 413.

The Gods of the Egyptians

The religion of ancient Egypt was a form of polytheism, belief in a number of gods. Not surprisingly, many of the Egyptians' gods were connected with death and the afterlife. Osiris (ō sī′ rĭs) was the chief god of the underworld, or home of the dead. One of Osiris's helpers was

▲ *The Egyptians' love for animals can be seen in their portrayal of gods with animal heads, their animal sculptures, and animal mummies like this one of a cat.*

Anubis (ə noo´bĭs), who had the body of a human and the head of a jackal. His job was to prepare the bodies of the dead for the afterlife.

The Egyptians had great gods that they believed created and ruled the world. One of these was Ra (rä) the sun god, who was later joined by another great god, Amon (ä´mən), to become Amon-Ra (ä´mən rä).

Some Egyptian gods, like Anubis, had a human body and the head of an animal.

■ *What religious beliefs account for the pyramids and mummies of ancient Egypt?*

Hathor (hă´thôr´), the goddess of love, had the head of a cow. Horus, the sky god, had the head of a hawk.

Each Egyptian village and city had its own local god. There were also gods of music and dancing, of love and beauty, and of healing and learning. Commoners in Egyptian society built small shrines at home and dedicated them to their favorite gods. Especially popular in households was a dwarflike god named Bes, the god of the family. ■

UNDERSTANDING THE IDEA OF AN AFTERLIFE

To us, the ancient Egyptians sometimes seem more interested in death than life. We marvel at the time, energy, and other resources they put into making pyramids and mummies. Yet we know that their love of life caused them to do these things. They thought an afterlife would be like this one, only better.

In every time and place, people have asked, "Is there life beyond this life?" and if so, "What kind of life is it?" These questions ask about the afterlife — life that continues after death.

A Place of Darkness

The Mesopotamians, the people of another ancient culture, painted a gloomy picture of the afterlife. For them, the world of the dead was under the earth. One of their stories called it a place "where they see no light and live in darkness." Their hero-king Gilgamesh tried but failed to gain a happy afterlife.

A Happy Afterlife

People's ideas about an afterlife are tied to their ideas about God or the gods. In our own twentieth-century

Western society, many people are believers in Judaism, Christianity, or Islam. Followers of these faiths believe in one God. Most of them also believe in a human soul that will never die. They look forward to an afterlife in which they will live with God and with other human souls. Like the Egyptians, many believe in an afterlife that will be happier and better than this life. However, few cultures have placed more importance on the idea of an afterlife than the ancient Egyptians.

A Writing System

The earliest Egyptian writing, called **hieroglyphics** (hī´ər ə glĭf´ĭks), used pictures to stand for objects, ideas, and sounds. The system was not easy to decipher. In fact, linguists and archaeologists studied the symbols for years without success.

Then, in 1799, French soldiers near Rosetta, a village in the Nile Delta, unearthed a black stone slab. On it the same passage was written in three ways: in Greek, in hieroglyphs, and in a cursive form of Egyptian.

For 20 years, scholars tried in vain to decode the hieroglyphic writing on the Rosetta Stone. Then a brilliant Frenchman named Jean Champollion found the key.

Champollion could read Greek. He knew that all three parts said the same thing, praising Ptolemy V for gifts he had given the temples in

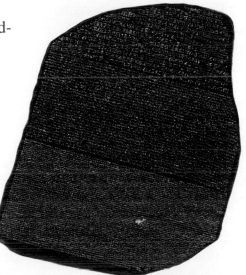

195 B.C. One summer day in 1822, Champollion was comparing the hieroglyphs with the Greek words. He identified

▲ *This picture, painted on papyrus around 1250 B.C., shows the jackal-headed god Anubis weighing the heart of a dead person named Ani against the feather of truth.*

◄ *The Rosetta Stone provided the key that unlocked the code of hieroglyphics.*

413

and compared proper names like *Ptolemy* and *Cleopatra*. He matched sounds from the names with the hieroglyphs that spelled them, as follows:

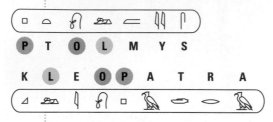

Now at last Champollion had the key he needed. He decoded the Rosetta stone and went on to publish a dictionary of ancient Egyptian.

Fortunately, the Egyptians left us many written texts. Once scholars could decode hieroglyphic writing, they could read laws, songs, tales, spells, jokes, and business contracts. From these texts and others, scholars have learned about Egypt's past.

The hieroglyphic system was complex. It had over 700 signs that a person must memorize to master it. Young peo-ple who wanted to be scribes spent years attending special schools. The school day was long, sometimes lasting from just after sunrise to sunset. Teachers expected their students to pay attention, and punishments could be harsh. One father sent these words of advice to his son, who was learning to be a scribe: "Learn to write, for this will be of greater advantage to you than all the trades. One day at school is useful to you and the work done there will last forever, like mountains."

Few Egyptian students, studying hard and copying the same lines over and over, would have found these words encouraging. However, those who completed the training would be well rewarded. Only a small number of dedicated ancient Egyptians learned to read and write. As experts with special skills, they would have good jobs and respected places in society. ■

■ *In what ways did the decoding of the Rosetta Stone expand our knowledge of ancient Egypt?*

A Social Pyramid

Scribes and farmers, potters and brickmakers — all Egyptians had a place in the social class system of ancient Egypt. A diagram of Egyptian society would look something like a pyramid.

Pharaoh and Priests

At the top of the social pyramid was the pharaoh. The Egyptians believed their pharaohs were gods.

The Egyptian pharaoh was all powerful. He owned all the land and had complete control of the people. All workers, from farmers to artists, served the pharaoh, directly or through royal officials. The members of the royal family were just below the pharaoh on the social pyramid.

The priests served the gods to which the temples were dedicated. Some people who worked at other occupations, such as law or medicine, also served in the temple.

Officials and Scribes

The pharaoh relied on government officials, who were also in the upper level of society. He counted on them to assist him in governing the country. Many were tax collectors. Some were responsible for the royal storehouses.

The scribes, another group of officials, held a privileged position. They were Egypt's writers and record keepers. Scribes might work at the pharaoh's palace, travel with high officials, or serve as public letter writers.

Skilled Workers and Farmers

Below scribes on the social pyramid were the artisans and other skilled workers. These included carpenters, painters, jewelers, brickmakers, and stonemasons. Many of these skilled workers provided goods for the pharaoh and his family.

For example, they might create furniture, make jewelry, weave fine cloth, and paint pictures inside the royal tombs.

Farmers formed the large base of the Egyptian social pyramid. Most people were farmers, and they spent their lives growing and marketing farm products. In this way, they supported all the other levels of Egyptian society.

But the farmers did not provide food only. During the flood season, they could not work in the fields. They were required to work on royal building projects. These included the irrigation works, the pyramids, and later the temples. The great stone monuments they helped to build have outlasted both pharaohs and commoners. ■

▲ *This fine painted woodcarving of a plowing scene was found in a Middle Kingdom tomb of around 2000 B.C. Why do you think it was put in the tomb? Where would these farmers have been on the social pyramid?*

■ *What were the occupations of people at the top, middle, and bottom of the Egyptian social pyramid?*

REVIEW

1. Describe the religious ideas and the social structure of the ancient Egyptians.
2. How did the annual flooding help the Egyptian pharaohs to complete their building projects?
3. What was the importance of farming to the economy of ancient Egypt?
4. Why do you think scribes hold privileged positions in ancient Egyptian society? What can be learned today from ancient texts?

Responding to "A Message of Ancient Days"

Thinking and Discussing

What are the many "gifts of the Nile" discussed in the text? Why is the Nile important to the people of Egypt?

How did the Nile's cycle of flooding give a pattern to life in ancient Egypt? What effect did the flooding cycle have on the building of pyramids and temples?

How did ancient Egyptian religious beliefs lead to the practices of mummification, tomb painting, and the stocking of tombs with the dead person's possessions?

Applying Historical Concepts

Drawing a Social Pyramid With a group of classmates, make a pyramid diagram that illustrates the social structure of ancient Egypt. Draw the pyramid and divide it into the various levels from top to bottom. For each level, draw pictures of what those people did as they went about their lives.

Being a Historian Historians often ask questions that begin with "What if . . ." in order to help themselves better understand historical events. Be a historian, and answer any of the following questions in a presentation to your classmates: What if the ancient Egyptians did not develop a writing system? What if Imhotep did not serve as Zoser's architect? What if ancient Egypt did not have a system of government?

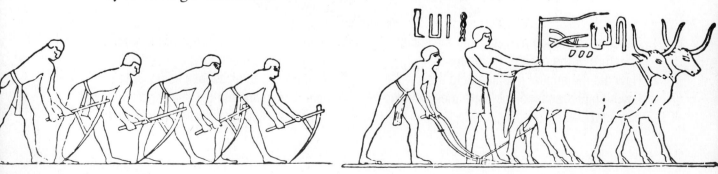

Advice to Schoolboys

In ancient Egypt, students learned to read and write by copying texts with messages like this one:

I place you at school along with the children of notables, to educate you and to have you trained for this enhancing calling.

Behold, I relate to you how it fares with the scribe when he is told: "Wake up and at your place! The books lie already before your comrades! Place your hand on your clothes and look to your sandals!"

When you get your daily task, be not idle and read diligently from the book. When you reckon in silence, let no word be heard.

Write with your hand and read with your mouth. Ask counsel of them who are clever. Be not slack, and spend not a day in idleness, or woe betide your limbs! Enter into the methods of your teacher and hear his instructions. Behold, I am with you every day!

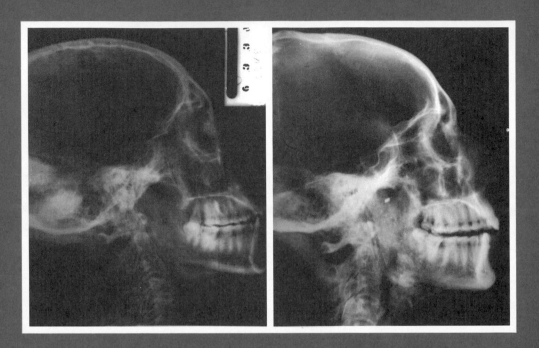

X-rays such as these, which show similarities in the skulls of Amenhotep II and his son Thutmosis IV, are one of the few means of identifying ancient Egyptian family relationships.

Seeing the
Unseen

from *Tales Mummies Tell* by Patricia Lauber

A single mummy can tell a lot about the life, health, and death of one person. The many, many mummies of ancient Egypt can tell about whole classes of people. What diseases did the Egyptians suffer from? How did diet affect their health? How long did they live? The answers to those and many other questions are in the mummies.

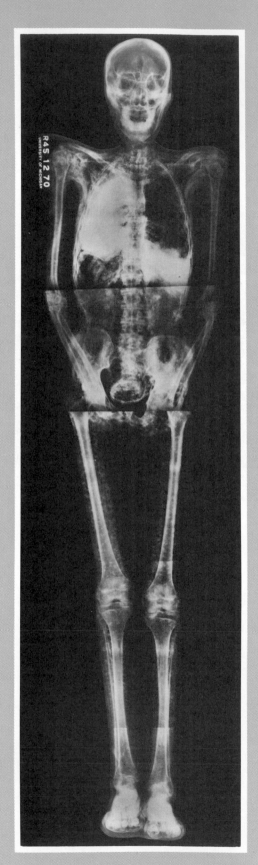

This mummy was once believed to be that of Thutmosis I, who died at the age of fifty after a very successful reign; however, x-rays of the mummy revealed a teen-ager's long leg bones. Was Thutmosis I a child-king? Did Thutmosis have a disease that affected his legs? Is this really the mummy of Thutmosis? Scientists have yet to solve this mystery.

Getting at the answers was a problem for many years. One way to study mummies is to unwrap them and do an autopsy,[1] but this destroys the mummies. Many mummies are too precious to destroy. Another way is to x-ray them. In the past this meant moving the mummies to hospitals or other places where the x-ray machines were. Many mummies were so fragile that moving them might have damaged them. Finally the development of a portable x-ray machine solved the problem. Now the machine can be taken to the mummies.

The x-ray pictures provide views of mummies never unwrapped — of pharaohs, queens, nobles, priests. The shape of the face appears, as do magic charms of gold and semiprecious stones within the wrappings. The pictures show that some mummies have been wrongly identified, that they cannot be the person they were thought to be. They have helped to clarify family relationships. They have produced some surprises and puzzles. Most of all, they have yielded important information about health in ancient Egypt. In the bones medical scientists can read age at death, signs of disease, fractures that healed.

X-rays show that the Egyptians suffered from many diseases known in the modern world — tuberculosis, polio, arthritis, gallstones, hardening of the arteries. They also show that the most serious health problems arose from the environment, from the Nile and the desert.

The Nile was the lifeblood of Egypt. Its yearly floods dropped soil that enriched the river valley. Its waters, drawn off in canals, irrigated fields and pastures. From the fields came barley and wheat, fruits, vegetables, herbs. The cattle grazing the pastures supplied milk and eventually became meat on the tables of the rich.

---

[1] **autopsy** (ô′tŏp′sē): a medical examination of a dead human body, especially to determine the cause of death.

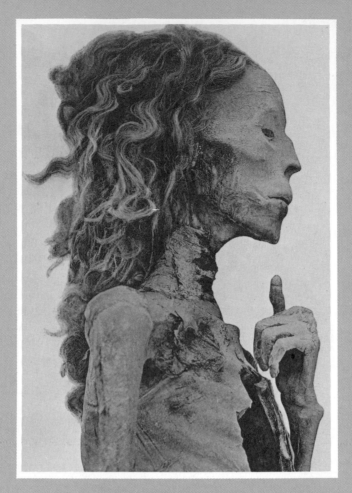

By studying x-rays and hair samples, scientists have concluded that the mummy above, known as the Elder Lady, is probably the mummy of Queen Tiye, Tut-ankh-Amen's grandmother. Small marks on the face of the mummy of Rameses V, pictured below, led scientists to believe that he may have contracted and died of smallpox.

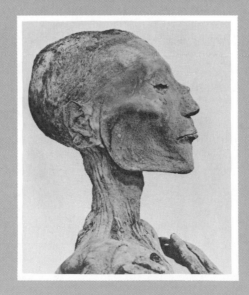

There were wild fowl to trap in the marshes of the Nile and fish from the river itself. The many tomb paintings of banquets and lists of grave foods make clear that the Egyptians enjoyed food and drink and that they ate well.

But the life-giving river was also a source of disease. It was a source of waterborne parasites — small animals that invade another creature, using its body as a place to live and feed but doing nothing that benefits the host. Most of the parasites that infected the ancient Egyptians were worms with complicated life cycles. But in general they spent part of their lives in human hosts and part in fresh water — canals, wet fields, marshes. Some kinds invaded their hosts through the skin, some were swallowed in drinking water. All caused misery, such as sores, rashes, and a growing weakness over a number of years. The remains of parasites and their eggs appear in x-rays of many mummies. They were a major reason why the life span of the average Egyptian was 35 to 40 years.

At the edge of the Nile Valley was the desert. Its dust storms filled the air with tiny particles of sand. The sand scarred the lungs of the Egyptians, and its effect on their teeth was equally serious.

The chief dental problem among the ancient Egyptians was extreme wear. It showed in the teeth of skeletons and mummies that medical scientists had examined earlier. Now the x-rays of pharaohs, priests, and nobles showed that their teeth too had rapidly worn down. The only possible explanation was sand. Somehow sand from the desert must have got into the food. As the Egyptians chewed, particles of sand ground down their teeth.

How that much sand got into their food was something of a puzzle until 1971. In that year the Manchester Museum in England was having an Egyptian exhibition. Among the displays were a large number of pieces of ancient Egyptian bread. X-rays showed that each piece contained vast quantities of mineral fragments. Some of the minerals were kinds that came from the soil in which the grain

A wooden model of a granary found in a tomb

had grown. Some came from the kind of stones used to grind the grain. But most of the fragments were the pure quartz of desert sand. Dust storms must have added sand to grain when it was being harvested, winnowed, and stored. The sand went into bread along with the flour. Because the Egyptians ate large amounts of bread, they also chewed large amounts of sand.

Sometimes sand may have been added on purpose. A scientist at the Manchester Museum tried making flour with ancient Egyptian grinding stones. After 15 minutes of work, the grain was still whole. But when he did what other ancient peoples are reported to have done and added sand to the grain, he was quickly able to make fine flour.

Sand in their daily bread caused serious tooth problems for peasants and pharaohs alike. It wore down the hard parts of their teeth, the outside enamel and the underlying dentine. In some people new dentine formed. In most, teeth wore down faster than new dentine could form. Then the inside of the tooth was exposed. This is the pulp chamber, which houses the nerves and blood supply for the tooth. Without dentine as a barrier, disease-causing bacteria could invade the tooth's root canals. Painful infections followed and sometimes led to death.

Responding to "Seeing the Unseen"

Thinking and Discussing

What were the main health problems suffered by the ancient Egyptians? Which were caused strictly by their environment?

Applying Historical Concepts

Charting the Help of X-rays Based on the selection, make a chart showing how effective x-rays have been in helping scientists who study ancient Egyptian mummies. Arrange your chart in two columns. In the left column, list the questions that scientists have been able to answer through the use of x-rays. In the right column, list the answers they found and the evidence that x-rays provided.

Giving Modern Medical Advice Imagine you could have given the ancient Egyptians some advice based on what you know about modern medicine and health concerns. What would you tell them? Write your recommendations in the form of a health newsletter.

An Egyptian grinding grain

426

Grave robbers stripped most of the tombs of ancient Egypt, but one royal burial place lay untouched for centuries. Its amazing treasure was unearthed in 1922 by English archaeologist Howard Carter and his partner Lord Carnarvon.

From *Lost Worlds: The Romance of Archaeology* by Anne Terry White

THE TOMB OF TUT-ANKH-AMEN

Now Carnarvon and Carter were not planning to dig at random in the Valley of the Tombs of the Kings. They were on the lookout for a particular tomb, the tomb of the Pharaoh Tut-ankh-Amen, and they believed they had worked out the very location where it lay.

To the eyes of most people their undertaking seemed absurd.

The solid gold death mask placed on Tut-ankh-Amen's mummy is perhaps the most famous treasure from the ancient Pharaoh's tomb. The mask is believed to be a good likeness of Tut-ankh-Amen.

Nearly everybody was convinced that Tut-ankh-Amen's tomb had already been found. But Lord Carnarvon and Mr. Carter were not to be dissuaded, for they believed that the pit-tomb containing the fragments bearing the figures and names of Tut-ankh-Amen and his queen was far too small and insignificant for a king's burial. In their opinion the things had been placed there at some later time and did not indicate that the Pharaoh himself had been buried on the spot. They were convinced that the tomb 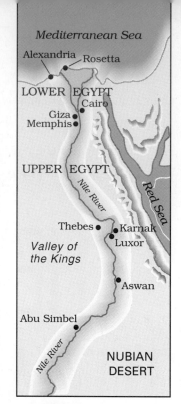 of Tut-ankh-Amen was still to be found, and that the place they had chosen — the center of the Valley — was the best place to look for it. In that vicinity had been unearthed something which they considered very good evidence — two jars containing broken bits of things that had been used at the funeral ceremonies of King Tut-ankh-Amen.

Nevertheless, when in the autumn of 1917 the excavators came out to look over the spot they had chosen and to begin their Valley campaign in earnest, even they thought it was a desperate undertaking. The site was piled high with refuse thrown out by former excavators. They would have to remove all that before they could begin excavating in virgin soil. But they had made up their minds and meant to go through with it; even though it took many seasons, they would go systematically over every inch of the ground.

In the years that followed, they did. They went over every inch, with the exception of a small area covered with the ruins of stone huts that had once sheltered workmen probably employed in building the tomb of Rameses VI. These huts lay very near the tomb of the Pharaoh on a spot which Carter and Carnarvon had not

In this photograph taken in the Valley of the Kings, the entrance to the tomb of Rameses VI is shown at the center. Buried beneath the huts of the workmen who built Rameses' tomb was the entrance to the tomb of Tut-ankh-Amen, discovered fifteen years after this picture was taken.

touched for reasons of courtesy. The tomb of Rameses VI was a popular show-place in the Valley, and digging in the area of the huts would have cut off visitors to the tomb. They let it be, and turned instead to another site which they felt had possibilities.

The new ground proved, however, no better than the old, and now Lord Carnarvon began to wonder whether with so little to show for six seasons' work they were justified in going on. But Carter was firm. So long as a single area of unturned ground remained, he said, they ought to risk it. There was still the area of the huts. He insisted on going back to it. On November first, 1922 he had his diggers back in the old spot.

And now things happened with such suddenness that Carter afterward declared they left him in a dazed condition. Coming to work on the fourth day after the digging on the little area had started, he saw at once that something extraordinary had happened. Things were too quiet; nobody was digging and hardly anybody was talking. He hurried forward, and there before him was a shallow step cut in the rock beneath the very first hut attacked! He could hardly believe his eyes. After all the disappointments of the past six seasons, was it possible that he was actually on the threshold of a great discovery? He gave the command to dig, and the diggers fell to work with a will. By the next afternoon Carter was able to see the upper edges of a stairway on all its four sides, and before very long there stood revealed twelve steps, and at the level of the twelfth the upper part of a sealed and plastered doorway.

Carter's excitement was fast reaching fever pitch. Anything, literally anything, might lie beyond. It needed all his self-control to keep from breaking the doorway down and satisfying his curiosity then and there. But was it fair to see what lay beyond that door alone? Although Lord Carnarvon was in England, was it not his discovery as much as Carter's? To the astonishment of the workmen, the excavator gave orders to fill the stairway in again, and then he sent the following cable off to Carnarvon: "At last have made wonderful discovery in Valley. A magnificent tomb with seals intact. Recovered same for your arrival. Congratulations."

In two weeks' time Lord Carnarvon and his daughter were on the spot. Carter now ordered his men to clear the stairway once more, and there on the lower part of the sealed doorway the explorers beheld what almost took their breath away — the seal of the Pharaoh Tut-ankh-Amen. Now they knew. Beyond this doorway lay either the Pharaoh's secret treasure store or else the very tomb for which they were searching. Yet one thing made them uneasy. They noticed that part of the door was patched up and that in the patched-up part there stood out clearly the seal of the cemetery. It was evident that the door had been partly broken down — by robbers, of course — and then patched up again by cemetery officials. Had the robbers been caught in time? Did at least some of Tut-ankh-Amen's glory yet remain behind that twice-sealed doorway? Or would perhaps only barren walls reward their years of tedious toil?

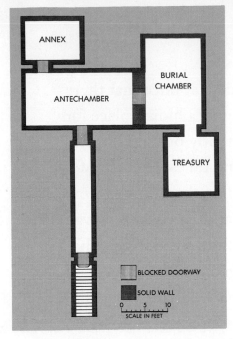

ANNEX

BURIAL CHAMBER

ANTECHAMBER

TREASURY

BLOCKED DOORWAY

SOLID WALL

0   5   10
SCALE IN FEET

With pounding hearts they broke down the door. Beyond lay only another obstacle to their progress — a passage filled with stone. Had the robbers got beyond that? They began slowly to clear away the stone, and on the following day — "the day of days," Carter called it, "and one whose like I can never hope to see again" — they came upon a second sealed doorway, almost exactly like the first and also bearing distinct signs of opening and reclosing.

His hands trembling so that he could scarcely hold a tool, Carter managed to make a tiny hole in the door and to pass a candle through it. At first he could see nothing, but as his eyes grew accustomed to the light, "details of the room slowly emerged from the mist, strange animals, statues, and gold — everywhere the glint of gold."

"Can you see anything?" Carnarvon asked anxiously as Carter stood there dumb with amazement.

"Yes, wonderful things!" was all the explorer could get out.

And no wonder. What he saw was one of the most amazing sights anybody has ever been privileged to see. It seemed as if a whole museumful of objects was in that room. Three gilt couches, their sides carved in the form of monstrous animals, and two statues of a king, facing each other like two sentinels,[1] were the most prominent things in the room, but all around and between were hosts of other things — inlaid caskets, alabaster vases, shrines, beds, chairs, a golden inlaid throne, a heap of white boxes (which they later found were filled with trussed ducks and other food offerings), and a glistening pile of overturned chariots. When Carter and Carnarvon

---

[1]**sentinel** (sĕn′tə nəl): something that serves to guard or give warning of approaching danger.

got their senses together again, they realized all at once that there was no coffin in the room. Was this then merely a hiding place for treasure? They examined the room very intently once again, and now they saw that the two statues stood one on either side of a sealed doorway. Gradually the truth dawned on them. They were but on the threshold of their discovery. What they saw was just an antechamber.[2] Behind the guarded door there would be other rooms, perhaps a whole series of them, and in one of them, beyond any shadow of doubt, they would find the Pharaoh lying.

But as they thought the thing over, the explorers were by no means certain that their first wild expectations would actually come to pass. Perhaps that sealed doorway, like the two before it, had also been re-opened. In that case there was no telling what lay behind it.

---

[2]**antechamber** (ăn′tē chām′bər): a waiting room at the entrance to a larger and more important room.

On the following day they took down the door through which they had been peeping, and just as soon as the electric connections had been made and they could see things clearly, they rushed over to the doubtful door between the royal sentinels. From a distance it had looked untouched, but when they examined it more closely, they saw that here again the robbers had been before them; near the bottom was distinct evidence that a small hole had been made and filled up and re-sealed. The robbers had indeed been stopped, but not before they had got into the inner chamber.

It took almost as much self-command not to break down that door and see how much damage the robbers had done as to have filled in the staircase after it had once been cleared. But Carter and Carnarvon were not treasure-seekers; they were archaeologists, and they would not take the chance of injuring the objects within the antechamber just to satisfy their curiosity. For the moment they let that go and turned their attention to the things already before them.

There was enough there to leave them altogether bewildered. But while they were yet going crazily from one object to another and calling excitedly to each other, they stumbled upon yet another discovery. In the wall, hidden behind one of the monstrous couches, was a small, irregular hole, unquestionably made by the plunderers and never re-sealed. They dragged their powerful electric light to the hole and looked in. Another chamber, smaller than

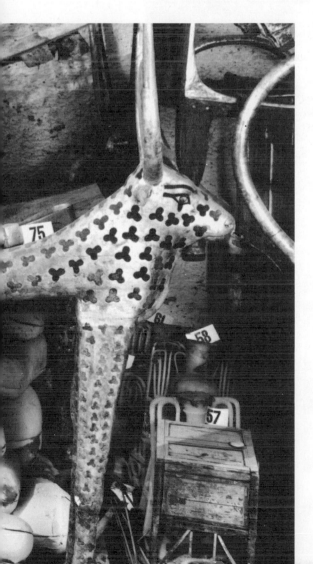

The treasures in the antechamber of Tut-ankh-Amen's tomb

433

Above, a child's gilt chair inlaid with ivory, perhaps used by the young Tut-ankh-Amen

At left, a carved relief of Tut-ankh-Amen making an offering to the god Osiris

the one they were in, but even more crowded with objects! And everything was in the most amazing mess they had ever seen. The cemetery officials had made some attempt to clean up the antechamber after the robbers and to pile up the funeral furniture in some sort of order, but in the annex they had left things just as they were, and the robbers had done their work "about as thoroughly as an earthquake." Not a single inch of floor space remained unlittered.

Carter and Carnarvon drew a long breath and sobered down. They realized now that the job before them was going to take months and months. It would be a monumental task to photograph, label, mend, pack and ship all this furniture, clothing, food, these chariots, weapons, walking sticks, jewels — this museumful of treasures.

All the time they were working, Carter and Carnarvon were, of course, feverishly anxious to know what lay beyond the guarded door. Many a time they glanced at it, but never once did they weaken. Not until every article was safely stowed away and the last bit of dust sifted for a possible bead or bit of inlay did they permit themselves to think of exploring farther.

But at length the day came, and in a hushed stillness — they had invited about twenty people to witness the opening of the door — Carter mounted a platform and with trembling hands very carefully chipped away the plaster and picked out the stones that made up the upper part. Then, when the hole was large enough to look through, he put his electric light on the other side and saw at a distance of a yard from him, and stretching as far as he could see, what appeared to be a wall of solid gold. He removed a few more stones, and then he understood. This was indeed the burial chamber, and the golden wall was an immense gilt shrine built to cover and protect the sarcophagus.[3]

---

[3]**sarcophagus** (sär kŏf′ə gəs): a stone coffin.

It took two hours to remove the doorway. Carter then let himself down into the burial chamber, which was some four feet below the level of the antechamber, and Lord Carnarvon came on behind through the narrow passage between the shrine and the wall. It was immense, that shrine. It practically filled the room, rising to nine feet and measuring seventeen on the long side and eleven on the short. And from top to bottom it was overlaid with gold.

Carter and Carnarvon did not stop to examine the decorations. At one end of the shrine were great folding doors, and to these they hurried, disregarding everything else. The all-absorbing question was: had the thieves got inside? They drew the bolts, swung back the doors. Inside was a second shrine with bolted doors just as before, and upon the bolts a seal — unbroken. The king was safe. In time they would remove one by one the encasing shrines and before them in full regalia[4] would lie a king of Egypt, unseen by human eyes, untouched by human hands, for three thousand and three hundred years.

With hearts at ease the explorers now moved to examine everything there was to see. They unrolled the wire of their electric light and passed on to the farthest end of the chamber.

To their astonishment, instead of coming to a dead wall, they saw a low door. It stood open as if inviting them into the room beyond, and passing through, they saw at the first glance that, though smaller than the outer ones, this room contained the greatest treasures of the tomb. Facing the doorway stood a monument so lovely that they gasped with wonder. It was a chest, shaped like a shrine, and overlaid with gold. On the top were sculptured cobras, and about them statues of the four goddesses of the dead, standing with outstretched arms, protecting and guarding the shrine. Directly in front of the entrance stood the emblems of the underworld — the jackal-god Anubis, lying on a shrine resting on

---

[4]**regalia** (rĭ gāl′yǝ): the emblems and symbols of royalty.

a sled, and behind him the head of a bull on a stand. A great number of black shrines and chests stood on one side of the chamber, all closed save one through the open doors of which the explorers could see statues of Tut-ankh-Amen standing on black leopards. Miniature coffins, model boats and yet another chariot stood in various places about the room, while in the center were a number of caskets of ivory and wood. The thieves had certainly been there, but they could not have taken much because the seals on most of the caskets were still intact.

Carter and Carnarvon felt now as Prince Yuaa's excavators had felt. These were not the relics of a life of three thousand years ago. These were the things of yesterday, of a year or two ago. Tut-ankh-Amen had not reigned from 1333 to 1323 B.C. He had but just died and they — two Englishmen strangely suspended in time and space — were taking part in the ceremonies of his burial. Not the unbelievable tomb, but the actual world of the twentieth century seemed unreal to these enchanted explorers.

It was their plan to go on immediately with the work of dismantling the shrines. But for some unfortunate reason the Government now started an argument with the excavators. The work had to be postponed. And months before the postponement, Lord Carnarvon had died.

It was thus with a heavy sense of loss that Carter returned to the tomb to dismantle the shrines — a hard task even for a light heart. The sarcophagus practically filled the chamber, leaving scarcely any room to work in. The sections of the outer shrine, moreover, weighed from a quarter to three-quarters of a ton each. They were almost impossible to handle without injury. And to prove his patience further, Carter found not two but four shrines about the sarcophagus. Eighty days passed before he could get them safely removed.

But at last the sarcophagus stood free, a magnificent chest carved from a single block of yellow quartzite, and sculptured in high relief[5] with goddesses so placed that their outstretched arms and wings encircled the sarcophagus. Strangely enough, the lid of the chest was made not of quartzite but of granite, cracked and patched, though stained to match the quartzite. The workmen, Carter decided, must have dropped the original lid, and there being no time to make another to match, granite had been used instead. That, too, had been cracked in the narrow quarters, and Carter, who had the task of removing the ton and a quarter of stone, understood why the Egyptians had decided to let well enough alone.

In all these many weeks the excavator's emotions had been steadily mounting, for with every day that passed the final mystery drew closer. Even the moment when he had first looked into the antechamber seemed to Carter less dramatic than the one he was looking forward to now as the workmen hauled up the lid of the sarcophagus. In an intense silence it was raised from its bed.

At first sight the contents were disappointing. Linen shrouds swathed whatever lay within and prevented his seeing anything. But when Carter had feverishly pushed back the folds on folds of linen, he saw a coffin of such unsurpassed beauty that he was speechless. It was in the form of the king himself and was decorated for the most part in low relief, but the head and hands were fully sculptured in the round, in massive gold. The hands, crossed over the breast, held the Crook and Flail, the face was wrought in sheet gold, the eyes were of aragonite and obsidian, the eyebrows and eyelids of lapis lazuli glass. Upon the forehead of the boy king in brilliant inlay were worked the Cobra and the Vulture, the symbols of Upper and Lower Egypt, and about these was twined a tiny wreath of flowers, which Carter guessed must have been the farewell offering of the widowed girl queen. "Among all that regal splendor," Carter afterwards said, "there was nothing so beautiful as those few withered flowers, still retaining their tinge of color.

---

[5]**relief:** the projection of a sculptured figure from a flat background.

The small wreath of flowers found on the forehead of Tut-ankh-Amen's likeness on the outermost coffin

The process of opening Tut-ankh-Amen's coffins in the burial chamber of his tomb was complicated. In the stage pictured, ropes lowered the bottom half of the outer coffin, while wires suspended the second coffin. Howard Carter wondered about the great weight of the coffins until he discovered that the third coffin was made of solid gold.

They told us what a short period three thousand three hundred years really was — but Yesterday and the Morrow."

To raise the lid of the coffin was the next task. Carter already guessed there would probably be another coffin nested inside. That is what he found. The inner coffin was also in human form, presenting another portrait of the king, and was sumptuously inlaid with colored glass on gold foil. But when the lid of this coffin was raised, there lay within it a third coffin, strangely heavy, and proving to be of solid gold.

The onlookers could not believe their eyes. They had been led to suppose that the funeral glory of the Pharaohs was very great, but so much they had not even dreamed. No wonder the robbers had always managed to find the royal tombs! The value of the gold in the coffin alone was $2,500,000. And Tut-ankh-Amen was but the least of Egypt's kings, a mere boy who ruled in the least glamorous period of Egypt's history. What must have been the funeral trappings of the great Pharaohs in the prime of Egypt's glory!

These were the thoughts that passed through the dazed spectators' minds while they stood awestruck about the innermost coffin of Tut-ankh-Amen. Then the final lid was raised by its golden handles. The mummy of the king lay disclosed. Over the face was a mask of beaten gold — another portrait of the ruler — while about the body was disposed layer after layer of beautiful objects. Beneath the mask was a lovely diadem, about the neck a heap of amulets[6] and necklaces, on the chest breastplates of gold, along the right thigh the Vulture of Upper Egypt, along the left thigh the Uraeus of Lower Egypt, emblems detached from the crown. Over the legs were four collarettes, over the feet were gold sandals, over the toes and fingers gold stalls,[7] about the arms bracelets of gold

---

[6]**amulet** (ăm′yə lit): a charm worn to ward off evil or injury, especially one worn around the neck.
[7]**stall:** a protective covering for a finger or thumb.

and silver inlaid with precious stones. Altogether one-hundred-and-forty-three objects were disposed about the body in one-hundred-and-one separate groups!

With trembling fingers Carter examined the treasures. How privileged above all men he had been to do that which others had dreamed of all their lives! Never before had such a find been made. Never had fancy even conjured up such magnificence. What was it worth? Fifteen million? Twenty? What did the money value matter! Carter knew that as an emblem of a lost civilization, the tomb of Tut-ankh-Amen was priceless. Of all those royal tombs it alone — and only in part — had baffled the greed of man, but it alone would suffice to bring to life the buried world of the Pharaohs, that never-equaled world of glamor and glitter and slavery and toil, of terror and magic and beauty and skill.

A painted frieze in the Pharaoh Tut-ankh-Amen's burial chamber pictures the following scenes, from right to left: Tut-ankh-Amen's successor Ay; the Pharaoh's mummy dressed as Osiris, the god of the dead; the Pharaoh standing before the goddess Nut; Tut-ankh-Amen, followed by his spirit double, being welcomed to the underworld by Osiris.

Thinking and Discussing

What was the reasoning that led Carter and Carnarvon to dig where they did, or even to dig for the tomb of Tut-ankh-Amen at all?

Why did Carter and Carnarvon not go on immediately from the antechamber to the inner chamber? Do you think they did the right thing in waiting? Why? Do you think you could have waited? Why or why not?

What did the vastness of Tut-ankh-Amen's treasures indicate about the wealth and burial customs of ancient Egyptian kings?

Applying Historical Concepts

Writing a News Story Carter and Carnarvon invited about twenty people to watch the opening of the burial chamber. Imagine that you, a newspaper reporter, are one of those people. Write a news story describing the two men as Carter pokes the hole in the door and peers into the chamber. Describe their actions and what they say to each other. Tell how the assembled people react. Give your story a headline.

Howard Carter and Lord Carnarvon at Tut-ankh-Amen's burial chamber entrance

TREASURES OF TUT-ANKH-AMEN'S TOMB

A gold collar in the shape of the vulture-goddess Nekhbet, inlaid with colored glass, was placed on Tut-ankh-Amen's mummy for magical protection.

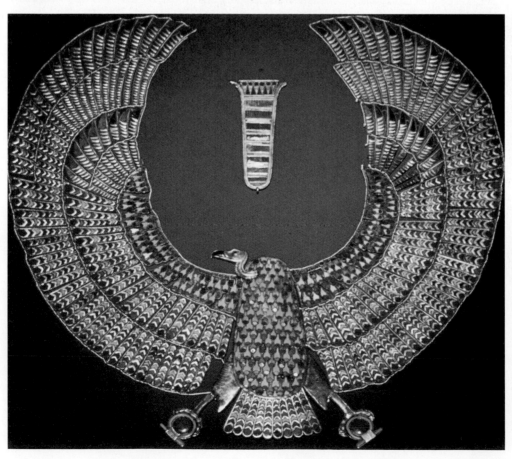

Above, royal emblems written in hieroglyphics stand for "Tut-ankh-Amen, ruler of On of Upper Egypt [Thebes]" and the Pharaoh's throne name, "Nebkheperura." At left, a sculpture of Tut-ankh-Amen depicts the Pharaoh moments before he throws a harpoon at a hippopotamus belonging to Seth, the god of evil.

At right, a gold buckle pictures Tut-
ankh-Amen as a triumphant warrior.
Below, a necklace represents the
moon's journey across the night sky.
Below right, a detail of the necklace
shows the moon floating above lotus
blossoms and poppies.

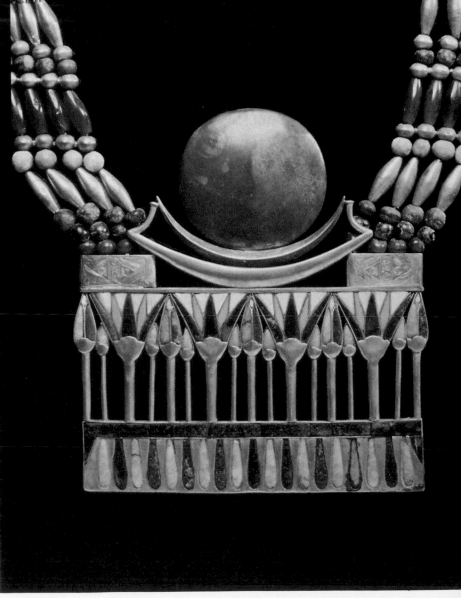

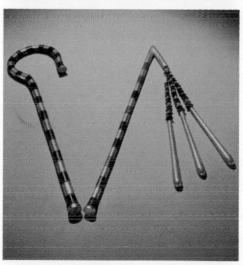

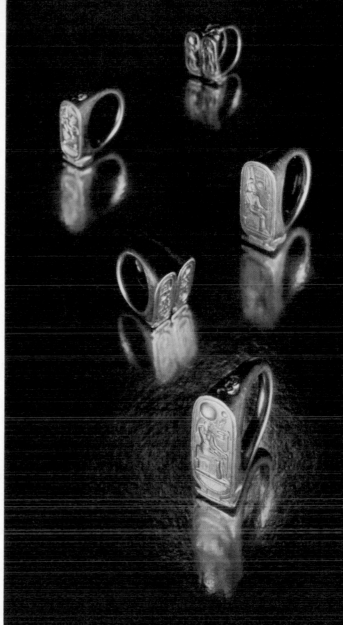

At left from top to bottom, a hand mirror is made in the shape of *ankh*, the hieroglyph meaning "life"; a crook is pictured with a flail that has the inscription "Tut-ankh-Aten," the original form of Tut-ankh-Amen's name; and an alabaster vase glows with light. Above, gold rings represent important ancient Egyptian gods.

About the Authors

 **Patricia Lauber** was born in New York City in 1924. Besides writing books, Lauber has been the chief editor of the science and mathematics division of *The New Book of Knowledge*. Her *Tales Mummies Tell* was named a New York Academy of Sciences Honor Book in 1986, and *Volcano: The Eruption and Healing of Mt. St. Helens* was named a Newbery Honor Book in 1987.

 **Anne Terry White** was born in 1896 in the Ukraine in Russia and raised in the United States. Most of her books grew out of her fascination with the geological history of the earth and the cultural history of its people. She has written a series of science books called *All About* that discusses stars, rocks, rivers, and mountains. Her other books include *Prehistoric America*, *North to Liberty: The Story of the Underground Railroad*, and *Lost Worlds: The Romance of Archaeology*.

Future Expeditions

Mummies, Tombs, and Treasure: Secrets of Ancient Egypt by Lila Perl (Clarion, 1987)   This is a fascinating, thorough description of Egyptian mummies. It explains how the process of mummifying was discovered, how mummies are prepared, and how theft of valuable items from burial places is prevented.

Pyramid by David Macaulay (Houghton, 1975)   Finely detailed drawings show the step-by-step process of pyramid building in ancient Egypt. The text describes the building process and the lives of the people who built the pyramids.

Hieroglyphs, the Writing of Ancient Egypt by Norma Jean Katan (Atheneum, 1981)   This introduction to hieroglyphs offers examples found on tombs, statues, and other objects.

His Majesty, Queen Hatshepsut by Dorothy Sharp Carter (Lippincott, 1987)   This fictionalized account tells the story of a queen in ancient Egypt who declared herself pharaoh.

Cat in the Mirror by Mary Stolz (Dell, 1978)   A time-travel fantasy follows the lives of two girls — one in New York City and the other in ancient Egypt.

Aïda told by Leontyne Price (Harcourt, 1990)   The famous opera singer Leontyne Price tells this classic story of a courageous heroine torn between her love of country and her love for an enemy military leader.

SCIENCE

EXPLORING THE OCEANS

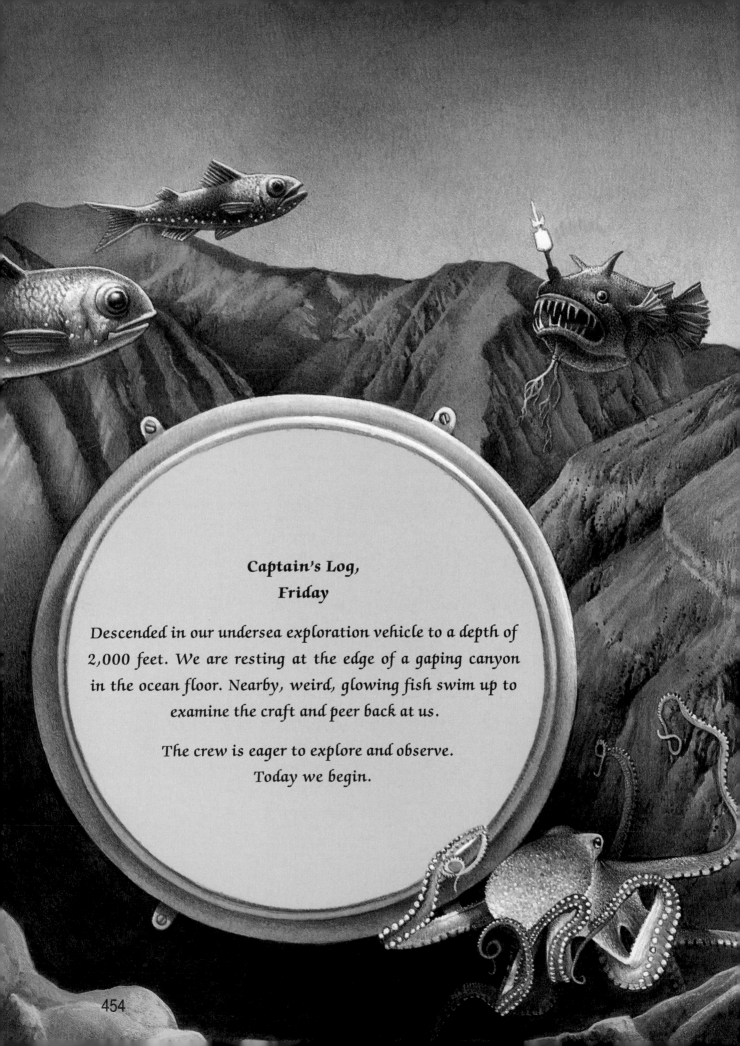

Captain's Log,
Friday

Descended in our undersea exploration vehicle to a depth of 2,000 feet. We are resting at the edge of a gaping canyon in the ocean floor. Nearby, weird, glowing fish swim up to examine the craft and peer back at us.

The crew is eager to explore and observe.
Today we begin.

ITINERARY

Treasure of the *Andrea Doria*   456
from *Treasures of the Deep:*
Adventures of Undersea Exploration
by Walter Oleksy

Oceans of the Earth   466
from *Earth Science*, a science textbook

Discovering the Oceans   476
from *Under the High Seas:*
New Frontiers in Oceanography
by Margaret Poynter and Donald Collins

Lurkers of the Deep: 486
Life Within the Ocean Depths
from the book by Bruce H. Robison

TREASURE
of the
ANDREA DORIA

by *Walter Oleksy*

illustrated by
Robert Gantt Steele

The *Andrea Doria*, an Italian luxury liner, was making her 101st crossing of the Atlantic Ocean in July 1956. She was a sleek beauty, 697 feet long and lavishly decorated by Italian artists. Her captain, Piero Calamai, called her "the prettiest ship in the world."

Nearing New York at night, the ship encountered dense fog. But the *Andrea Doria* was considered one of the safest ships afloat. She carried a crew of 572 and 1,134 passengers and was equipped with the most modern safety equipment. She was considered unsinkable because watertight doors could divide the ship into eleven watertight compartments. Just in case, the boat deck housed sixteen lifeboats capable of carrying 2,000 persons.

At about 10:20 P.M. on July 25, the *Andrea Doria* passed about a mile from the Nantucket lighthouse off the coast of Massachusetts, and entered an area of very heavy marine traffic. Some people called it "the Times Square of the Atlantic," so many ships plied the area's waters.

Fifteen minutes later, an officer on the *Andrea Doria* bridge spotted another ship on the radar screen. The approaching ship was about seventeen miles away and moving almost directly in the *Andrea Doria*'s path. Rules of the sea are that when two ships meet head-on in open water, they should pass port-to-port (left side to left side), unless that would force them to cross.

Captain Calamai was notified of the approaching ship. He saw that the oncoming ship appeared to be already well to the starboard (right) side of the *Doria*. He felt there was no reason to swing the *Doria* to the right for normal port-to-port passing. It would be just as safe, he thought, to pass starboard-to-starboard.

At about the same time, about twenty-five miles west of the Nantucket lighthouse, and not yet in fog, a duty officer aboard the oncoming ship, the *Stockholm*, of the Swedish American Line, sighted the *Doria* on that ship's radar. He estimated the *Doria* to be about twelve miles away and slightly to the port of the *Stockholm*. The ships, it was expected, would follow the correct passing procedure, although it might be a little too close for comfort.

By 11 P.M., the two ships were about seven miles apart. They were sailing at a combined speed of forty knots and closing two miles every three minutes.

Without seeing each other, because the *Doria* was in heavy fog, Calamai and the *Stockholm*'s Third Officer, Johan-Ernst Carstens Johannsen, both made a decision to put a little more distance between the two ships. When the ships were only 3.5 nautical miles[1] apart, Calamai ordered the *Doria* turned four degrees to port. Two minutes later, while only two miles apart, the *Stockholm* was turned 20 degrees to starboard.

Moments later, through the fog, each ship's officer spotted the lights of the other ship. Both realized they were on a collision course. Calamai ordered the *Doria* into an even harder left turn. The *Stockholm*'s engines were put into full reverse. But momentum kept the ship moving toward the *Doria*'s broad starboard side.

At exactly 11:09 P.M., the *Stockholm*'s sharp icebreaker bow sliced into the starboard side of the *Andrea Doria*. It cut a V-shaped gash about forty feet wide at the top and thirty feet deep, demolishing nearly fifty cabins on five decks, killing many of the occupants who were sleeping.

The sea flooded in below the waterline of the damaged compartments. The *Doria* had been designed to stay afloat with a maximum list[2] of 15 degrees. But within only minutes of being rammed, she listed at 20 degrees.

---

[1]**nautical miles:** units of length used when traveling by sea or air; 3.5 nautical miles equals about four land miles.

[2]**list:** tilt.

SOS messages immediately sent out from both ships were picked up by a Coast Guard monitoring station on Long Island. One of the most dramatic sea rescue operations in modern history went into effect.

Within minutes of the SOS (a marine emergency call), Navy and private ships in the area hurried to the rescue. But between the three rescue ships, they only had six lifeboats.

Having been radioed that help was on its way, Calamai called back that danger was immediate, and more boats were needed to rescue about 1,500 persons.

Now a bit of good luck happened. The great French luxury liner, *Ile de France*, had just left New York. She was about forty-five miles from the scene of the collision when her captain, Baron Raoul de Beaudean, got the *Doria*'s distress message. He turned his ship around and came to the rescue with many lifeboats.

But the *Andrea Doria* was listing badly and in great danger of sinking, even though help was hurrying on its way.

Calamai radioed frantically to the *Stockholm*, urging that it come immediately to pick up the *Doria*'s passengers.

Captain Harry Gunner Nordenson of the *Stockholm* radioed back that he couldn't do that. His ship's whole bow was crushed. The number-one hold was filled with water. He had to stay in his present position. But he told the Italian captain that if he could lower his lifeboats, *Stockholm*'s crew would pick up his passengers. Nordenson had to keep his own lifeboats for his own crew and passengers, should his ship sink.

Precious minutes passed. Calamai radioed Nordenson desperately: "We are listing too much. Impossible to put boats over side. Please send lifeboats immediately."

Luckily, Nordenson was now certain his own ship would not sink. He got ready to launch seven lifeboats, three of them with motors. By now, it had been three hours since the collision.

Doria passengers saw a most welcome sight. Crowded onto the decks awaiting rescue into lifeboats, they saw the brightly lighted *Ile de France* loom out of the early morning fog. Its powerful searchlights pierced the dark to lighten up the rescue scene.

Some terrified passengers aboard the *Doria* were too frightened to wait for lifeboats as the ship listed further toward the sea. They jumped overboard and had to be fished out of the dark water. Many more were lowered into lifeboats from the *Ile de France* and the *Stockholm*.

As the rescue operation continued, day began to break. At about 10 A.M., the foundering[3] *Andrea Doria* gave up her fight to stay afloat. Turning over, she slid prow-first[4] into her watery grave.

About fifty persons aboard the *Doria* lost their lives in the collision. The weary survivors were taken aboard the *Ile de France*, the *Stockholm*, and smaller ships. Two Coast Guard cutters helped the crippled *Stockholm* sail slowly back to New York.

The *Andrea Doria* remains over 200 feet below the surface of the ocean off the coast of Nantucket. It was a quiet, solitary grave until about a quarter of a century later. Then, during the summer of 1980, divers began searching for the *Andrea Doria* in hopes of reclaiming some of its lost treasure, including two safes believed to be holding between $1 million and $4 million.

Nick Caloyianis, a diver and photographer, and three others formed a team to film the salvage operation under the leadership and sponsorship of Peter Gimbel, of the famous Gimbel's Department Store in New York.

Finding the *Andrea Doria* and recovering her safes had been Gimbel's dream since the sinking. Only two days after the tragedy,

---

[3]**foundering:** sinking due to flooding.

[4]**prow** (prou): the bow of a ship.

Gimbel, then a young scuba diver, made a dive down to find the wreck. For the next twenty-five years, Gimbel, now an underwater filmmaker, would attempt to recover the safes. He also hoped to prove his theory that a missing watertight door caused the *Doria* to sink so fast.

In 1975, Gimbel made a documentary film for television that showed how difficult it was to explore the wreck of the *Doria*. But the project failed to prove his theory about the missing door. And divers failed to bring up or open the ship's safes.

During the summer of 1981, Gimbel launched a second project to recover the safes. Gimbel and his wife, Elga Anderson, an actress and diver, began "The *Doria* Project" with Caloyianis and two other photographer-divers, Jack McKinney and Bob Hollis. McKinney, editor of *Skin Diver* magazine, and Hollis had been with Gimbel on previous *Doria* expeditions. Gimbel financed the latest expedition, which cost nearly $1.75 million.

A support crew of thirty-two people was hired to work from a 180-foot trawler,[5] the *Sea Level II*, which became the base of operation for the project. The crew included welders, electricians, and a medic, as well as commercial divers hired

[5] **trawler (trô′lər):** a boat equipped to tow a fishing net along the ocean floor.

to tend equipment, feed lines to divers, and assist the underwater cameramen.

Before heading for the wreck site in the Atlantic, the four photographer-divers prepared themselves for the project by going to Long Beach, California, where they underwent training in bell saturation diving, a system that allows divers to remain in the water at great depths for long periods of time.

In twenty-five years, the *Andrea Doria* had become an artificial reef. Schools of fish swam in and out of the wreckage and nested there. But the ship was not so safe for humans. A week after the sinking, a sport diver drowned trying to swim into the *Doria*. Other divers consider it a deathtrap.

Each dive was dangerous. A twenty-eight-pound camera was weightless under water, but a pair of scuba tanks as a reserve air supply and 500 feet of air hose to the surface trawler made the swimming difficult and tiring.

Worst of all, the ocean was stormy that August and September. Hurricane Dennis whipped up powerful winds and brought down heavy rains. Nets became entangled in the ship, taking days to untwine. Visibility was often as little as five feet. Sharks swam dangerously close before they were spotted and scared away with stun guns.

463

Dives usually lasted a little more than half an hour and were exhausting, though exhilarating.[6] Twice a day, a giant steel bell weighing three-and-a-half tons and measuring seven feet in diameter was lowered into and out of the water. A cameraman and diver rode the bell to 160 feet beneath the surface. There the pressure in the bell equaled the pressure outside. Then the diver would swim out and stay underwater for up to five hours.

After three weeks of diving at the wreck site, one of the two safes was found in the *Doria*'s first-class lounge in a mass of debris that had to be picked through by hand and with suction hoses. A special rig was constructed to withstand the heavy ocean swells and the safe was lifted to the surface. Nick Caloyianis photographed the raising of the safe and also Elga Anderson's dive on that expedition. She became only the second woman to dive on the *Andrea Doria* wreck. While divers continued searching for the second safe, the one that was found was brought ashore and put in a tank of sharks in a Coney Island aquarium for safekeeping.

Did the *Doria* have a missing door that caused the ship to sink so fast? Gimbel now believes that a missing watertight door probably would not have made much difference. The hole opened up by the *Stockholm* was big enough to sink the *Andrea Doria*.

The 1981 expedition lasted thirty-five days. Between that and previous trips, Gimbel and his helpers made forty-nine dives on the wreck. He says the *Andrea Doria* is rapidly breaking down, and it may be too dangerous to risk any further dives. After twenty-five years, Gimbel believes the *Andrea Doria* will be left to her peaceful grave at the bottom of the Atlantic, to keep her treasure and secrets.

---

[6]**exhilarating** (ĭg zĭl´ə rāt´ ĭng): exciting.

TREASURE OF THE ANDREA DORIA

Thinking and Discussing

Think of what you learned about the ocean in "Treasure of the *Andrea Doria*." How did the characteristics of the ocean make the underwater expedition a difficult and dangerous task?

Notice that the author provides the reader with historical information about the *Andrea Doria* and a description of the ships' collision. How would the story have been different if the author had merely provided an account of Peter Gimbel's salvaging operation?

Applying Science Concepts

Protecting the Safe Did you think Peter Gimbel's idea of putting the safe into a shark-filled aquarium tank was ingenious? In a small group, brainstorm other creative ideas for protecting the safe. Share your ideas with your classmates.

Thinking and Writing

Imagine that you are Peter Gimbel. Write a letter to a friend describing how you found and explored the *Andrea Doria*. Explain why the wreck is important to you and how it felt when you discovered the treasure.

From *Earth Science*, a science textbook

OCEANS

of the

EARTH

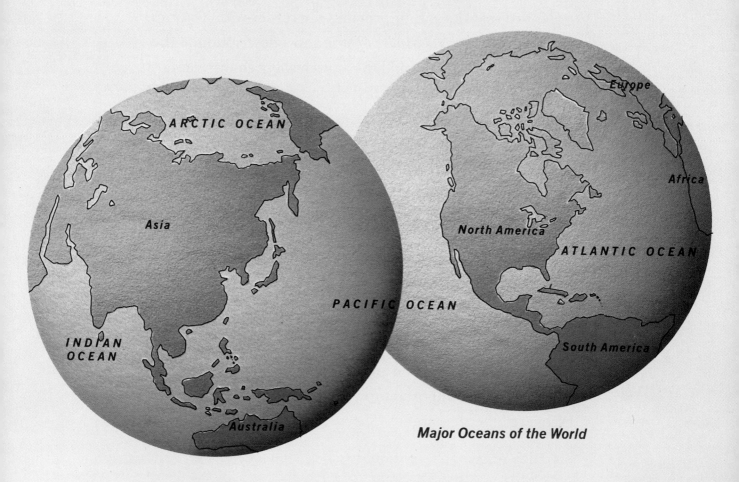

Major Oceans of the World

Illustrations by Joseph LeMonnier

Of all the planets in our solar system, only earth is covered by vast oceans of liquid water. This water is like a thin soup. It teems with living things and is seasoned with salt and other minerals. As you read about the ocean, keep the following questions in mind:

    a. How much of the world is covered by oceans?

    b. What are the major oceans of the earth?

Oceans Cover Most of the Earth

Oceans cover more than 70 percent of the earth's surface. Astronauts looking at the Pacific Ocean from space see only cloud-covered water dotted with small islands and ringed with continents. The other side of the globe contains almost all the earth's land.

The oceans contain 97 percent of all the water on earth. Rivers, lakes, streams, and ponds hold less than 1 percent of the earth's water. The remaining 2 percent is frozen into ice in glaciers and around the North and South Poles. Water circulates among the oceans, the land, and the air by means of precipitation and evaporation in the water cycle.

Major Oceans of the World

The water of all the oceans circulates in one vast ocean. Geographers divide this great ocean into four separate bodies of water, as shown on the map. The Pacific is the largest and deepest ocean. It covers more than a third of the earth's surface. Next in size is the Atlantic. The third largest is the Indian Ocean. The Arctic is the smallest ocean. Much of the surface water in the Arctic is frozen most of the year.

Scientists who study the movements of the earth's crust find that the Pacific Ocean is getting smaller. Most of the crust beneath the Pacific is one huge plate. At its boundaries, the Pacific plate sinks under the surrounding continental plates. In the center of the Atlantic Ocean's floor, however, two plates are moving apart. The

Atlantic is slowly getting larger because new crust forms at the spreading boundary. The plates of the ocean floor move at about the same speed your fingernails grow.

REVIEW IT

1. How much of the earth's surface do oceans cover?
2. Name the four major oceans, from largest to smallest.

WATERS OF THE OCEAN

A mouthful of seawater tastes saltier than a mouthful of potato chips. To understand why, you must know about the minerals in ocean water. Keep these questions in mind:

a. What is salinity?

b. How do the temperature and pressure of seawater vary?

Dissolved Salts Make Seawater Salty

Dissolved salts and minerals make ocean water salty. Notice in the table that sodium chloride — common table salt — is the most abundant salt in the ocean. Almost all elements found on earth are also found in seawater.

The ocean's crust is the main source of the minerals in seawater. Water seeps down through pores and tiny cracks in the ocean floor. Minerals in the crust dissolve in this water. The kinds of minerals and their ratio to each other are the same in seawater everywhere. An amount of water equal to the entire ocean filters into and out of the crust every eight million years.

Salinity (sə lĭn′ĭ tē) is a measure of how salty seawater is. If you boil away all the water from 1,000 grams of seawater, about 35 grams of salt will remain. Only 965 grams is water. The average salinity of the oceans is 35 parts of salt in 1,000 parts of seawater.

The most abundant minerals in seawater

	Parts per thousand
Sodium chloride	27.2
Magnesium chloride	3.8
Magnesium sulfate	1.7
Calcium sulfate	1.3
Potassium sulfate	0.9
Calcium carbonate	0.1
Magnesium bromide	0.1

In warm, dry climates, such as near the Mediterranean Sea, ocean water evaporates rapidly. The salts that remain make the water saltier than average. Salinity is low where rivers, melting ice, or heavy rains pour fresh water into the ocean.

Temperature and Pressure of Ocean Water

Temperature The sun warms the water on the ocean's surface. Wind and waves mix the heated surface water with cold water beneath it. Notice in the diagram that water temperature is almost the same throughout the top layer of water. The temperature of this layer — the **mixed layer** — is different in different parts of the ocean. At the poles, it is usually colder than 0° C. Near the equator, surface water can be as warm as 30° C. In the middle latitudes, the surface temperature changes with the seasons. The mixed layer is 100 to 300 meters deep.

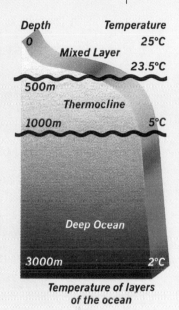

Temperature of layers of the ocean

Beneath the mixed layer is the **thermocline (thûr′mə klīn′)** — a layer of water that rapidly gets colder with increasing depth. Seawater at the bottom of the thermocline is very cold. Even near the equator, the bottom of the thermocline is colder than 5° C. The thermocline can be as deep as 1,000 meters.

Below the thermocline, temperatures drop slowly. The freezing point of seawater of average salinity is -2° C. The temperature of deep ocean water is always near freezing.

Pressure Air above the earth presses on the earth's surface. The air pressure that results can be measured in "atmospheres." Average air pressure at sea level is one atmosphere. In the same way that air presses on the earth's surface, water presses on the ocean's bottom. Pressure becomes greater with depth. Water pressure on the sea floor increases by an amount equal to one atmosphere of pressure for every increase of 10 meters beneath the ocean's surface. Forty atmospheres of water press on objects 400 meters below the surface. Deeper in the ocean, pressures are even greater.

REVIEW IT

1. What is the average salinity of seawater?
2. What is the thermocline?
3. How many atmospheres of pressure would the ocean put on an object 6,000 meters beneath the surface?

EXPLORING THE OCEAN FLOOR

Most people know more about the surface of the near side of the moon than they know about the bottom of the ocean. Answer these questions as you read about the ocean floor:

   a. How do oceanographers measure the depth of the ocean?
   b. How is sediment brought up from the ocean bottom?
   c. What are the features of the sea floor?

Measuring the Water's Depth

Soundings are measurements of the depth of water. In the past, sailors took soundings by lowering ropes with weights. When the weight touched bottom, the length of wet rope showed the depth of the water. In deep water, a sounding was inaccurate because of the water's movement.

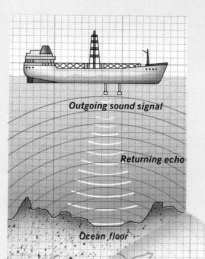

Outgoing sound signal

Returning echo

Ocean floor

Profile of the ocean floor

Today, scientists find the depth of water by using an **echo sounder**. This device measures depth by bouncing sound waves off the ocean floor. Notice in the diagram to the left that sound waves hit the ocean bottom and bounce back to the ship as an echo. The echo sounder measures how long a sound wave takes to reach the ocean bottom and return to the ship. Since the speed of sound in seawater is known, the sounder can calculate the ocean's depth at that spot. As the ship moves, the echo sounder makes a map.

Sediments on the Ocean Bottom

The layers of rock that make up the sea floor are covered with **sediments,** or material that has settled to the bottom of the ocean. Near the continents, most of these sediments were washed off the land as sand, clay, dust, or volcanic ash. Far from land, however, many sediments are the remains of organisms — or living things. As sea organisms die, their bodies fall to the ocean floor. Some parts of the ocean are so deep that bodies of organisms dissolve before they reach the bottom.

A core

The deepest sea floors are covered by tiny particles of clay carried from the continents by rivers. The particles slowly drift through the ocean until they sink to the bottom. It can take 1,000 years for two millimeters of sediment to accumulate on the bottom of the sea floor.

Scientists use several devices to gather samples from the ocean bottom. A grab sampler has jaws that close when they reach bottom. It takes bites out of the sediment beneath shallow water. A dredge is like a bag made of steel links. A ship drags the dredge along the ocean bottom. Dredges pick up large objects, such as loose rocks.

A corer works like a huge hollow drill. It brings long cylinders of sediment — **cores** — up to the surface in metal tubes. Special research ships bring up cores from beneath the water along the edges of continents. Scientists learn about the history of the sea floor by studying the layers of sediments in cores.

The Features of the Sea Floor

The drawing below shows a side view of the ocean's floor. At the far left is the **continental shelf** — a broad, gently sloping plain near the shoreline. Its width ranges from less than 3 kilometers off the west coast of Peru and Chile to more than 1,000 kilometers off the northeastern coast of Siberia. In most places, the shelf extends about 75 kilometers from the shoreline. The ocean averages 135 meters deep on the shelf. Scientists believe that fast-flowing currents containing mud or sand erode deep valleys — or submarine canyons — into the continental shelf. The Hudson River Canyon, for example, is a deep cut in the continental shelf off New York City.

The slightly steeper **continental slope** begins beyond the continental shelf. It drops to a depth of about 4,000 meters. Sand or mud washed down from the slope may form a gentle **continental rise** at the base of the slope.

The **ocean basin** extends hundreds of kilometers beyond the continental slope. Its depth averages more than 4,000 meters. Low hills, called **abyssal** (ə bĭs´əl) hills, cover parts of the ocean basin. If a hill is more than 1,000 meters high, it is called a **seamount**. The ocean floor is flat where sediment collects and covers the hills. These large flat regions are abyssal plains.

Sea Level

Shoreline

Land

Abyssal Hills

Continental Shelf

Continental Slope

Abyssal Plain

472

Volcanoes rise from the ocean basin in many areas. Some reach above the ocean's surface to form volcanic islands, such as the Hawaiian Islands. A volcano with a flat top is called a **guyot** (gē′ō). Oceanographers believe guyots are volcanoes that rose above the ocean's surface until waves eroded and leveled their tops.

Underwater earthquakes and volcanoes often occur at mid-ocean **trenches** and **ridges.** Trenches are deep cracks in the ocean floor where two plates are colliding. Trenches are the deepest places in the ocean. Most trenches cut 2 to 4 kilometers down into the ocean floor. They may be thousands of kilometers long, but only about 100 kilometers wide. Deep ocean trenches run around the edges of the Pacific Ocean.

Mid-ocean ridges are mountain ranges that zigzag along the ocean floor. Ridges form where plates are spreading apart. Magma is the molten material under the earth's crust. It pushes up into rifts — or valleys — that cut through the center of the ridges. This magma forms new sea floor. The Mid-Atlantic Ridge runs along the center of the Atlantic Ocean. Spreading boundaries with lower, less rugged mountains are called rises.

REVIEW IT

1. How do oceanographers use sound waves to measure the depth of the ocean?
2. What is a source of sediment found in the deepest part of the ocean?
3. Name three types of features on the ocean floor.

Volcano

Mid-Ocean Ridge

Guyot

Trench

OCEANS OF THE EARTH

Thinking and Discussing

According to the text, the Pacific Ocean is getting smaller, and the Atlantic Ocean is growing larger. What is causing these changes?

What are the three main characteristics of ocean water discussed in the text?

What terms have you learned to describe features of the ocean floor? Which explanations of the causes of these features do you find most interesting? Why?

Applying Science Concepts

Performing a Salt-Water Experiment Leave a container of salt water on a sunny windowsill for a few days. Observe the water daily and record your observations. When all the water has evaporated, observe and record the results. What has happened to the water? What has happened to the salt? What conclusions can you draw from the experiment to explain why the ocean stays salty?

Creating a Graphic Look at the graphics — maps, charts, and graphs — in this textbook chapter. They all help you understand important facts about the ocean. Alone or with a group of classmates, create another graphic that presents information about the ocean in a clear and organized way. You could, for example, make a chart that shows the pressure of the water beneath the ocean's surface or, with a little research, a map of ocean currents. You might want to explain your graphic to the class and display it in the classroom.

The diving bell was first suggested by the ancient Greek philosopher Aristotle. It finally came into being in the seventeenth century. Made of metal, the bell could be the size of a helmet, or it could be large enough to hold two people. The bell was lowered into the water with the open end downward so that the inside remained filled with air.

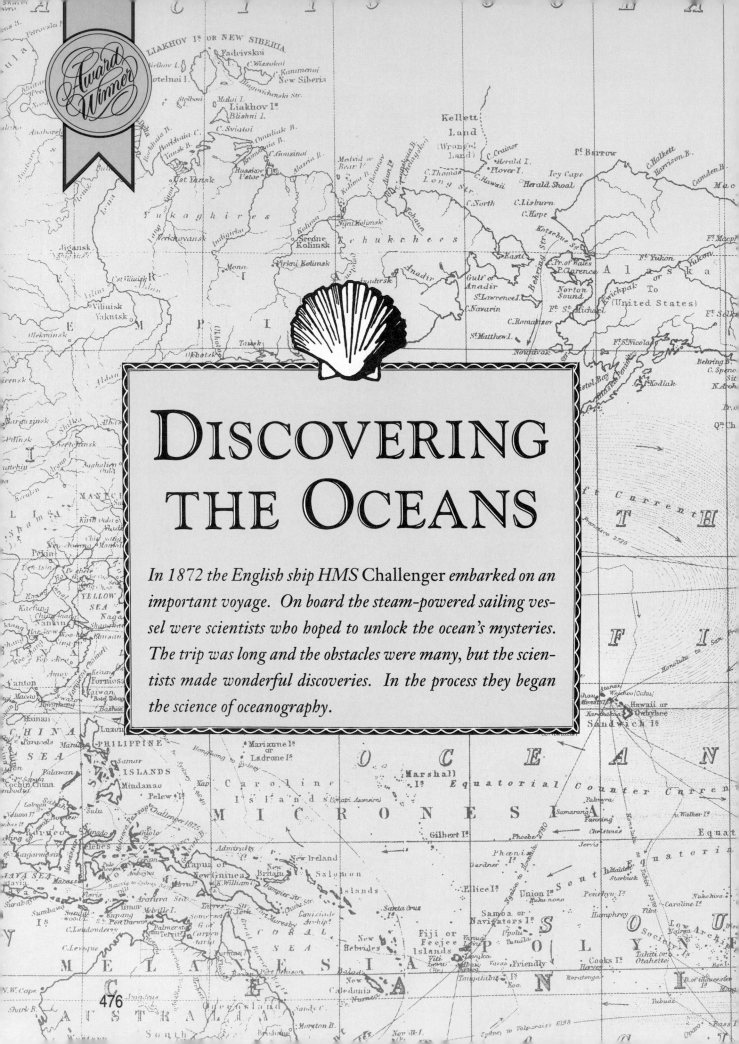

DISCOVERING THE OCEANS

In 1872 the English ship HMS Challenger embarked on an important voyage. On board the steam-powered sailing vessel were scientists who hoped to unlock the ocean's mysteries. The trip was long and the obstacles were many, but the scientists made wonderful discoveries. In the process they began the science of oceanography.

From *Under the High Seas*
by Margaret Poynter and Donald Collins

A giant step in the study of the world ocean was taken after the telegraph was invented in 1837. European and American businessmen were eager to use this speedy method of communication, so they enthusiastically supported the plans to lay a transatlantic cable. The success of the project depended upon finding the answers to some questions about the proposed cable route. What sort of water movement exists there? How is the ocean floor contoured? Are there any animals inhabiting the region, and if so, what kind? Will they chew the cable's covering? Or will they deposit their wastes upon it, thus causing it to rot?

Biologists, botanists, zoologists and oceanographers went to work to find the answers to these and other questions. They took soundings at regular intervals all along the route. They analyzed sediments from the sea floor. They made charts of the currents.

One weight that had been left on the sea floor for an hour came back to the surface with thirteen starfish clinging to it. The captain was delighted at what he considered proof that abundant life existed at great depths.

"The sea has sent forth its long coveted[1] message," he wrote in his log that night.

Some of the scientists weren't certain that the starfish had actually lived on the sea floor. "Couldn't they have clung to the weight as it passed through the water at a much higher level?" they asked.

---

[1]**coveted (kŭv′** ĭt əd)**:** desired or craved.

In 1860, their doubts were partially resolved. At that time, a submerged cable broke and was brought up for repair. Several sea creatures were clinging to it, one of which was a coral which could only have grown into place as the cable lay on the ocean bottom.

By the time the Atlantic cable project was completed, this particular section of the sea floor had been mapped in a detail that had never before been attempted. A vague picture of deep coastal trenches and a central plateau began to emerge. Until that time, it had been assumed that the sea floor sloped gradually down to its lowest point about halfway between the two continents, then climbed back up to meet the opposite shore. It now appeared that the middle of the ocean floor wasn't its lowest point, but perhaps its highest.

As usually happens in a scientific investigation, these discoveries led to a host of questions that cried out to be answered. What does the presence of these undersea mountains and valleys mean? Are they part of the lost continent of Atlantis?[2] Or are they part of a newly emerging landform, one which will appear above the surface of the sea millions of years hence?

To solve these and other mysteries, the world's major seafaring countries joined in the search for more facts. The "space race" of the nineteenth century began, but instead of competing, the participants cooperated with each other.

In 1872, England launched the HMS *Challenger*, which was to "investigate the condition of the Deep Sea throughout the entire Oceanic Basin." An old naval sailing ship with auxiliary steam power, it was an unlikely vessel to perform such a monumental task.

---

[2] **Atlantis:** a fabled island or continent of ancient times, said to have sunk beneath the sea during an earthquake.

Besides being clumsy and slow, it had an alarming tendency to pitch and roll much more than most ships.

As the *Challenger* groped its way across unknown seas using inaccurate and partially blank maps, the members of its crew often had to call upon all of their skills of seamanship. In the Antarctic, the ship was caught amid icebergs that were drifting in the gale force wind. By artfully navigating between two icebergs that were used as a windbreak, the sailors were able to escape the precarious situation.

Each time the *Challenger* had to "take a station" to make a depth sound, the sails had to be shortened, and the ship brought into the wind. Twin propellers, which were driven by the steam engines, were used to keep the craft steady in the water. Steam-powered winches creaked and groaned as the lines went slowly over the sides.

Each line could hold a variety of primitive gear. The nets that gathered the plankton and other forms of small marine life were muslin or silk bags attached to iron rings one foot in diameter. Water samples were collected in glass bottles that could be opened underwater by the men on the ship. Mercury recording thermometers measured the water temperature. These readings were far from accurate, and the instruments were often broken when they struck the side of the ship.

From the time the *Challenger* furled its sails to take a station to the time when the last foot of line was wound laboriously back onto the reel, two days sometimes passed. Stations were often held in the fury of a raging blizzard and in below-freezing temperatures. As the scientists waited for the dredging to be completed, they suffered agonies of frustration and uncertainty. Would the steam engine break down at a crucial moment? Or would the winches jam? What if the nets came up empty? Even the ship's parrot seemed uneasy. "What?" he echoed. "Two thousand fathoms and no bottom?"

The *Challenger*'s ordinary seamen had little understanding of the reasons behind the grueling search for bits of coral and shell and mud and clay. They knew only that they had to work long hours under the worst of conditions and that they were often on the receiving end of the scientists' anger when something went wrong. It was hard for them to understand how a man's happiness could depend to such a great extent on some slimy bit of muck, or a particularly unattractive sea worm.

The HMS *Challenger* returned to England in May of 1876. During the three and one-half years of its voyage, it had logged almost sixty-nine thousand miles and had taken over 360 stations, having stopped on the average every 200 miles.

The scientists were jubilant. They had measured the structure of the ocean all around the world and had found it to be marvelously complicated. They had analyzed the chemical composition of hundreds of water samples and saw that the sea contained many of the earth's minerals in solution. They had dredged up thousands of species of animal life that were new to the scientific world. Their findings had indicated that life exists in a myriad[3] of forms in all of the measured depths of the sea. They had dredged

[3]**myriad (mîr′ē əd):** a very large, indefinite number.

481

up strange, charred-looking rocks that ranged in size from cinders to potatoes. These were put on display in the British Museum, but otherwise received little attention.

The *Challenger*'s scientists had felt the thrill of handling ooze that had lain hidden under thousands of fathoms of water for millions of years. This sediment was composed largely of the corpses of microscopic creatures that constantly filter like an endless snowfall to the ocean floor.

One of the most awesome results of the *Challenger*'s voyage was the partial uncovering of the hidden world of the ocean floor. This world contained a tantalizing mixture of tall mountain ranges, wide plateaus, and deep, plunging trenches. Far from being flat and uninteresting, the sea floor apparently rivaled the continents in the majesty of its landforms.

The *Challenger* had collected so much information that it took scores of experts twenty years to sort it out. The data eventually filled fifty thick volumes, and the study of the material kept the oceanographers of the world busy for many decades.

"Never did one expedition cost so little and produce such momentous results for human knowledge," wrote a scientist. "Indeed, the science of oceanography began the day the *Challenger* was launched."

Despite such words of praise, the *Challenger*'s voyage was only the beginning. The experts who had been on the vessel readily admitted that they had been "like blind men, groping about in the water with white sticks three-and-a-half miles long." Many of the mysteries that were found to exist at that time remain unsolved today.

DISCOVERING THE OCEANS

Thinking and Discussing

Evaluate the methods of collecting data used by the scientists aboard the *Challenger*. Were they impressive, or surprising, or were they what you would expect? Support your answers with examples.

The selection is divided into two parts. The first part tells mainly about the *Challenger* scientists and the ways in which they conducted research on their voyage. What do you read about in the second part? Why do you think the author arranged the selection in this way?

A biologist studies living things, a botanist studies plants, and a zoologist studies animals. Why are these scientists — as well as oceanographers — concerned with ocean study?

Applying Science Concepts

Identifying Scientific Accomplishments The text discusses the accomplishments of the scientists aboard the *Challenger*. Make a list of these discoveries and accomplishments. Present your list to the class. Discuss the accomplishments you think are the most important or interesting.

The Johnson Sea Link, first launched in 1971, is a modern vessel for deep-sea exploration. The Sea Link can dive to a depth of 3000 feet. Its acrylic sphere gives explorers a total view of their underwater environment.

DIVING SUITS

Early diving suits were bulky, and the diver depended on getting air from the surface through a hose or tube. In 1943, the famous French sea pioneer Jacques Cousteau made it possible for divers to carry their own air supply. Cousteau invented the **self-c**ontained **u**nderwater **b**reathing **ap**paratus, or *scuba*. Today, for exploring deeper parts of the ocean, divers sometimes still use suits and helmets with air supplied through a hose.

485

LURKERS OF THE DEEP

People have always been curious about the depths of the ocean: what is the bottom like, what — if anything — lives there? Technology has allowed us to probe ever deeper, to satisfy our curiosity and add to our store of knowledge. We know that the bottom is not a level, sloping plain but is rather a rugged terrain made up of features like those found on land. We have also learned much about the fish that dwell in the deepest parts of the ocean. In their way, they are as strange and fantastic as the legendary sea monsters of human imagination.

Photograph by Bruce Robison

Illustrations by Robert Hynes

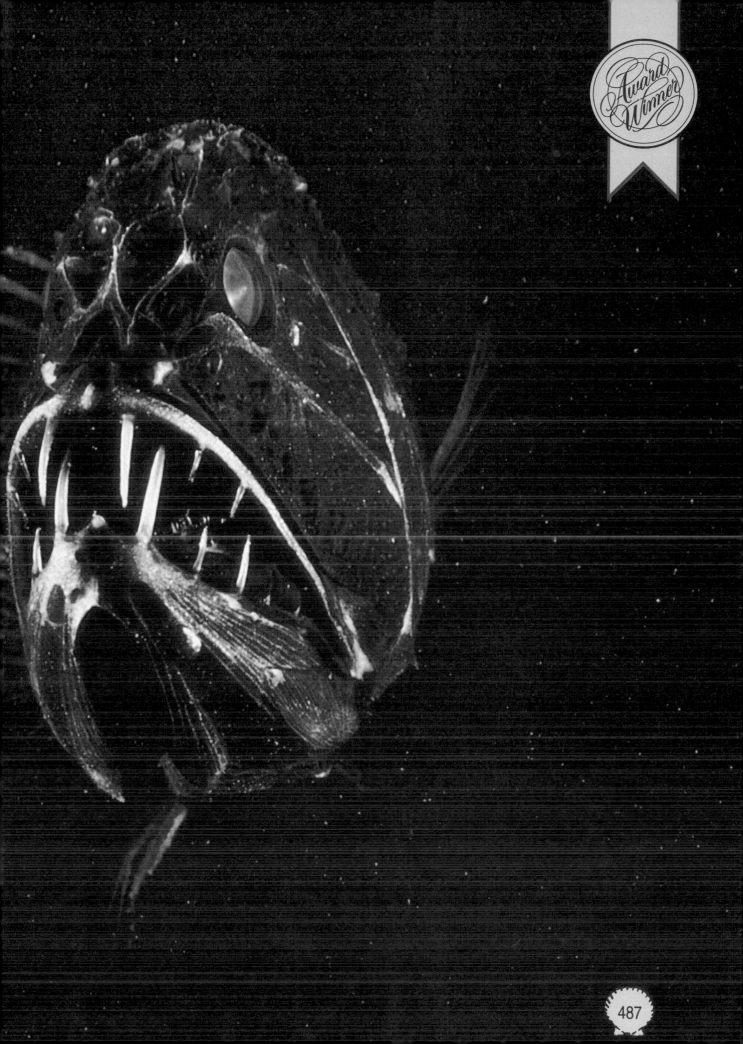

From *Lurkers of the Deep*
by Bruce H. Robison

Gulper

Lurking in the still, dark waters of the deep sea are some of the strangest creatures on our planet. Fishes with huge teeth and glowing lights cruise through a cold blackness that is studded with small blue lights like the galaxies of space. Bright red shrimp, oddly shaped squid, and transparent animals made of jelly also live at these depths. To those of us who live on the land, the deep ocean is an alien environment, almost as harsh as that of the moon or Mars.

Only a few people have ever seen the creatures of the deep sea with their own eyes. Oceanographers, riding in tiny submarines, are some of the lucky explorers who have seen these animals. In these pages we will discover what deep-sea scientists have learned about the fishes and other animals they study. In many ways it will seem like a report on the exploration of another world.

Lanternfish

Let's start with the sun. Sunlight is radiant energy that travels 150 million kilometers (93 million miles) from the sun to the earth. We know the energy in sunshine as light and heat. Sunlight is the basic source of energy for all of the plants on our planet. Plants receive the energy of sunshine, and through a series of chemical reactions called *photosynthesis* (fō′tō **sĭn′**thĭ sĭs), they use the energy to make food from chemicals in their surroundings.

Sunshine and plants may seem an odd place to begin a discussion of deep-sea fishes, who live where there are no plants and where there is no sunlight. But the food that plants make with sunshine is important to every animal on earth, even those living deep in the ocean.

When sunlight reaches the surface of the earth it falls on grasses, trees, and other land plants and on plants that live in the ocean. Most of the oceanic plants are very small, no bigger than the period at the end of this sentence. These tiny plants are made up of only one cell, but each of them can perform the magic of photosynthesis. They are called *phytoplankton* (fī′tō **plăngk′**tən). There are so many of them in the ocean that counting them would be like trying to count the grains of sand on a beach.

Phytoplankton are usually found near the surface of the ocean. The surface waters have the most sunlight, and in order to produce food, the phytoplankton need to be in the light. Sunlight strong enough for photosynthesis reaches down only about 150 meters (nearly 500 feet) in clear oceanic water. Below this depth the dim light gradually fades to nothing. At depths of 600 meters (about 2000 feet) the water is as dark as the blackest night.

Because the oceans of the world occupy so much of its surface, more than half of the sunlight that falls on our planet lights up the waters where phytoplankton live. These billions of one-celled plants produce most of the food energy used by all of the animals of the ocean — from shrimp to whales.

But there is a lot more to the ocean than just the layer near the surface where plants can live. Down in the dim, dark waters below the plant layer lives a strange and wonderful group of animals: the creatures of the deep sea.

Most people see only the edges of the ocean. We see beaches where the ocean meets the land; in boats we can sail along the ocean's upper edge where it meets the air. In shallow water near the shore we can swim or wade; and by using scuba gear, it is possible to swim down to depths of 50 meters (more than 150 feet). But out beyond the shore the ocean gets very deep, going down about 4000 meters (more than 2 miles) in most places.

Hatchetfish

It is almost as difficult for people to explore the deep ocean as it is for them to explore the moon. One of the main reasons for this

is that the deep ocean is always dark. Sunlight reaches only a short way down, and the long stretch of water between the sunlit part and the bottom is dark except for the lights produced by the animals that live there.

Another important thing about the deep sea is its coldness. With no sunlight to heat it, the temperature of the water is usually between 1° and 5° centigrade (34° to 41° Fahrenheit). Just as the light gets dimmer as depth increases, so does the temperature get colder.

Hunter

Gravity, the force that gives us weight by pulling us toward the center of the earth, also affects the animals that live in the deep sea. The deeper we go in the ocean the more the water above us weighs. The weight of the water is felt as pressure.

Creatures on the land have only the weight of the air above pressing on them. At sea level the weight is described as one atmosphere of pressure. High in the mountains or flying in an airplane at great altitude, the pressure is less. Because water is thicker, or denser, than air, pressure increases very quickly with greater depth in the ocean. At a depth of 10 meters (about 33 feet) the weight of the water above is equal to one atmosphere. At 100 meters (330 feet) the pressure is 10 atmospheres plus the weight of the air above the ocean — a total of 11 atmospheres. One atmosphere of pressure weighs about one kilogram per square centimeter (15 pounds per square inch), so a fish living at a depth of 1000 meters in the ocean has a pressure of 101 atmospheres (1650 pounds per square inch) on it.

All of these things — the darkness, the cold, and the pressure — make it difficult for scientists to study the animals of the deep sea. They also make the deep sea a difficult place for most animals to live in. The result is that we don't know a great deal about deep-sea creatures but what we do know shows us that they are very unusual animals.

Lanternfish, like many deep-sea fishes, have light-producing spots on their bodies. Some lanternfish have large lights on their heads between their eyes, lighting the dark water in front of them much like the headlights on a car.

Hatchetfish share the deep-sea living space with the lanternfish. Their bodies are shaped like hatchet blades, and their small tails look like handles. Hatchetfish spend most of their time at depths of about 400 to 800 meters (1300 to 2500 feet).

The eyes of some species of hatchetfish point straight up. Their eyes help the fish to see well in dim light and to judge distances accurately.

Bristlemouth fishes are found in nearly all oceans. Most are quite small — about 5 centimeters (or 2 inches) long. When two similar species inhabit the same area, they generally divide the living space into two layers. The darker species lives in the lower, more dimly lit layer, and the lighter species lives above. In this way, the fishes match the light levels of their environment.

Dragonfish get their name from their ferocious appearance. They seldom grow longer than 60 or 70 centimeters (about two feet). The long, flexible projections called *barbels* (**bär′**bəlz) that hang from their lower jaws end in light-producing bulbs. The light seems to attract other fish that the dragonfish eat.

Most species of dragonfish have mouths filled with jagged rows of long, sharp teeth. In some species, the teeth are hinged so that they will fold inward toward the throat but not forward to allow escape. Anything that finds itself in such a mouth is trapped.

Anglerfish are ambushers. They have long projections, like

Anglerfish

fishing rods, growing from their heads. At the tip of the rods are glowing baits. Anglers have large mouths filled with long, sharp teeth. They quickly gobble up anything that is attracted to their bait.

Most anglerfish live in depths below 1000 meters (3300 feet), where the water is inky black. Like most fish that live in the cold depths, anglerfish swim rather slowly. While awaiting their prey, they probably stay motionless in the dark water with only the lights of their lures to indicate their presence. But they spring into action when their lures are touched.

In some species of anglerfish, the female is much larger than the male. Once the tiny male anglerfish has found his mate, he attaches himself to her body with his teeth. For some species, this is the end of the male's life as a separate fish. The male is a permanent attachment to the female, nourished by the female's blood supply. Female anglers have been caught with as many as eleven attached males. However, in some species, the male lets go and swims away after mating.

Hunters are deep-sea predators. Some actively seek out and chase their prey through a range of depths, from black depths below 1000 meters (3300 feet) to twilight depths above 600 meters (about 2000 feet). They go through greater changes in temperature and pressure than most other deep-sea fishes. Because they are fast-moving, they are harder to catch than most other deep-water fishes. Fewer of them have been captured for scientific study. Most of what is known about them is based on the smaller varieties of hunter.

Gulpers [ambush predators] are fishes with huge mouths, tiny eyes, and long, slender bodies that seem to be at least half stomach. Some species have luminous organs at the tip of a long tail, used to attract prey. Like many other deep-sea predators, the gulpers have stomachs with black walls. Thus, the lights of an eaten fish do not shine through the stomach wall to reveal the gulper's location.

Dragonfish

494

LURKERS OF THE DEEP

Thinking and Discussing

The selection discusses two layers of the ocean. What are the different layers? What kinds of life are to be found in each layer?

The text points out that many deep-sea fish have light-producing spots on their bodies. In terms of survival, why are the lights a good thing for some fish, but not such a good thing for others?

Applying Science Concepts

Diagramming the Food Chain Imagine that you have just eaten an ocean fish for dinner. Draw a diagram that shows how energy was transferred from the sun to your body through the food chain of the ocean.

Charting Deep-Sea Life Make a chart that compares and contrasts how the fishes discussed in the selection have adapted to life in the deep ocean. Include such categories as the food the fish eats, how it swims, where it lives, and what it looks like. Research any categories you cannot complete with information from the selection. Give your chart a title such as "Deep-Sea Fish Adaptation" and display it in the classroom.

Donald Collins received his Ph.D. from the California Institute of Technology in 1969. He currently works at the Jet Propulsion Laboratory at the California Institute of Technology and lives in Altadena, California, with his wife and two sons. In his spare time, Dr. Collins is active in Scouting.

Walter Oleksy was born in Chicago in 1930 and started writing stories when he was a child. He spent seven years working as a reporter and editor for the *Chicago Tribune*. His first book for preteens, *Laugh, Clown, Cry: The Story of Charlie Chaplin*, was published in 1976. Oleksy's books for young adults include *Visitors from Outer Space?*, *Paramedics*, and *Treasures of the Deep*.

Margaret Poynter was born in Long Beach, California, in 1927. She became a free-lance writer in 1972 and joined the staff of the *Pasadena/Altadena Weekly* in 1979. Her first book, *Frisbee Fun*, was published in 1977. She has since published more than twenty books, including *The Zoo Lady, Search and Rescue, Volcanoes: The Fiery Mountains* (named an outstanding science book for children by the National Science Teachers Association in 1980), *Voyager: The Story of a Space Mission* (named an outstanding science book in 1981), and *Cosmic Quest*.

Bruce H. Robison works as a research biologist at the Marine Science Institute of the University of California at Santa Barbara. He has spent several years aboard research vessels, conducting hundreds of deep-sea trawl hauls to study the fish that live at great depths. One of his most exciting experiences was a dive in the three-man submersible *Alvin*, in which he descended to a depth of over a mile in the Atlantic Ocean.

The Black Pearl

by Scott O'Dell   (Houghton, 1967)

Ramón Salazar realizes his dream of diving for pearls when he finds the great pearl — the magnificent, dusky Pearl of Heaven — in a sea creature's cave. But Ramón knows no peace as long as he possesses the gem.

The Great Barrier Reef: A Treasure in the Sea

by Alice Gilbreath   (Dillon, 1986)

Off the coast of Australia lies the Great Barrier Reef, one of the natural wonders of the world. This informative book explains how the reef was formed and focuses on creatures living on the reef.

Incredible Facts About the Ocean: The Land Below, the Life Within

by W. Wright Robinson   (Dillon, 1987)

Excellent photographs, many taken from outer space, help readers discover how the oceans create deltas, islands, and sandbars, and how land below sea level shapes bays, gulfs, and seas.

How Did We Find Out About Life in the Deep Sea?

by Isaac Asimov   (Walker, 1981; Avon, 1982)

The popular author describes the discovery of life beneath the sea and the extraordinary creatures that dwell there.

The Mysterious Undersea World

by Jan Leslie Cook   (National Geographic Society, 1980)

Striking color photographs help the reader investigate the sea, its plants and animals, and coral reefs. Submersibles, ocean pets, and aquariums are also explained briefly.

Glossary

Some of the words in this book may have pronunciations or meanings you do not know. This glossary can help you by telling you how to pronounce those words and by telling you the meanings with which those words are used in this book.

You can find out the correct pronunciation of any glossary word by using the special spelling after the word and the pronunciation key that runs across the bottom of the glossary pages.

The full pronunciation key opposite shows how to pronounce each consonant and vowel in a special spelling. The pronunciation key at the bottom of the glossary pages is a shortened form of the full key.

FULL PRONUNCIATION KEY

Consonant Sounds

b	**bib**	k	**c**at, **kick**, pi**que**	th	pa**th**, **th**in
ch	**church**	l	**l**id, need**l**e	*th*	ba**th**e, **th**is
d	**deed**	m	a**m**, **m**an, **mum**	v	ca**v**e, **v**al**v**e,
f	**f**ast, **fif**e, o**ff**,	n	**n**o, sudde**n**		**v**ine
	phase, rou**gh**	ng	thi**ng**	w	**w**ith
g	**g**a**g**	p	**p**o**p**	y	**y**es
h	**h**at	r	**r**oa**r**	z	**r**ose, **s**ize,
hw	**wh**ich	s	mi**ss**, **s**auce, **s**ee		**x**ylophone,
j	**j**u**dg**e	sh	di**sh**, **sh**ip		**z**ebra
		t	**t**igh**t**	zh	gara**g**e,
					plea**s**ure, vi**s**ion

Vowel Sounds

ă	p**a**t	î	d**ea**r, d**ee**r,	ou	c**ow**, **ou**t
ā	**ai**d, th**ey**, p**ay**		f**ie**rce, m**e**re	ŭ	c**u**t, r**ou**gh
â	**ai**r, c**a**re, w**ea**r	ŏ	p**o**t, h**o**rrible	û	f**i**rm, h**ea**rd,
ä	f**a**ther	ō	g**o**, r**ow**, t**oe**		t**e**rm, t**u**rn,
ĕ	p**e**t, pl**ea**sure	ô	**a**lter, c**au**ght,		w**o**rd
ē	b**e**, b**ee**, **ea**sy,		f**o**r, p**aw**	yo͞o	ab**u**se, **u**se
	s**ei**ze	oi	b**oy**, n**oi**se, **oi**l	ə	**a**bout, sil**e**nt,
ĭ	p**i**t	o͝o	b**oo**k		penc**i**l, lem**o**n,
ī	b**y**, g**uy**, p**ie**	o͞o	b**oo**t		circ**u**s
				ər	butt**er**

STRESS MARKS

Primary Stress '	Secondary Stress '
bi•ol•o•gy [bī **ŏl**′ə jē]	bi•o•log•i•cal [bī′ə **lŏj**′ĭ kəl]

A

ACCUSATION

The word **accusation** *and its root* accuse *come from the Latin word* accusare, *from* ad-, *"to"* + causa, *"lawsuit," meaning "to call to account."*

a·ban·doned (ə bǎn′dənd) *adj.* Recklessly unrestrained; free from self-control: *The players' **abandoned** joy after their win was understandable.*

a·brupt·ly (ə brŭpt′lē) *adv.* Unexpectedly; suddenly: *Lightning caused the lights to go out **abruptly**.*

a·bun·dant (ə bŭn′dənt) *adj.* Existing in great supply; very plentiful: *In April there is usually **abundant** rainfall.*

ac·com·pa·ny (ə kŭm′pə nē) *v.* **ac·com·pa·nied, ac·com·pa·ny·ing, ac·com·pa·nies.** To support (a singer, musician, etc.) by playing or providing music: *I **accompanied** Mike on the piano when he sang.*

ac·cu·sa·tion (ăk′yōō zā′shən) *n.* A statement or formal declaration that a person has been guilty of wrongdoing: *Her **accusation** of theft took me by surprise.*

ac·knowl·edge (ăk nŏl′ ĭj) *v.* **ac·knowl·edged, ac·knowl·edg·ing.** To admit the existence or truth of: *Did she **acknowledge** that we were right?*

ad·dle (ăd′l) *v.* **ad·dled, ad·dling.** To mix up, confuse, or muddle.

ad·van·tage (ăd vǎn′tĭj) *or* (-vän′-) *n.* A benefit that puts one in a favorable position: *This year's team has the **advantages** of several returning players and an experienced coach.*

af·ter·life (ăf′tər līf′) *or* (äf′-) *n.* Life or existence after death.

ag·i·ta·tion (ăj′ ĭ tā′shən) *n.* Great emotional disturbance or excitement: *His **agitation** grew as he realized he was losing the contest.*

a·li·en (ā′ lē ən) *or* (āl′yən) *adj.* Not natural; not characteristic: *The desert is an **alien** place to a person from a wet climate.* —*n.* A person living in one country though a citizen of another; a foreigner: *It is important for **aliens** and tourists to have up-to-date passports.*

ă pat / ā **pay** / â care / ä father / ě pet / ē be / ǐ pit / ī pie / î fierce / ŏ pot / ō go / ô paw, for /

a•mi•a•ble (ā′mē ə bəl) *adj.*
Friendly; good-natured.

an•guish (ăng′gwĭsh) *n.* A
pain of the body or mind that
causes one agony.

ap•pre•ci•ate (ə prē′shē āt′)
v. **ap•pre•ci•at•ed,
ap•pre•ci•at•ing.** To
recognize the worth,
quality, importance, etc., of;
value highly: *The manager
appreciated the work her
assistant did.*

ar•chae•ol•o•gist
(är′kē ŏl′ə jĭst) *n.* A person
engaged in the scientific
study of the remains of past
human activities, such as
burials, buildings, tools, and
pottery.

as•ton•ish•ing•ly
(ə stŏn′ ĭ shĭng lē) *adv.* In a
surprising or amazing manner: *Astonishingly, they
caught the largest shark on
record.*

a•stound (ə stound′) *v.*
a•stound•ed, a•stound•ing.
To strike with sudden wonder; astonish: *The magician's
trick astounded the crowd.*

at•mos•phere (ăt′mə sfîr′)
n. A unit of pressure equal to
the pressure of the air at sea
level, about 14.7 pounds per
square inch.

a•vi•a•tor (ā′vē ā′tər) *or*
(ăv′ē-) *n.* A person who
flies or is capable of flying
aircraft; a pilot.

B

bar•ren (băr′ən) *adj.* **1.** Lacking or unable to produce
growing plants or crops.
2. Empty; bare: *With no
furniture, the house looked
barren.*

bar•ri•er (băr′ē ər) *n.* A
fence, wall, or other structure
that holds back or blocks
movement or passage: *The
highway crew put up a barrier
around the pothole.*

be•fall (bĭ fôl′) *v.* **be•fell**
(bĭ fĕl′), **be•fall•en**
(bĭ fôl′ən), **be•fall•ing.** To
happen to: *Disasters have
befallen many ships in these
waters.*

ben•e•fit (bĕn′ ə fĭt) *n.*
Something that is of help; an
advantage: *The field trip was
of great benefit to the students.*

archaeologists

ASTOUND

The word **astound**
comes from the word
astone, *"to amaze."*
Astone *developed
from the Vulgar
Latin* extonāre, *"to
strike and make
senseless." This word
developed from the
Latin word* tonare,
"to thunder."

BENEFIT

The word **benefit**
*developed from the
Latin* benefactum,
*"a good deed," which
came from* bene
facere, *"to do well."*

---

oi **oil** / ŏŏ **book** / ōō **boot** / ou **out** / ŭ **cut** / û **fur** / *th* **the** / th **thin** / hw **which** /
zh **vision** / ə **ago, item, pencil, atom, circus**

buoy

be•tray (bǐ trā´) *v.* **be•trayed, be•tray•ing.** To give evidence of; indicate: *Do not let any noise betray our hiding place.*

be•wil•dered (bǐ wǐl´dərd) *adj.* Feeling greatly confused or puzzled: *The bewildered players needed help understanding the game's directions.*

boar (bôr) *or* (bōr) *n.* A wild pig with dark hair or bristles.

bois•ter•ous (boi´stər əs) *or* (-strəs) *adj.* Noisy and lacking restraint or discipline.

bolt (bōlt) *v.* **bolt•ed, bolt•ing.** To make off suddenly; run.

bot•a•nist (bŏt´n ĭst) *n.* A scientist who specializes in the study of plants.

bound•a•ry (boun´də rē) *or* (-drē) *n., pl.* **bound•a•ries.** An edge, limit, or dividing line marking the place where a region ends.

bridge (brĭj) *n.* A platform above the main deck of a ship from which the ship is controlled.

bris•tling (brĭs´lĭng) *adj.* Raising the hair stiffly.

brows•ing (brouz´ĭng) *n.* The act of looking over goods in a store casually without seriously intending to buy them: *Browsing in the bookstore is one of her favorite activities.*

buoy (bōō´ē) *or* (boi) *n.* A float used to mark a channel or a place for boats to anchor.

C

ca•dence (kād´ns) *n.* The beat or rhythm of music, dancing, marching, walking, etc.: *The cadence of the drums set the pace of the parade.*

cas•ket (kăs´kĭt) *or* (kä´skĭt) *n.* A small case or chest for jewels or other valuables.

cas•u•al•ly (kăzh´ōō əl lē) *adv.* With little interest; unconcernedly; nonchalantly: *She casually tossed the wrapper into a trash can.*

cat•a•ract (kăt´ə răkt´) *n.* A very large waterfall formed from steep rapids.

ă pat / ā pay / â care / ä father / ĕ pet / ē be / ĭ pit / ī pie / î fierce / ŏ pot / ō go / ô paw, for /

cer•e•mo•ny (sĕr´ə mō´nē) *n.* A formal act or set of acts performed in honor or celebration of an occasion, such as a wedding, funeral, etc.: *The graduation* **ceremony** *marked the finish of our years in elementary school.*

chal•lenge (chăl´ənj) *v.* **chal•lenged, chal•leng•ing.** To call to engage in a contest or fight: *They* **challenged** *us to a game of volleyball.*

clam•or•ing (klăm´ər ĭng) *adj.* Making or full of a loud, continuous, and usually confused noise: *The* **clamoring** *crowd disrupted the speech.*

clus•ter (klŭs´tər) *n.* A group of similar things growing or grouped close together: *That* **cluster** *of flowers is made up of daisies and petunias.*

coarse (kôrs) *or* (kōrs) *adj.* Not refined; crude; rude.

codg•er (kŏj´ər) *n.* An old or somewhat eccentric man.

col•lec•tive (kə lĕk´tĭv) *adj.* Of a number of persons or things acting as one: *Our* **collective** *opinion will add weight to the decision.*

col•li•sion (kə lĭzh´ən) *n.* The act or process of bumping together; a crash.

com•pas•sion (kəm păsh´ən) *n.* The feeling of sharing the suffering of another.

com•pe•tent (kŏm´pĭ tnt) *adj.* Able to do what is required; capable.

com•pre•hend (kom´prĭ hĕnd´) *v.* **com•pre•hend•ed, com•pre•hend•ing.** To grasp mentally; understand: *He finally* **comprehended** *the main idea of the story.*

con•cen•trate (kŏn´sən trāt´) *v.* **con•cen•trat•ed, con•cen•trat•ing.** To keep or direct one's thoughts, attention, or efforts: *She is* **concentrating** *on making the free throw.*

con•duct (kən dŭkt´) *v.* **con•duct•ed, con•duct•ing.** To direct the course of; manage: *As president, Ylena is supposed to* **conduct** *the club's meetings.*

con•tour (kŏn´ toor´) *v.* **con•toured, con•tour•ing.** To shape the surface of: *The field is* **contoured** *in ridges and furrows.*

CHALLENGE

The word **challenge** *comes from French and Latin words that mean "to accuse." These words developed from the Latin* calvi, *"to deceive."*

CONCENTRATE

Concentrate *probably comes from the Latin word* concentrare, *a combination of* com-, *"together" +* centrum, *"center."*

oi **oi**l / o͝o **book** / o͞o **boot** / ou **out** / ŭ **cut** / û **fur** / *th* **the** / th **thin** / hw **which** / zh **vision** / ə **ago, item, pencil, atom, circus**

505

cove (kōv) *n.* A small, sheltered bay or inlet: *We sailed around the cove several times.*

crit·i·cal (krĭt´ĭ kəl) *adj.* Likely to find fault: *He is always critical of the things I do.*

crude·ly (krōōd´lē) *adv.* In an unskilled manner; roughly.

crust (krŭst) *n.* Any hard outer layer or covering.

cul·prit (kŭl´prĭt) *n.* A person guilty or believed to be guilty of a crime or offense: *The culprit received a prison sentence.*

curl·i·cue (kûr´lĭ kyōō´) *n.* A fancy twist or curl, such as a flourish made with a pen.

cur·rent (kûr´ənt) *or* (kŭr´-) *n.* A mass of liquid or gas that is in motion: *Swimmers can be swept off balance by a river's current.*

cut·ter (kŭt´ər) *n.* A Coast Guard vessel of more than 65 feet in length.

> ### CRUST
> **Crust** *comes from Middle English and Old French words that developed from the Latin word* crusta, *"shell."*

curlicue

daw·dle (dôd´l) *v.* **daw·dled, daw·dling.** To move slowly and aimlessly; loiter: *We dawdled over dinner.*

de·bris (də brē´) *or* (dā´brē´) *n.* The scattered remains of something broken, destroyed, or discarded; fragments; rubble: *We began cleaning up the debris left by the tornado.*

de·ci·pher (dĭ sī´fər) *v.* **de·ci·phered, de·ci·pher·ing.** To change (a message) from a code or cipher to ordinary language; decode.

ded·i·cate (dĕd´ĭ kāt´) *v.* **ded·i·cat·ed, ded·i·cat·ing.** To set apart for a special purpose, such as worship: *The ministers and members dedicated the new church last Sunday.*

de·gree (dĭ grē´) *n.* A unit of arc or angular measure equal to 1/360 of a complete revolution: *A right angle measures 90 degrees.*

ă pat / ā pay / â care / ä father / ĕ pet / ē be / ĭ pit / ī pie / î fierce / ŏ pot / ō go / ô paw, for /

del·i·ca·cy (dĕl´ĭ kə sē) *n.*, *pl.* **del·i·ca·cies.** A choice food: *They served many delicacies at the party.*

del·ta (dĕl´tə) *n.* A usually triangular mass of sand, mud, and earth at the mouth of a river.

de·mol·ish (dĭ mŏl´ish) *v.* **de·mol·ished, de·mol·ish·ing.** To tear down completely; wreck; destroy.

dem·on·stra·tion (dĕm´ən strā´shən) *n.* A display of how something proceeds or operates.

depth (dĕpth) *n.* A distance downward or inward from a surface.

des·per·a·tion (dĕs´pə rā´shən) *n.* Despair or extreme action resulting from it.

des·tine (dĕs´tĭn) *v.* **des·tined, des·tin·ing.** To determine beforehand, as if by some force or power over which one has no control: *She was destined to become a great ruler.*

de·test (dĭ tĕst´) *v.* **de·test·ed, de·test·ing.** To dislike strongly; abhor; loathe.

det·o·na·tion (dĕt´n ā´shən) *n.* An explosion: *The detonation caused a large fire.*

de·vot·ed (dĭ vō´tĭd) *adj.* Giving or applying (one's time, attention, or self) entirely to a specified activity, cause, person, etc.: *That devoted author spends seven hours a day writing.*

de·vour (dĭ vour´) *v.* **de·voured, de·vour·ing.** To swallow or eat up greedily.

di·a·dem (dī´ə dĕm´) *n.* A crown or ornamental band worn on the head as a sign of royalty.

di·et (dī´ ĭt) *n.* The usual food and drink consumed by a person or animal.

dig·ni·fied (dĭg´nə fīd´) *adj.* Having or expressing honor; serious and stately; poised: *Crowds cheered as the dignified soldiers marched proudly in the parade.*

dire (dīr) *adj.* Having dreadful or terrible consequences; disastrous: *The earthquake was a dire catastrophe.*

diadem

---

oi **oil** / o͝o **book** / o͞o **boot** / ou **out** / ŭ **cut** / û **fur** / *th* **the** / th **thin** / hw **which** / zh **vision** / ə **ago, item, pencil, atom, circus**

dis•a•bil•i•ty (dĭs´ə bĭl´ĭ tē) *n.* Something that disables; a handicap: *People with hearing loss can use hearing aids to cope with this disability.*

dis•grun•tled (dĭs grŭn´tld) *adj.* Discontented; unsatisfied.

dis•man•tle (dĭs măn´tl) *v.* **dis•man•tled, dis•man•tling.** To take apart: *Workers were dismantling the exhibits at the science museum.*

doc•u•men•ta•ry (dŏk´yə měn´tə rē) *n.* A motion picture giving a factual account of some subject and often showing actual events: *We watched a documentary on the eruption of Mount St. Helens.*

doomed (do͞omd) *adj.* Fated for an unhappy end, especially death.

dredg•ing (drĕj´ĭng) *n.* The act of fishing up from or as if from the bottom of a river, lake, etc., with a machine that uses scooping or suction devices.

drone (drōn) *n.* A continuous low humming or buzzing sound: *We went into the house when we heard the drone of the mosquitos.*

droop (dro͞op) *v.* **drooped, droop•ing.** To bend or hang downward; sag.

dy•nas•ty (dī´nə stē) *n.* A succession of rulers from the same family or line.

ee•rie (îr´ē) *adj.* Strange; unsettling; weird: *The old, empty house gave us an eerie feeling.*

el•e•gance (ĕl´ĭ gəns) *n.* Refinement and grace in appearance or manner: *He always noticed her unaffected elegance.*

el•e•gant (ĕl´ĭ gənt) *adj.* Refined or tastefully lavish: *The queen's elegant dress was decorated with jewels.*

em•balm (ĕm bäm´) *v.* **em•balmed, em•balm•ing.** To treat (a corpse) with substances that prevent or retard decay.

DOCUMENTARY

Documentary *and its root* document *developed from Middle English and Old French words based on the Latin* documentum, *"lesson."*

EERIE

Eerie *comes from the Middle English* eri, *"fearful," which came from the Old English* earg, *"cowardly."*

---

em•brace (ĕm brās´) *v.*
em•braced, em•brac•ing.
To clasp or hold with the
arms as a sign of affection:
She was **embracing** *the crying
child.*

e•merge (ĭ mûrj´) *v.*
e•merged, e•merg•ing. To
come into view; appear: *The
hermit crab* **emerged** *from its
shell.*

e•merg•ing (ĭ mûrj´ ĭng)
adj. Coming into view;
appearing.

en•a•ble (ĕn ā´bəl) *v.*
en•a•bled, en•a•bling. To
give the means, ability, or
opportunity to do something:
The award **enabled** *him to
travel across the country.*

en•thu•si•as•ti•cal•ly
(ĕn thoo´zē ăs´tĭk lē) *adv.*
In an interested, eager, or
admiring manner: *The crowd
cheered the victorious team*
enthusiastically.

en•vel•op (ĕn vĕl´əp) *v.*
**en•vel•oped,
en•vel•op•ing.** To enclose
completely with or as if with
a covering: *Clouds* **enveloped**
the mountains.

e•rode (ĭ rōd´) *v.* **e•rod•ed,
e•rod•ing.** To wear away by
or as if by rubbing or bom-
bardment with small parti-
cles: *High winds can* **erode** *the
hillside.*

es•cort (ĭ skôrt´) *v.*
es•cort•ed, es•cort•ing. To
accompany in order to
provide protection or to pay
honor: *The police* **escorted** *the
president through the crowded
lobby.*

es•tab•lish (ĭ stăb´lĭsh) *v.*
**es•tab•lished,
es•tab•lish•ing.** To show to
be true; prove: *The lawyer's
job is to* **establish** *that the man
is not guilty.*

e•vac•u•ate (ĭ văk´yoo āt´) *v.*
**e•vac•u•a•ted,
e•vac•u•at•ing.** To send
away or withdraw (inhabi-
tants or troops) from an
area: *The townspeople were*
evacuated *because of the flood.*

e•ven•tu•al•ly
(ĭ vĕn´choo əl ē) *adv.* In a
future time not yet set or
specified: *She never lost hope of*
eventually *becoming a movie
star.*

ex•ca•va•tor (ĕks´ kə vā´tər)
n. One who uncovers or
exposes to view by digging.

EMERGE

Emerge *is from the
Latin* emergere, *"to
un-sink, to rise to the
surface, to come out,"
formed by combining
e-, "out" + mergere,
"to sink."*

ERODE

The word **erode**
comes from the Latin
erodere, *meaning
"to eat away" or "to
gnaw off."*

---

oi **oil** / oŏ **book** / ōō **boot** / ou **out** / ŭ **cut** / û **fur** / *th* **the** / th **thin** / hw **which** /
zh **vision** / ə **ago, item, pencil, atom, circus**

fam•ine (**făm´**ĭn) *n.* A serious shortage of food resulting in widespread hunger and starvation.

fea•ture (**fē´**chər) *n.* A prominent part, quality, or characteristic: *The main **features** of the desert are rock, sand, and wind.*

fi•nal•i•ty (fī **năl´**ĭ tē) *n., pl.* **fi•nal•i•ties.** The quality of being at the end; decisiveness: *At the end of the game, the buzzer sounded with **finality**.*

flinch (flĭnch) *v.* **flinched, flinch•ing.** To shrink or wince, as from pain or fear: *He **flinched** at the unexpected sound of the firecracker.*

fo•li•age (**fō´**lē ĭj) *n.* The leaves of plants or trees; leaves in general.

for•lorn•ly (fôr **lôrn´** lē) *adv.* In a manner that is wretched or pitiful in appearance or condition: *The little lost dog whined **forlornly**.*

for•sak•en (fôr **sā´**kən) *adj.* Deserted, abandoned, or lonely; uncared for: *The **forsaken** boat rotted in its spot near the dock.*

fu•gi•tive (**fyoō´**jĭ tĭv) *n.* A person who flees; a runaway; refugee: *The police caught the **fugitive** after a two-day search.*

furl (fûrl) *v.* **furled, furl•ing.** To roll up and fasten (a flag or sail) to a pole, yard, or mast: *While the ship was in port, its sails were **furled**.*

gal•va•nized (**găl´**və nīzd) *adj.* Coated with zinc in order to prevent rust: *It is best to use **galvanized** nails when building an outdoor deck of wood.*

gape (gāp) *or* (găp) *v.* **gaped, gap•ing.** To open wide: *Holes were **gaping** where the floor had rotted away.*

ges•ture (**jĕs´**chər) *n.* A motion of the hands, arms, head, or body used while speaking or in place of speech to help express one's meaning: *The actor used a dramatic **gesture**.*

FAMINE

Famine *is from Middle English and Old French words that developed from the Latin* fames, *"hunger."*

ă pat / ā pay / â care / ä father / ĕ pet / ē be / ĭ pit / ī pie / î fierce / ŏ pot / ō go / ô paw, for /

glare (glâr) *v.* **glared, glar•ing.** To stare fiercely or angrily: *She **glared** at him with resentment.*

glis•ten (glĭs´ən) *v.* **glis•tened, glis•ten•ing.** To shine with reflected light: *The snow-covered mountains **glistened** in the sunshine.*

goal (gōl) *n.* A desired result or purpose toward which one is working; an objective: *His **goals** are to go to college and to become a doctor.*

grade (grād) *n.* A slope or an incline, as of a road: *Trailer trucks have trouble climbing the steep **grade** of the mountain pass.*

hal•lu•ci•nate (hə lōō´sə nāt´) *v.* To see, hear, or otherwise sense something that does not really exist.

har•bor (här´bər) *v.* **har•bored, har•bor•ing.** To give shelter and lodging to; take in.

has•ten (hā´sən) *v.* **has•tened, has•ten•ing.** To move or act swiftly; hurry: *He **hastened** home to tell the family the news.*

haunch (hônch) *or* (hänch) *n.* The hip, buttock, and upper thigh of a person or animal: *The cat sat on its **haunches** and bathed.*

he•ro•ic (hĭ rō´ ĭk) *adj.* Having or showing the qualities of a hero; courageous; noble: *We read about the **heroic** voyages of the astronauts.*

hes•i•tant•ly (hĕz´ ĭ tənt lē) *adv.* In a slow or doubtful manner: *The hikers **hesitantly** approached the old wooden footbridge.*

hi•er•o•glyph•ics (hī´ər ə glĭf´ĭks) *or* (hī´rə-) *n.* A system of writing, used in ancient Egypt, in which pictures or symbols are used to represent words or sounds.

host (hōst) *n.* A living plant or animal on or in which a parasite or other organism lives and from which it usually gets its nourishment.

GRADE

Grade *is from French and developed from the Latin* gradus, *"step."*

HIEROGLYPHIC

Hieroglyphic *developed from the Greek* hieros, *"sacred"* + gluphē, *"carving." The Greek word passed through the Latin and French languages before becoming part of English.*

hieroglyphics

oi **oil** / ŏŏ **book** / ōō **boot** / ou **out** / ŭ **cut** / û **fur** / *th* **the** / th **thin** / hw **which** / zh **vision** / ə **ago, item, pencil, atom, circus**

hov•er (hŭv´ər) *or* (hŏv´-) *v.* **hov•ered, hov•er•ing.** To be in a condition of uncertainty; waver: *They* **hovered** *over the test questions before they started.*

hurl (hûrl) *v.* **hurled, hurl•ing.** To throw with great force; fling: *The waterfall* **hurled** *the ice into the pool below.*

hur•tle (hûr´tl) *v.* **hur•tled, hur•tling.** To move or cause to move with or as if with great speed: *The wind* **hurtled** *leaves into the air.*

hy•giene (hī´ jēn´) *n.* Scientific methods for the promotion of good health and the prevention of disease: *We learned about killing germs in our class on* **hygiene.**

ig•no•rant (ĭg´ nər ənt) *adj.* Showing lack of education or knowledge: *The ignorant person signed the document with an* x.

ig•nore (ĭg nôr´) *or* (-nōr´) *v.* **ig•nored, ig•nor•ing.** To pay no attention to; disregard.

il•lu•sion (ĭ lōō´zhən) *n.* An appearance or impression that has no real basis; false perception: *The artist used shading to create the* **illusion** *of depth.*

im•i•tate (ĭm´ ĭ tāt´) *v.* **im•i•tat•ed, im•i•tat•ing.** To copy the actions, appearance, function, or sounds of.

im•mense (ĭ měns´) *adj.* Of great, often immeasurable, size, extent, degree, etc.: *It was difficult to climb such* **immense** *rocks.*

im•mu•ni•za•tion (ĭm´yə nə **zā´**shən) *n.* A medicine that helps people and animals resist disease, in whole or in part: *This* **immunization** *will protect children from the measles.*

im•pul•sive (ĭm **pŭl´**sĭv) *adj.* Tending to act on an urge or whim rather than careful thought: *Impulsive shoppers sometimes buy things they don't need.*

in•de•struc•ti•ble (ĭn´dĭ **strŭk´**tə bəl) *adj.* Not capable of being destroyed.

IMMUNIZATION
Immunization *and its root* immune *come from the Latin* in-, *"not"* + munia, *"duties," meaning "free from service, as in the military."*

ă pat / ā pay / â care / ä father / ĕ pet / ē be / ĭ pit / ī pie / î fierce / ŏ pot / ō go / ô paw, for /

in·dig·na·tion
(ĭn´dĭg nā´shən) *n.* Anger aroused by something unjust, mean, etc.: *Her indignation was caused by his insulting remarks.*

in·fect (ĭn fĕkt´) *v.* **in·fect·ed, in·fect·ing.** To transmit a disease to: *Cover your mouth when you sneeze so that you do not infect the class.*

in·lay (ĭn´ lā´) *n.* Contrasting material set into a surface in pieces to form a design: *The bracelets were made of turquoise inlay.*

in·stinct (ĭn´stĭngkt´) *n.* An inner influence, feeling, or drive that may result in automatic behavior: *Instinct told me to stay away from the stranger.*

in·stinc·tive·ly
(ĭn´ stĭngk´ tĭv lē) *adv.* In a manner showing instinct: *Many birds instinctively fly south for the winter.*

in·tact (ĭn tăkt´) *adj.* Not impaired, injured, or damaged.

in·ter·pret (ĭn tûr´prĭt) *v.* **in·ter·pret·ed, in·ter·pret·ing.** To translate from one language to another.

in·vol·un·tar·i·ly
(ĭn vŏl´ən târ´ə lē) *adv.* Automatically; not subject to the person's will or choice: *She blinked involuntarily in the glare.*

J

jeer·ing·ly (jîr´ ĭng lē) *adv.* With a mocking or disapproving tone of voice: *The crowd roared jeeringly when the forward lost the basketball.*

jos·tle (jŏs´əl) *v.* **jos·tled, jos·tling.** To come into contact; crowd or brush against: *Hundreds of people jostled to find their theater seats.*

ju·bi·lant (joo´ bə lənt) *adj.* Full of joy; rejoicing. **—ju·bi·lant·ly** *adv.* In a joyful or rejoicing manner: *The astronaut waved jubilantly to the crowd.*

INFECT

Infect *comes from the Latin* infectus, *"to stain."*

inlay

JOSTLE

Jostle *developed from the Latin root* juxtā, *which means "close together."*

---

oi **oil** / o͝o **book** / o͞o **boot** / ou **out** / ŭ **cut** / û **fur** / *th* **the** / th **thin** / hw **which** / zh **vision** / ə **ago, item, pencil, atom, circus**

ka•lei•do•scope

(kə lī´də skōp´) *n.* A tube-shaped toy in which bits of loose, colored glass contained at one end reflect light into changing patterns visible from a hole at the other end.

knot

(nŏt) *n.* A unit of speed equal to one nautical mile per hour, used especially by ships and aircraft: *That plane can travel at 250 knots.*

laugh•ing•stock

(lăf´ĭng stŏk) *or* (lä´fĭng-) *n.* An object of mocking laughter, jokes, or ridicule.

lav•ish•ly

(lăv´ĭsh lē) *adv.* In an extravagant, luxurious, or showy manner: *The costume was gold trimmed and lavishly embroidered.*

lin•guist

(lĭng´gwĭst) *n.* A specialist in the science of language and the study of the nature and structure of human speech.

list•less

(lĭst´ lĭs) *adj.* Lacking energy or enthusiasm; lethargic: *I often feel listless on hot summer days.*

log•i•cal

(lŏj´ĭ kəl) *adj.* Reasonable: *The logical thing to do was to ask for help.*

loi•ter

(loi´tər) *v.* **loi•tered, loi•ter•ing.** To stand about idly; linger: *They were loitering in the schoolyard when the tardy bell rang.*

long

(lông) *or* (lŏng) *v.* **longed, long•ing.** To have a strong desire; wish for very much; want: *She longed to go back home.*

long•ing

(lông´ĭng) *or* (lŏng´-) *n.* A deep yearning; a strong desire: *The longing he felt to see his parents grew stronger.*

lounge

(lounj) *v.* **lounged, loung•ing.** To pass time idly: *His employer said he was lounging on the job.*

lu•mi•nous

(loo´mə nəs) *adj.* Giving off light, especially light that is self-generated rather than reflected; shining.

KALEIDOSCOPE

The **kaleidoscope** *was invented in 1816 by Sir David Brewster. The name came from a combination of the Greek words* kalos, *"beautiful" +* eidos, *"form" +* skopos, *"watcher."*

LONG

Long *is from the Old English* langian, *which originally meant "to grow longer." It was used in phrases like "it longs me for (something)," meaning "it makes me wish for, I yearn for." The key idea is that when one yearns for something, it makes time seem to pass slowly.*

ă pat / ā pay / â care / ä father / ĕ pet / ē be / ĭ pit / ī pie / î fierce / ŏ pot / ō go / ô paw, for /

lure (lŏŏr) *n.* Something that tempts or attracts with the promise of giving pleasure or reward.

lurk•er (lûrk´ər) *n.* Someone or something that moves about furtively or sneaks.

lus•trous (lŭs´trəs) *adj.* Having a gloss or sheen; gleaming: *She wore a **lustrous** silk dress to the party.*

mag•ma (măg´mə) *n.* The hot melted material under the earth's crust that often cools and hardens to form igneous rock.

mag•nif•i•cent (măg nĭf´ĭ sənt) *adj.* Splendid in appearance; grand; remarkable: *We visited a **magnificent** cathedral in Mexico City.*

ma•rine (mə rēn´) *adj.* Of shipping or navigation; maritime: ***Marine** engineers could not explain why the ship sank.*

mar•vel (mär´vəl) *v.* **mar•veled, mar•vel•ing.** To be filled with surprise, astonishment, or wonder: *She **marveled** at the dinosaur skeletons in the museum.*

mas•sive (măs´ĭv) *adj.* Large, heavy, and solid; bulky: *An elephant is a **massive** animal.*

maze (māz) *n.* A complicated, usually confusing network of passageways or pathways.

me•chan•i•cal (mə kăn´ĭ kəl) *adj.* Like a machine in operation: *He swung his arms repeatedly in a **mechanical** motion.*

min•er•al (mĭn´ər əl) *n.* Any natural substance that has a definite chemical composition and characteristic physical structure: *The country is rich in **minerals** such as coal, zinc, and gold.*

min•i•mum (mĭn´ə məm) *adj.* Representing the least possible or allowed: *That laundry will take a **minimum** bundle of three shirts to be ironed.*

mol•ten (mōl´tən) *adj.* Made liquid by heat; melted.

LURKER

Lurker *and the verb* lurk *developed from the Middle English* lurken, *from the Scandinavian word* lurka, *"move slowly, creep forward."*

MARINE

Marine *is a Middle English word that comes from Old French and developed from the Latin* mare, *"sea."*

MAZE

In Middle English the word **maze** *meant "confusion," from the Old English* amasian, *which meant "to bewilder." When lost in a maze, a person may feel bewildered.*

---

oi **oil** / ŏŏ **book** / ōō **boot** / ou **out** / ŭ **cut** / û **fur** / *th* **the** / th **thin** / hw **which** / zh **vision** / ə **ago, item, pencil, atom, circus**

mo•men•tar•y
(mō´ mən tĕr´ē) *adj.* Lasting only an instant or moment: *I suffered a **momentary** loss of confidence when I fumbled the ball.*

mo•men•tum (mō mĕn´təm) *n.* The force of motion that keeps a speeding object moving: *The bicyclist coasted awhile after she had built up **momentum**.*

mum•my (mŭm´ē) *n., pl.* **mum•mies.** The body of a human being or animal that was embalmed after death, according to the practice of the ancient Egyptians.

mus•ter (mŭs´tər) *v.* **mus•tered, mus•ter•ing.** To call forth or bring forth: *He could barely **muster** enough courage to apply for a job.*

nui•sance (noo´səns) *or* (nyoo´-) *n.* A source of irritation or annoyance; a bother: *She felt her little brother was a terrible **nuisance**.*

o•bliv•i•ous (ə blĭv´ē əs) *adj.* Unaware or unmindful: *The sleeping guard remained **oblivious** to the cry for help.*

ob•struc•tion (əb strŭk´shən) *n.* Something that blocks or gets in the way: *The **obstruction** on the highway caused a traffic jam.*

o•ce•a•nog•ra•pher (ō´shē ə nŏg´rə fər) *or* (ō´shə nŏg´-) *n.* A scientist who specializes in the study and exploration of the ocean.

pa•py•rus (pə pī´rəs) *n., pl.* **pa•py•rus•es** *or* **pa•py•ri.** A tall, reedlike water plant of northern Africa and nearby regions from which a kind of paper was made by the ancient Egyptians.

pe•di•a•tri•cian (pē´ dē ə trĭsh´ən) *n.* A physician who specializes in the care of infants and children and the treatment of their diseases.

oceanographer

ă pat / ā pay / â care / ä father / ĕ pet / ē be / ĭ pit / ī pie / î fierce / ŏ pot / ō go / ô paw, for /

peer (pîr) *v.* **peered, peer•ing.** To look intently, searchingly, or with difficulty: *She **peered** carefully at the bird so she could draw a picture of it.*

per•sist (pər **sĭst´**) *v.* **per•sist•ed, per•sist•ing.** To insist or repeat stubbornly; to continue: *The men **persisted** in declaring their innocence.*

pet•ri•fied (pĕt´rə fīd´) *adj.* Stunned or paralyzed, as with fear or astonishment.

phar•aoh (fâr´ō) *or* (fā´ rō) *n.* A king of ancient Egypt.

pile (pīl) *n.* A heavy beam of timber, concrete, or steel, driven into the ground as a foundation or support for a structure: *Once the **piles** were set, work began on the rest of the dock.*

pitch (pĭch) *v.* **pitched, pitch•ing.** To plunge forward and backward alternately.

plank•ton (plăngk´tən) *n.* Plants and animals, usually of very small size, that float or drift in great numbers in bodies of salt or fresh water.

pleat•ed (plēt´əd) *adj.* Arranged in flat folds made by doubling a material, such as cloth, on itself and pressing or sewing it in place.

plun•der•er (plŭn´dər ər) *n.* One who steals property or valuables; robber.

ply (plī) *v.* **plied, ply•ing, plies.** To travel (a route or course) regularly: *Steamers **plied** trade routes to the Far East.*

poise (poiz) *v.* **poised, pois•ing.** To remain in one spot as if suspended: *The hummingbird **poised** over a flower.*

pred•a•tor (prĕd´ə tər) *or* (-tôr´) *n.* An animal that lives by capturing and feeding on other animals; a preying animal: *The rancher protected his sheep from **predators.***

pre•pos•ter•ous (prĭ **pŏs´**tər əs) *adj.* Completely unreasonable or incredible; nonsensical; absurd: *His **preposterous** idea was to build a spaceship in the back yard.*

pres•sure (prĕsh´ər) *n.* The amount of force applied per unit of area of a surface.

PLANKTON

Plankton *is a German word that comes from the Greek* planktos, *"wandering." This word came from* plazein, *"to drive astray."*

PLUNDER

Plunder *comes from the German* plündern, *which came from the Middle High German* plunder, *"household goods."*

PREDATOR

Predator *is from the Latin* praedator, *"pillager," which came from* praedari, *"to plunder." This word came from* praeda, *"booty."*

---

oi **oil** / ŏŏ **book** / ōō **boot** / ou **out** / ŭ **cut** / û **fur** / *th* **the** / th **thin** / hw **which** / zh **vision** / ə **ago, item, pencil, atom, circus**

pre•vi•ous (prē´vē əs) *adj.*
Existing or occurring before
something else: *You can look
back to find the answer in the
previous chapter.*

prof•it (prŏf´ ĭt) *n.* The
money made in a business
venture, sale, or investment
after all expenses have been
met: *The increase in rent
meant less profit for the
storekeeper.*

pro•jec•tion (prə jĕk´shən)
n. Something that thrusts or
juts outward: *That insect uses
the spiny projections on its back
to trap its prey.*

prom•i•nent (prŏm´ə nənt)
adj. Highly noticeable;
readily evident; conspicuous:
*Move this exhibit to a more
prominent location.*

prop•er (prŏp´ər) *adj.*
Strictly following rules or
conventions, especially in
social behavior; seemly: *A
suit and tie is the proper dress
for a man who is applying for
a job.*

pro•posed (prə pōzd´) *adj.*
Put forward for consideration or acceptance;
suggested.

psy•chol•o•gy (sī kŏl´ə jē) *n.*
The scientific study of mental processes and behavior.

puce (pyo͞os) *n.* A deep,
grayish red or purple.

qual•i•ty (kwŏl´ ĭ tē) *n., pl.*
qual•i•ties. A personal trait,
especially a character trait:
*Her greatest quality is her
sense of fairness.*

quan•da•ry (kwŏn´drē) *or*
(-də rē) *n., pl.* **quan•da•ries.**
A condition of uncertainty or
doubt; a dilemma: *The puzzle
left us in a quandary over
what to do next.*

ra•tio (rā´shō) *or* (-shē ō´) *n.*
A relationship between the
amounts or sizes of two
things; proportion: *The ratio
of girls to boys in our class is
three to one.*

PUCE

Puce *is from a
French word
meaning "flea" that
was used to designate
the color of a flea.
The French word
came from the Latin
word for "flea,"*
pulex.

QUALITY

Quality *is from the
Latin* qualitas, *from*
qualis, *"of what
kind."*

ă pat / ā pay / â care / ä father / ĕ pet / ē be / ĭ pit / ī pie / î fierce / ŏ pot / ō go /
ô paw, for /

ra•tion (**răsh´**ən) *or*
(**rā´**shən) *n.* A fixed amount,
especially of food, issued
regularly: *People in deserts may
have to live on a limited* **ration**
of water.

re•as•sure (rē´ə **shoor´**) *v.*
re•as•sured, re•as•sur•ing.
To assure again; renew confidence: *He sat in the front row
to* **reassure** *his daughter, who
was in the show.*

ref•u•gee (**rĕf´**yoo **jē´**) *n.* A
person who flees, especially
from his country, to find
safety from oppression,
persecution, etc.: ***Refugees***
*are sometimes people who leave
battle areas during war.*

rel•a•tive•ly (**rĕl´**ə tĭv lē) *adv.*
In comparison with other
persons or things: *The tap
dancer found ballet to be
relatively difficult.*

rel•ic (**rĕl´**ĭk) *n.* An object or
custom surviving from a
culture or period that has
disappeared.

re•lief map (rĭ **lēf´** **măp´**) *n.*
A map that shows the physi-
cal features of land, as by
using lines, colors, or
shading.

re•luc•tant (rĭ **lŭk´**tənt) *adj.*
Unwilling; averse: *They were
reluctant to leave the park and
go home.*

re•mote•ness (rĭ **mōt´**nəs) *n.*
The state of being distant or
standoffish in manner; aloof-
ness: *Few people spoke to the
woman because of her quiet
remoteness.*

rep•li•ca (**rĕp´**lĭ kə) *n.* Any
copy or close reproduction:
*We built a **replica** of an early
telephone.*

re•solve (rĭ **zŏlv´**) *v.*
re•solved, re•solv•ing. To
remove or dispel; explain
away: *He **resolved** his concerns
at the meeting.*

re•splen•dent (rĭ **splĕn´**dənt)
adj. Shining with brilliance
and splendor; dazzling: *She
was **resplendent** in her jeweled
gown.*

re•sume (rĭ **zoom´**) *v.*
re•sumed, re•sum•ing. To
begin again or continue after
a break.

re•volve (rĭ **vŏlv´**) *v.*
re•volved, re•volv•ing. To
turn or cause to turn on an
axis; rotate: *Fan blades are
meant to **revolve** and stir up a
breeze.*

RELIC

Relic *is from the Old
French word* relique,
*derived from the
Latin* reliquiae,
*"remains, relics,"
which in turn came
from* relinquere, *"to
leave behind":* re-,
"back, behind" +
linquere, *"to leave."*

RESUME

Resume *comes from
the Latin verb*
sumere, *"to take hold
of." From* sumere
*was formed the
compound verb that
was borrowed into
English:* resumere,
*meaning "to take up
again."*

---

oi **oil** / oŏ **boo**k / oō **boo**t / ou **out** / ŭ **cut** / û **fur** / *th* **the** / th **thin** / hw **which** /
zh **vision** / ə **ago, item, pencil, atom, circus**

rig (rĭg) *n.* Any special equipment or gear: *A drilling **rig** is used to dig an oil well.*

rig•id (rĭj´ĭd) *adj.* **1.** Not changing shape or bending; stiff; inflexible: *The **rigid** soldiers were standing at attention.* **2.** Strict; unchanging: *We follow a **rigid** schedule in school.*

rut (rŭt) *n.* A track, as in a dirt road, made by the passage of wheeled vehicles: *Everyone bounced when the school bus hit that **rut.***

S

sa•cred (sā´krĭd) *adj.* Dedicated or devoted to a religious use or purpose.

sa•lin•i•ty (sə lĭn´ĭ tē) *n.* The degree to which something is saline or salty: *Ocean water has a high **salinity.***

sal•vage (săl´vĭj) *n.* A rescue of a wrecked, damaged, or sunken ship or of its cargo or parts: *__Salvage__ workers are usually highly trained divers.*

sa•vor (sā´vər) *v.* **sa•vored, sa•vor•ing.** To enjoy heartily; relish: *She is **savoring** the idea of beginning high school.*

scant•y (skăn´tē) *adj.* Barely sufficient or enough; meager: *The sailors had a **scanty** supply of fresh water.*

scar•i•fy (skâr´ə fī´) *v.* **scar•i•fied, scar•i•fy•ing.** To shock or frighten: *Volunteers created a haunted house to **scarify** the children on Halloween.*

scru•ti•nize (skrōōt´n īz´) *v.* **scru•ti•nized, scru•ti•niz•ing.** To observe or examine with great care: *The collector **scrutinized** the baseball cards carefully.*

scu•ba (skōō´bə) *n.* Equipment used by divers to breathe underwater, including a tank or tanks of compressed air worn on the back and fitted with a regulator, a hose, and a mouthpiece.

scur•ry (skûr´ē) *v.* **scur•ried, scur•ry•ing.** To race about in a hurried or confused manner; rush: *The dogs **scurried** back into their pen.*

sed•i•ment (sĕd´ə mənt) *n.* Finely divided solid matter that falls to the bottom of a liquid.

RUT

*The word **rut** comes from the Old French word rote or rute, which meant "beaten path, track broken through forest or wilderness."*

SCANTY

Scanty *and its root* scant *are from a Middle English word that developed from the Old Norse* skamt, *"short."*

SCUBA

Scuba *is an acronym, a word made up of the first letters of several words. It stands for "self-contained underwater breathing apparatus."*

ă pat / ā pay / â care / ä father / ĕ pet / ē be / ĭ pit / ī pie / î fierce / ŏ pot / ō go / ô paw, for /

share·crop·per
(**shâr´**krŏp´ər) *n.* A tenant
farmer who pays a share of
the crops as rent to the
owner: *As a **sharecropper**,
Dad pays one third of his crops
to the landlord as rent.*

shrine (shrīn) *n.* **1.** A place
devoted to worship or religious observances. **2.** A
container or receptacle for
sacred relics. **3.** A receptacle
(as a casket or tomb) for the
dead.

shroud (shroud) *n.* A cloth
used to wrap a body for
burial.

shuf·fle (**shŭf´**əl) *v.*
shuf·fled, shuf·fling. To
move with a shambling, idle
gait: *The tired hikers **shuffled**
into the dusty campground.*

sil·hou·ette (sĭl´ōō ĕt´) *n.*
An outline of something that
appears dark against a light
background.

sin·ew (**sĭn´**yōō) *n.* A ten-
don, or the tough fibrous
tissue that connects a muscle
and a bone.

snarl (snärl) *n.* Any confused, complicated, or tan-
gled situation: *The traffic
snarl in the intersection caused
a huge traffic jam.*

snor·kel (**snôr´**kəl) *v.*
snor·keled, snor·kel·ing.
To swim using a snorkel,
which is a breathing apparatus consisting of a plastic
tube curved at one end and
fitted with a mouthpiece.

sol·i·tar·y (**sŏl´**ĭ tĕr´ē) *adj.*
Remote; secluded; lonely:
*She likes to paint pictures of
solitary mountain scenes.*

sound·ing (**soun´**dĭng) *n.* A
measurement of depth,
especially of a body of water,
by means of a weighted line.

source (sôrs) *or* (sōrs) *n.* A
place or thing from which
something comes; a point of
origin: *This power station is the
main **source** of electricity.*

spe·cies (**spē´**shēz´) *or*
(-sēz´) *n.* A group of similar
animals or plants that are
regarded as of the same kind
and that are able to breed
with one another.

spec·ter (**spĕk´**tər) *n.* A
phantom; apparition.

spig·ot (**spĭg´**ət) *n.* A faucet.

splen·dor (**splĕn´**dər) *n.*
Magnificent appearance
or display; grandeur: *The
splendor of the palace was
breathtaking.*

snorkel

---

oi **oil** / ŏŏ b**oo**k / ōō b**oo**t / ou **out** / ŭ **cut** / û **fur** / *th* **the** / th **thin** / hw **which** /
zh **vision** / ə **ago, item, pencil, atom, circus**

stren•u•ous•ly
(**strĕn´**yōō əs lē) *adv.* In a manner that requires great effort, energy, or exertion: *She exercises* **strenuously** *for a half-hour each day.*

stride (strīd) *v.* **strode, strid•den, strid•ing.** To walk vigorously with long steps: *The new principal* **strode** *through the halls between classes.*

strip min•ing
(**strĭp´ mī´**nĭng) *n.* A method in which a mineral, especially coal, that lies close to the surface of the earth is mined by stripping off the topsoil, rock, etc., that covers it, leaving the earth barren after the mineral is removed.

suit•or (**sōō´**tər) *n.* A man who is courting a woman: *She said yes to her* **suitor's** *proposal of marriage.*

sur•plus (**sûr´**plŭs) *or* (-pləs´) *n.* An amount or quantity greater than what is needed or used: *Brazil produces a large* **surplus** *of coffee for export.*

sus•pect (sə **spĕkt´**) *v.* **sus•pect•ed, sus•pect•ing.** To think or have an idea about someone or something: *In spite of our secrecy, she did* **suspect** *that we were planning a surprise party for her.*

sus•pi•cion (sə **spĭsh´**ən) *n.* Doubt; distrust: *He eyed the stranger with* **suspicion.**

taint (tānt) *v.* **taint•ed, taint•ing.** To touch or affect, as with something undesirable: *The bad news* **tainted** *the celebration.*

taunt (tônt) *n.* A scornful remark.

te•di•ous (**tē´**dē əs) *adj.* Tiresome because of slowness or length; boring.

teem (tēm) *v.* **teemed, teem•ing.** To be full of; abound: *A tropical forest* **teems** *with plant and animal life.*

tel•e•graph (**tĕl´** ĭ grăf´) *or* (-gräf´) *n.* A communications system in which a message is sent, either by wire or radio, to a receiving station.

ă pat / ā pay / â care / ä father / ĕ pet / ē be / ĭ pit / ī pie / î fierce / ŏ pot / ō go / ô paw, for /

the•o•ry (**thē´**ə rē) *or* (**thîr´** ē) *n.* An assumption or guess based on limited information or knowledge: *The detective's* **theory** *is that wind, not a burglar, broke the window.*

ther•mo•cline (**thûr´**mə klīn´) *n.* A layer of water in a body of water that separates an upper, warmer layer from a lower, colder layer and in which the temperature rapidly declines in increasing depth.

thresh•old (**thrĕsh´** ōld) *or* (-hōld) *n.* The place or point of beginning; the outset: *Scientists are on the* **threshold** *of understanding the earth's atmosphere.*

thrift (thrĭft) *n.* Careful management of money and other resources: *His* **thrift** *has helped to make him a rich man.*

thrust (thrŭst) *v.* **thrust, thrust•ing.** To push or drive forcefully: *She* **thrust** *her hands into her pockets.*

tim•id (**tĭm´** ĭd) *adj.* Easily frightened; hesitant and fearful; shy: *The* **timid** *rabbit hid deep in its hole.*

tim•id•ly (**tĭm´** ĭd lē) *adv.* In an easily frightened, hesitant, or fearful manner; shyly: *The squirrel* **timidly** *peered out of its hole.*

tog (tŏg) *or* (tôg) *v.* **togged, tog•ging.** To clothe oneself; dress up: *She was* **togged** *out in her best dress for the party.*

trace (trās) *n.* A visible mark or sign of the former presence or passage of some person, thing, or event: *The thief escaped without leaving a* **trace.**

trans•ac•tion (trăn **săk´** shən) *or* (-**zăk´**-) *n.* The act or process of carrying out or conducting a matter, as in business: *Both people made money on this unusual business* **transaction.**

trap•pings (**trăp´** ĭngz) *pl.n.* Articles of dress or ornamentation: *She wanted a wedding with all the* **trappings.**

tri•umph (**trī´** əmf) *n.* Victory; success: *Her performance at the piano competition was a* **triumph.**

tum•bler (**tŭm´** blər) *n.* A drinking glass having no handle or stem: *Fill this* **tumbler** *with iced tea.*

TOG

Tog *is from the French for "cloak,"* toge, *which is from the Latin* toga, *"garment."*

TRAPPINGS

The word **trappings** *comes from the Middle English word* trappe *and the Old French* drap, *meaning "cloth." Its root probably extends back to the Late Latin* drappus, *for "drape or cloth."*

---

oi **oil** / o͝o **book** / o͞o **boot** / ou **out** / ŭ **cut** / û **fur** / *th* **the** / th **thin** / hw **which** / zh **vision** / ə **ago**, **item**, **pencil**, **atom**, **circus**

un•ion (yōōn´ yən) *n.* A combination formed by joining people or things together into a whole: *The states banded together to form a* **union**.

vague (vāg) *adj.* Lacking definite shape, form, or character: *Through the fog we could see the* **vague** *outline of a ship.*

vein (vān) *n.* A long, regularly shaped deposit of an ore, mineral, etc., in the earth.

vet•er•an (vĕt´ər ən) *or* (vĕt´ rən) *n.* A former member of the armed forces: *Grandfather is a* **veteran** *of the Korean War.*

vig•or (vĭg´ər) *n.* Strong feeling; enthusiasm; intensity: *The crowd cheered the team with great* **vigor**.

vir•tu•ous (vûr´chōō əs) *adj.* Having or showing goodness, righteousness, or moral excellence: *No one could find fault with her* **virtuous** *actions.*

winch

wake (wāk) *n.* The visible track of waves, ripples, or foam left behind something moving through water: *The boat's* **wake** *overturned the water-skier.*

wa•ver (wā´ vər) *v.* **wa•vered, wa•ver•ing.** To tremble or flicker, as sound or light: *The sound of the radio seemed to* **waver** *in the wind.*

wheeze (hwēz) *v.* **wheezed, wheez•ing.** To breathe with difficulty, producing a hoarse whistling or hissing sound: *She caught a cold and* **wheezed** *for two days.*

winch (wĭnch) *n.* A machine for pulling or lifting, consisting of a drum around which a rope or cable attached to the load is wound as the load is moved.

win•now (wĭn´ ō) *v.* **win•nowed, win•now•ing.** To separate the lighter chaff, or husks, from the heavier grain by using the air currents of the wind.

ă pat / ā pay / â care / ä father / ĕ pet / ē be / ĭ pit / ī pie / î fierce / ŏ pot / ō go /
ô paw, for /

yearn•ing (yûr´nĭng) *n.* A deep feeling that something is desired or wanted: *The detective felt a deep* **yearning** *to discover the truth*.

zo•ol•o•gist (zō ŏl´ə jĭst) *n.* A scientist who specializes in the study of animals.

oi **oil** / ŏŏ **book** / ōō **boot** / ou **out** / ŭ cut / û fur / *th* **the** / th **thin** / hw **which** / zh vision / ə ago, item, pencil, atom, circus

action   The series of events that make up a **plot.**

alliteration   The repetition of a consonant sound, usually the first sound in a group of words, as in "trumpeted two times."

allusion   A brief mention of a person or thing with which the reader is presumed to be familiar.

anecdote   A short account that gives details of an interesting event.

antagonist   The character who opposes the main character, or **protagonist,** in a story, play, or poem.

archaic language   Words and expressions that once were part of the language, but are no longer in use.

author's purpose   What the author means to say or accomplish in his or her work.

autobiography   A person's account of his or her own life.

ballad   A fairly short poem that tells a story. Ballads typically consist of **stanzas** and a **refrain.** They were originally meant to be sung.

biography   The factual account of a person's life, written by someone else.

blank verse   A form of poetry that does not rhyme and has five beats per line.

chapter   One of the main sections of a book, usually labeled with a number or title.

characterization   The process of making a character seem real and lifelike. An author uses description of the character's physical features, personality traits, actions, thoughts, speech, and feelings to achieve characterization.

characters   The people or animals in a story. The main character handles the problem or **conflict** in the story. Minor characters help advance the **plot** and reveal information about the main character's personality.

character traits Qualities that make one character different from another. Such qualities — bravery, intelligence, stinginess, and so on — are as various in literature as they are in real life.

climax The point in a play or story where the **conflict** reaches its highest intensity and must be resolved. The climax is the most exciting moment in a story and holds the most interest for the reader. (See also **turning point.**)

comedy Writing that is designed to amuse. Comedy uses such devices as sarcasm, **exaggeration, satire,** and **wit.** Comedies typically have happy endings.

conclusion In dramatic structure, the part of a story or play that gives the final results; the ending.

conflict The problem in a story faced by the main character. The character may face one (or more) of the following four kinds of conflict: a struggle against nature, a struggle against another character, a struggle against society, or a struggle against himself or herself.

connotation The feelings, emotions, and ideas associated with a word, as opposed to its dictionary definition. (See also **denotation.**)

context The words and ideas that surround a particular word. A reader can often figure out the meaning of a new word from its context.

denotation The exact meaning of a word as it might appear in a dictionary. (See also **connotation.**)

description Writing that provides details of time, place, character, and setting. An author uses description to create images of the "world" in which the story takes place.

descriptive language Language that is rich in sensory details. It evokes sights, smells, sounds, and textures.

dialect The way of speaking used by the people of a particular region or group. A writer achieves a dialect by using words that are spelled differently to show local or regional pronunciations, and by using words and sentence structures that are part of local or regional sayings and manners of speaking.

dialogue The words spoken by characters to one another in a story or play.

diction **1.** The choice and arrangement of words in a story or play. **2.** The quality of speech or singing judged by clearness and distinctness of pronunciation.

drama A serious play designed to be acted on a stage.

dramatize **1.** To turn a story into a play or screenplay. **2.** To relate an incident in a very dramatic way.

epic A long poem or literary work, usually written in a formal style, about heroes and their adventures. Ancient epics, such as Homer's *Iliad* and *Odyssey*, are often written versions of the oral legends of a nation or culture.

essay A brief piece of prose writing about a specific topic. An essay usually expresses the opinions of its author.

exaggeration Deliberate overstatement used for emphasis, effect, or **humor.**

expository writing Informational writing that enlightens or explains. Most **nonfiction prose** is expository.

fable A short story, often with animal characters who speak and act like humans, that teaches a lesson about human nature.

falling action In dramatic structure, the part of a story or play that tells what happens after the **climax.**

fantasy Fiction that tells about events that are impossible in the real world because they do not obey known scientific laws. **Science fiction** and fairy tales are types of fantasy writing.

fiction Stories created from the imagination of the author. **Novels, short stories,** and **fables** are all forms of fiction.

fictionalized biography An account of a person's life that is based on facts but includes some imagined elements.

figurative language Writing that uses figures of speech such as metaphors, similes, and personification. (See also **metaphor, simile,** and **personification.**)

figures of speech Various imaginative uses of language that create special effects or meanings. (See also **metaphor, simile,** and **personification.**)

first person The **point of view** from which one of the characters tells the story using the pronoun *I.* This character may experience the events of the story personally or may simply be a witness to them. (See also **narrator** and **third person.**)

flashback A writing technique that interrupts the present action to explain something that happened earlier.

folklore Traditions, beliefs, legends, customs, and stories handed down by a particular people from generation to generation by word of mouth. Folklore includes folk **ballads,** folk **dramas,** folk **heroes,** and **folktales.**

folktale A traditional story of a particular place or people, handed down from generation to generation and eventually written down.

foreshadowing A writing technique involving clues that a writer gives early in a selection to hint at future events.

formal language Careful, precise language, more frequently used in writing than in everyday speech. (See also **informal language.**)

free verse Poetry that does not follow a regular pattern of rhythm or line, and has either irregular rhyme or no rhyme.

genre A category or type of literary work. Works can be grouped into genres by form, technique, or type of subject. Thus, the adventure story, the **folktale,** and the **novel** are all examples of literary genres.

haiku A **lyric** poem of three lines and usually seventeen syllables. Traditionally, a haiku expresses a person's feelings inspired by nature.

hero/heroine **1.** The central character in a work of fiction, poetry, or drama. **2.** A strong and courageous man or woman who performs brave deeds or who risks his or her life for a good cause. In mythology, heroes and heroines were descended from gods.

historical fiction A story based partly on historical events and people and partly on the author's imagination.

humor **1.** A type of writing intended to make people laugh. **2.** The quality of being funny.

idiom A use of words, such as a **figure of speech** or a common saying, that is unique to one language and cannot be translated literally into another.

image A mental picture of something not present or real.

imagery Word pictures; mental images. In writing or speech, the use of **figurative language,** vivid **description,** or **sensory words** to produce **images.**

informal language Casual language used mainly in conversation. (See also **formal language.**)

interpretation The art of understanding what a work of literature means. Complex works can be interpreted in several different ways.

introduction In dramatic structure, the part of a story or play that creates the mood, presents some of the characters, and supplies background information.

irony The use of words or situations to contrast what is expected with what is actually meant or occurs. In *verbal irony*, the speaker says the opposite of what he or she means. In *dramatic irony*, the audience knows more about events than the characters do, which makes for **suspense** as the characters act out the story.

jargon Special or technical language used by people in a particular job or by people with a particular hobby or interest.

legend An imaginative story that is often connected with a national hero or a historical event and may be based on truth.

literature Imaginative writing that possesses recognized artistic value.

lyric poetry Poetry that expresses personal feelings and thoughts.

memoir A form of **autobiography,** usually written by someone famous or by someone who has witnessed an important event. A memoir focuses on other people and events, rather than on the writer, as in autobiography.

metaphor An implied comparison between very different things, used to add vividness to writing. In a metaphor, the two things compared are said to be the same, as in "Her mind is a computer." (See also **simile.**)

monologue A long speech delivered by one character in a play, story, or poem.

mood The effect of a story, poem, or play on the feelings of a reader or an audience; the emotional **tone** of a piece of writing.

moral A lesson taught by a story or **fable.**

motivation The combination of plot events and personality traits that determines a character's actions.

motive A reason, a need, or an emotion that causes a character to act in a certain way.

mystery novel Fiction that deals with a puzzling event, often a crime. (See also **novel.**)

myth A story handed down from the past that gives an imaginary explanation of how certain things in nature, such as the moon, the sun, and the stars, came to be.

narration The act or example of narrating, or telling a story.

narrative In an account of an event, the description of characters, scenes, or events that is not dialogue.

narrative poetry A type of poetry, sometimes rather long, that tells a story.

narrator The character who tells the story or, in a play, who explains the events to the audience by addressing them directly. (See also **point of view, first person, third person.**)

nonfiction   Writing that is about the real world rather than an imagined one.

novel   A long fictional **narrative,** usually showing how a **character** develops as a result of events or actions, and organized around a **plot** or **theme.**

onomatopoeia   The use of a word that imitates the sound it describes. *Buzz, splash,* and *honk* are all onomatopoetic words. In poetry, onomatopoeia may be more subtle, as the sound of the verses may help create a particular mood.

oral tradition   A tradition in which songs and tales are passed by word of mouth from one generation to another.

outcome   The final result; how something ends.

personification   A **figure of speech** in which human traits are given to something that is not human.

plot   The action or series of events in a story. The plot is traditionally divided into sections. The **introduction** creates the mood, presents some of the characters, and supplies background information. The **rising action** establishes and develops the **conflict.** At the **climax,** or turning point, the conflict is resolved through a key event or through the actions of the main character. In the **falling action,** the reader learns what happens as a result of the climax. The **conclusion** gives the final results.

point of view   The position from which a story is told. A story may be told from the point of view of one of its characters, or from the position of an observer who is outside the action. (See also **first person, third person,** and **narrator.**)

prose   Ordinary speech or writing as distinguished from verse or poetry.

protagonist   The main character in a story. (See also **antagonist.**)

proverb   A sentence or phrase that expresses a truth about life. "The early bird catches the worm" is a proverb.

realism   Fiction that tells about true-to-life people, places, or events that could actually exist or happen.

refrain A phrase or verse repeated several times, usually at regular intervals throughout a song or poem.

repetition A writing technique in which a word or phrase is repeated for emphasis.

rhyme The repetition of the same or similar sounds of syllables, often at the ends of lines of verse.

rhyme scheme The pattern in which rhymes occur in a poem.

rhythm In poetry, a regular pattern of accented and unaccented syllables.

rising action In dramatic structure, the part of a story or play that establishes and develops the **conflict.**

romance novels **Novels** about extraordinary events in extraordinary settings. Romance novels are more concerned with action — love, adventure, combat — than with characters.

satire The use of **humor** or **irony** to expose hypocrisy or foolishness.

scene A section of a novel or play that focuses on the actions of one or several characters in one place and time.

science fiction Imaginative writing that has some basis in scientific fact and usually takes place in a time other than the present. Science fiction writing is sometimes used by an author as a vehicle for making a statement about society.

sensory words Words that appeal to one or more of the five senses (hearing, sight, smell, touch, and taste).

setting The time and place in which events in a story or play occur.

short story A brief fictional **narrative** in prose. It has unity in **theme, tone, plot,** and **character.** Often a short story reveals a character's true nature through a series of events.

simile A comparison of two unlike things, using *like* or *as*. "He was as brave as a lion" is a simile. (See also **metaphor.**)

slang   Words and phrases that occur most often in **informal language.** Slang is often humorous, vivid, and extremely casual. Slang tends to be in a state of constant change, words and phrases experiencing popularity for a time, only to be replaced by new terms.

stage directions   Instructions in the script of a play that tell the characters their movements on the stage. They also describe the use of props and sound effects.

stanza   In poetry, a group of lines united by a pattern of rhyme and rhythm.

subplot   An additional, but secondary **plot,** that makes the action in a work of fiction more complex and more interesting.

suspense   Uncertainty, on the part of the reader or the audience, about what will happen in a story or play. Authors deliberately create suspense to hold the reader's or audience's interest.

symbolism   The use of an object, character, or incident to represent something else.

symbols   Objects, characters, or incidents that represent something else.

synopsis   A summary of a story's events.

theme   The underlying idea or message in a story. The theme may be directly or indirectly stated.

third person   The **point of view** in which the author acts as an unidentified **narrator** to tell the story about the characters. (See also **first person.**)

tone   The attitude toward the subject and the reader in a work of literature. The tone of a work may be formal or informal, for example, or light-hearted or serious. (See also **mood.**)

tragedy   A serious play that ends with a great misfortune that could not have been prevented. In a classic tragedy, the main character, a worthy, noble person, meets his or her fate with courage and dignity.

turning point An important moment in the **plot,** when events that have led to the moment of greatest intensity in the story come to a peak, and the main conflict must be resolved. (See also **climax.**)

universal themes Themes that occur in the stories of every culture, in every time. The conflict between good and evil is a traditional theme. Universal themes are particularly apparent in traditional tales.

verse 1. A part of a poem, such as a line or a **stanza.** 2. Rhythmic, and usually rhymed, poetry.

wit The ability to describe events that are amusing or odd, or to point out similarities in things that seem to be very different. Wit is a type of humor that depends mainly on the clever use of words.

Acknowledgments

For each of the selections listed below, grateful acknowledgment is made for permission to excerpt and/or reprint original or copyrighted material as follows:

Major Selections

"Advice to Schoolboys" from *Wings of the Falcon: Life and Thought of Ancient Egypt*, translated and edited by Joseph Kaster. Copyright © 1968 by Joseph Kaster. Reprinted by permission of Henry Holt and Company, Inc.

"The Alligator War" by Horacio Quiroga. Attempts to locate the rightsholder of this work were unsuccessful. If the rightsholder should read this, please contact Houghton Mifflin Company, School Permissions, One Beacon Street, Boston, MA 02108.

From *Barrio Boy* by Ernesto Galarza. Copyright © 1971 by University of Notre Dame Press, Notre Dame, Indiana 46556. Reprinted by permission.

"Boar Out There" from *Every Living Thing* by Cynthia Rylant. Copyright © 1985 by Cynthia Rylant. Reprinted with permission of Bradbury Press, an affiliate of Macmillan, Inc.

"The Bracelet" by Yoshiko Uchida in *The Scribner Anthology For Young People*, edited by Anne Diven. Copyright © 1976 by Yoshiko Uchida. Reprinted with permission of Charles Scribner's Sons, an imprint of Macmillan Publishing Company.

"Brer Rabbit and Brer Cooter Race" from *The Days When the Animals Talked* by William J. Faulkner. Copyright © 1977 by William J. Faulkner. Reprinted by permission of Marie F. Brown, Executor of the Estate of William J. Faulkner.

"The Circuit" by Francisco Jiménez from *The Arizona Quarterly*, Autumn 1973. Copyright © 1973 by *The Arizona Quarterly*. Reprinted by permission of *The Arizona Quarterly* and the author.

"Daddy" by Yolanda King in collaboration with Hilda R. Tompkins. Copyright © 1989 by Yolanda King and Hilda R. Tompkins. Reprinted by permission of Yolanda King and Hilda R. Tompkins.

"Discovering the Oceans" from *Under the High Seas: New Frontiers in Oceanography* by Margaret Poynter and Donald Collins. Copyright © 1983 by Margaret Poynter and Donald Collins. Reprinted with permission of Atheneum Publishers, an imprint of Macmillan Publishing Company.

"The Figgerin' of Aunt Wilma" by James Thurber from *Thurber Country*. Copyright © 1953 by James Thurber. Copyright © 1981 Helen Thurber and Rosemary A. Thurber. Published by Simon & Schuster.

"The Headless Rider" from *Stories That Must Not Die, Volume Two* by Juan Sauvageau. Copyright © 1976, Juan Sauvageau, Kingsville, Texas. Published by The Oasis Press, Austin Texas. Reprinted by permission of Pan American Publishing Company.

From *Homesick: My Own Story* by Jean Fritz, text copyright © 1982 by Jean Fritz. Reprinted by permission of G.P. Putnam's Sons and Gina Maccoby Literary Agency.

"The Hunter Who Wanted Air" from *Voices In The Wind* by Alex Whitney. Copyright © 1976 by Alex Whitney. Reprinted by permission of David McKay Co., a division of Random House, Inc.

Long Claws by James Houston. Copyright © 1981 by James Houston. Reprinted by arrangement with Margaret K. McElderry, an imprint of Macmillan Publishing Company, and the Canadian publishers, McClelland and Stewart.

From *Lurkers of the Deep: Life Within the Ocean Depths* by Bruce H. Robison. Copyright © 1978 by Dr. Bruce Robison (David McKay Company, New York). Reprinted by permission of Dr. Bruce H. Robison.

"Oceans of the Earth" from *Scott, Foresman Earth Science* by Jay M. Pasachoff, Naomi Pasachoff, and Timothy M. Cooney. Copyright © 1983 by Scott, Foresman and Company. Reprinted by permission.

"Old Plott" from *Tall Tales from the High Hills* by Ellis Credle. Copyright © 1957 by Ellis Credle. Reprinted by permission of the author.

"Papa's Parrot" from *Every Living Thing* by Cynthia Rylant. Copyright © 1985 by Cynthia Rylant. Reprinted with permission of Bradbury Press, an affiliate of Macmillan, Inc.

Credits